Ancient Prophecies Revealed

by Ken Johnson, Th.D.

Copyright 2010 by Ken Johnson, Th.D.

Ancient Prophecies Revealed
by Ken Johnson, Th.D.

Printed in the United States of America

ISBN 143825346X
EAN13 9781438253466

Unless otherwise indicated,
"Scripture quotations taken from the New American Standard Bible®,
Copyright © 1960, 1962, 1963, 1968, 1971, 1972, 1973,
1975, 1977, 1995 by The Lockman Foundation
Used by permission." (www.Lockman.org)

Table of Contents

Introduction *4*

Creation to the Egyptian Exodus *10*
   3924 BC The Curse & Redeemer 10
   2994 BC Adam's Death 11
   2268 BC Noah's Flood 12
   1476 BC The Exodus 14
   Witnessing to Muslims 15

Egyptian Exodus to the Rise of Babylon *18*
   1436 BC The 40-year Wandering 19
   1040 BC David Becomes King 20
   989 BC Solomon Builds the Temple 22
   711 BC Destruction of the Assyrian Army ... 30

The Rise of Babylon to the Messiah *33*
   612 BC Destruction of the Assyrian Empire 34
   607 BC Babylonian Empire 34
   537 BC Cyrus of Persia 38
   326 BC Alexander the Great 40
   587-326 BC The Destruction of Tyre 41
   323-64 BC The Age of Greece 43
   64 BC Rise of the Roman Empire 46

The Messiah's First Coming *47*
   2 BC Messiah's Birth & Childhood 48
   AD 28 Messiah's Ministry 53
   AD 32 Messiah's Death 62
   AD 32 Messiah's Resurrection 67
   Spring Festivals 68

The Messiah to the Great Dispersion *71*
   AD 32 Pentecost, Birth of the Church 71
   AD 70 Destruction of the Temple 74
   AD 132 Great Dispersion 76

The Great Dispersion *79*
   AD 395-476 Fall of Rome 85
   AD 476 Fall of Constantinople 86
   AD 476-1423 Rise of Papal Rome 86
   AD 1423 to 1917 Rise of Germany 87
   AD 1917 to 1945 Rise of Russia 87

Modern Israel *89*
   AD 1948 The Rebirth of Israel 93
   AD 1948 The Four Craftsmen 96
   AD 1948-1981 Seven Shepherds 97
   AD 1949 Yemenite Jews Return 100
   AD 1951-2005 Ashdod, Ashkalon, and Gaza ... 101
   AD 1967 The Temple Mount Taken 102
   AD 1967 The Five Cities 103

   AD 1989 Fall of the Berlin Wall 104
   AD 1990 Ethiopian Jews Fly Home 105
   AD 2000 Multiple Points 106
   AD 2004 The Sanhedrin Reestablished ... 108
   AD 2005 Palestinians Claim Jerusalem ... 109
   AD 2006 Second Lebanese War 110

Future Events - Post 2008 .... *111*
   4, 5, & 6 Shepherds 111
   West Bank Becomes a Sovereign State ... 112
   Lebanese-Jordanian War 112
   Sephardic Jews Return 114
   Destruction of Damascus, Syria 115
   First Gog-Magog War 115
   Ten Kingdoms Arise 118
   Miscellaneous Points 119
   The Birth Pangs 120

The Apostasy of the Church *122*
   AD 32-Present Seven Church Ages 122
   AD 32 Ephesus – The Nicolaitans 125
   AD 64 Smyrna – The Synagogue of Satan ... 125
   AD 312 Pergamos – Balaam's Stumbling Block ... 127
      Amillennialism 127
      Cessationism 129
      Church Tradition 130
   AD 606 Thyatira – Jezebel, Depths of Satan ... 131
      Gnosticism 132
   Sardis – Dead Ritual 135
   AD 1750 Philadelphia – Missionary Church ... 135
   AD 1948 Laodicea – Lukewarm Church ... 135
   Unsound Doctrines of Demons 136
   Master Chart 141

The Rapture of the Church *143*

The Tribulation *148*
   First 3.5 years of the Tribulation 148
   Tribulation Temple/Peace Plan 151
   The Middle of the Tribulation 157
   The Desolating Abomination 159
   The Second 3.5 Years 161
   The Festival of Yom Kippur 164

The Millennial Reign *166*
   Israeli Borders 169
   The Last Gog-Magog War 170

Other Books by Ken Johnson *171*

Bibliography *174*

Introduction

What Is Prophecy?
God, who created all things in the universe, is all knowing. In some cases, He has told His servants, the people whom we call prophets, what is going to take place in the future.

> "Behold, the former things have come to pass, now I declare new things; before they spring forth I proclaim *them* to you." *Isaiah 42:9 KJV*

> "Thus says the LORD, the King of Israel and his Redeemer, the LORD of hosts: 'I am the first and I am the last, and there is no God besides Me. Who is like Me? Let him proclaim and declare it; yes, let him recount it to Me in order, from the time that I established the ancient nation. And let them declare to them the things that are coming and the events that are going to take place. Do not tremble and do not be afraid; have I not long since announced it to you and declared it? And you are My witnesses. Is there any God besides Me, or is there any *other* Rock? I know of none.'" *Isaiah 44:6-8*

> "From now on I am telling you before *it* comes to pass, so that when it does occur, you may believe that I am *He*." *Jesus – John 13:19*

True prophecy came by the inspiration of the Holy Spirit to prophets and apostles. It was recorded in the Scriptures, in both the Old and New Testaments in the Bible. True prophecy does not originate from man, but from God alone.

> "But know this first of all, that no prophecy of Scripture is *a matter* of one's own interpretation, for no prophecy was ever made by an act of human will, but men moved by the Holy Spirit spoke from God." *2 Peter 1:20-21*

No other religion has written prophecies, like Christianity, that have been fulfilled during our lifetime. In Isaiah 41:17-20, Isaiah the prophet shows us a glimpse of our time, when the Jews would be regathered to their land and the forests reappear in Israel. (For full details see the section on Modern Israel.) Isaiah predicted that during the last days there would be those who live in that land (Muslims) who have perverted the prophecies. In reality Muslims can't tell us anything that will happen in the future because their holy book (the Qur'an) is nothing but falsehood and their religion is an abomination to God.

> "'Present your case,' the LORD says. 'Bring forward your strong arguments,' the King of Jacob says. Let them bring forth and declare to us what is going to take place; as for the former events, declare what they were, That we may consider them and know their outcome. Or announce to us what is coming; declare the things that are going to come afterward, That we may know that you are gods; indeed, do good or evil, that we may anxiously look about us and fear together. Behold, you are of no account, and your work amounts to nothing; he who chooses you is an abomination." *Isaiah 41:21-24*

In the book of Revelation, the apostle John states we are to be careful to properly interpret the prophecies. If we are careless or deliberately change the prophecies to lead others astray, we will suffer the consequences!

> "I testify to everyone who hears the words of the prophecy of this book: if anyone adds to them, God will add to him the plagues which are written in this book; and if anyone takes away from the words of the book of this prophecy, God will take away his part from the tree of life and from the holy city, which are written in this book." *Revelation 22:18-19*

In this book we will learn the different types of prophecy and how to correctly interpret them. We will even learn about the prophecies that predict that in the last days prophecies will be twisted! They even tell us what they will be twisted into!

In this book we will use both the American calendar and the Jewish calendar to calculate dates. Historical calculations are based on the books *Ancient Post-flood History* and *Ancient Seder Olam* by the author. Using these, Creation would be placed about 3924 BC.

Introduction

Elijah the prophet formed the "school of the prophets." Formal training on what real prophesies are and how to properly interpret them is essential to following the will of God. We are not to be ignorant of Satan's devices. Satan uses false prophets and false kinds of prophecies. Once we know his tactics, we can easily find true prophecy and know the correct interpretation. Let's look at the different kinds of prophecy used in Scripture.

Literal Prophecy

There are six main types of real prophecy. The seventh type is twisted or false prophecy. The first and most common form of prophecy in the Bible is called Literal Prophecy. This is a prophecy where the prediction needs no explanation and the fulfillment occurs exactly as predicted.

Examples:
- Micah 5 says the Eternal Shepherd would come out of Bethlehem.
- In Matthew 2, Jesus, who is God incarnate or from eternity, was literally born in the town of Bethlehem, a town six miles south of Jerusalem.

Timeline Prophecy

A Timeline Prophecy occurs when you are told that from the time a certain event takes place there will be so many days until another event occurs. If the first event happened in the past, you can calculate the exact day the future prophecy will occur.

Example:
- Daniel 9 records the angel's prophecy telling the number of days from the command to rebuild the Temple to the death of the Messiah. This came to pass exactly on the day it was supposed to be fulfilled: April 6, AD 32.

Inscription Prophecy

The third kind of prophecy is called an Inscription Prophecy. An Inscription Prophecy occurs when we are given a word or group of words that in Hebrew or Greek have various meanings. It is a kind of riddle. In these we have to find the correct translation to understand what is being prophesied. This is not to be confused with Bible codes, which we will discuss under Twisted Prophecy.

Example:
- Enoch's son was named Methuselah, a name which is created from two Hebrew words, "meth" meaning *death* and "salah" meaning *sent*. His name, if formed into a sentence, would read "when he is dead, it shall be sent." Methuselah died exactly one week before Noah's Flood occurred. His name and life were a prediction of the destruction of the whole world.

Symbolic Prophecy

A fourth kind of prophecy seen in the Bible is called Symbolic Prophecy. This is a prophecy where the prediction is not clearly spoken, as in the literal kind, but God causes the prophet or ruler to act a certain way or do something odd. His action forms a riddle for us to figure out. Also when a prophet has a dream or vision, parts of it are usually symbolic. Several Symbolic Prophecies substitute a day for a year.

Examples:
- Revelation 12 records a dream of a seven-headed red dragon. Since there are no seven-headed creatures on earth, we know this has to be symbolic of something else.
- In Ezekiel 4, God instructs the prophet to lay on one side for 390 days and his

---

Types of Prophecies

1. Literal
2. Timeline
3. Inscription
4. Symbolic
5. Typological
6. Duel-Purpose
7. Twisted

Literal Prophecies

Messiah born in Bethlehem – Mic. 5
Messiah is God Incarnate – Isa. 7

Timeline Prophecies

Messiah's death in AD 32 – Dan. 9
Israel restored in AD 1948 – Dan. 4

Inscription Prophecies

Single-Word Inscription
Methuselah – Gen. 5
   When he is dead it shall be sent
Immanuel – Isa. 7
   God with us or God incarnate

Quad-Word Inscription
Maher Shalal Haz Baz – Isa. 8
Mene Mene Tekel Uparsin – Dan. 5
Zurubabbel Shealtial – Hag. 2

Phrase Inscription
The Inscription – Zech. 3

Symbolic Prophecies

Seven-headed Dragon – Rev. 13
Ezekiel's 390 & 40 days – Ezek. 4
Insane Nebuchadnezzar – Dan. 4

Ancient Prophecies Revealed

other side for 40 days, symbolizing the years of judgment on Israel and Judah.
- In Daniel 4, God causes King Nebuchadnezzar to become insane for seven years. Then God restores him to his throne. This action teaches Nebuchadnezzar a lesson on humility but also gives us a symbolic prophecy about the restoration of the nation of Israel.

Typological Prophecies

Single Typological
Passover Lamb

Double Typological
Antiochus Epiphanies abomination
John the Baptist & Elijah

Typological Prophecy
The fifth kind of prophecy is Typological Prophecy. This is a literal prophecy fulfilled at one time in history, then fulfilled again *in exactly the same way* by someone else, sometimes centuries later. This is also referred to as a Double Fulfillment Prophecy. There are no triple fulfilled prophecies, to my knowledge.

Examples:
- In Daniel 11, Antiochus Epiphanes placed the abomination in the Temple.
- In Matthew 24, Jesus said Daniel's prophecy also referred to the future Antichrist placing the abomination into the Temple.
- The Bible said John the Baptist came in the spirit and power of Elijah, but it also says another "Elijah" will come before the Day of the Lord. We know him to be one of the two witnesses of Revelation.

Duel-Purpose Prophecies

Mene mene tekel uparsin – Dan. 5
Inscription and Typological

Nebuchadnezzar – Dan. 4
Symbolic and Typological

70 years of captivity – Jer. 23
Literal and Timeline

Woman sitting on 7 Hills – Rev. 13

Duel-Purpose Prophecy
In this form, a prophecy is given and fulfilled at one time in history. That, in turn, is typological of a future prophecy. It differs from the double fulfillment prophecy in that the second or future prophecy is not an *exact copy* of the first, but *a totally different prophecy*.

Examples:
- The handwriting on the wall is an Inscription Prophecy that gives one current prophecy (the overthrow of the Babylonians) *and* is also an Inscription Prophecy that is a typological prophecy about the future (a Timeline Prophecy predicting when Modern Israel would gain control of the Temple Mount).
- Nebuchadnezzar's insanity contains Literal, Symbolic, and Duel-purpose Prophecies.
- Jeremiah 23 predicts that the Israelites will spend 70 years in Babylonian captivity. In Daniel 9, the angel Gabriel uses the 70-year captivity prophecy to reveal the 70 weeks of years prophecy.
- Revelation 17 explains that the seven heads of the beast represent the seven hills on which the woman (city of Rome) sits, *and* it also represents seven ancient empires.

All of these prophecies will be examined in detail later in this book. But before we go on, it is important to see how Satan twists *true* prophecies into *false* prophecies.

Twisted Prophecies
Long ago, false teachers "despised the real prophecies" as Paul warned us not to do in 1 Thessalonians 5:20. They did not like what was prophesied to take place, so they twisted them to mean something else. In time these false ideas became common place.

Twisted Prophecies

Amillennialism
Replacement Theology
The USA being Babylon
Bible Codes
JW's and the 144,000
Serpent seed doctrine

Here are just a few examples to show how *NOT* to interpret a prophecy.

Changing the fulfillment of a prediction from a specific meaning to a vague one
A great example of Twisted Prophecy is the change from pre-millennialism to amillennialism. This is discussed in detail in the section on the apostasy of the church. These false teachers did not like the idea of the book of Revelation referring to the

Introduction

church-state combination as the Harlot of Babylon, so they spiritualized it away by saying it was symbolic of what happened in the first century. The ancient church recorded in great detail how this happened. In spite of the 53 prophecies fulfilled from AD 1948 to 2006, some today *still* maintain the modern rebirth of Israel means nothing to God. This is called Replacement Theology and is actually a fulfillment of another prophecy. We will discuss all these prophecies in great detail later in this book. Along this venue, others have taught the Babylonian commercial system is not in Babylon but the United Nations, which exists in New York, in the USA. This will be explained in great detail in the section on the *Apostasy of the Church*.

Looking For Things That Are Not There
In Revelation 13, the Holy Spirit gives us a riddle that the name of the Antichrist is somehow 666. This is fully detailed in the section on the Tribulation period. Since we are told this is a riddle and the mind that has wisdom can figure it out, we should try; but that doesn't mean any and all numbers can be used like this. This 666 riddle has led some into the error of what today is referred to as "Bible codes."

In both the Hebrew and Greek languages, the characters that represent their alphabet also represent their numbers. The idea behind modern-day Bible codes is based on the kabala of medieval times. First, you obtain the Hebrew or Greek Old Testament or the Greek New Testament with all the letters running together. Then, by starting at a certain letter and hopping every so many letters, the sequence is supposed to come out with a secret sentence.

Church father Irenaeus believed in pre-millennialism. He related to us though his writings, the apostle John's instructions on how to properly interpret the 666 riddle. But he was opposed to creating riddles out of the Scripture. Of the Bible code idea he said:

"God is not to be sought after by means of letters, syllables, and numbers." *Against Heresies 2.25*, AD 177

He did not mean for us *not* to follow Scripture when it tells us to do so. Irenaeus simply meant looking where you were not told to look is *usually* a trick of Satan to get us to waste our time.

Mixing Symbolic Prophecies With Literal Prophecies
In Revelation 7 there is a prophecy that 12,000 people from each of the 12 tribes of Israel will be witnesses for God during the Tribulation. This totals 144,000 Jewish people. Today a cult called "Jehovah's Witnesses" misinterprets this prophecy. They say the number is literal. There really will be 144,000 people; but they ignore or spiritualize away the fact that these are 12,000 from each of the 12 tribes of Israel. They say these 144,000 people are simply Jehovah's Witnesses. Either both the number *and* the tribes are literal or they are both symbolic. You can't just mix and match pieces of a prophecy like that.

Another example of this is twisting the prophecy about the seed of the woman from Genesis. This will be discussed in detail in the first chapter, *Creation to the Egyptian Exodus*. This prophecy predicts the Messiah will triumph over the kingdom of Satan. Some cultic groups teach the seed of the serpent is not the Antichrist in Satan's kingdom, but blacks and Jews. The Klu Klux Klan teaches the serpent's seed is the black race and the mark of Cain, referred to in Genesis, is black skin. Skinheads and neo-Nazis have taught the Jewish people are the descendant of the serpent. Other aberrant teachers like William Branham and Armstrong have taught variants of the serpent seed doctrine. This may sound so crazy that no one would really believe it, but I want you to see the pattern involved. You can't just change a symbol or change a literal meaning into a symbolic one in the same prophecy.

Exaggerating a Prophecy
In Zechariah 5 there is a prophecy about a flying scroll that is 10x20 cubits in size. The words "liar" and "thief" are written on the front and back of the scroll. We are told that the scroll represents judgment. If it falls on you, you will be destroyed. The size of the scroll, 10x20 cubits, is the size of the holy place of the Tabernacle. The Israelites who returned to Jerusalem did so under the edict of Cyrus. They swore an oath to restore the Temple of God, *then* build the rest of the city. After a few years their houses were restored but the temple still lay in ruins.

This scroll prophecy is showing that God considered His people to be liars and thieves because they broke their oath to restore His house first. They used the money King Cyrus gave them for the Temple to build their homes. Knowing that the

Ancient Prophecies Revealed

10x20 size symbolized the Tabernacle, some groups have used this part of the prophecy to justify their theory that all the measurements in the Tabernacle represent a timeline prophecy. They say this tells us when certain events will occur. The same thing is done with the measurements of the Great Pyramid. Just because one prophecy used numbers does not mean we can arbitrarily take another set of numbers and make then into what we want them to be.

Many other examples of twisted prophecy can be shown. These examples are given to provide you with some basic ideas of how *not* to twist a prophecy.

General Rules for Interpreting Prophecies:

1. New prophecies can't contradict the old ones.
2. The phrase "this *then* that" gives an order, but a simple list of events does not necessarily imply an order.
3. An ancient name given in a prophecy indicates the *area* in which the prophecy will occur, not where the ancient people are now, for example, Gomer (Ezekiel 38) and Assyria (Numbers 24)

Extra-Biblical History Books

There are several ancient history books quoted in this book. These are to be considered just history, not inspired works. They may contain errors just as any other history book can. Here is a brief history of each historian and book cited in this work:

Josephus
Josephus was a historian who wrote about AD 70. He is best known for *Antiquities of the Jews* and *Wars of the Jews*. These works are divided into books, chapters, and sections. When you see an abbreviation like "Ant. 5.3.2" that means *Antiquities of the Jews*, book 5, chapter 3, section 2.

Jasher
The book of Jasher is the only ancient history book still in existence that is recommended reading by the Scriptures. See Joshua 10:13 and 2 Samuel 1:18.

Ancient Church Fathers
Eerdmans Publishing has produced a ten volume set called the *Ante-Nicean Fathers*. This set contains all the existent writings from the ancient church fathers dating from AD 32 to AD 325.

Septuagint
The Septuagint, abbreviated LXX, is the copy of the Old Testament translated into Greek. It dates from about the year 300 BC. It contains numerous scribal errors. However, it is quoted by Jesus and the apostles and contains one prophecy that seems to be slightly more accurate than the Hebrew version we use today. In general, the Hebrew version is much more accurate than the Greek. The Hebrew version is the basis for the Old Testament used in most English versions today; including the KJV, NKJV, NASB, NIV, etc.

Seder Olam
The Seder Olam is a Jewish history book dated from AD 169. It agrees with the Bible and Jasher up to the period of the Persians. At that point it tries to alter the timeline to argue that Jesus was not the Messiah.

Introduction

Outline of the Prophetical Ages

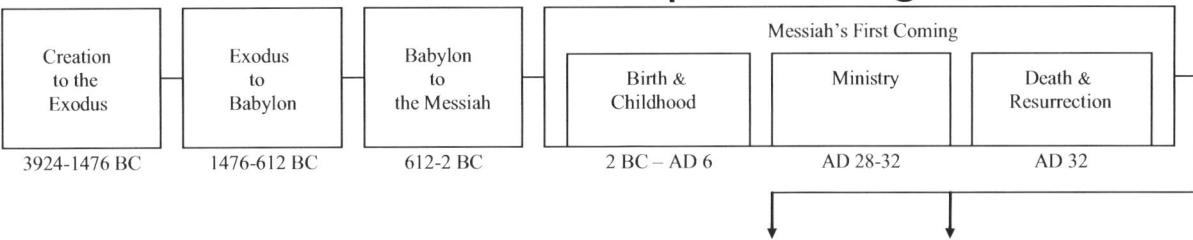

Creation to the Exodus	Exodus to Babylon	Babylon to the Messiah	Messiah's First Coming		
			Birth & Childhood	Ministry	Death & Resurrection
3924-1476 BC	1476-612 BC	612-2 BC	2 BC – AD 6	AD 28-32	AD 32

In this book we will list the biblical prophecies in the order in which they were fulfilled. The prophecies are placed in twelve ages. Some ages are subdivided further into periods.

From AD 32 to the Rapture there are prophecies dealing with the church's descent into apostasy, side-by-side with prophecies dealing with Israel. The church age is subdivided into seven periods and the Israeli age is subdivided into three periods.

Two prophetic lines develop at AD 32. The First Crossover Period takes place when Israel exists along with the church; this corresponds to the Ephesus period of church history. The great dispersion of the nation of Israel covers the years between when the Romans desolved the nation until the nation was recreated in 1948. The Second Crossover Period starts in 1948, covering the period between the birth of the modern nation of Israel to the Rapture of the church.

These two prophetic lines converge back into one at the Second Coming of the Messiah.

The following is an outline of chapters found in this book:

1. Creation to the Exodus from Egypt
2. The Exodus to the Babylonian Captivity
3. The Babylonian Captivity to the birth of the Messiah
4. First Coming of the Messiah
    a. Messiah's Birth and Childhood
    b. Messiah's three and a half year ministry
    c. Messiah's Death, Burial, & Resurrection
5. First Crossover Period, from the birth of the church to the dispersion of the nation of Israel
6. The Great Dispersion of Israel among the nations
7. Second Crossover Period
    a. Birth of modern Israel to 2008
    b. 2008 to the beginning of the Tribulation period
8. The Apostasy of the Church
    a. Ephesus – First Crossover Period
    b. Smyrna, Pergamos, Thyatira, Sardis, Philadelphia
    c. Laodicea – Second Crossover Period
9. The Rapture of the Church
10. The Seven-Year Tribulation
11. The Second Coming of the Messiah
12. The Millennium

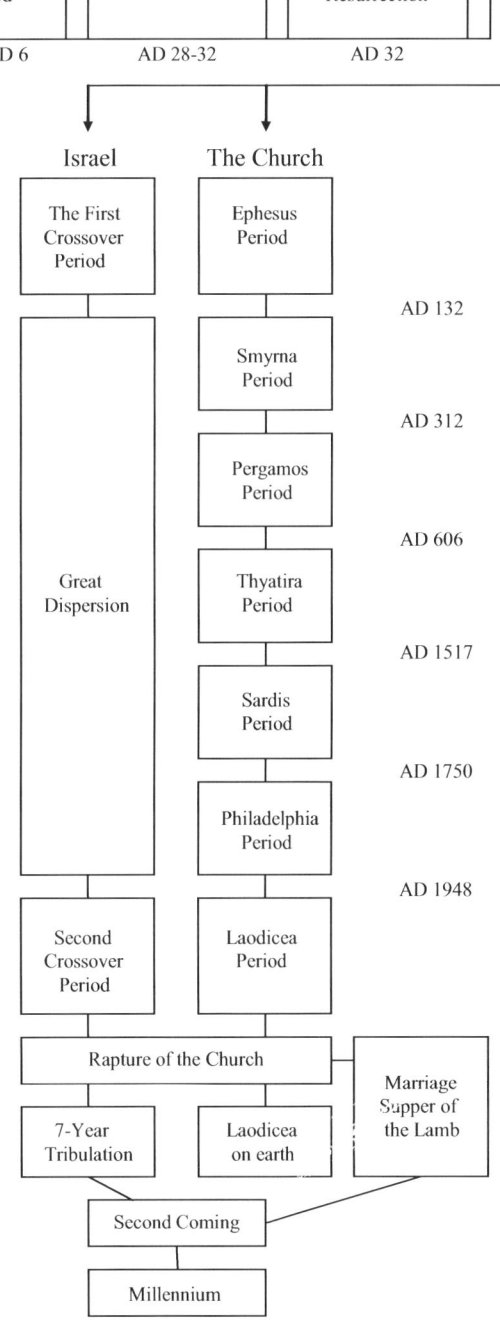

Israel branch: The First Crossover Period → Great Dispersion → Second Crossover Period → 7-Year Tribulation → Second Coming → Millennium

The Church branch: Ephesus Period — AD 132 — Smyrna Period — AD 312 — Pergamos Period — AD 606 — Thyatira Period — AD 1517 — Sardis Period — AD 1750 — Philadelphia Period — AD 1948 — Laodicea Period → Rapture of the Church → Laodicea on earth / Marriage Supper of the Lamb → Second Coming → Millennium

Ancient Prophecies Revealed

Creation to the Egyptian Exodus

3924-1476 BC – 28 prophecies in 2,448 years

Date	Prophecy	Prediction	Fulfillment
3924	Creation occurs		
3924	1. The curse of the Fall and the promise of a Redeemer	Gen. 3:14-19	Matt. 28
	2. Cain will be a vagabond	Gen. 4:11-14	Gen. 4:16
2994	3. Adam will die if he eats of the Tree of Knowledge	Gen. 3:1; 2:16-17	Gen. 5:5, 14
2268	4. Flood will destroy the earth if mankind does not repent within 120 years	Gen. 6:3	Gen. 7:11
	5. Adam predicts worldwide destructions by fire and water	Josephus Ant. 1.2.3	Gen. 7:11
	6. Canaanites will become slaves to Shem	Gen. 9:18-29	
1931	7. Confusion of languages will occur – Tower of Babel	Gen. 11:7	Gen. 11:8
1877	8. Barren Sarah will conceive Isaac	Gen. 15:4-5; 18:10	Gen. 21:2
	9. Sodom and Gomorrah will be destroyed	Gen. 18:20-33	Gen. 19:24
1876	10. Isaac will be born on the exact day prophesied	Gen. 17:21	Gen. 21:2
	11. Abraham will become the father of many nations	Gen. 17:4	Gen. 35:11; 48:19
	12. Ishmael will be a wild man and beget 12 nations	Gen. 17:20	Gen. 25:12-16
	13. Ishmael will become a great nation	Gen. 21:13	Gen. 25:12-16
	14. God tells Joseph in a dream that he will rule over his family	Gen. 37:9	Gen. 42:6; 44:26
1698	15. Joseph interprets pharaoh's dream of a seven-year famine	Gen. 41:1-25	Gen. 41:54
1686	16. Jacob will be in Egypt with Joseph before he dies	Gen. 46:4	Gen. 46:29
1669	17. Joseph will be with Jacob when Jacob dies	Gen. 46:4	Gen. 49:33-50:2
1476	18. Abraham will be blessed by becoming a great nation	Gen. 12:2	Exod. 12:33-41
	19. Abraham's great nation will inherit all the land of Canaan	Gen. 13:14	Exod. 12:33-41
	20. The great nation will come though the seed of Isaac	Gen. 21:12	Rom. 9:7; Heb. 11:18
	21. The great nation will come though Jacob/Israel and his descendants	Gen. 28:13	Exod. 12:33-41
	22. The great nation, Israel, will be enslaved	Gen. 15:13-14	Exod. 1:8-12
	23. God will send plagues on Egypt to force pharaoh to let the Israelites go	Exod. 3:20	Exod. 7-12
	24. Israel will leave Egypt with spoil	Exod. 3:21-22	Exod. 11:2; 12:35,36
	25. Israel will return to the land of Canaan (Israel)	Gen. 15:9-21	Josh. 1:1-5
	26. Israel will be blessed and became numerous	Gen. 12:1-3	Exod. 12:33-41
	27. Abraham's descendants will be brought out of captivity after 430 years	Gen. 15:13	Exod. 12:41; Gal. 3:16-17
	28. Jews will always keep the Passover	Exod. 12:23-24	

3924 BC
The Curse & Redeemer

The first prophecy recorded in the Bible is found in Genesis 3:15. This curse/prophecy states that because of disobedience, men were cursed to work hard to get food to grow and women would have increased pain in childbirth. Both men and women will die. The serpent would no longer walk, but was cursed to crawl along the ground. Seen any walking snakes lately? God literally fulfilled these prophecies.

"The LORD God said to the serpent, 'Because you have done this, cursed are you more than all cattle, and more than every beast of the field; on your belly you will go, and dust you will eat all the days of your life; and I will put enmity Between you and the woman, and between your seed and her seed; He shall bruise you on the head, and you shall bruise him on the heel.' To the woman He said, 'I will greatly multiply your pain in childbirth, in pain you will bring forth

children; yet your desire will be for your husband, and he will rule over you.' Then to Adam He said, 'because you have listened to the voice of your wife, and have eaten from the tree about which I commanded you, saying, 'you shall not eat from it'; cursed is the ground because of you; In toil you will eat of it all the days of your life. Both thorns and thistles it shall grow for you; and you will eat the plants of the field; by the sweat of your face you will eat bread, till you return to the ground, because from it you were taken; for you are dust, and to dust you shall return.'"
Genesis 3:14-19

The rest of the prophecy for the serpent states "I will put enmity between you and the woman, and between your seed and her seed; He shall bruise you on the head, and you shall bruise him on the heel." This has been taught that it vaguely refers to the crucifixion when Jesus crushed the "head of the serpent" or Satan's kingdom. Critics of literal interpretation will argue that Jesus was never really bit on the heel by a snake and never stepped on the head of one, either. So, they reason that the fulfillments of some prophecies are not literal one-time events, but a general vague conception of a future event. This is twisting prophecies and is how the church turned away from premillennialism to amillennialism.

"And I will put enmity between thee and the woman, and between thy seed and her seed; it shall bruise thy head, and thou shalt bruise his heel." *Genesis 3:15 KJV*

So, how could Genesis 3:15 be a literal prophecy? We need to look at the Hebrew words used for "head," "heel," and "bruise" to see the literal meaning. In Hebrew the word for "head" is ראש (rash), which can mean a "head," the "head/top of a mountain," or "kingdom." The word translated "bruise" is שוף (shuph), which can be translated, "bruised" or simply "hurt/injure." The word for "heel" is עקב (oqb). In verb form it can be translated "consequence." So the literal meaning from the Hebrew of this part of the prophecy can read "God will put enmity between Satan and the woman, and between Satan's seed and her seed; the Messiah shall injure Satan's kingdom, but Satan shall injure the Messiah as a consequence."

We now see every part in this entire prophecy points to a one-time specific event. We will see all the other prophecies point to one-time specific events as well. In many cases they are fulfilled on the *exact day* they were prophesied to occur.

Cain a Vagabond
God cursed Cain to wander the earth as punishment for killing his brother Abel. God said to Cain:

"Now you are cursed from the ground, which has opened its mouth to receive your brother's blood from your hand. When you cultivate the ground, it will no longer yield its strength to you; you will be a vagrant and a wanderer on the earth." *Genesis 4:11-12*

Jasher 1:34 records Cain wandered many years without peace, but in the latter years God granted him some rest. Cain built the city of Enoch, naming it after his firstborn son.

2994 BC
Adam's Death

God created Adam and Eve to live forever in the Garden of Eden. Because they disobeyed God, God cursed them and all mankind with death. The Hebrew of this verse explains much more clearly why they did not die immediately. The Hebrew literally says, "in dying you shall die." In other words, the dying process began when they ate of the tree, but took several hundred years to finish. Today we call this aging. If something else does not kill you, you will eventually die of old age. God said:

"but from the tree of the knowledge of good and evil you shall not eat, for in the day that you eat from it you will surely die." *Genesis 2:17*

Ancient Prophecies Revealed

> 2268 BC
> Noah's Flood

"Then the LORD said, 'My Spirit shall not strive with man forever, because he also is flesh; nevertheless his days shall be one hundred and twenty years...' Now Noah was six hundred years old when the flood of water came upon the earth." *Genesis 6:3; 7:6*

God gave this prophecy to Noah in 2388 BC, 120 years before the Flood. God said he would give mankind 120 years to repent or the world would be destroyed by a flood of water. By the end of the 120 years, mankind had not repented. Noah's Flood occurred on the 17th day of the second month (Heshvan 17) in the year 2268 BC, *on the very day* prophesied.

Adam's Prediction of the Flood
Josephus stated in his *Antiquities of the Jews 1.2.3* that Adam prophesied to his children that the world would be destroyed twice – once by fire and once by a flood of water, but was unsure which would come first.

Cainan Interprets Adam's Prophecy Correctly
Cainan was the son of Enos, son of Seth, son of Adam. Cainan by his "wisdom" came to know God well. He understood that a judgment would come. Knowing Adam's prophecy of the two judgments, Cainan correctly understood God's warning that the destruction by water would come first; and much later, the destruction by fire. Notice these prophecies were put into writing before the Flood. This shows us that if we pay close attention to the Scriptures, the Holy Spirit will teach us all things, including the correct interpretation of the prophecies.

> "And Cainan grew up and he was forty years old, and he became wise and had knowledge and skill in all wisdom, and he reigned over all the sons of men, and he led the sons of men to wisdom and knowledge... And Cainan knew by his wisdom that God would destroy the sons of men for having sinned upon earth, and that the Lord would in the latter days bring upon them the waters of the flood. And in those days Cainan wrote upon tablets of stone, what was to take place in time to come, and he put them in his treasures." *Jasher 2:11-13*

Canaanites Became Slaves
After the Flood, Noah divided the earth into three parts for his three sons, Ham, Shem, and Japheth, to inhabit. Noah gave Ham Africa, and Shem received the Middle East. Canaan, the firstborn son of Ham, went into Shem's territory and founded the land of Canaan, later to be called Israel. Noah cursed the descendants of Canaan to slavery if they continued to inhabit the land they illegally occupied. In his history of Ireland, Geoffrey Keeting states the Famorians were Canaanites that did not want to live in slavery and believed they could not win a war with the sons of Shem because the Semites were blessed. They took to ships to look for another land because of Noah's curse. Some of them went as far as Ireland and became raiders of the seacoasts there. These were the first pirates. They were called the "Famorians" in Irish history. In one ancient dialect, "Famorian" means "pirate." See *Ancient Post-Flood History* for more details.

> "When Noah awoke... he said, 'Cursed be Canaan; a servant of servants he shall be to his brothers.' He also said, 'Blessed be the LORD, the God of Shem; and let Canaan be his servant. May God enlarge Japheth, and let him dwell in the tents of Shem; and let Canaan be his servant.'" *Genesis 9:24-27*

Notice this prophecy shows what becomes of the Canaanites; but it also states that the Lord God of Shem would come to dwell in Shem's tents. In other words, the Messiah will be a descendant of Shem and dwell in the land of Israel.

Tower of Babel
The confusion of languages occurred during the building of the Tower of Babel. Until that time all peoples spoke one language. At this point God broke the people into groups that spoke different languages. There are several ancient records that mention there was one original language. See *Ancient Post-Flood History* for more details. Later in this book we will

Creation to the Egyptian Exodus

examine a prophecy that tells us God will reverse this multi-language curse and we all will again speak the original language during the millennial reign.

"'Come, let Us go down and there confuse their language, so that they will not understand one another's speech.' So the LORD scattered them abroad from there over the face of the whole earth; and they stopped building the city."
Genesis 11:7-8

Sodom and Gomorrah Destroyed
God told Abraham He was going to destroy Sodom, Gomorrah, and the cities of the plains because of their wickedness. That same year the cities were destroyed. The remains of the cities are under what is now called the Dead Sea.

"And the LORD said, 'The outcry of Sodom and Gomorrah is indeed great, and their sin is exceedingly grave. I will go down now, and see if they have done entirely according to its outcry, which has come to Me; and if not, I will know.' …Then the LORD rained on Sodom and Gomorrah brimstone and fire from the LORD out of heaven… Thus it came about, when God destroyed the cities of the valley…" *Genesis 18:20-21, 19:24,29*

Isaac's Birth
In Genesis 15:4-5, 17:21, and 18:10, we learn Sarah was 90 years old and barren. God prophesied to Abraham and Sarah that she would conceive and bear a son at that exact time in the next year. This was fulfilled on the *exact day* it was prophesied to occur.

"Then the LORD took note of Sarah as He had said, and the LORD did for Sarah as He had promised. So Sarah conceived and bore a son to Abraham in his old age, at the appointed time of which God had spoken to him. Abraham called the name of his son who was born to him, whom Sarah bore to him, Isaac." *Genesis 21:1-3*

Abraham and Ishmael
In Genesis 17:4, God promised Abraham would became the father of many nations. Through Abraham's first wife, Sarah, Isaac was born. Isaac was the father of Jacob who fathered the nation of Israel. Through his second wife, Hagar, Ishmael was born. Ishmael fathered the 12 Arab nations. The 12 Arab nations were prophesied in Genesis 17:20. Through his third wife, Keturah, Abraham fathered Zimran, Jokshan, Medan, Midian, Ishbak, and Shuah. These sons fathered additional Arab peoples. Midian fathered the Midianites and Jokshan fathered Sheba and Dedan in modern Arabia.

"I will make you exceedingly fruitful, and I will make nations of you, and kings will come forth from you. I will establish My covenant between Me and you and your descendants after you throughout their generations for an everlasting covenant, to be God to you and to your descendants after you. I will give to you and to your descendants after you, the land of your sojournings, all the land of Canaan, for an everlasting possession; and I will be their God."
Genesis 17:6-8

Joseph
Genesis 37 records that God told Joseph in a dream that he would rule over his family. The fulfillment occurred after he was sold into slavery in Egypt and rose to be the second most powerful man in Egypt. His rise to power occurred when he interpreted pharaoh's dream of the seven-year famine. When this occurred, Joseph's position in the government was secured.

"Then Joseph had a dream… Now he had still another dream, and related it to his brothers, and said, 'Lo, I have had still another dream; and behold, the sun and the moon and eleven stars were bowing down to me.' He related it to his father and to his brothers; and his father rebuked him and said to him, 'What is this dream that you have had? Shall I and your mother and your brothers actually come to bow ourselves down before you to the ground?'"
Genesis 37:5,9-10

"Now it happened at the end of two full years that Pharaoh had a dream… Joseph said to Pharaoh… Behold, seven years of great abundance are coming in all the land of Egypt; and after them seven years of famine will come, and all the abundance will be forgotten in the land of Egypt, and the famine will ravage the land… Then Pharaoh said to his servants, 'Can we find a man like this, in whom is a divine spirit?' So Pharaoh said to Joseph, 'Since God has informed

Ancient Prophecies Revealed

you of all this, there is no one so discerning and wise as you are. You shall be over my house, and according to your command all my people shall do homage; only in the throne I will be greater than you.' Pharaoh said to Joseph, 'See, I have set you over all the land of Egypt.'" *Genesis 41:1,25,29-30,38-41*

Joseph to Lay Jacob to Rest
God appeared to Jacob in a dream and told him not to be afraid to go to Egypt, because he and his descendants would be brought back from Egypt. Jacob would spend the rest of his life with his son Joseph and that Joseph would lay him to rest. This was fulfilled when Jacob died in Egypt. Joseph took Jacob's body back to Canaan and buried him in the cave of Macpelah.

"God spoke to Israel in visions of the night and said, 'Jacob, Jacob.' And he said, 'Here I am.' He said, 'I am God, the God of your father; do not be afraid to go down to Egypt, for I will make you a great nation there. I will go down with you to Egypt, and I will also surely bring you up again; and Joseph will close your eyes.'" *Genesis 46:2-4*

"When Jacob finished charging his sons, he drew his feet into the bed and breathed his last, and was gathered to his people. Then Joseph fell on his father's face, and wept over him and kissed him. Joseph commanded his servants the physicians to embalm his father. So the physicians embalmed Israel... Thus his sons did for him as he had charged them; for his sons carried him to the land of Canaan and buried him in the cave of the field of Machpelah before Mamre, which Abraham had bought along with the field for a burial site from Ephron the Hittite. After he had buried his father, Joseph returned to Egypt..." *Genesis 49:33-50:2,50:12-14*

Isaac to father the Great Nation
God's special blessing of one great nation came though Abraham, as we have seen; but Genesis 21 adds the blessing would pass only through Abraham's son, Isaac, not Ishmael. This blessing includes the promise that the Messiah would be his descendant and his descendants would inherit the Land of Canaan.

"Now Sarah saw the son of Hagar the Egyptian, whom she had borne to Abraham, mocking. Therefore she said to Abraham, 'Drive out this maid and her son, for the son of this maid shall not be an heir with my son Isaac.' The matter distressed Abraham greatly because of his son. But God said to Abraham, 'Do not be distressed because of the lad and your maid; whatever Sarah tells you, listen to her, for through Isaac your descendants shall be named.'" *Genesis 21:9-12*

Jacob to father the Great Nation
The blessing was given to Jacob, son of Isaac, not Esau, his older twin. From here on out the Ishmaelites and Edomites had a perpetual hatred for Israel. Jacob's name was changed to Israel and thereafter the great nation of his descendants was called Israel after him.

"And behold, the LORD stood above it and said, 'I am the LORD, the God of your father Abraham and the God of Isaac; the land on which you lie, I will give it to you and to your descendants. Your descendants will also be like the dust of the earth, and you will spread out to the west and to the east and to the north and to the south; and in you and in your descendants shall all the families of the earth be blessed. Behold, I am with you and will keep you wherever you go, and will bring you back to this land; for I will not leave you until I have done what I have promised you.'"
Genesis 28:13-15

1476 BC
The Exodus

Before looking at the Exodus, we must list several points of prophecy. First, Abraham was to become the father of many nations (Genesis 17:4). Second, Abraham was to father one *special* great nation that would be as numerous as the stars and through whom the Messiah would come (Genesis 12:1-3). Third, this great nation would be enslaved in a land not their own

Creation to the Egyptian Exodus

(Genesis 15). Fourth, after four generations, this great nation would return and inherit all the land of Canaan, having the right to rule it (Genesis 15:9-21).

> "God said to Abram, 'Know for certain that your descendants will be strangers in a land that is not theirs, where they will be enslaved and oppressed four hundred years. But I will also judge the nation whom they will serve, and afterward they will come out with many possessions. As for you, you shall go to your fathers in peace; you will be buried at a good old age. Then in the fourth generation they will return here, for the iniquity of the Amorite is not yet complete.'" *Genesis 15:13-16*

The children of Israel entered Egypt after Joseph began ruling there. In time, the Israelites became enslaved. Then God raised up Moses to deliver them. God forced Pharaoh to let the Israelites leave Egypt by sending the ten plagues upon Egypt. The Israelis took spoil as their wages and returned to the land of Canaan.

> "I know that the king of Egypt will not permit you to go, except under compulsion. So I will stretch out My hand and strike Egypt with all My miracles which I shall do in the midst of it; and after that he will let you go. I will grant this people favor in the sight of the Egyptians; and it shall be that when you go, you will not go empty-handed. But every woman shall ask of her neighbor and the woman who lives in her house, articles of silver and articles of gold, and clothing; and you will put them on your sons and daughters. Thus you will plunder the Egyptians." *Exodus 3:19-22*

Exodus Occurred on the Exact Day Prophesied

Galatians 3:16-17 records that from the time when the promise/prophecy was given to Father Abraham unto the time of the Exodus was 430 years. Exodus 12:41 tells us the prophecy was fulfilled *on the very day* it was prophesied to take place. See *Ancient Post-Flood History* for complete details. When God gives details or dates, He means exactly what He says!

> "Now the promises were spoken to Abraham and to his seed He does not say, 'And to seeds,' as *referring* to many, but *rather* to one, 'And to your seed,' that is, Christ. What I am saying is this: the Law, which came four hundred and thirty years later, does not invalidate a covenant previously ratified by God, so as to nullify the promise." *Galatians 3:16-17*

> "And at the end of four hundred and thirty years, to the very day, all the hosts of the LORD went out from the land of Egypt." *Exodus 12:41*

Witnessing to Muslims

The Bible is divided into 66 books. Each book contains a number of chapters and each chapter contains a number of verses. The holy book of the Muslims, called the Qur'an, is only *one* book which is divided into chapters called "suras." Each sura is divided into verses. The chart below gives a sample of prophecies verified in the Qur'an. We need to use the Qur'an to witness to Muslims, since they think the Bible was tampered with.

It is interesting to note that Abraham, Isaac, Jacob, and Moses are mentioned in the Qur'an. One has to question why Muslims deny this when they are so clearly written in their own holy book. Since the Qur'an verifies Moses led the Israelites from Egypt to the Promised Land and that God gave the Land of Canaan to them under a special covenant, a true Muslim would have to acknowledge the modern state of Israel is Allah's will and submit to Israeli authority!

Ancient Prophecies Revealed

Notable witnessing points from the Qur'an

Event	Qur'an : Sura
Moses led the Exodus	2
Allah has a special covenant with the Children of Israel	5:70
Children of Israel were brought from Egypt into the land promised to them by Allah	10:91,94; 17:103-104
Children of Israel were chosen above all other nations for a special purpose	44:30-32
Israel is favored by Allah above all peoples	45:16
Allah ordained the Holy Land for Israel and no one else	95:20-21
There is no God except that of the Jews	10:91
The God of Abraham, Ishmael, and Isaac is the one true God	2:133
You *must* believe what was revealed to Abraham, Ishmael, Isaac, Jacob, the tribes of Israel, Moses, and Jesus (no one has any record of revelations given to Ishmael)	2:136
Joseph becomes ruler in Egypt	12:4-102
Solomon, David, and Lot really existed	27

Other Notable Points
Passover will be kept forever by Jews; therefore, it is a sign that the land of Canaan/Israel is theirs. Muslims never have kept the Passover, neither have Christians.

> "For the LORD will pass through to smite the Egyptians; and when He sees the blood on the lintel and on the two doorposts, the LORD will *pass over* [author's emphasis] the door and will not allow the destroyer to come in to your houses to smite *you*. And you shall observe this event as an ordinance for you and your children forever."
> *Exodus 12:23-24*

The Bible calls God the God of Jacob and the God of Israel, but *never* the God of Ishmael. The pagans of Arabia practiced Ramadan (they fast during the day for one whole month) and the Hajj (a pilgrimage to Mecca) long before the time of Muhammad. The Hajj was a pagan ritual dedicated to the 300 plus gods of the Kaaba. Muhammad adopted these rituals for Islam. Even today Saudi Arabia still beheads Muslims who convert to another faith, and allows a man to have four wives. This is part of what is called Shari'a Law (pronounced Shä rē ä).

Allah vs. Yahweh
You often hear that "Allah" is just the Arabic word for God. This is not true. In Hebrew the word for God is "El" and the Jewish/Christian God's name is "Yahweh" or "Jehovah." In Arabic, the word for god is "Ilaha" and the Muslim God's name is "Allah." Allah was the name of the pagan moon god worshiped in the Kabba, along with the other 300 gods, long before Islam came. The pagan moon god Allah had no son, but had three daughters named al-Lat, al-Uzza, and Manat. What is interesting is that the Qur'an states in Sura 4:171 Allah has no son. In Sura 53 it records the names of Allah's three daughters. The famous statement "There is no ilaha but Allah" proves that Allah is not the Arabic word for God. This phrase is found in many places in the Qur'an, Sura 2:255; 4:171; 5:73; 6:102; 10:69-70; etc.

The main excuse that Muslims give for all the discrepancies in the Qur'an is that the Bible *was* God's Word but over the centuries became corrupted. However, the Qur'an itself says this would never happen.

> "We did indeed aforetime give the Book (Torah) to Moses: be then not in doubt of its (The Torah) reaching (you): and We made it a Guide to the Children of Israel." *Qur'an Sura 32:23*

> "If thou wert in doubt as to what We have revealed unto thee, then ask those who have been reading the Book (the Bible) from before thee: the Truth hath indeed come to thee from thy Lord: so be in no way one of those in doubt. Nor be of those who reject the Signs of 'I AM' (the God of the Bible), or thou shalt be of those who perish."
> *Qur'an Sura 10:94-95*

Creation to the Egyptian Exodus

This quote from the Qur'an shows clearly that the Bible will be guarded from corruption. Modern Muslims try to say that the Bible was guarded from corruption by the Qur'an, which shows how to correct it. This is illogical. It is kept from corruption by another book that shows how to correct the corruption that never occurred?

"We have, without doubt, sent down the Message (Moses and the prophets and the apostles); and we will assuredly guard it (from corruption)." *Qur'an Sura 15:9*

These are just a few passages that prove Islam to be a false religion. It is a cult born out of Christianity and Judaism. In the section on Modern Israel, we will see over 50 prophecies that prove Israelis are still blessed by God and that the Bible is 100% accurate, while all other religions have holy books that are in error. It should be noted that, other than the Bible, there are no religious holy books that contain prophecies verified by modern history.

Accurately Interpreting Prophecy

We must be careful to properly interpret biblical prophecies. If we misinterpret them, we may find ourselves in trouble or even forfeit our lives. One such example is recorded in the ancient Jewish history book of Jasher 75 (Jasher is one of the few remaining history books recommended by Scripture). Joseph understood the prophecies well and taught them to his children. The descendants of Joseph's son Ephraim had grown into a large tribe. They knew that at the end of the 430 years they would go free from Egypt, but they miscalculated the date of the end of the 430 years. Part of the tribe tried to leave, thinking God would be behind them. Instead they were almost annihilated.

"At that time, in the hundred and eightieth year of the Israelites going down into Egypt, there went forth from Egypt valiant men, thirty thousand on foot, from the children of Israel, who were all of the tribe of Joseph, of the children of Ephraim the son of Joseph. For they said the period was completed which the Lord had appointed to the children of Israel in the times of old, which he had spoken to Abraham. And these men girded themselves, and they put each man his sword at his side, and every man his armor upon him, and they trusted to their strength, and they went out together from Egypt with a mighty hand. But they brought no provision for the road, only silver and gold, not even bread for that day did they bring in their hands, for they thought of getting their provision for pay from the Philistines, and if not they would take it by force. And these men were very mighty and valiant men, one man could pursue a thousand and two could rout ten thousand, so they trusted to their strength and went together as they were. And they directed their course toward the land of Gath, and they went down and found the shepherds of Gath feeding the cattle of the children of Gath… And these men were engaged in battle with the children of Ephraim, and the Lord delivered the children of Ephraim into the hands of the Philistines. And they smote all the children of Ephraim, all who had gone forth from Egypt, none were remaining but ten men who had run away from the engagement. For this evil was from the Lord against the children of Ephraim, for they transgressed the word of the Lord in going forth from Egypt, before the period had arrived which the Lord in the days of old had appointed to Israel… And the men who had escaped from the battle came to Egypt, and told all the children of Israel all that had befallen them." *Jasher 75:1-6,15-17,20*

Later in this book we will see how to properly interpret timeline prophecies by converting the dates from the prophetical Jewish calendar to our standard calendar.

Ancient Prophecies Revealed

Egyptian Exodus to the Rise of Babylon
1476 BC to 612 BC – 50 prophecies in 864 years

Date	Prophecy	Prediction	Fulfillment
1476	29. Israel will wander in the desert for 40 years	Num. 14:20-23,34	Num. 26:63-65
1436	30. Jericho will be destroyed	Josh. 6:1-5	Josh. 6:21
1054	31. Eli's sons will be cursed	1 Sam. 2:31-34	1 Sam. 3:11-14
1042	32. A Benjamite, Saul, will be the first king	1 Sam. 9:15-15	1 Sam. 10:17-24
1040	33. Samuel predicts Saul will lose the kingdom	1 Sam. 15:22-23	1 Sam. 15:35
1040	34. David will be king	1 Sam. 16:13	2 Sam. 2:1-7
1040	35. Saul and his sons will die	1 Sam. 28:15-19	1 Sam. 31:6-9
1012	36. David's sin will cause his child to die	2 Sam. 12:13-18	2 Sam. 12:18-23
1012	37. David's sin will cause constant violence in his house	2 Sam. 12:10-12	2 Sam. 15-20
	38. David's throne will continue forever	2 Sam. 7:16	
989	39. Solomon will take the throne and build the Temple	2 Sam. 7:12-13	2 Sam. 12:24
	40. Priestly linage from Eli will be destroyed	1 Sam. 2:31-35	1 Kings 2:26-27
964	41. Prophet Iddo will be killed for disobedience	1 Kings 13:8-22	1 Kings 13:23-31
938	42. Jeroboam's dynasty will be destroyed	1 Kings 14:1-16	1 Kings 15:29
914	43. Jehu predicts Baasha's dynasty will be destroyed	1 Kings 16:1-4	1 Kings 16:11-13
887	44. Elijah predicts a drought will occur in Israel (3-year drought, 890-887 BC)	1 Kings 17:1	1 Kings 18:36-45
	45. The meal and oil of the widow will not fail	1 Kings 17:7-14	1 Kings 17:15-16
887	46. Ahab to have victory over Syria	1 Kings 20:13-14	1 Kings 20:21
	47. Ruins of cursed Jericho will be rebuilt	Josh. 6:26	1 Kings 16:34
883	48. Ahab/Israel will suffer because of sparing Ben-Hadad	1 Kings 20:42	1 Kings 22:31-37
883	49. Micaiah predicts Ahab & Jehoshaphat will be defeated	1 Kings 22:13-28	1 Kings 22:37-38
883	50. Ahab will die and dogs will lick up his blood	1 Kings 21:17-20	2 Kings 10:1-11
883	51. Jezebel will be eaten by dogs	1 Kings 21:23	2 Kings 9:30-37
881	52. Elijah predicts Ahaziah I will die because of consulting Baal-Zebub	2 Kings1:4,16	2 Kings1:17
881	53. Elijah will be taken to heaven on a certain day	2 Kings 2:5	2 Kings 2:11
881	54. Elijah predicted Elisha will receive a double portion of Elijah's spirit	2 Kings 2:9-10	2 Kings 2:12-14
881	55. Elisha predicts the Moabites will be conquered though a miracle of water	2 Kings 3:15-19	2 Kings 3:20-27
	56. Elisha predicts Naaman will be healed if Naaman obeys him	2 Kings 5:1-10	2 Kings 5:11-14
890	57. Moab, Ammon, & Edom will be destroyed without Judah fighting them	2 Chron. 20:15-17	2 Chron. 20:20-25
875	58. Elisha predicts his servant, Gehazi, will become leprous because of greed	2 Kings 5:19-27	2 Kings 5:27
875	59. A seven-year famine predicted (881-875 BC)	2 Kings 8:1	2 Kings 8:3
875	60. Elisha predicts Hazael will become king of Aram	2 Kings 8:7-13	2 Kings 8:14-15
869	61. Jehu will become king of Israel	2 Kings 9:1-10	2 Kings 9:14-28
869	62. Elijah predicts Jehoram will die of a disease & his family taken captive	2 Chron. 21:12-16	2 Chron. 21:17-20
839	63. Elisha predicted Israel will defeat Aram three times	2 Kings 13:14-19	2 Kings 13:25
824	64. God will abandon Joash because he killed the prophet Zechariah	2 Chron. 24:20-22	2 Chron. 24:23-24
809	65. Amaziah will be killed because of sin	2 Chron. 25:15-17	2 Chron. 25:27
770	66. Jehu's descendants will sit on the throne for four generations	2 Kings 10:30	2 Kings 15:12
750	67. Jonah warns the Assyrians of destuction	Book of Jonah	
732	68. Moab will be captured by Assyria within three years of this prophecy	Isa. 16:14	
	69. Moab and Edom will be destroyed	Num. 24:17-20	
722	70. Kenites will be taken captive by Assyria	Num. 24:21-22	
715	71. Arabia will fall to Assyria	Isa. 21:13-17	
711	72. Assyria will besiege Jerusalem (185,000 Assyrians died)	2 Kings 19:5-7; 20-36	Isa. 36-37
	73. Sennacherib will be assassinated	2 Kings 19:5-7	2 Kings 19:36-37
701	74. Shebna will die because of disrespect	Isa. 22:15-25	
700	75. Amalekites' final destruction predicted	Exod. 17:8-15; Num. 24:20	1 Chron. 4:43
696	76. Hezekiah will live another 15 years (711-696 BC)	2 Kings 20:1-19	2 Kings 20:20-21
641	77. Manasseh's downfall predicted	2 Kings 21:10-15	2 Kings 21:17-18
639	78. A man named Josiah will arise and destroy the idolaters	1 Kings 13:1-3	2 Kings 23:15-17

Dates given are BC.

Egyptian Exodus to the Rise of Babylon

> 1436 BC
> The 40-year Wandering

Scripture records that because of their unbelief in refusing to take the Promised Land, the Israelites would wander in the wilderness for 40 years. Everyone above the age of 20 would die except for Joshua and Caleb. Then the Lord would bring the survivors into the land of Canaan. In Chapter 10 of the *Ancient Seder Olam,* it is recorded that the children of Israel entered the land exactly 40 years *to the day* they were prophesied to enter.

> "But as for you, your corpses will fall in this wilderness. Your sons shall be shepherds for forty years in the wilderness, and they will suffer for your unfaithfulness, until your corpses lie in the wilderness. According to the number of days which you spied out the land, forty days, for every day you shall bear your guilt a year, *even* forty years, and you will know My opposition." *Numbers 14:32-34*

> "But among these there was not a man of those who were numbered by Moses and Aaron the priest, who numbered the sons of Israel in the wilderness of Sinai. For the LORD had said of them, 'They shall surely die in the wilderness' And not a man was left of them, except Caleb the son of Jephunneh and Joshua the son of Nun." *Numbers 26:64-65*

> "The manna stopped coming down the same day Moses died. When it says 'they did eat Manna, until they came to the borders of the land of Canaan,' (Exodus 16:35) it means on that day all the manna they had on hand simply vanished. If we subtract the last 30 days and then add the 30 days they ate from the Egyptian cakes they brought with them at the start, we have *exactly* 40 years." *Ancient Seder Olam, pg. 56*

Jericho Destroyed
God told Joshua he would give the city of Jericho into the hand of the Israelites. God then told them to march around the city and shout for six days. On the seventh day, after they had marched around the city seven times, the Lord caused the walls of the city to fall flat and Israel took the city.

> "Now Jericho was tightly shut because of the sons of Israel; no one went out and no one came in. The LORD said to Joshua, 'See, I have given Jericho into your hand, with its king *and* the valiant warriors. You shall march around the city, all the men of war circling the city once. You shall do so for six days...' So the people shouted, and *priests* blew the trumpets; and when the people heard the sound of the trumpet, the people shouted with a great shout and the wall fell down flat, so that the people went up into the city, every man straight ahead, and they took the city."
> *Joshua 6:1-3, 20*

Eli's Sons Cursed
Eli was a faithful priest, but his sons were not; they angered the Lord with their evil ways. God told Eli that his two sons, Hophni and Phinehas, would die in a single day. When the Philistines attacked and captured the Ark of the Covenant, they killed Hophni and Phinehas on the same day, just as predicted. God then promised to raise up a faithful priest, Zadok, who would follow His ways.

> "This will be the sign to you which will come concerning your two sons, Hophni and Phinehas: on the same day both of them will die. But I will raise up for Myself a faithful priest who will do according to what is in My heart and in My soul; and I will build him an enduring house, and he will walk before My anointed always." *1 Samuel 2:34-35*

> "So the Philistines fought and Israel was defeated, and every man fled to his tent; and the slaughter was very great, for there fell of Israel thirty thousand foot soldiers. And the ark of God was taken; and the two sons of Eli, Hophni and Phinehas, died." *1 Samuel 4:10-11*

Ancient Prophecies Revealed

Saul to be the First King
The people rejected the Lord's rule over them by asking for a king. The Lord predicted that a human king would take their sons and daughters and land, but they insisted they still wanted a human king like other nations. So the Lord gave them a Benjaminite named Saul for their first king.

> "Now a day before Saul's coming, the LORD had revealed *this* to Samuel saying, 'About this time tomorrow I will send you a man from the land of Benjamin, and you shall anoint him to be prince over My people Israel; and he will deliver My people from the hand of the Philistines. For I have regarded My people, because their cry has come to Me.' When Samuel saw Saul, the LORD said to him, 'Behold, the man of whom I spoke to you! This one shall rule over My people.'" *1 Samuel 9:15-17*

Saul Lost his Kingdom
The Lord commanded Saul to utterly destroy all the Amalekites. Instead of obeying, Saul conquered them and took their king, Agag, prisoner. This disobedience caused Saul to loose the kingdom. The prophet Samuel killed Agag as the Lord had commanded and sought a new king for Israel.

> "Then Saul said to Samuel, 'I have sinned; I have indeed transgressed the command of the LORD and your words, because I feared the people and listened to their voice. Now therefore, please pardon my sin and return with me, that I may worship the LORD.' But Samuel said to Saul, 'I will not return with you; for you have rejected the word of the LORD, and the LORD has rejected you from being king over Israel.' As Samuel turned to go, Saul seized the edge of his robe, and it tore. So Samuel said to him, 'The LORD has torn the kingdom of Israel from you today and has given it to your neighbor, who is better than you. Also the Glory of Israel will not lie or change His mind; for He is not a man that He should change His mind.'" *1 Samuel 15:24-29*

1040 BC
David Becomes King

The Lord chose David, son of Jesse, to be the next king.

> "Thus Jesse made seven of his sons pass before Samuel. But Samuel said to Jesse, 'The LORD has not chosen these.' And Samuel said to Jesse, 'Are these all the children?' And he said, 'There remains yet the youngest, and behold, he is tending the sheep.' Then Samuel said to Jesse, 'Send and bring him; for we will not sit down until he comes here.' So he sent and brought him in. Now he was ruddy, with beautiful eyes and a handsome appearance. And the LORD said, 'Arise, anoint him; for this is he.' Then Samuel took the horn of oil and anointed him in the midst of his brothers; and the Spirit of the LORD came mightily upon David from that day forward. And Samuel arose and went to Ramah."
> *1 Samuel 16:10-13*

Saul and Family to Die
Saul refused to accept the word of the Lord and tried to take David's life several times. Ultimately, Saul and his posterity had to be removed for all of Israel to accept David as the true God-ordained king. The Lord would no longer speak to Saul; so Saul found a medium to conjure up the ghost of the prophet Samuel who then gave this prophecy:

> "Then Samuel said to Saul, 'Why have you disturbed me by bringing me up?' And Saul answered, 'I am greatly distressed; for the Philistines are waging war against me, and God has departed from me and no longer answers me, either through prophets or by dreams; therefore I have called you, that you may make known to me what I should do.' Samuel said, 'Why then do you ask me, since the LORD has departed from you and has become your adversary? The LORD has done accordingly as He spoke through me; for the LORD has torn the kingdom out of your hand and given it to your neighbor, to David. As you did not obey the LORD and did not execute His fierce wrath on Amalek, so the LORD has done this thing to you this day. Moreover the LORD will also give over Israel along with you into the hands

of the Philistines, therefore tomorrow you and your sons will be with me. Indeed the LORD will give over the army of Israel into the hands of the Philistines!'" *1 Samuel 28:15-19*

This prophecy was fulfilled to the letter. The very next day they all died and were with the prophet Samuel:

"The Philistines overtook Saul and his sons; and the Philistines killed Jonathan and Abinadab and Malchi-shua the sons of Saul. The battle went heavily against Saul, and the archers hit him; and he was badly wounded by the archers. Then Saul said to his armor bearer, 'Draw your sword and pierce me through with it, otherwise these uncircumcised will come and pierce me through and make sport of me' But his armor bearer would not, for he was greatly afraid. So Saul took his sword and fell on it. When his armor bearer saw that Saul was dead, he also fell on his sword and died with him. Thus Saul died with his three sons, his armor bearer, and all his men on that day together." *1 Samuel 31:2-6*

David's Son to Die
David sinned by commiting adultery with Bathsheba. When Bathsheba became pregnant, David engineered the murder of her husband, Uriah. The prophet Nathan told David that the Lord would spare King David, but the child would die.

"Then David said to Nathan, 'I have sinned against the LORD.' And Nathan said to David, 'The LORD also has taken away your sin; you shall not die. However, because by this deed you have given occasion to the enemies of the LORD to blaspheme, the child also that is born to you shall surely die.' So Nathan went to his house. David therefore inquired of God for the child; and David fasted and went and lay all night on the ground. The elders of his household stood beside him in order to raise him up from the ground, but he was unwilling and would not eat food with them. Then it happened on the seventh day that the child died. And the servants of David were afraid to tell him that the child was dead, for they said, 'Behold, while the child was still alive, we spoke to him and he did not listen to our voice. How then can we tell him that the child is dead, since he might do himself harm!' But when David saw that his servants were whispering together, David perceived that the child was dead; so David said to his servants, 'Is the child dead?' And they said, 'He is dead.' So David arose from the ground, washed, anointed *himself*, and changed his clothes; and he came into the house of the LORD and worshiped. Then he came to his own house, and when he requested, they set food before him and he ate." *2 Samuel 12:13-20*

The Sword would not Depart from David's House
Nathan prophesied that because David had Uriah killed, the sword would never depart from David's house. The Lord allowed constant strife in David's family. Absalom formed a rebellion against David, his own father.

"Nathan then said to David '… I gave you the house of Israel and Judah; and if that had been too little, I would have added to you many more things like these! Why have you despised the word of the LORD by doing evil in His sight? You have struck down Uriah the Hittite with the sword, have taken his wife to be your wife, and have killed him with the sword of the sons of Ammon. Now therefore, the sword shall never depart from your house, because you have despised Me and have taken the wife of Uriah the Hittite to be your wife.' Thus says the LORD, 'Behold, I will raise up evil against you from your own household; I will even take your wives before your eyes and give them to your companion, and he will lie with your wives in broad daylight.'" *2 Samuel 12:7-11*

David's Throne Would Continue Forever
The Lord promised David that his throne and house would continue forever and that his son would build the Temple of the Lord on Mount Zion. Solomon fulfilled this prophecy. God said to David:

"When your days are complete and you lie down with your fathers, I will raise up your descendant after you, who will come forth from you, and I will establish his kingdom. He shall build a house for My name, and I will establish the throne of his kingdom forever. I will be a father to him and he will be a son to Me; when he commits iniquity, I will correct him with the rod of men and the strokes of the sons of men, but My lovingkindness shall not depart from him, as I took *it* away from Saul, whom I removed from before you. Your house and your kingdom shall endure before Me forever; your throne shall be established forever." *2 Samuel 7:12-16*

Ancient Prophecies Revealed

In the section on the Messiah's First Coming, we will see a prophecy about Israel always having a Jewish king up until the time 'Shiloh' would come and the kingship will be given to him. The kingly line continued though the Hasmonean kings all the way to the first century when Jesus, the Messiah, came. Since that time, there have been no Jewish kings. Even today, modern Israel has prime ministers instead of kings. After the Second Coming, Jesus will be crowned king and rule from Jerusalem.

**989 BC
Solomon Builds the Temple**

Solomon Built the Jerusalem Temple
The verse above prophesied that David's son would build the Temple. In 1 Kings 6, we see that it was David's son, Solomon, who took the throne, fulfilled the prophecy, and built the Temple.

"Now it came about in the four hundred and eightieth year after the sons of Israel came out of the land of Egypt, in the fourth year of Solomon's reign over Israel, in the month of Ziv which is the second month, that he began to build the house of the LORD… In the fourth year the foundation of the house of the LORD was laid, in the month of Ziv. In the eleventh year, in the month of Bul, which is the eighth month, the house was finished throughout all its parts and according to all its plans. So he was seven years in building it." *1 Kings 6:1,37-38*

Priestly Linage of Eli Destroyed
Because Eli did not restrain his children, but allowed them to practice sin in the Tabernacle, the priesthood of Eli was cut off. This was fulfilled over 50 years later, when King Solomon cut off Eli's linage for betraying David and put Zadok and his descendants in their place. (See John the Baptist baptizing Jesus, in the section on the Messiah's First Coming for more details.) This example teaches us we must show proper respect to the Lord and to the Scripture.

"Behold, the days are coming when I will break your strength and the strength of your father's house so that there will not be an old man in your house. You will see the distress of *My* dwelling, in *spite of* all the good that I do for Israel; and an old man will not be in your house forever. Yet I will not cut off every man of yours from My altar so that your eyes will fail *from weeping* and your soul grieve, and all the increase of your house will die in the prime of life. This will be the sign to you which will come concerning your two sons, Hophni and Phinehas: on the same day both of them will die. But I will raise up for Myself a faithful priest who will do according to what is in My heart and in My soul; and I will build him an enduring house, and he will walk before My anointed always." *1 Samuel 2:31-35*

"Then to Abiathar the priest the king said, 'Go to Anathoth to your own field, for you deserve to die; but I will not put you to death at this time, because you carried the ark of the Lord GOD before my father David, and because you were afflicted in everything with which my father was afflicted.' So Solomon dismissed Abiathar from being priest to the LORD, in order to fulfill the word of the LORD, which He had spoken concerning the house of Eli in Shiloh."
1 Kings 2:26-27

Disobedient Prophet Iddo Killed by a Lion
God commanded an unnamed prophet to go down and prophesy against Jeroboam, then leave Jeroboam's country and never return. Jewish tradition identifies this man as the prophet Iddo. Iddo did exactly what he was told until another prophet in that country invited Iddo to come to his house for fellowship. When Iddo told him he was forbidden to come back into that country, that prophet lied, saying an angel told him to request this. So Iddo, believing the prophet instead of God, came back into the land. While there, the Holy Spirit prophesied though the native prophet that Iddo would be attacked and killed by a lion for his disobedience. This is a good lesson for us to never assume that God has changed his mind because a man/prophet tells us so.

Egyptian Exodus to the Rise of Babylon

"Now an old prophet was living in Bethel... So he went after the man of God and found him sitting under an oak; and he said to him, 'Are you the man of God who came from Judah?' And he said, 'I am.' Then he said to him, 'Come home with me and eat bread.' He said, 'I cannot return with you, nor go with you, nor will I eat bread or drink water with you in this place. For a command came to me by the word of the LORD, 'You shall eat no bread, nor drink water there; do not return by going the way which you came.'' He said to him, 'I also am a prophet like you, and an angel spoke to me by the word of the LORD, saying, 'Bring him back with you to your house, that he may eat bread and drink water.'' *But* he lied to him. So he went back with him, and ate bread in his house and drank water. Now it came about, as they were sitting down at the table, that the word of the LORD came to the prophet who had brought him back; and he cried to the man of God who came from Judah, saying, 'Thus says the LORD, 'Because you have disobeyed the command of the LORD, and have not observed the commandment which the LORD your God commanded you, but have returned and eaten bread and drunk water in the place of which He said to you, 'Eat no bread and drink no water'; your body shall not come to the grave of your fathers.' It came about after he had eaten bread and after he had drunk, that he saddled the donkey for him, for the prophet whom he had brought back. Now when he had gone, a lion met him on the way and killed him." *1 Kings 13:11,14-24*

Jeroboam's Dynasty Destroyed
Jeroboam was the first king of Israel after the nation split into two countries. Jeroboam quickly fell into idolatry and was judged by God. Ahijah the prophet gave the following prophecy, which was fulfilled by Baasha, the next king of Israel.

"...you also have done more evil than all who were before you, and have gone and made for yourself other gods and molten images to provoke Me to anger, and have cast Me behind your back-- therefore behold, I am bringing calamity on the house of Jeroboam, and will cut off from Jeroboam every male person, both bond and free in Israel, and I will make a clean sweep of the house of Jeroboam, as one sweeps away dung until it is all gone. Anyone belonging to Jeroboam who dies in the city the dogs will eat. And he who dies in the field the birds of the heavens will eat; for the LORD has spoken it. Now you, arise, go to your house. When your feet enter the city the child will die... Moreover, the LORD will raise up for Himself a king over Israel who will cut off the house of Jeroboam this day and from now on." *1 Kings 14:9-12,14*

"So Baasha killed him in the third year of Asa king of Judah and reigned in his place. It came about as soon as he was king, he struck down all the household of Jeroboam. He did not leave to Jeroboam any persons alive, until he had destroyed them, according to the word of the LORD, which He spoke by His servant Ahijah the Shilonite," *1 Kings 15:28-29*

Baasha's Dynasty Destroyed
Baasha, however, also did evil in the sight of the Lord. Baasha's dynasty would suffer the same fate as that of Jeroboam.

"Now the word of the LORD came to Jehu the son of Hanani against Baasha, saying, 'Inasmuch as I exalted you from the dust and made you leader over My people Israel, and you have walked in the way of Jeroboam and have made My people Israel sin, provoking Me to anger with their sins, behold, I will consume Baasha and his house, and I will make your house like the house of Jeroboam the son of Nebat. Anyone of Baasha who dies in the city the dogs will eat, and anyone of his who dies in the field the birds of the heavens will eat.'" *1 Kings 16:1-4*

"Then Zimri went in and struck him and put him to death in the twenty-seventh year of Asa king of Judah, and became king in his place. It came about when he became king, as soon as he sat on his throne, that he killed all the household of Baasha; he did not leave a single male, neither of his relatives nor of his friends. Thus Zimri destroyed all the household of Baasha, according to the word of the LORD, which He spoke against Baasha through Jehu the prophet, for all the sins of Baasha and the sins of Elah his son, which they sinned and which they made Israel sin, provoking the LORD God of Israel to anger with their idols." *1 Kings 16:10-13*

Three-Year Famine
The prophet Elijah predicted a drought that would last until he prophesied its end. This drought started when he predicted it; and it lasted for three and one half years. This prophecy turned the hearts of the Israelites toward God. Elijah confronted the

Ancient Prophecies Revealed

priests of Baal and destroyed them. Then the Lord sent rain. The fulfillment is recorded in 1 Kings 18. This three-year drought ended about three years before the death of Ahab in the second battle against Aram, approximately 889-886 BC.

> "Now Elijah the Tishbite, who was of the settlers of Gilead, said to Ahab, 'As the LORD, the God of Israel lives, before whom I stand, surely there shall be neither dew nor rain these years, except by my word.'" *1 Kings 17:1*

Meal and Oil
Elijah approached a widow in the city of Zarephath, and asked her to make him some food. She replied that she did not even have enough for her own family, so she could not. Elijah prophesied that if she put the Lord and his servant first, she would have plenty. The widow fed Elijah in faith and the Lord miraculously increased the portion of food that she had. It was more than enough for all. This lesson teaches us that if we put the Lord first, he will always take care of us.

> "It happened after a while that the brook dried up, because there was no rain in the land. Then the word of the LORD came to him, saying, 'Arise, go to Zarephath, which belongs to Sidon, and stay there; behold, I have commanded a widow there to provide for you.' So he arose and went to Zarephath, and when he came to the gate of the city, behold, a widow was there gathering sticks; and he called to her and said, 'Please get me a little water in a jar, that I may drink.' As she was going to get *it*, he called to her and said, 'Please bring me a piece of bread in your hand.' But she said, 'As the LORD your God lives, I have no bread, only a handful of flour in the bowl and a little oil in the jar; and behold, I am gathering a few sticks that I may go in and prepare for me and my son, that we may eat it and die.' Then Elijah said to her, 'Do not fear; go, do as you have said, but make me a little bread cake from it first and bring it out to me, and afterward you may make one for yourself and for your son. For thus says the LORD God of Israel, 'The bowl of flour shall not be exhausted, nor shall the jar of oil be empty, until the day that the LORD sends rain on the face of the earth.'' So she went and did according to the word of Elijah, and she and he and her household ate for many days. The bowl of flour was not exhausted nor did the jar of oil become empty, according to the word of the LORD which He spoke through Elijah." *1 Kings 17:7-16*

Ahab Victorious over Syria
Ben-Hadad king of Aram conquered Syria, then went to attack Israel. Through a prophet, the Lord told Ahab he would defeat Ben-Hadad and that he should start the battle. Ahab won the war, but did not pursue Ben-Hadad, which ultimately cost him the kingdom and his life.

> "Now behold, a prophet approached Ahab king of Israel and said, 'Thus says the LORD, 'Have you seen all this great multitude? Behold, I will deliver them into your hand today, and you shall know that I am the LORD.'' Ahab said, 'By whom?' So he said, 'Thus says the LORD, 'By the young men of the rulers of the provinces.'' Then he said, 'Who shall begin the battle?' And he answered, 'You.'" *1 Kings 20:13-14*

Ruins of Jericho Rebuilt
Joshua placed a curse/prophecy on the ruins of Jericho. Joshua prophesied that whoever rebuilt Jericho would lose both his firstborn son and his youngest son. This was fulfilled about 883 BC, over 550 years after the prophecy was made!

> "Then Joshua made them take an oath at that time, saying, 'Cursed before the LORD is the man who rises up and builds this city Jericho; with *the loss of his* firstborn he shall lay its foundation, and with *the loss of his* youngest son he shall set up its gates.' So the LORD was with Joshua, and his fame was in all the land." *Joshua 6:26-27*

> "In his days Hiel the Bethelite built Jericho; he laid its foundations with the *loss of* Abiram his firstborn, and set up its gates with the *loss of* his youngest son Segub, according to the word of the LORD, which He spoke by Joshua the son of Nun." *1 Kings 16:34*

Ahab's Death
Several things were prophesied about the death of Ahab. Ahab would die because of idolatry, for sparing Ben-Hadad, and for killing Naboth (1 Kings 20:42). Micaiah prophesied, in 1 Kings 22, that the Lord allowed a lying spirit to go into the false prophets to convince Ahab to go to battle so that he would be slain. This teaches us a valuable lesson. There will always be

false and true prophets that contradict each other. If you make a mistake and side with the wrong one you will suffer for it! A true prophet never contradicts the written word, and knows the written word well.

"You shall speak to him, saying, 'Thus says the LORD, "Have you murdered and also taken possession?' And you shall speak to him, saying, 'Thus says the LORD, 'In the place where the dogs licked up the blood of Naboth the dogs will lick up your blood, even yours.'"" *1 Kings 21:19*

"So the king died and was brought to Samaria, and they buried the king in Samaria. They washed the chariot by the pool of Samaria, and the dogs licked up his blood (now the harlots bathed themselves *there*), according to the word of the LORD which He spoke." *1 Kings 22:37-38*

Jezebel Eaten by Dogs
Jezebel, the wicked wife of Ahab, practiced the religion of Baal. She sought to put the prophet Elijah to death. Elijah prophesied Jezebel would be eaten by dogs.

"Of Jezebel also has the LORD spoken, saying, 'The dogs will eat Jezebel in the district of Jezreel.'" *1 Kings 21:23*

When Jehu took power, he commanded Jezebel to be thrown down from her palace window:

"He said, 'Throw her down.' So they threw her down, and some of her blood was sprinkled on the wall and on the horses, and he trampled her under foot. When he came in, he ate and drank; and he said, 'See now to this cursed woman and bury her, for she is a king's daughter.' They went to bury her, but they found nothing more of her than the skull and the feet and the palms of her hands. Therefore they returned and told him. And he said, 'This is the word of the LORD, which He spoke by His servant Elijah the Tishbite, saying, 'In the property of Jezreel the dogs shall eat the flesh of Jezebel; and the corpse of Jezebel will be as dung on the face of the field in the property of Jezreel, so they cannot say, 'This is Jezebel.'" *2 Kings 9:33-37*

Ahaziah I Died
Elijah prophesied that King Ahaziah would die because he consulted the false god Baal-Zebub, which was idolatry.

"Ahaziah fell through the lattice in his upper chamber which was in Samaria, and became ill. So he sent messengers and said to them, 'Go, inquire of Baal-zebub, the god of Ekron, whether I will recover from this sickness.' But the angel of the LORD said to Elijah the Tishbite, 'Arise, go up to meet the messengers of the king of Samaria and say to them, 'Is it because there is no God in Israel that you are going to inquire of Baal-zebub, the god of Ekron?' Now therefore thus says the LORD, 'You shall not come down from the bed where you have gone up, but you shall surely die.'' Then Elijah departed… So Ahaziah died according to the word of the LORD which Elijah had spoken. And because he had no son, Jehoram became king in his place in the second year of Jehoram the son of Jehoshaphat, king of Judah." *2 Kings 1:2-4,17*

Elijah Taken to Heaven on a Certain Day
We are not told the date, but one of the sons of the prophets asked Elisha if he knew that Elijah will be taken to heaven later on that day. Elisha responded that he already knew it would happen that day. So the exact date had already been prophesied.

"The sons of the prophets who *were* at Jericho approached Elisha and said to him, 'Do you know that the LORD will take away your master from over you today?' And he answered, 'Yes, I know; be still.'" *2 Kings 2:5*

"As they were going along and talking, behold, *there appeared* a chariot of fire and horses of fire which separated the two of them. And Elijah went up by a whirlwind to heaven." *2 Kings 2:11*

Elisha to Receive a Double Portion of Elijah's Spirit
Elisha asked for a double portion of the spirit of Elijah. Elijah predicted that if Elisha saw him depart for heaven, his request of God would be granted. Elisha did see him depart and received his request from the Lord. Elisha did exactly twice as many miracles as Elijah did. One of these occured after his own death!

Ancient Prophecies Revealed

"As they were going along and talking, behold, *there appeared* a chariot of fire and horses of fire which separated the two of them. And Elijah went up by a whirlwind to heaven. Elisha saw *it* and cried out, 'My father, my father, the chariots of Israel and its horsemen!' And he saw Elijah no more. Then he took hold of his own clothes and tore them in two pieces. He also took up the mantle of Elijah that fell from him, and returned and stood by the bank of the Jordan. He took the mantle of Elijah that fell from him and struck the waters and said, 'Where is the LORD, the God of Elijah?' And when he also had struck the waters, they were divided here and there; and Elisha crossed over. Now when the sons of the prophets who *were* at Jericho opposite *him* saw him, they said, 'The spirit of Elijah rests on Elisha.' And they came to meet him and bowed themselves to the ground before him." *2 Kings 2:11-15*

Moabites Conquered though a Miracle in Water
Elisha prophesied that God would go before the kings of Israel and Judah and cause a flood that would fill the battleground with water. While Israel and Judah saw only water, God caused the Moabites to see something different:

"They rose early in the morning, and the sun shone on the water, and the Moabites saw the water opposite *them* as red as blood. Then they said, 'This is blood; the kings have surely fought together, and they have slain one another. Now therefore, Moab, to the spoil!' But when they came to the camp of Israel, the Israelites arose and struck the Moabites, so that they fled before them; and they went forward into the land, slaughtering the Moabites." *2 Kings 3:22-24*

Naaman Healed of Leprosy
Naaman was a captain in the army of Aram, who contracted leprosy. His servant girl, who was a Hebrew, told him about the Israelite prophet, Elisha. She said he should go to Elisha to be healed. This account teaches us to avoid pride and simply obey God, whether we understand God's plan or not.

"So Naaman came with his horses and his chariots and stood at the doorway of the house of Elisha. Elisha sent a messenger to him, saying, 'Go and wash in the Jordan seven times, and your flesh will be restored to you and *you will* be clean.' But Naaman was furious and went away and said, 'Behold, I thought, He will surely come out to me and stand and call on the name of the LORD his God, and wave his hand over the place and cure the leper. Are not Abanah and Pharpar, the rivers of Damascus, better than all the waters of Israel? Could I not wash in them and be clean?' So he turned and went away in a rage. Then his servants came near and spoke to him and said, 'My father, had the prophet told you *to do some* great thing, would you not have done *it*? How much more *then*, when he says to you, 'Wash, and be clean'?' So he went down and dipped *himself* seven times in the Jordan, according to the word of the man of God; and his flesh was restored like the flesh of a little child and he was clean." *2 Kings 5:9-14*

Moab, Ammon, and Edom Destroyed Without Judah Fighting
The Lord delivered Judah from a coalition of Edom, Moab, and Ammon. The Lord had Judah go out *just to watch* the destruction. He sent confusion on Moab and Ammon so that they attacked and destroyed all the Meunites (Meunites had inherited Edom by this time). When the last of the Meunites were dead, God caused Moab and Ammon to destroy each other.

"Now it came about after this that the sons of Moab and the sons of Ammon, together with some of the Meunites, came to make war against Jehoshaphat... Then in the midst of the assembly the Spirit of the LORD came upon Jahaziel... 'Tomorrow go down against them. Behold, they will come up by the ascent of Ziz, and you will find them at the end of the valley in front of the wilderness of Jeruel. You *need* not fight in this *battle*; station yourselves, stand and see the salvation of the LORD on your behalf'... They rose early in the morning... the LORD set ambushes against the sons of Ammon, Moab and Mount Seir, who had come against Judah; so they were routed. For the sons of Ammon and Moab rose up against the inhabitants of Mount Seir destroying *them* completely; and when they had finished with the inhabitants of Seir, they helped to destroy one another. When Judah came to the lookout of the wilderness, they looked toward the multitude, and behold, they *were* corpses lying on the ground, and no one had escaped."
2 Chronicles 20:1,14,16-17,20,22-24

Gehazi Becomes Leprous
Gehazi, the servant of Elisha, heard that Elisha had healed Naaman and that he also refused Naaman's gifts of silver. So Gehazi followed Naaman and told him Elisha had changed his mind and would take the silver. Naaman gladly gave it to

Gehazi. Elisha predicted Gehazi would become a leper because of his greed. Gehazi's punishment teaches us valuable lessons about greed and reliance on the Lord.

"But he went in and stood before his master. And Elisha said to him, 'Where have you been, Gehazi?' And he said, 'Your servant went nowhere.' Then he said to him, 'Did not my heart go *with you*, when the man turned from his chariot to meet you? Is it a time to receive money and to receive clothes and olive groves and vineyards and sheep and oxen and male and female servants? Therefore, the leprosy of Naaman shall cling to you and to your descendants forever.' So he went out from his presence a leper *as white* as snow." 2 Kings 5:25-27

Seven-Year Famine
Elisha predicted a seven-year famine in the land of Israel. The occurred in 881-875 BC.

"Now Elisha spoke to the woman whose son he had restored to life, saying, 'Arise and go with your household, and sojourn wherever you can sojourn; for the LORD has called for a famine, and it will even come on the land for seven years.' So the woman arose and did according to the word of the man of God, and she went with her household and sojourned in the land of the Philistines seven years. At the end of seven years, the woman returned from the land of the Philistines; and she went out to appeal to the king for her house and for her field." 2 Kings 8:1-3

Hazael Became King of Aram
Elisha went to Aram to see Ben-Hadad, who was sick; Hazael went out to meet him. Hazael asked Elisha if King Ben-Hadad would recover. Elijah knew Ben-Hadad would recover from the illness if left alone. He also knew that Hazael would murder Ben-Hadad and ascend to the throne and do horrible things to the Israelites.

"Then Elisha said to him, 'Go, say to him, 'You will surely recover,' but the LORD has shown me that he will certainly die.' He fixed his gaze steadily *on him* until he was ashamed, and the man of God wept. Hazael said, 'Why does my lord weep?' Then he answered, 'Because I know the evil that you will do to the sons of Israel: their strongholds you will set on fire, and their young men you will kill with the sword, and their little ones you will dash in pieces, and their women with child you will rip up.' Then Hazael said, 'But what is your servant, *who is but* a dog, that he should do this great thing?' And Elisha answered, 'The LORD has shown me that you will be king over Aram.' So he departed from Elisha and returned to his master, who said to him, 'What did Elisha say to you?' And he answered, 'He told me that you would surely recover.' On the following day, he took the cover and dipped it in water and spread it on his face, so that he died. And Hazael became king in his place." 2 Kings 8:10-15

Jehu Became King of Israel
Elisha sent a son of a prophet to anoint Jehu to be the next king and to prophecy over him. Elisha told the son of the prophet to run quickly back home so that he would not be put to death.

"He arose and went into the house, and he poured the oil on his head and said to him, 'Thus says the LORD, the God of Israel, 'I have anointed you king over the people of the LORD, *even* over Israel. You shall strike the house of Ahab your master, that I may avenge the blood of My servants the prophets, and the blood of all the servants of the LORD, at the hand of Jezebel. For the whole house of Ahab shall perish, and I will cut off from Ahab every male person both bond and free in Israel. I will make the house of Ahab like the house of Jeroboam the son of Nebat, and like the house of Baasha the son of Ahijah. The dogs shall eat Jezebel in the territory of Jezreel, and none shall bury *her*.'' Then he opened the door and fled." 2 Kings 9:6-9

Jehu became the next king of Israel. He assassinated the current king, along with all the descendants of Ahab, thus completely destroying Ahab's dynasty.

Jehoram Died of a lingering Disease
Elisha predicted that Jehoram would die from a lingering disease and that his family would go into captivity. This was fulfilled when the Lord turned away from Jehoram because of his idolatry, and caused the Philistines and Arabs to attack and

Ancient Prophecies Revealed

take captive his whole family, except for his youngest son, Jehoahaz. Then Jehoram contracted a disease of the bowls. It took him two years to die.

"Then a letter came to him from Elijah the prophet saying, 'Thus says the LORD God of your father David, "Because you have not walked in the ways of Jehoshaphat your father and the ways of Asa king of Judah, but have walked in the way of the kings of Israel, and have caused Judah and the inhabitants of Jerusalem to play the harlot as the house of Ahab played the harlot, and you have also killed your brothers, your own family, who were better than you, behold, the LORD is going to strike your people, your sons, your wives and all your possessions with a great calamity; and you will suffer severe sickness, a disease of your bowels, until your bowels come out because of the sickness, day by day."' Then the LORD stirred up against Jehoram the spirit of the Philistines and the Arabs who bordered the Ethiopians; and they came against Judah and invaded it, and carried away all the possessions found in the king's house together with his sons and his wives, so that no son was left to him except Jehoahaz, the youngest of his sons. So after all this the LORD smote him in his bowels with an incurable sickness. Now it came about in the course of time, at the end of two years, that his bowels came out because of his sickness and he died in great pain. And his people made no fire for him like the fire for his fathers. He was thirty-two years old when he became king, and he reigned in Jerusalem eight years; and he departed with no one's regret, and they buried him in the city of David, but not in the tombs of the kings." *2 Chronicles 21:12-20*

Israel Defeats Aram Three Times
Elisha asked the king to shoot some arrows. The king shot three times. God wanted to test his resolve. If he had shot five or six times, he would have completely wiped out the enemy; but his three shots were enough to take back the conquered Israelite cities.

"When Elisha became sick with the illness of which he was to die, Joash the king of Israel came down to him and wept over him and said, 'My father, my father, the chariots of Israel and its horsemen!' Elisha said to him, 'Take a bow and arrows.' So he took a bow and arrows. Then he said to the king of Israel, 'Put your hand on the bow.' And he put his hand *on it*, then Elisha laid his hands on the king's hands. He said, 'Open the window toward the east,' and he opened *it*. Then Elisha said, 'Shoot!' And he shot. And he said, 'The LORD'S arrow of victory, even the arrow of victory over Aram; for you will defeat the Arameans at Aphek until you have destroyed *them*.' Then he said, 'Take the arrows,' and he took them. And he said to the king of Israel, 'Strike the ground,' and he struck it three times and stopped. So the man of God was angry with him and said, 'You should have struck five or six times, then you would have struck Aram until you would have destroyed *it*. But now you shall strike Aram *only* three times.' …When Hazael king of Aram died, Ben-hadad his son became king in his place. Then Jehoash the son of Jehoahaz took again from the hand of Ben-hadad the son of Hazael the cities which he had taken in war from the hand of Jehoahaz his father Three times Joash defeated him and recovered the cities of Israel." *2 Kings 13:14-19, 24-25*

Joash Abandoned for Killing Zechariah
Joash started out well, bringing back the Temple worship and the study of the Scriptures, but afterwards slacked off. Not being as familiar with the teaching of Scripture as he once was, Joash made the mistake of ordering the death of the priest/prophet Zechariah. God abandoned him for the murder. Many people get involved in church but then dislike something the preacher said and abandon the church. If the preacher is speaking the Word of God, then leaving the church amounts to rebellion against God. If they do so, they will suffer for it. If the preacher is not speaking the Word of God, then no harm will come to them for abandoning a false teacher. The only way to know the correct action for sure, is to continually study the Scriptures.

"They abandoned the house of the LORD, the God of their fathers, and served the Asherim and the idols; so wrath came upon Judah and Jerusalem for this their guilt. Yet He sent prophets to them to bring them back to the LORD; though they testified against them, they would not listen. Then the Spirit of God came on Zechariah the son of Jehoiada the priest; and he stood above the people and said to them, 'Thus God has said, 'Why do you transgress the commandments of the LORD and do not prosper? Because you have forsaken the LORD, He has also forsaken you.'' So they conspired against him and at the command of the king they stoned him to death in the court of the house of the LORD."
2 Chronicles 24:18-21

Egyptian Exodus to the Rise of Babylon

Amaziah Killed Because of His Sin
Joash was murdered while he slept. Amaziah succeeded him. Amaziah followed in the ways of the Lord until after a battle with the Edomites. After the battle, he brought back the Edomite gods and began worshiping them. As a result, God abandoned him and he was assassinated.

"Now after Amaziah came from slaughtering the Edomites, he brought the gods of the sons of Seir, set them up as his gods, bowed down before them and burned incense to them. Then the anger of the LORD burned against Amaziah, and He sent him a prophet who said to him, 'Why have you sought the gods of the people who have not delivered their own people from your hand?' As he was talking with him, the king said to him, 'Have we appointed you a royal counselor? Stop! Why should you be struck down?' Then the prophet stopped and said, 'I know that God has planned to destroy you, because you have done this and have not listened to my counsel.'" *2 Chronicles 25:14-16*

Jehu's Great-Great Grandson
Jehu's descendants would sit on the throne of Israel for only four generations. The last of his line was his great-great grandson, Azariah. Shallum formed a conspiracy and assassinated Azariah, and started a new dynasty in Israel.

"The LORD said to Jehu, 'Because you have done well in executing what is right in My eyes, and have done to the house of Ahab according to all that *was* in My heart, your sons of the fourth generation shall sit on the throne of Israel.'" *2 Kings 10:30*

"In the thirty-eighth year of Azariah king of Judah, Zechariah the son of Jeroboam became king over Israel in Samaria *for* six months. He did evil in the sight of the LORD, as his fathers had done; he did not depart from the sins of Jeroboam the son of Nebat, which he made Israel sin. Then Shallum the son of Jabesh conspired against him and struck him before the people and killed him, and reigned in his place... This is the word of the LORD which He spoke to Jehu, saying, 'Your sons to the fourth generation shall sit on the throne of Israel.' And so it was." *2 Kings 15:8-10,12*

Jonah Warns the Assyrians
The book of Jonah gives details about how God gave the Assyrians a chance to repent and they did. Jonah preached in Nineveh about 758 BC during the reign of Jeroboam II. Eventually the sin of the inhabitants of Nineveh returned and grew to the point where God stepped in and sent the Babylonian Empire to destroy them.

Moab Captured by Assyria
Isaiah prophesied that within three years the Assyrian Empire would displace the Moabites. The nation of Moab fell to the Assyrians about the year 732 BC.

"But now the LORD speaks, saying, 'Within three years, as a hired man would count them, the glory of Moab will be degraded along with all *his* great population, and *his* remnant will be very small *and* impotent.'" *Isaiah 16:14*

Balaam predicted the destruction of Edom and Moab in this way:

"I see him, but not now; I behold him, but not near; A star shall come forth from Jacob, A scepter shall rise from Israel, And shall crush through the forehead of Moab, and tear down all the sons of Sheth. Edom shall be a possession, Seir, its enemies, also will be a possession, while Israel performs valiantly. One from Jacob shall have dominion, and will destroy the remnant from the city." *Numbers 24:17-19*

Kenites
The Kenites remained friendly to the Israelites, but ultimately lost their identity as a people when Assyria took them captive about 722 BC.

"Then he looked over toward the Kenites and delivered this message: 'Your home is secure; your nest is set in the rocks. But the Kenites will be destroyed when Assyria takes you captive.'" *Numbers 24:21-22 NLT*

Ancient Prophecies Revealed

Arabia Fell to Assyria
About seven years after the fall of the Kenites, Assyria conquered Arabia. Called "Kedar and Dedan" in this prophecy, the final invasion occurred in 715 BC.

"The oracle about Arabia. In the thickets of Arabia you must spend the night, O caravans of Dedanites. Bring water for the thirsty, O inhabitants of the land of Tema, meet the fugitive with bread. For they have fled from the swords, from the drawn sword, and from the bent bow, and from the press of battle. For thus the Lord said to me, 'In a year, as a hired man would count it, all the splendor of Kedar will terminate; and the remainder of the number of bowmen, the mighty men of the sons of Kedar, will be few; for the LORD God of Israel has spoken.'" *Isaiah 21:13-17*

---

711 BC
Destruction of the Assyrian Army

After the conquest of Arabia, the Assyrian army marched into Judah and besieged Jerusalem. Recorded in both Isaiah and 2 Kings, by 711 BC the Assyrians had besieged Jerusalem. The people in the city were starving. The Lord sent the prophet Isaiah to tell King Hezekiah that by the next day they would have plenty to eat. The Lord would deliver them that night. During the night, the Lord sent just *one* angel into the Assyrian camp. The angel killed 185,000 troops, which was the whole camp!

"Therefore thus says the LORD concerning the king of Assyria, 'He will not come to this city or shoot an arrow there; and he will not come before it with a shield or throw up a siege ramp against it. By the way that he came, by the same he will return, and he shall not come to this city,' declares the LORD. 'For I will defend this city to save it for My own sake and for My servant David's sake.' Then it happened that night that the angel of the LORD went out and struck 185,000 in the camp of the Assyrians; and when men rose early in the morning, behold, all of them were dead. So Sennacherib king of Assyria departed and returned home, and lived at Nineveh." *2 Kings 19:32-36*

King Sennacherib Assassinated
The news of the defeat of such a large portion of the Assyrian army at Jerusalem started a rumor of a rebellion. Sennacherib left off the battle for Jerusalem and went back to Assyria. It is interesting to note that the God of Israel defended Jerusalem against Sennacherib; but Sennacherib's god could not save him. While Sennacherib was worshiping his false god in his pagan temple, he was assassinated!

"Isaiah said to them, 'Thus you shall say to your master, "Thus says the LORD, 'Do not be afraid because of the words that you have heard, with which the servants of the king of Assyria have blasphemed Me. Behold, I will put a spirit in him so that he will hear a rumor and return to his own land. And I will make him fall by the sword in his own land.'"' …So Sennacherib king of Assyria departed and returned *home*, and lived at Nineveh. It came about as he was worshiping in the house of Nisroch his god, that Adrammelech and Sharezer killed him with the sword; and they escaped into the land of Ararat. And Esarhaddon his son became king in his place." *2 Kings 19:6-7,36-37*

Shebna Died Because of Disrespect
Shebna was a high official in the Jewish court of King Hezekiah. He became arrogant and built for himself a tomb in the area of the kings of Israel, even though he was not an Israelite, but a foreigner. Isaiah prophesied that he would not be buried in that tomb, but God would cast him into a distant land and he would die there. Shebna was removed from his office. His position was filled by Eliakim Ben-Hilkiah as predicted.

"Thus says the Lord GOD of hosts, 'Come, go to this steward, to Shebna, who is in charge of the *royal* household, 'what right do you have here, and whom do you have here, that you have hewn a tomb for yourself here, you who hew a tomb on the height, you who carve a resting place for yourself in the rock? Behold, the LORD is about to hurl you headlong, O man. And He is about to grasp you firmly *and* roll you tightly like a ball, *to be cast* into a vast country; there you will die… Then it will come about in that day, that I will summon My servant Eliakim the son of Hilkiah, and I will clothe him with your tunic, and tie your sash securely about him. I will entrust him with your authority," *Isaiah 22:15-18,20-21*

Amalekites Final Destruction
Amalek was the grandson of Esau. His descendants became the Amalekites. In Numbers 24, Balaam prophesied the entire race of Amalekites would cease to exist.

"And he looked at Amalek and took up his discourse and said, 'Amalek was the first of the nations, but his end *shall be* destruction.'" *Numbers 24:20*

In Exodus 17 God said that He would war with Amalek from generation to generation. He promised to utterly blot out Amalek so that he would not even be remembered. Their destruction occurred over several successive wars. In the first war the Amalekites came down and met the Israelites at Rephidim. This is the battle recorded in Exodus 17 when Aaron and Hur had to hold up Moses' hands for the Israelites to prevail over the Amalekites. They were driven back. God said to Moses:

"Then the LORD said to Moses, 'Write this in a book as a memorial and recite it to Joshua, that I will utterly blot out the memory of Amalek from under heaven.' …and he said, 'The LORD has sworn; the LORD will have war against Amalek from generation to generation.'" *Exodus 17:14,16*

Much later, King Saul drove the Amalekites back and took their king, Agag, prisoner (1 Samuel 15). Since Saul did not obey God by completely destroying the Amalekites, Saul lost his kingdom. David, in his day, completely crushed the Amalekite nation, as recorded in 1 Samuel 30:1-20. The remnant of the Amalekites tried reforming their nation but was destroyed by Simeonites in the days of Hezekiah of Judah, sometime before 700 BC. From that time forward only a few Amalekite people remained.

"…in the days of Hezekiah king of Judah, …from the sons of Simeon, five hundred men went to Mount Seir, with Pelatiah, Neariah, Rephaiah and Uzziel, the sons of Ishi, as their leaders. They destroyed the remnant of the Amalekites who escaped, and have lived there to this day." *1 Chronicles 4:41-43*

Hezekiah Lives Another 15 Years
King Hezekiah lay dying. He prayed to the Lord to heal him. The Lord healed him and also added 15 years to his life. Unfortunately, during this 15 years, Hezekiah fathered Judah's most evil king: Manasseh.

"In those days Hezekiah became mortally ill. And Isaiah the prophet the son of Amoz came to him and said to him, 'Thus says the LORD, "Set your house in order, for you shall die and not live."' Then he turned his face to the wall and prayed to the LORD... Before Isaiah had gone out of the middle court, the word of the LORD came to him, saying, 'Return and say to Hezekiah the leader of My people, 'Thus says the LORD, the God of your father David, I have heard your prayer, I have seen your tears; behold, I will heal you. On the third day you shall go up to the house of the LORD. I will add fifteen years to your life, and I will deliver you and this city from the hand of the king of Assyria; and I will defend this city for My own sake and for My servant David's sake.'" *2 Kings 20:1-2,4-6*

Manasseh's Death
Because of all the evil Manasseh did, the Lord destroyed him and placed his son on the throne instead. Manasseh was more evil than all the kings that came before him. According to Jewish legend (Ascension of Isaiah and others), he ordered the prophet Isaiah to be put into a hollow log and sawn in two. Paul alludes to Isaiah dying in this way in Hebrews 11.

"Now the LORD spoke through His servants the prophets, saying, 'Because Manasseh king of Judah has done these abominations, having done wickedly more than all the Amorites did who *were* before him, and has also made Judah sin with his idols... Moreover, Manasseh shed very much innocent blood until he had filled Jerusalem from one end to another; besides his sin with which he made Judah sin, in doing evil in the sight of the LORD.' Now the rest of the acts of Manasseh and all that he did and his sin which he committed, are they not written in the Book of the Chronicles of the

Ancient Prophecies Revealed

Kings of Judah? And Manasseh slept with his fathers and was buried in the garden of his own house, in the garden of Uzza, and Amon his son became king in his place." *2 Kings 21:10-11,16-18*

Josiah Destroys the Idols

This prophecy was given when Jeroboam became king about 950 BC. It was fulfilled over 300 years later in 639 BC. Notice that God called Josiah *by name* 300 years *before he was born*. God did the same with Cyrus, also calling him by name before he was born. After Josiah was born, he fulfilled the prophecy in every detail.

"Now behold, there came a man of God from Judah to Bethel by the word of the LORD, while Jeroboam was standing by the altar to burn incense. He cried against the altar by the word of the LORD, and said, 'O altar, altar,' thus says the LORD, 'Behold, a son shall be born to the house of David, Josiah by name; and on you he shall sacrifice the priests of the high places who burn incense on you, and human bones shall be burned on you.' Then he gave a sign the same day, saying, This is the sign which the LORD has spoken, 'Behold, the altar shall be split apart and the ashes which are on it shall be poured out.'" *1 Kings 13:1-3*

"He broke in pieces the *sacred* pillars and cut down the Asherim and filled their places with human bones. Furthermore, the altar that *was* at Bethel *and* the high place which Jeroboam the son of Nebat, who made Israel sin, had made, even that altar and the high place he broke down. Then he demolished its stones, ground them to dust, and burned the Asherah. Now when Josiah turned, he saw the graves that *were* there on the mountain, and he sent and took the bones from the graves and burned *them* on the altar and defiled it according to the word of the LORD which the man of God proclaimed, who proclaimed these things. Then he said, 'What is this monument that I see?' And the men of the city told him, 'It is the grave of the man of God who came from Judah and proclaimed these things which you have done against the altar of Bethel.' He said, 'Let him alone; let no one disturb his bones.' So they left his bones undisturbed with the bones of the prophet who came from Samaria." *2 Kings 23:14-18*

The Rise of Babylon to the Messiah

612 BC to 2 BC – 45 prophecies in 610 years

Date	Prophecy	Prediction
612	79. Nineveh (Assyria) will be permanently destroyed	Nah. 1:8-9
	80. Assyrians will be drunk the night of the Babylonian attack	Nah. 1:10
	81. Ninevites will be completely wiped out	Nah. 1:14
	82. Nineveh's fortresses will be easily captured	Nah. 3:12
	83. Nineveh will be destroyed by fire	Nah. 3:15
607	84. 70-year Babylonian captivity will begin	Jer. 25:11-12
	85. Judah will be taken captive to Babylon because of idolatry	Deut. 31:16-17
	86. After three Babylonian rulers, Persian Empire will take over	Jer. 27:6-7
582	87. Babylonian King Nebuchadnezzar will go insane for seven years (582-575 BC)	Dan. 4:4-37
544	88. The kingdom of Lydia will fall to the Persians	Dan. 7:5
537	89. After 70 years, the Babylonian captivity will end	Jer. 25:11-12; 32:36-37
	90. Babylon will fall to the Medes and Persians	Isa. 13:17, 21:2,9; Dan. 5:30-31; Hab. 2
	91. Cyrus will take Babylon (gates will be open before Cyrus)	Isa. 45:1
	92. Cyrus will free the Jews - Josephus Ant 11:1	Dan. 5:30 (Isa. 41:25; 44:28-45:6)
	93. Israel and Judah will come back as one nation from Assyria and Babylon	Jer. 50:4
	94. Temple vessels will be restored	Jer. 27:19-22
523	95. Kingdom of Egypt will fall to the Persians	Dan. 7:5
480	96. After four kings, Persian Empire will attack Greece (537-465 BC)	Dan. 11:1-2
465	97. Ezra will restore the Temple services	Ps. 20:1-3
326	98. Alexander the Great will conquer the known world	Dan. 11:3
	99. Tyre will be destroyed	Ezek. 26:4-14
	100. Ekron will be destroyed, never to rise again	Zech. 9:1-8
	101. Ashkalon and Gaza will be destroyed	Zech. 9:1-8
	102. Ashdod will be taken over	Zech. 9:1-8
	103. God will protect Jerusalem from Alexander's army	Zech. 9:1-8
323	104. Alexander's empire will be split into four smaller empires	Dan. 11:4
323	105. Ptolemy I Soter will help Seleucus Nicator retake Syria (323-285 BC)	Dan. 11:5
285	106. Berenice will marry Antiochus II ~285-246 BC	Dan. 11:6
	107. Berenice and Antiochus will be poisoned	Dan. 11:6
246	108. Ptolemy II will die	Dan. 11:6
	109. Ptolemy III will avenge Berenice's death by killing Laodece	Dan. 11:7
	110. Ptolemy will take Syrian and Egyptian idols back home	Dan. 11:8
217	111. Seleucus III and Antiochus III will attack Egypt at the "battle of Raphia"	Dan. 11:10
204	112. Antiochus III will attack Egypt	Dan. 11:13
	113. False Prophet will arise and mislead many	Dan. 11:14
197	114. Antiocus III will gain complete control of Israel	Dan. 11:16
194	115. Cleopatra I will marry Ptolemy V	Dan. 11:17
190	116. Battle of Magnesia will occur	Dan. 11:18
175	117. Seleucus IV will order an attack on the Jerusalem Temple	Dan. 11:20
	118. Antiochus Epiphanes will rise to power	Dan. 11:21
	119. Antiochus Epiphanes will assassinate Onias	Dan. 11:22
	120. Antiochus Epiphanes will deceive Rome into officially recognizing him	Dan. 11:23
165	121. Maccabees will revolt against Greek-ruled Syria	Dan. 11:32; Zech. 9:13

Ancient Prophecies Revealed

Date	Prophecy	Prediction*
64	122. Grecian Empire will fall to Rome	Dan. 11:33
40	123. Rome will destroy Ashur (Syria/Assyria)	Num. 24:23-24; Isa. 7:14

*In this chart only the prophecy of Cyrus freeing the Jews at the end of the 70-year Babylonian captivity has its fulfillment recorded in Scripture. Therefore we left out the column for the fulfillments.

612 BC
Destruction of the Assyrian Empire

The great Assyrian Empire captured the ten northern tribes of Israel in 722 BC. A decade later, in 711 BC, Assyria attacked Judah. The prophet Isaiah recorded the Assyrian besiegement of Jerusalem ended when the Lord sent an angel that killed 185,000 Assyrian solders in one night. The Assyrians retreated and their leader, Sennacherib, was assassinated.

The prophet Nahum describes the destruction of Nineveh (Assyria's capital) by the Babylonians in 612 BC. Nahum wrote Nineveh would be taken easily at night while the guards were drunk and the city burned with fire.

> "...He will make a complete end of its site ...Like tangled thorns, and like those who are drunken with their drink, they are consumed as stubble completely withered... The LORD has issued a command concerning you: 'Your name will no longer be perpetuated. I will cut off idol and image From the house of your gods. I will prepare your grave, For you are contemptible.' ...All your fortifications are fig trees with ripe fruit-- when shaken, they fall into the eater's mouth... There fire will consume you, the sword will cut you down; it will consume you as the locust does."
> *Nahum 1:8,10,14, 3:12,15*

Ancient historian Diodorus of Sicily, who wrote about 30 BC, records that the night Nineveh fell the Assyrian king had given "much wine to the solders." The ancient Babylonian records describe how the fortified cities began to fall about 614. By 612 Nineveh fell, marking the total defeat of the Assyrian Empire. The Encyclopedia Britannica states "...Extensive traces of ash, representing the sack of the city by Babylonians, Scythians, and Medes in 612 BC, have been found in many parts of the Acropolis. After 612 BC the city ceased to be important..." All of Nahum's prophecies had now been proven true.

607 BC
Babylonian Empire

Nabopolassar, Nebuchadnezzar, and Belshazzar

Nabopolassar was the first king of the neo-Babylonian empire. He ruled from 628-607 BC. Nabopolassar defeated the Assyrian Empire as prophesied. He then handed the kingdom over to his son Nebuchadnezzar, who ruled 45 years, from 607-561 BC. Nebuchadnezzar defeated Judah and Aram. Evil-merodach, Nebuchadnezzar's son, ruled 23 years, from 561-537 BC. Belshazzar, Nebuchadnezzar's grandson, co-ruled with his father during the last three years of the kingdom. Then the Babylonian kingdom fell to the Persians in 537 BC. See *Ancient Seder Olam* for more historical details.

Jeremiah recorded that the Babylonian Empire would end after three generations, starting with Nebuchadnezzar. Some secular historians try to say Belshazzar was actually someone else's son, but according to Scripture he was the grandson of Nebuchadnezzar.

"Now I have given all these lands into the hand of Nebuchadnezzar king of Babylon… All the nations shall serve him and his son and his grandson until the time of his own land comes; then many nations and great kings will make him their servant." *Jeremiah 27:6-7*

The Babylonian king, Nebuchadnezzar, went insane for seven years as was prophesied and fulfilled in Daniel 4. These dates would have been 582-575 BC.

The book of Habakkuk recorded that Judah would be overturned by the Babylonians, who in turn would be overthrown by another nation. Isaiah 13:17 and 21:2,9 recorded Babylon would be destroyed by the Medes and Persians more then 300 years before the overthrow took place.

70-Year Captivity
Israel failed to allow the land to rest one year in seven, as God had commanded through Moses. God judged Judah by allowing Nebuchadnezzar, king of Babylon, to carry the nation away into captivity for 70 years.

"The LORD then spoke to Moses at Mount Sinai, saying… 'Six years you shall sow your field, and six years you shall prune your vineyard and gather in its crop, but during the seventh year the land shall have a sabbath rest, a sabbath to the LORD; you shall not sow your field nor prune your vineyard. Your harvest's aftergrowth you shall not reap, and your grapes of untrimmed vines you shall not gather; the land shall have a sabbatical year. *Leviticus 25:1,3-5*

Instead of obeying God's command, they planted crops every year. After 490 years, Israel owed the land 70 years of rest. Jeremiah wrote that the Babylonian captivity would last *exactly* 70 years. Then Israel would be allowed to return home. Daniel confirmed this when he stated the 70 years were fulfilled in the first year of the reign of Cyrus and Darius.

"'This whole land will be a desolation and a horror, and these nations will serve the king of Babylon seventy years. Then it will be when seventy years are completed I will punish the king of Babylon and that nation,' declares the LORD, 'for their iniquity, and the land of the Chaldeans; and I will make it an everlasting desolation.'"
Jeremiah 25:11-12

God also caused the 70-year captivity because of idolatry.
"The LORD said to Moses, "Behold, you are about to lie down with your fathers; and this people will arise and play the harlot with the strange gods of the land, into the midst of which they are going, and will forsake Me and break My covenant which I have made with them. Then My anger will be kindled against them in that day, and I will forsake them and hide My face from them, and they will be consumed, and many evils and troubles will come upon them; so that they will say in that day, 'Is it not because our God is not among us that these evils have come upon us?' But I will surely hide My face in that day because of all the evil which they will do, for they will turn to other gods."
Deuteronomy 31:16-18

Daniel records the fulfillment of the 70 years.
"In the first year of Darius the son of Ahasuerus, of Median descent, who was made king over the kingdom of the Chaldeans-- in the first year of his reign, I, Daniel, observed in the books the number of the years which was *revealed as* the word of the LORD to Jeremiah the prophet for the completion of the desolations of Jerusalem, *namely*, seventy years. So I gave my attention to the Lord God to seek *Him by* prayer and supplications, with fasting, sackcloth and ashes. *Daniel 9:1-3*

On the following page there is an outline of prophecies given by the prophet Daniel. In chapter 2 of the Book of Daniel, he interprets King Nebuchadnezzar's dream about a great statue. The statue represents four major empires that will rule before the Messiah will set up his kingdom. In chapters 7 and 8, Daniel has a series of dreams detailing these empires.

Ancient Prophecies Revealed

Babylonian
Both the golden head of the statue and the winged lion represent the Babylonian Empire which ruled over Israel from 607 to 537 BC.

Medio-Persian
The statue's silver chest and arms, the bear, and the ram all represent the empire of the Medes and Persians. They ruled over Israel from 537 to 326 BC. The bear has three ribs in its mouth, representing the three-nation coalition of Lydia, Babylon, and Egypt that tried to stop Persia, but failed. Lydia fell first in 544 BC, then Babylon in 537 BC, and finally, Egypt in 523 BC. The bear had one side higher than the other and the ram had one horn higher than the other. These represent the fact that the Persians were the dominate power in the Medio-Persian Empire.

Grecian
Next, the statue's brass belly and thighs, along with the prophecies of the four-headed leopard and the goat represent the Grecian Empire begun by Alexander the Great. The leopard has four heads, and the goat had one great horn that crushed the ram and then was broken. In the place of the great horn grew four little horns. The meaning of these is that the Grecian Empire, under Alexander the Great, would replace the Persian Empire. This occurred in 326 BC, but within three years Alexander died and the empire was split into four smaller empires. Two of these empires were Greek-ruled Syria, called the Seleucid Empire, and Greek-ruled Egypt, called the Ptolemaic Empire. These two would rule over Israel from 323 to 64 BC when the Roman Empire would take control of the nation of Israel.

Roman
The Roman Empire was represented by the iron legs, and a beast that is not described by Daniel. Just as the two arms of the silver chest represented an empire formed from two nations (the Medes and the Persians), the two iron legs also represent a division: the Roman Empire splitting in two. Rome took Israel in 64 BC and continued until AD 395 when the empire was split in two. Rome ruled the western empire, while Constantinople ruled the eastern empire. This continued until AD 476 when the old Roman Empire dissolved. Sometime in the future it will revive in the form of ten nations. In their days the Messiah will return. See the section on Post-2008 Prophecies for further details.

Daniel chapter 11 describes in great detail the period between 537 BC and AD 1948. The Romans dispersed the nation of Israel in AD 132. They remained expelled from their land until the nation of Israel was reestablished in AD 1948. See the section on Modern Israel for more details on their return.

The Rise of Babylon to the Messiah

World Empires
Daniel 2,7,8 Rev 13

These drawings are from Clerance Larkin's book *Dispensational Truth*, published in 1907.

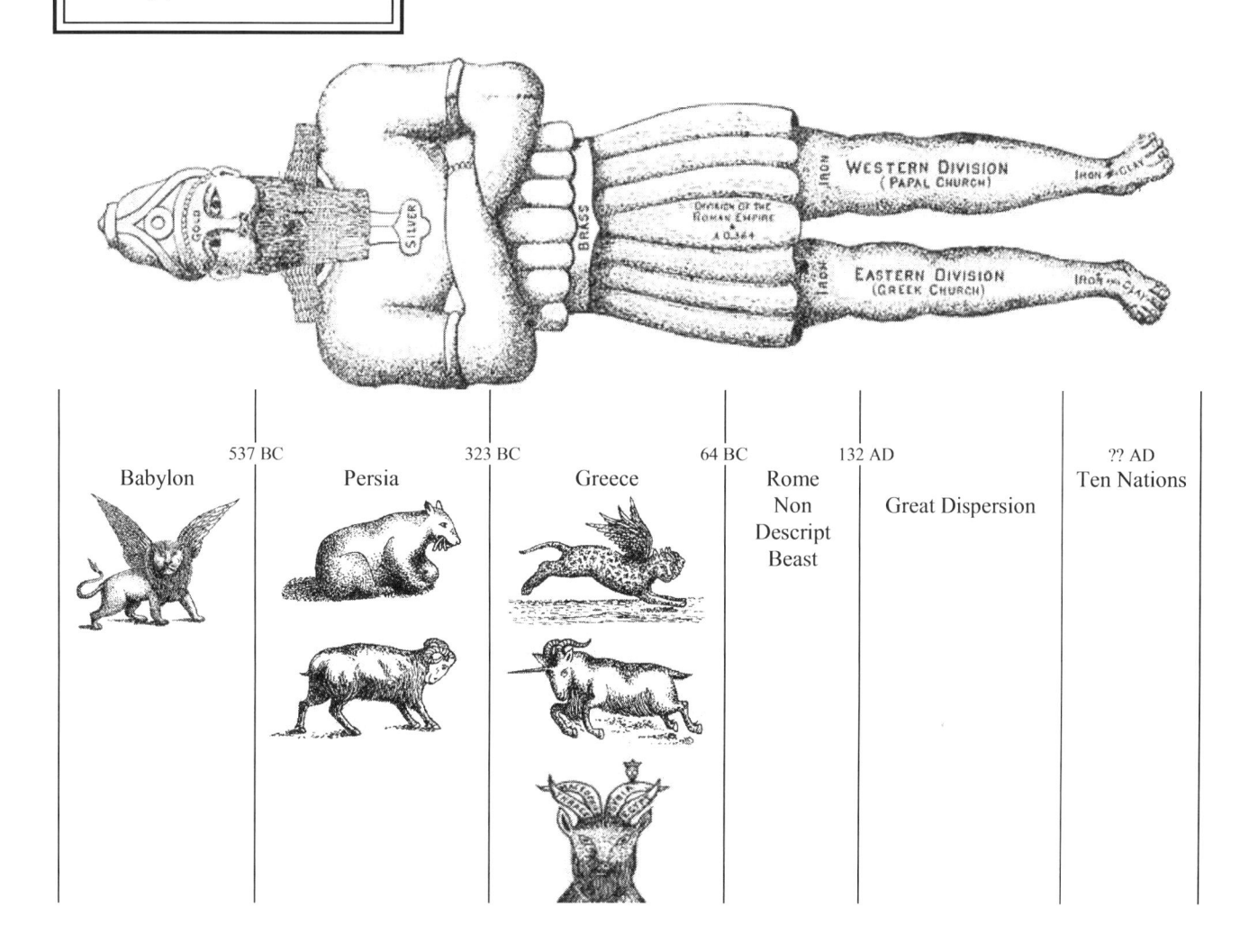

537 BC	323 BC	64 BC	132 AD	?? AD
Babylon	Persia	Greece	Rome Non Descript Beast	Great Dispersion	Ten Nations

37

Ancient Prophecies Revealed

---
537 BC
Cyrus of Persia

Isaiah wrote his prophecies between 800-700 BC. Centuries before Cyrus was born Isaiah called him by name and prophesied that he would be protected by God, allowed to destroy the Babylonian Empire, free the Jews, and finance the rebuilding of the Temple in Jerusalem. Cyrus became King of Persia in 559 BC and took Babylon in 537 BC. Isaiah even gives details describing how Cyrus would capture the city of Babylon!

The prediction that the Persians, along with the Medes, would replace the Babylonian Empire is recorded in Isaiah 13:17, 21:2,9 and Daniel 2:39, 5:30-31. Jeremiah prophesied this would occur at the end of 70 years of the Israelites being held captive in Babylon (Jeremiah 25:11-12). The fulfillment is also recorded in Daniel 9:1-3. How did Cyrus accomplish this? Notice Isaiah prophesied Cyrus would dry up or divert a river.

> "*It is I* who says to the depth of the sea, 'Be dried up!' And I will make your rivers dry. *It is I* who says of Cyrus, '*He is* My shepherd! And he will perform all My desire' And he declares of Jerusalem, 'She will be built,' and of the temple, 'Your foundation will be laid.'" *Isaiah 44:27-28*

Cyrus besieged Babylon but could not conquer the city. The city of Babylon had outer walls that were more than 70 feet thick, 300 feet high, with more than 250 watchtowers. It had motes and many other defenses. Since the city sat on the Euphrates River, the inhabitants had all the water and food they needed. They could withstand a siege indefinitely. If Cyrus could not scale the walls or wait them out, how could he conquer the city? Josephus writes that a group of Jews showed the prophecies to Cyrus. He learned of his destiny and was even told by Isaiah's prophecy how to breach the walls of Babylon!

> "Thus says the LORD to Cyrus His anointed, whom I have taken by the right hand, to subdue nations before him, and to loose the loins of kings; to open doors before him so that gates will not be shut: I will go before you and make the rough places smooth; I will shatter the doors of bronze and cut through their iron bars. I will give you the treasures of darkness, and hidden wealth of secret places, so that you may know that it is I, the LORD, the God of Israel, who calls you by your name. For the sake of Jacob My servant, And Israel My chosen *one*, I have also called you by your name; I have given you a title of honor though you have not known Me. I am the LORD, and there is no other; besides Me there is no God. I will gird you, though you have not known Me; that men may know from the rising to the setting of the sun that there is no one besides Me. I am the LORD, and there is no other," *Isaiah 45:1-6*

Notice in these two prophecies Isaiah says God would "go before him and open the gates." He was to command that a "river be dried up." Cyrus believed what the Scripture literally said. Upstream, out of the sight of the Babylonians, his men created a dam and trench that led into a dry river basin. When it was ready, under cover of darkness, he opened the dam and diverted the water. Cyrus' troops marched quietly along the center of the river *under* the walls of the city. Sure enough, God went before them and caused the brass gates in the water way to be left unlocked. His men entered

---
Prophecies Cyrus fulfilled:
Loosed the loins of kings
The Jews freed
State of Israel was recreated
Funded the rebuilding of the Temple
Destroyed Babylonian Empire
Took Babylon by diverting a river

---

the city. They opened the main city gates and took the city. The Encyclopedia Judaica records this event occurred on the 14th of Tishrei, the evening before the first day of the Jewish festival of Tabernacles.

The ancient historian Herodotus also records the taking of the city by diverting the water. He adds that when the dam was opened, the water level of the river dropped "to the height of the middle of a man's thigh," *Herodotus 1.191*

The ancient historian, Josephus, wrote that Cyrus conquered Babylon by believing the literal interpretation of Scripture:

> "'Thus saith Cyrus the king: Since God Almighty hath appointed me to be king of the habitable earth, I believe that he is that God which the nation of the Israelites worship; for indeed he foretold my name by the prophets, and that I should

build him a house at Jerusalem, in the country of Judea.' This was known to Cyrus by his reading the book which Isaiah left behind him of his prophecies; for this prophet said that God had spoken thus to him in a secret vision: 'My will is, that Cyrus, whom I have appointed to be king over many and great nations, send back my people to their own land, and build my temple.' This was foretold by Isaiah one hundred and forty years before the temple was demolished." *Josephus Antiquities 11.1.1-3*

Isaiah says Cyrus would "loose the loins of kings." This was fulfilled in Daniel 5:6, when Belshazzar realized that very night Cyrus would take the city and kill him. Daniel says:

"the joints of his loins were loosed, and his knees smote one against another." *Daniel 5:6 KJV*

Cyrus' decree to free the Jews and rebuild the Jerusalem Temple is recorded in Ezra 1:1-4. Daniel 5:30 records the fall of Babylon. Daniel explains how Darius the Mede, under the direction of Cyrus, took control of Babylon. In addition to funding the rebuilding of the Temple, Cyrus also arranged for the sacred vessels from Solomon's Temple to be returned to the Jews. Jeremiah prophesied this and Josephus recorded its fulfillment.

"For thus says the LORD of hosts concerning the pillars, concerning the sea, concerning the stands and concerning the rest of the vessels that are left in this city, which Nebuchadnezzar king of Babylon did not take when he carried into exile Jeconiah the son of Jehoiakim, king of Judah, from Jerusalem to Babylon, and all the nobles of Judah and Jerusalem. Yes, thus says the LORD of hosts, the God of Israel, concerning the vessels that are left in the house of the LORD and in the house of the king of Judah and in Jerusalem, 'They will be carried to Babylon and they will be there until the day I visit them,' declares the LORD 'Then I will bring them back and restore them to this place.'"
Jeremiah 27:19-22

"upon the rebuilding of their city, and the revival of the ancient practices relating to their worship, Cyrus also sent back to them the vessels of God which King Nebuchadnezzar had pillaged out of the temple, and had carried to Babylon."
Josephus Antiquities 11.1.1-3

First Return (from Babylon)
Jeremiah also relates how the ten tribes were captured by Assyria and Judah was taken by Babylon. After the 70 years, both nations returned *together*.

"The word which the LORD spoke concerning Babylon… For a nation has come up against her out of the north; it will make her land an object of horror, and there will be no inhabitant in it. Both man and beast have wandered off, they have gone away! 'In those days and at that time,' declares the LORD, 'the sons of Israel will come, *both* they and the sons of Judah as well; they will go along weeping as they go, and it will be the LORD their God they will seek.'"
Jeremiah 50:1,3-4

Persia (536-326 BC)
"In the first year of Darius the Mede, I arose to be an encouragement and a protection for him. And now I will tell you the truth. Behold, three more kings are going to arise in Persia. Then a fourth will gain far more riches than all *of them*; as soon as he becomes strong through his riches, he will arouse the whole *empire* against the realm of Greece."
Daniel 11:1-2

Darius the Meade ruled from 536 to 530 BC. The four kings were: Cambyses (530-522 BC); Pseudo-Smerdis (522 BC); Darius (522-486 BC); Xerxes I (486-465 BC, See Esther 1:1). Xerxes I, after growing rich, attacked Greece at Sardis of Asia Minor with 60,000 men and 1200 ships. It was the largest invasion force the world had ever seen up to that time. The Greeks stood their ground. The Persians lost the war. This battle occurred in 480 BC.

Ancient Prophecies Revealed

Ezra Restores Services – 465BC
Is Psalm 20 the Hebrew word for "help" is "Ezra." So in this passage, Ezra the scribe is actually mentioned by name. In the day when they have trouble reestablishing the Temple services, God will send Ezra to restore them. Notice this passage ends with 'Selah,' which means this is a riddle. See the biblical book of Ezra for more details.

> "May the LORD answer you in the day of trouble! May the name of the God of Jacob set you *securely* on high! May He send you help [Ezra] from the sanctuary, And support you from Zion! May He remember all your meal offerings, and find your burnt offering acceptable! Selah." *Psalm 20:1-3*

Greece under Alexander the Great (326-323 BC)
> "And a mighty king will arise, and he will rule with great authority and do as he pleases. But as soon as he has arisen, his kingdom will be broken up and parceled out toward the four points of the compass, though not to his *own* descendants, nor according to his authority which he wielded, for his sovereignty will be uprooted and *given* to others besides them." *Daniel 11:3-4*

Alexander the Great was born in Pella in 356 BC. Upon taking the throne of Greece, he began a campaign against the Persian Empire. He entered Asia in 334 BC with 34,000 men against Darius' 400,000 men. Within a year he captured control of Syria.

Alexander the Great died at the age of 33, only three years after gaining control of the known world. At the time of his death in 323 BC, none of his children took the throne. Instead, Alexander's kingdom was split into four parts. Each of the four ruling generals of his empire took part of the empire for his own. Seleucus Nicator took Syria, Cassander took Macedonia (Greece), Lysimachus took Thrace (Turkey), and Ptolemy took Egypt. There was a fifth general, but he died in a battle just before Alexander did.

```
326 BC
Alexander the Great
```

> "The burden of the word of the LORD is against the land of Hadrach, with Damascus as its resting place (for the eyes of men, especially of all the tribes of Israel, are toward the LORD), and Hamath also, which borders on it; Tyre and Sidon, though they are very wise. For Tyre built herself a fortress and piled up silver like dust, and gold like the mire of the streets. Behold, the Lord will dispossess her and cast her wealth into the sea; and she will be consumed with fire. Ashkelon will see it and be afraid. Gaza too will writhe in great pain; also Ekron, for her expectation has been confounded. Moreover, the king will perish from Gaza, and Ashkelon will not be inhabited. And a mongrel race will dwell in Ashdod, and I will cut off the pride of the Philistines. And I will remove their blood from their mouth and their detestable things from between their teeth. Then they also will be a remnant for our God, and be like a clan in Judah, and Ekron like a Jebusite. But I will camp around My house because of an army, because of him who passes by and returns; and no oppressor will pass over them anymore," *Zechariah 9:1-8*

The fulfillment of this prophecy begins with Alexander the Great destroying Tyre. His men threw all of her rubble into the sea (See section on The Destruction of Tyre for full details).

Josephus, in his *Antiquities 11.8.3-7*, tells of how Alexander came to Jerusalem. He relates that Alexander came into Syria and captured Damascus, then Sidon, and then besieged Tyre for seven months. He sent word to the high priest of Jerusalem demanding supplies for his troops. But the high priest, Jaddua, refused, saying he was under obligation to Darius of Persia and could not help. After Alexander destroyed Tyre, he proceeded south along the border and conquered all of Gaza. He destroyed all of the cities except Ashdod, which he used for his own port city.

Notice Ekron would be like the Jebusite, utterly destroyed. Ekron is still in ruins to this day. The rest of these cities have been rebuilt.

After these things, Alexander went to besiege Jerusalem, put the high priest to death for disobedience, and sack the Temple for gold. The high priest was warned by God in a dream not to resist Alexander. When he saw the army approaching, he opened the gates and sent out the priests in white robes in two rows then he went out to meet Alexander in front of the procession. When Alexander saw this, he stated that he had seen this man with the breastplate of crystals in a dream. In his dream, the high priest told him he would subjugate Persia. So Alexander respectfully greeted the high priest and made a sacrifice to God as Gentiles do. The high priest then showed Alexander the prophecies recorded in Daniel 11. Daniel prophesied that the fourth Persian king, after Cyrus, would attack Greece, which had been fulfilled by that time. After this attack on Greece, a mighty Greek king would rise up and defeat the Persians (See Daniel 11:3 later in this section). Alexander believed the prophecies and went on to conquer the Persian Empire. One more prophecy was fulfilled. Truly God camped around Jerusalem and protected it from Alexander's army!

587-326 BC
The Destruction of Tyre

The prophecies about the ancient Phoenician city of Tyre come from both Ezekiel and Isaiah. Ezekiel's prophecy actually has two separate parts intertwined. When referring to Nebuchadnezzar, king of Babylon, Ezekiel uses the word "he." When referring to Alexander the Great and his troops, Ezekiel uses the word "they." History bears out this two-part prophecy. Ezekiel 26:3-5 shows the ultimate destruction of Tyre by Alexander. Then Ezekiel gives, in detail, how this would be accomplished. Verses 6-11 have Nebuchadnezzar setting the stage for Alexander to finish the destruction prophesied in verses 12-21.

After Noah's Flood, Canaan, son of Ham, son of Noah, traveled to the land of Israel and named it after himself, the land of Canaan. Canaan's first-born son, Sidon, founded the city of Sidon. Years later a great grandson founded the city of Tyre about 40 km south of Sidon. In 586 BC, the Israelites were transported to Babylon and Nebuchadnezzar destroyed Solomon's Temple. Nebuchadnezzar then proceeded to the mainland city of Tyre and besieged it for 13 years, 587-574 BC. He eventually broke though the wall and destroyed the gates, but the city of Tyre was composed of two parts: one on the mainland and one on a small island off the coast of the mainland. The Tyrians had moved all the people and merchandise to the island for safety. Nebuchadnezzar left at that point and invaded Egypt. Ezekiel 29:17 shows God allowed him to plunder Egypt as payment for his 13-year siege. This was all part of God's master plan to punish the nations that came against Israel. In 332 BC, 254 years later, Alexander the Great fulfilled the rest of this prophecy, after besieging the island port for only seven months.

Tyre spurned Alexander, thinking they could never be conquered. Alexander ordered his troops to take all the rubble – including the dirt – and throw it into the sea. This made the old mainland site a barren rock and created an Isthmus to the island fortress. He then marched his troops to the city and breached the walls. In his anger he destroyed 1/3 of the city itself, slew over 30,000 inhabitants, and sold the rest into slavery. He then proceeded to destroy the last of the Phoenicians. Even though we have a modern city named after the old city of Tyre, the ancient Phoenician city of Tyre was never rebuilt. See Encyclopedia Britannica for further details.

Alexander (332 BC)
"...'Behold, I am against you, O Tyre, and I will bring up many nations against you, as the sea brings up its waves. They will destroy the walls of Tyre and break down her towers; and I will scrape her debris from her and make her a bare rock. She will be a place for the spreading of nets in the midst of the sea, for I have spoken,' declares the Lord GOD, 'and she will become spoil for the nations.'" *Ezekiel 26:3-5 prophecy given about 586 BC*

Ancient Prophecies Revealed

Nebuchadnezzar (586-574 BC)
"Also her daughters who are on the mainland will be slain by the sword, and they will know that I am the LORD.' For thus says the Lord GOD, 'Behold, I will bring upon Tyre from the north Nebuchadnezzar king of Babylon, king of kings, with horses, chariots, cavalry and a great army. He will slay your daughters on the mainland with the sword; and he will make siege walls against you, cast up a ramp against you and raise up a large shield against you. The blow of his battering rams he will direct against your walls, and with his axes he will break down your towers. Because of the multitude of his horses, the dust raised by them will cover you; your walls will shake at the noise of cavalry and wagons and chariots when he enters your gates as men enter a city that is breached. With the hoofs of his horses he will trample all your streets. He will slay your people with the sword; and your strong pillars will come down to the ground.'"
Ezekiel 26:6-11

Alexander (332 BC)
"Also they will make a spoil of your riches and a prey of your merchandise, break down your walls and destroy your pleasant houses, and throw your stones and your timbers and your debris into the water. [13]"So I will silence the sound of your songs, and the sound of your harps will be heard no more. [14]"I will make you a bare rock; you will be a place for the spreading of nets. You will be built no more, for I the LORD have spoken," declares the Lord GOD."
Ezekiel 26:12-14

"For thus says the Lord GOD, "When I make you a desolate city, like the cities which are not inhabited, when I bring up the deep over you and the great waters cover you, [20]then I will bring you down with those who go down to the pit, to the people of old, and I will make you dwell in the lower parts of the earth, like the ancient waste places, with those who go down to the pit, so that you will not be inhabited; but I will set glory in the land of the living. [21]"I will bring terrors on you and you will be no more; though you will be sought, you will never be found again," declares the Lord GOD."
Ezekiel 26:19-21

Today you can go to the spot where Tyre used to be, approximately two miles south of the modern city of Tyre. The original location has never been rebuilt. Today you will still see fishermen casting nets off the isthmus. Isaiah gives even more details in this prophecy:

"Behold, the land of the Chaldeans--this is the people *which* was not; Assyria appointed it for desert creatures--they erected their siege towers, they stripped its palaces, they made it a ruin. Wail, O ships of Tarshish, for your stronghold is destroyed. Now in that day Tyre will be forgotten for seventy years like the days of one king. At the end of seventy years it will happen to Tyre as *in* the song of the harlot: take *your* harp, walk about the city, O forgotten harlot; pluck the strings skillfully, sing many songs, that you may be remembered. It will come about at the end of seventy years that the LORD will visit Tyre. Then she will go back to her harlot's wages and will play the harlot with all the kingdoms on the face of the earth. Her gain and her harlot's wages will be set apart to the LORD; it will not be stored up or hoarded, but her gain will become sufficient food and choice attire for those who dwell in the presence of the LORD." *Isaiah 23:13-18 prophecy given about 800 BC*

Timeline	
586 BC	Nebuchadnezzar destroyed Solomon's Temple
586-574	Nebuchadnezzar besieged Tyre for 13 years
586-516	Mainland Tyre forgotten for 70 years
516	Tyre restored and hired by decree of Cyrus
323	Alexander destroyed the island city of Tyre
after 323	Remnant of the Philistines destroyed

Assyria destroyed Babylon. They decreed that it be left desolate for 70 years. After Babylon was restored to full strength, the Babylonians attacked and destroyed the Assyrian Empire. King Nebuchadnezzar then destroyed Solomon's Temple and took the Jews into captivity. Then he besieged Tyre for 13 years, finally capturing the mainland city, to no avail. The mainland city lay desolate for the remainder of the 70 years that God decreed the nations could not trade with her, until 516 BC. Isaiah's prophecy states the 70 years will be "like the days of one king" or kingdom. Just as the Babylonian kingdom would only last 70 years, 607 BC to 537 BC, so Tyre would be forgotten for 70 years.

Ezra 3:7 shows that in Cyrus' decree the Tyrians would be hired to supply cedar for the rebuilding of the Jerusalem Temple. This was put on hold until Darius allowed the decree to take place. The Temple building commenced in 516 BC – See *Ancient Seder Olam 28*. In order to supply cedar for the Temple, Tyre was restored as an independent city with all its rights

The Rise of Babylon to the Messiah

and privileges. Notice that from the destruction of the Temple to its rededication was 70 years, 586 to 516 BC. It was during those same 70 years that Tyre was "forgotten."

Isaiah 23:18a points out the fact that when Tyre is restored, its riches were not stored up; but its profits would be used for the rebuilding of the Jerusalem Temple. Verse 18b shows at Tyre's destruction her riches were taken by Alexander's troops, which were then used in Jerusalem as payment for food supplies and for offerings to God by Alexander. See Josephus *Antiquities of the Jews 11.8.3-11*.

Notes:
Tyre has a lot in common with the Babylonian harlot in Revelation 17. Tyre is called a harlot and fornicates with the kings of the earth though her commerce. Some teach the 'song of the harlot' is Job 29:2.

The book of Daniel was written in the 500's BC, centuries before these events took place. After the break up of Alexander the Great's kingdom, the following prophecies from Daniel 11 were fulfilled.

323-64 BC
The Age of Greece

Ptolemy I Soter (323-285)
"Then the king of the South will grow strong, along with *one* of his princes who will gain ascendancy over him and obtain dominion; his domain *will be* a great dominion *indeed*." Daniel 11:5

Seleucus Nicator took control of Syria. Then he was deposed and fled to Egypt. He became a general/prince for Ptolemy and recaptured control of Syria. Seleucus ruled Syria from 311-280 BC.

Berenice Marries Antiochus II & the Reign of Ptolemy III Euergetes (246-221 BC)
"After some years they will form an alliance, and the daughter of the king of the South will come to the king of the North to carry out a peaceful arrangement. But she will not retain her position of power, nor will he remain with his power, but she will be given up, along with those who brought her in and the one who sired her, as well as he who supported her in *those* times. But one of the descendants of her line will arise in his place, and he will come against *their* army and enter the fortress of the king of the North, and he will deal with them and display *great* strength. [8]"Also their gods with their metal images *and* their precious vessels of silver and gold he will take into captivity to Egypt, and he on his part will refrain from *attacking* the king of the North for *some* years. Then the latter will enter the realm of the king of the South, but will return to his *own* land." Daniel 11:6-9

Berenice, daughter of Ptolemy II, married Antiochus II to form an alliance between Syria and Egypt. Laodice, Antiochus II's first wife, had Berenice and her son put to death. She then poisoned Antiochus II and placed her son, Seleucus II Callinicus, on the throne (246-226 BC). Berenice's brother, Ptolemy III Philadelphus (285-246 BC), attacked the Syrian fortress of Antioch. He captured and put to death Laodice. Berenice's father, Ptolemy II, died about the same time. Ptolemy III took back the Syrian & Egyptian gods, as spoil, that the Persian king Cambyses carried off after conquering Egypt in 525 BC.

Seleucus III Ceaunus (226-223 BC) & **Antiochus III the Great** (223-187 BC)
"His sons will mobilize and assemble a multitude of great forces; and one of them will keep on coming and overflow and pass through, that he may again wage war up to his *very* fortress." Daniel 11:10

Seleucus II had two sons, Seleucus III and Antiochus III. They started a war with Egypt but Seleucus III died half way in to the battle. Antiochus II made it all the way to the Egyptian fortress at Raphia in south Israel by 218 BC.

Ancient Prophecies Revealed

Ptolemy IV Philopator (221-203 BC)
"The king of the South will be enraged and go forth and fight with the king of the North. Then the latter will raise a great multitude, but *that* multitude will be given into the hand of the *former*. When the multitude is carried away, his heart will be lifted up, and he will cause tens of thousands to fall; yet he will not prevail." *Daniel 11:11-12*

Ptolemy IV defeated Antiochus III at Raphia in 217 BC. Historian Polybius records over 10,000 solders were killed in the battle. Ptolemy drove Antiochus III back, but "did not prevail" or conquer Syria. He went back to Egypt.

Ptolemy V Epiphanes (203-181 BC)
"For the king of the North will again raise a greater multitude than the former, and after an interval of some years he will press on with a great army and much equipment. Now in those times many will rise up against the king of the South; the violent ones among your people will also lift themselves up in order to **fulfill the vision**, but they will fall down. Then the king of the North will come, cast up a siege ramp and capture a well-fortified city; and the forces of the South will not stand *their ground*, not even their choicest troops, for there will be no strength to make a stand."
Daniel 11:13-15

Thirteen years after the battle of Raphia, Ptolemy IV died. Antiochus III then attacked Egypt. A false prophet arose and caused the people to err. The "many" included Philip of Macedon who entered into an agreement to divide Egypt between himself and Antiochus, but the Ptolemic general Scopas crushed the rebellion. Having lost the battle in the south, Antiochus turned back north and captured the port city of Sidon.

Antiochus gave Cleopatra I to Ptolemy V (194 BC)
"But he who comes against him will do as he pleases, and no one will *be able* to withstand him; he will also stay *for a time* in the Beautiful Land, with destruction in his hand. He will set his face to come with the power of his whole kingdom, bringing with him a proposal of peace which he will put into effect; he will also give him the daughter of women to ruin it. But she will not take a stand *for him* or be on his side." *Daniel 11:16-17*

Antiochus was in full control of Israel, the "Beautiful Land," by 197 BC. When Antiochus learned Egypt had made an alliance with Rome, he did not attack Egypt but tried gaining control of Egypt by giving his daughter Cleopatra to the 7-yr-old Ptolemy V in marriage. Cleopatra, however, did what was right for Egypt and did not listen to her father.

Roman Consul Defeats Antiochus (190 BC)
"Then he will turn his face to the coastlands and capture many. But a commander will put a stop to his scorn against him; moreover, he will repay him for his scorn. So he will turn his face toward the fortresses of his own land, but he will stumble and fall and be found no more." *Daniel 11:18-19*

Antiochus attacked the coastlands with 300 ships; but the Roman consul Lucius Cornelius Scipio Asiaticus defeated him at Magnesia, in Asia Minor, in 190 BC. Antiochus died in 187 BC while trying to plunder the temple of Bel, in the province of Elymais.

Seleucus IV Philopator (187-175 BC)
"Then in his place one will arise who will send an oppressor through the Jewel of *his* kingdom; yet within a few days he will be shattered, though not in anger nor in battle." *Daniel 11:20*

Seleucus IV, son of Antiochus the Great, gave orders to his finance minister to have the Jerusalem Temple, the "Jewel of his kingdom", plundered. Heliodorus, his finance minister, quickly formed a conspiracy, and within "a few days" Seleucus IV was poisoned.

Antiochus IV Epiphanes (175-164 BC)
"In his place a despicable person will arise, on whom the honor of kingship has not been conferred, but he will come in a time of tranquility and seize the kingdom by intrigue. The overflowing forces will be flooded away before him and shattered, and also the prince of the covenant. After an alliance is made with him he will practice deception, and he will go up and gain power with a small *force of* people. In a time of tranquility he will enter the richest *parts* of the realm, and he will accomplish what his fathers never did, nor his ancestors; he will distribute plunder, booty and possessions

The Rise of Babylon to the Messiah

among them, and he will devise his schemes against strongholds, but *only* for a time. He will stir up his strength and courage against the king of the South with a large army; so the king of the South will mobilize an extremely large and mighty army for war; but he will not stand, for schemes will be devised against him. Those who eat his choice food will destroy him, and his army will overflow, but many will fall down slain. As for both kings, their hearts will be *intent* on evil, and they will speak lies to each other at the same table; but it will not succeed, for the end is still *to come* at the appointed time." *Daniel 11:21-27*

Antiochus Epiphanes "seized" the "honor of kingship" from his brother Demetrius I, and had Onias III, the "prince of the covenant" assassinated. See 2 Maccabees 4:4-10 for full details. Antiochus Epiphanes deceived Rome into officially recognizing him. He invaded Israel and most of Egypt. Ptolemy VI Philometer mobilized a large army to stop Antiochus but his younger brother Ptolemy VII Physcon entered into a conspiracy with Antiocus. As a result, Ptolemy VI Philometer was overthrown.

Antiochus IV Epiphanes Attacked Jerusalem
"Then he will return to his land with much plunder; but his heart will be *set* against the holy covenant, and he will take action and *then* return to his *own* land." *Daniel 11:28*

Antiochus Epiphanes had high priest, Jason, deposed. Jason thinking Antiochus was now powerless, started a rumor that he had died, in hopes of getting the priesthood back. When Antiochus heard all of Israel rejoiced over his supposed death, he attacked with fury, in 169 BC. See 1 Maccabees 1:19-20 for full details.

Antiochus IV Epiphanes Attacked Egypt and was Repelled by Rome
"At the appointed time he will return and come into the South, but this last time it will not turn out the way it did before. For ships of Kittim will come against him; therefore he will be disheartened and will return and become enraged at the holy covenant and take action; so he will come back and show regard for those who forsake the holy covenant." *Daniel 11:29-30*

Antiochus attacked Egypt again in 168 BC. "Kittim" is the Hebrew word for Rome – see Jasher, Josephus, and the Septuagint. The Roman vessels under the command of Popilius Laenas drove Antiochus back.

Antiochus typifies the Antichrist (165 BC)
"Forces from him will arise, desecrate the sanctuary fortress, and do away with the regular sacrifice. And they will set up the abomination of desolation." *Daniel 11:31*

From 158 to 165 BC, Antiochus occupied Jerusalem. He even sacrificed a pig on the alter in the Temple! For three years he controlled Jerusalem. Then Judas Maccabee started a rebellion that drove Syrian forces out of Jerusalem and all of Israel.

The Maccabees (164-64 BC)
"By smooth *words* he will turn to godlessness those who act wickedly toward the covenant, but the people who know their God will display strength and take action." *Daniel 11:32*

After Antiochus' three-year occupation, he was driven out by the Maccabees. News of the Israelite rebellion crushed his empire. He died a natural death in 164 BC in the city of Tabae. The Macabees then ruled in peace from 164 to 64 BC when Roman General Pompey conquered Jerusalem. Another prophecy about the war between Greek-ruled Syria and the Macabees is found in Zechariah.

"For I will bend Judah as My bow, I will fill the bow with Ephraim. And I will stir up your sons, O Zion, against your sons, O Greece; And I will make you like a warrior's sword." *Zechariah 9:13*

Ancient Prophecies Revealed

> 64 BC
> Rise of the Roman Empire

We have already discussed the nondescript beast of Daniel's visions and the iron legs which represented the Roman Empire. In Daniel 11:30 we see the coming of the ships of Kittim. We learned that Kittim was the ancient Hebrew name for Rome. The Septuagint version of the Old Testament, which is written in Greek, actually says ships of Rome. We know from history Rome did conquer Egypt, Israel, and Syria in the year 64 BC. General Pompey of the Roman army marched into Jerusalem and simply announced that Israel was now "Roman Territory!"

Another prophecy about Rome was given by Balaam in the book of Numbers. This prophecy states the Romans will occupy and then destroy the territory of "Ashur" and "Eber." Ashur is the ancient Hebrew name for Assyria, and later Syria. Eber is an ancient name for the Hebrews themselves. Eber was a forefather of Abraham, and is where the name "Hebrews" comes from. We will see in the next section a prophecy from Isaiah that describes the same events. We know the nation of Israel was scattered by the Romans in AD 132. In this case, Ashur is the land of Assyria (Syria). The Romans fought wars with Parthia, also called Persia, from 60 to 40 BC. In these wars the land of Assyria and the Syrian people (who were ruled by Greeks during the Seleucid Empire) were totally devastated by the wars between Rome and Parthia.

> "But ships *shall come* from the coast of Kittim, and they shall afflict Asshur and will afflict Eber; so they also *will come* to destruction." Numbers 24:24

Messiah came during the Time of the Roman Empire
In the next section we will show all the prophecies concerning the first coming of the Messiah, which occurred during the Roman occupation of the land of Israel.

We will follow the Roman Empire through the Middle Ages in the section on the Great Dispersion.

✡

The Messiah's First Coming

2 BC to AD 32 – 122 prophecies in 34 years

We will divide this section into three portions. First, we will look at the prophecies fulfilled from the events surrounding Messiah's birth and childhood. Second, we will look at the events surrounding His ministry. Third, we will look at the events surrounding His crucifixion and resurrection. There are over 300 prophecies fulfilled by Jesus in His first coming, if you count each occurrence per prophet. For simplicity's sake I will list each point only once with the multiple occurrences listed to the side.

Prophecies surrounding the birth of Jesus and His childhood

Date	Prophecy	Prediction	Fulfillment
2	124. The Messiah will be the One who has existed from eternity	Mic. 5:2; cmp Ps. 90:2	John 1:1, 14
	125. The Messiah is the preexistent Son of God	Ps. 102:25-27; 2 Sam. 7:14	Heb. 1:10-11
	126. The Messiah is God	Isa. 9:6; 40:9; Jer. 23:5-6b	John 1:1
	127. The only begotten Son of God will be called the Messiah	Ps. 2:2	John 1:14
	128. The Messiah will incarnate into human form (lower than the angels)	Ps. 8:5-6	1 Cor. 15:27; Phil. 2
	129. The Messiah is both God and Man	Zech. 13:7c; Jer. 23:5-6	John 14:9
	130. The Messiah will be called "The mighty God, the everlasting Father"	Isa. 9:6	Matt. 1:23
	131. The Messiah will be called Immanuel, "God with us"	Isa. 7:14; 8:8	Matt. 1:23
	132. The Messiah will be a decendant of Eve	Gen. 3:15	Matt. 1:1-16
	133. The Messiah will be a decendant of Shem	Gen. 9:26-27	Matt. 1:1-16
	134. The Messiah will be a decendant of Abraham	Gen. 12:3,7	Matt. 1:1-16
	135. The Messiah will be a decendant of Isaac	Gen. 22:18; Gen. 26:2-5	Heb. 11:18
	136. The Messiah will be from the tribe of Judah (Shiloh)	Gen. 49:10	Matt. 1:1-3
	137. Jewish kings will not cease until the First Coming of the Messiah	Gen. 49:10	
	138. The Messiah will be a decendant of David	2 Chron. 17:11; Ezek. 17:22-24	Luke 3:23-31
	139. The Messiah will be heir to the throne of David	Isa. 9:6-7; 2 Sam. 7:16	Matt. 1:1
	140. The Messiah will not be from Jeconiah's linage (virgin born)	Jer. 2:28-30	Matt. 1:1-17
	141. The Messiah will be born of a virgin	Isa. 7:14; Jer. 31:22; *Gen. 3:15*	Matt. 1:18
	142. Gabriel predicts the birth of Jesus while Mary was still a virgin	Luke 1:26-38	Matt. 1:18
	143. Jesus will be conceived by the Holy Spirit	Matt. 1:20	Matt. 1:18-21
	144. The Messiah will be holy	Dan. 9:24b	Luke 1:35
	145. The Messiah's name will be Jesus/Joshua	Isa. 12:2-3; Zech. 3:8-10	Matt. 1:21
	146. Angel Gabriel predicts John the Baptist's birth to Zachariah	Luke 1:57-66	Luke 1:5-25
	147. Elisabeth predicts Jesus' birth and Mary's future honor	Luke 1:39-45	Matt. 1:18
	148. Zachariah will not speak until John's birth	Luke 1:20	Luke 1:64
	149. Zachariah's prophetic song	Luke 1:67-79	Luke 1:80
	150. Mary will be a prophetess	Isa. 8:3	Luke 1:46
	151. Child of the prophetess will be called Mahr-Shalal-Hash-Baz	Isa. 8:3,18 {Isa. 53:3 despised}	Matt. 27:33
	152. Mary predicts her blessedness and Jesus' rule	Luke 1:46-56	
	153. Simeon predicts a sword shall pierce Mary's heart	Luke 2:21-35	
	154. Prophetess Anna confirms Simeon's prophecy	Luke 2:38	
	155. The Messiah will be born in Bethlehem	Mic. 5:2a	Matt. 2:1-2
	156. Angels tell the shepherds Jesus will be found in Bethlehem	Luke 2:8-14; Isa. 60:7	Luke 2:15-20
	157. A star will mark the Messiah's birth	Num. 24:17-19	Matt. 2:2
	158. The Messiah will be visited by Magi (given gifts of frankincense)	Isa. 60:3	Matt. 2:1
	159. Magi warned in a dream that Herod will try to kill Jesus	Matt. 2:12	Matt. 2:18
	160. Bethlehem children will be slaughtered	Jer. 31:15	Matt. 2:18
4	161. The Messiah will be called out of Egypt	Hos. 11:1; Num. 24:8	Matt. 2:14-15
	162. The Messiah will be called a Nazarene (Branch)	Isa. 11:1; Zec 3:8; 6:12	Matt. 2:23
6	163. Kings of Syria and Samaria will cease before Jesus is 12 yrs old.	Isa. 7:14-17	
10	164. Jesus' Bar Mitzvah in the Temple at the age of 12	Isa. 7:14-17	Luke 2:41-50

Ancient Prophecies Revealed

---
2 BC
Messiah's Birth & Childhood

Messiah would be God Incarnate
The following prophesies describe that the Messiah is both fully God and fully Man. The Scriptural teaching that Jesus is God is called the doctrine of the deity of Christ. The Scriptural teaching that Jesus is fully God and fully man is called the doctrine of the hypostatic union. In Hebrews 1, Paul quotes Psalms 2:7; 97:7; 45:6; 102:25 and 2 Samuel 7:14 as prophecies that show what the Messiah will be. Paul shows Jesus is the Creator of the world, is called God, is worshiped by the angels, and is called the Son of God.

"God, after He spoke long ago to the fathers in the prophets in many portions and in many ways, in these last days has spoken to us in *His* Son, whom He appointed heir of all things, through whom also He made the world… For to which of the angels did He ever say, "YOU ARE MY SON, TODAY I HAVE BEGOTTEN YOU"? And again, "I WILL BE A FATHER TO HIM AND HE SHALL BE A SON TO ME"? And when He again brings the firstborn into the world, He says, "AND LET ALL THE ANGELS OF GOD WORSHIP HIM." …But of the Son *He says*, "YOUR THRONE, O GOD, IS FOREVER AND EVER… And, "YOU, LORD, IN THE BEGINNING LAID THE FOUNDATION OF THE EARTH, AND THE HEAVENS ARE THE WORKS OF YOUR HANDS;" *Hebrews 1:1-2,5-6,8,10*

Other passages that clearly show the Messiah is God are: Isaiah 9:6; 40:9; 44:6; Jeremiah 23:5-6b; Zechariah 12:10b. Micah says that the Messiah, the one born in Bethlehem, has always existed from the days of eternity. These passages show that Jesus is the eternal Son of God, who exists in the form of God. In numerous places Jesus is referred to as "Immanuel," which means "God with us." Jesus is never referred to as "Immanumelech," which means "angel with us." Jesus was not an incarnate angel, but incarnate God.

"But as for you, Bethlehem Ephrathah, *too* little to be among the clans of Judah, from you One will go forth for Me to be ruler in Israel. His goings forth are from long ago, from the days of eternity." *Micah 5:2*

In Psalm 2 we see that the only begotten Son of God is the King Messiah. This as another reference to the Trinity in Scripture:

"…And the rulers take counsel together against the LORD and against His Anointed (Messiah)… 'But as for Me, I have installed My King upon Zion, My holy mountain.' I will surely tell of the decree of the LORD: He said to Me, 'You are My Son, today I have begotten You.'" *Psalm 2:2,6-7*

Genealogy of the Messiah
The complete genealogy of Jesus is written in Matthew 2:1-16. Through the ages the genealogy of the Messiah was revealed piece by piece. It was first revealed that He would be a descendant of Adam and Eve (Genesis 3:15); then a descendant of Shem. Genesis 9:26-27 declares the Messiah will come though Shem's line, even though the Messiah is the God of Shem!

"He also said, 'Blessed be the LORD, the God of Shem; and let Canaan be his servant. May God enlarge Japheth, and let him [God – the Messiah] dwell in the tents of Shem; and let Canaan be his servant.'" *Genesis 9:26-27*

Then it was revealed that the Messiah would be a descendant of Abraham (Genesis 12:3,7), Isaac (Genesis 22:18, 26:2-5), and Judah (Genesis 49:10). When Jacob prophesied over his son Judah he said:

"The scepter shall not depart from Judah, nor the ruler's staff from between his feet, until Shiloh comes, and to him *shall be* the obedience of the peoples." *Genesis 49:10*

The Messiah's First Coming

Shiloh is a name for the Messiah. This prophecy is not only saying the Messiah would be a descendant of Judah, but that Jewish rulers would come from the tribe of Judah until the Messiah comes. Historically we have seen this to be true. After the Messiah's death, the nation of Israel was dispersed and did not return until 1948. The modern state of Israel is a democracy. There are no longer Jewish kings ruling in Israel, and there will not be a king in Israel until the Second Coming of the Messiah. See the section on Modern Israel for more details. The prophets declared the Messiah would be a descendant of King David (2 Chronicles 17:11; Ezekiel 17:22-24; 34:23-24; Jeremiah 33:14-15; Psalm 110:1; Isaiah 11:1) and heir to his throne but would not be a descendant of Jeconiah (Jeremiah 2:28-30).

Messiah not from Jeconiah's linage
One will notice that the genealogy of Jesus is the same in Luke 3:23-37 and Matthew 1:1-17 until you get to David. Luke continues the genealogy from David though his son Nathan, while Matthew continued the genealogy though David's son, Solomon. Ancient church father Eusebius, in his *Ecclesiastical History 1.7,* explains it this way:

Luke lists the grandfather of Joseph as Melchi. Melchi married a woman named Estha and they had a child named Eli. After the death of Melchi, Estha married Matthan, the grandfather of Joseph listed in Matthew. They had a child named Jacob. Eli married but died childless. According to the Law of Moses, the nearest of kin must marry a childless widow and raise up seed in his brother's name. So Jacob married the widow of Eli and had a child named Joseph. This Joseph was the wife of Mary, the mother of Jesus the Messiah. So Matthew recorded the *biological* linage of Joseph while Luke recorded his *legal* linage. Matthew's genealogy shows Joseph was a biological descendant of Jeconiah.

Muslims will say this proves Jesus can't be the Messiah because Jeremiah records God placed a curse on Jeconiah, saying that none of his descendants will ever sit on the throne of David. What this *actually* proves is that Joseph was the legal father of Jesus, but not the biological father. In other words, this proves the virgin birth. Mary's genealogy is different from that of Joseph. Even the Qur'an, the holy book of the Muslims, states that Mary gave birth to Jesus when she was still a virgin (Sura 3:47, 9:20-31)!

Virgin Birth
The Old Testament prophecies show that Mary, a descendant of David – but not though the linage of Jeconiah, would conceive the Messiah, not though sexual intercourse but by a special miracle from the Holy Spirit. In addition to these prophecies, the angel Gabriel came and directly told Joseph and Mary these things.

> "But when he had considered this, behold, an angel of the Lord appeared to him in a dream, saying, 'Joseph, son of David, do not be afraid to take Mary as your wife; for the Child who has been conceived in her is of the Holy Spirit. She will bear a Son; and you shall call His name Jesus, for He will save His people from their sins.' Now all this took place to fulfill what was spoken by the Lord through the prophet: 'BEHOLD, THE VIRGIN SHALL BE WITH CHILD AND SHALL BEAR A SON, AND THEY SHALL CALL HIS NAME IMMANUEL,' which translated means, 'GOD WITH US.'"
> Matthew 1:20-23

The Messiah will be Protected
The Messiah would be protected by angels until the time for his crucifixion. Satan actually quoted this verse in Luke 4:10-11 while trying to tempt Jesus to sin!

> "No evil will befall you, nor will any plague come near your tent. For He will give His angels charge concerning you, to guard you in all your ways. they will bear you up in their hands, that you do not strike your foot against a stone."
> Psalm 91:10-12

The Messiah's name will be Jesus/Yeshua
The Messiah's name in English is "Jesus." In Hebrew it is "Yeshua." Yeshua is one of the Hebrew words that mean "salvation." In Isaiah 12 the words for salvation are actually Yeshua. See also the section on the Apostasy of the Church to see a prophecy in Zechariah that also shows His name will be Jesus. John the Baptist's father, Zachariah, called the Messiah by name when he mentioned the "horn of Yeshua" in Luke 1:69.

Ancient Prophecies Revealed

"'Behold, God is my salvation [Yeshua], I will trust and not be afraid; for the LORD GOD is my strength and song, and He has become my salvation [Yeshua].' Therefore you will joyously draw water from the springs of salvation [Yeshua]." *Isaiah 12:2-3*

John the Baptist
God ordained John the Baptist to be the forerunner of the Messiah. The forerunner is prophesied in Malichi 4:5-6. The angel Gabriel quotes this Old Testament passage when telling Zachariah that his son would fulfill this prophecy. Gabriel instructed Zachariah to name his son "John," which in Hebrew means "gift of Yahweh." In order to prove John indeed was the one prophesied, the angel predicted Zachariah would not speak until John was born. This was fulfilled exactly as prophesied.

"It is he who will go *as a forerunner* before Him in the spirit and power of Elijah, TO TURN THE HEARTS OF THE FATHERS BACK TO THE CHILDREN, and the disobedient to the attitude of the righteous, so as to make ready a people prepared for the Lord." *Luke 1:17*

Elisabeth, John the Baptist's mother, also prophesied in Luke 1:39-45 about the birth of John and Jesus and the honor to be bestowed on Mary as the mother of the Messiah. Zachariah predicted in Luke 1:67-79 the Old Testament prophecies were about to be fulfilled by the Messiah and that his son John would be both a prophet and the forerunner of the Messiah.

Quad-Word Inscription Prophecies
You will remember that an inscription prophecy is one in which a series of words are grouped together and form a sentence that is a riddle. An example from the first chapter was the name "Methuselah." The most complex one is the Zechariah 3 inscription prophecy that will be given in the section on the Apostasy of the Church.

A quad-word prophecy is an inscription prophecy that consists of just four words. This creates a duel-purpose prophecy. The prophet gives the last three words as a prophecy for his time. This proves it is a truly inspired word from the Lord. We are to look at all four words to see another prophecy for the last days.

I have given three examples in the chart below so you can see the quad-word Inscription prophecies are real and always follow the same pattern. Daniel's quad-word Inscription will be fully explained in the section on Modern Israel. Haggai's quad-word Inscription will be seen with the Zechariah 3 inscription prophecy in the section on the Apostasy of the Church. Let's look at the quad-word Inscription from Isaiah 8.

A few Quad-Word Inscription Prophecies

Isaiah 8:3					
Hebrew	בז	חש	שלל	מהר	
Given	plunder	hurry	loot	–	• Loot and spoil will be hurried off (by Assyria)
Prophetic	despised one	hurry	captivity	from the Mountain	• From the Mountain (Golgotha) the despised one (Jesus) will hurriedly lead captivity captive.
Daniel 5:25					
Hebrew	פרס	תקל	מנא	מנא	
Given	divided	weighed	numbered	–	• You have been weighed and are found deficient, the days of your kingdom are at an end, and it shall be divided
Prophetic	500	20	1000	1000	• 2520 Jewish years till Israel is reestablished
Haggai 2:23					
Hebrew	אל	שאלתי	בל	זרב	
Given	God	I have asked	Lord	–	• I have asked God for the Lord (to send the Messiah)
Prophetic	God	I have asked	Lord	infilling	• I have asked God for the infilling of the Lord

Mary a Prophetess
The Holy Spirit told Simeon that he would see the Messiah before he died. Upon seeing Jesus, he prophesied that Jesus would bring salvation to many, but a sword would pierce Mary's heart. The prophetess Anna later confirmed this. Mary

would have to see her son crucified. In Luke 1:46-56, Mary predicted Jesus' messianic rule on earth and that future generations would call her blessed. Elisabeth, John the Baptist's mother, also prophesied in Luke 1:39-45 about Jesus and Mary's honor. Isaiah referred to Mary as the virgin who was to give birth. Isaiah also stated the virgin who would give birth to Immanuel would be a prophetess and that one of the names for her child would be Mahr-Shalal-Hash-Baz.

> "So I approached the prophetess, and she conceived and gave birth to a son. Then the LORD said to me, 'Name him Maher-shalal-hash-baz.'" *Isaiah 8:3*

This is a duel-purpose prophecy and an inscription prophecy. Isaiah gives the explanation that the *loot* will be *hurried* off by the *despised* king of Assyria. "Shalal" means loot or captivity, "hash" means hurry, and "baz" means despised one. The word "maher" is left out of this prophecy altogether. When "maher" is added to the other three words, it forms a different sentence. "Har" is the Hebrew word for mountain and attaching an "m" onto "Har" would mean "from the mountain." So the complete sentence is "from the mountain (Golgotha) the despised one (Jesus) will hurriedly lead captivity captive." Isaiah describes Jesus as the "despised one" in Isaiah 53:3, and Paul mentioned "leading captivity captive" in Ephesians 4:8.

Born in Bethlehem
When Herod's scribes checked, they found the prophet Micah predicted the Messiah would be born in Bethlehem. Micah 5:2 is partly quoted here in Matthew.

> "Gathering together all the chief priests and scribes of the people, he inquired of them where the Messiah was to be born. They said to him, 'In Bethlehem of Judea; for this is what has been written by the prophet: AND YOU, BETHLEHEM, LAND OF JUDAH, ARE BY NO MEANS LEAST AMONG THE LEADERS OF JUDAH; FOR OUT OF YOU SHALL COME FORTH A RULER WHO WILL SHEPHERD MY PEOPLE ISRAEL.'" *Matthew 2:4-6*

Star of Bethlehem
Balaam saw the coming of the Messiah in a vision, which is recorded in the book of Numbers. He saw that Jesus' birth would be many years from his time. A sign of the Messiah's birth would be the appearance of a very bright star. Jesus was born over 1400 years after Balaam gave this prophecy.

> "Now after Jesus was born in Bethlehem of Judea in the days of Herod the king, magi from the east arrived in Jerusalem, saying, Where is He who has been born King of the Jews? For we saw His star in the east and have come to worship Him." *Matthew 2:1,2*

> "I see him, but not now; I behold him, but not near; a star shall come forth from Jacob, a scepter shall rise from Israel, and shall crush through the forehead of Moab, and tear down all the sons of Sheth. Edom shall be a possession, Seir, its enemies, also will be a possession, while Israel performs valiantly. One from Jacob shall have dominion, and will destroy the remnant from the city." *Numbers 24:17-19*

Visited by Magi
Isaiah shows that Jesus would be visited by Kings from Midian, Epheh, and Sheba at His birth. They would bring Him gifts of gold and frankincense. Notice also that shepherds from Kedar will also visit Him.

> "Nations will come to your light, and kings to the brightness of your rising… The young camels of Midian and Ephah; all those from Sheba will come; they will bring gold and frankincense, and will bear good news of the praises of the LORD. All the flocks of Kedar will be gathered together to you…" *Isaiah 60:3,6-7*

Slaughter of the Bethlehem Children
When King Herod heard of the birth of a King (the Messiah), he wanted to kill Him, so he would not lose his throne. Learning from the scribes that the Messiah would be born in Bethlehem and knowing that the wise men had been searching for him for two years, Herod gave orders to slaughter all the male children two years and younger. His actions unwittingly fulfilled Jeremiah's prophecy.

Ancient Prophecies Revealed

"Then when Herod saw that he had been tricked by the magi, he became very enraged, and sent and slew all the male children who were in Bethlehem and all its vicinity, from two years old and under, according to the time which he had determined from the magi. Then what had been spoken through Jeremiah the prophet was fulfilled: 'A VOICE WAS HEARD IN RAMAH, WEEPING AND GREAT MOURNING, RACHEL WEEPING FOR HER CHILDREN; AND SHE REFUSED TO BE COMFORTED, BECAUSE THEY WERE NO MORE.'" *Matthew 2:16-18*

Called out of Egypt – AD 4
This prophecy was made cryptic in Hosea to conceal the whereabouts of the Messiah until it would be safe. Herod would not be able to ask the sages where the Messiah would flee to from Bethlehem; otherwise Herod would have sent assassins to Egypt to kill Him.

"He remained there until the death of Herod. This was to fulfill what had been spoken by the Lord through the prophet: 'OUT OF EGYPT I CALLED MY SON.'" *Matthew 2:15*

Jesus Called a Nazarene – AD 4
The Messiah is referred to as God's branch in several places in the Old Testament. Zechariah 3 is one primary example, where we see the actual name of the Messiah will be "Yeshua" or "Jesus" and his title is "the branch." There are several words for branch in Hebrew, just like in English, for example, branch, limb, twig, bough. One such Hebrew word is *netzer*. This is the word Isaiah used to designate the Messiah. In Hebrew you add a "y" or "i" to the end of a word to designate ownership. So when God says 'my branch' it would be *netzeri*. So Yeshua Ha Netzeri would be the full title of the Messiah. In English this translates as "Jesus the Nazarene."

"Then a shoot will spring from the stem of Jesse, and a branch (*netzer*) from his roots will bear fruit." *Isaiah 11:1*

"and came and lived in a city called Nazareth. This was to fulfill what was spoken through the prophets: 'He shall be called a Nazarene.'" *Matthew 2:23*

Samaria & Syria destroyed – AD 6
Isaiah 7:14-16 predicts the virgin birth of Jesus. It goes on to predict that before Jesus knows good from evil, (or has His Bar Mitzvah), that the two kings bothersome taszo Judah in that day would cease to be a power. These were Syria and Ephraim. During Jesus' lifetime these kingdoms were called Syria and Samaria.

"…Behold, a virgin will be with child and bear a son, and she will call His name Immanuel… For before the boy will know *enough* to refuse evil and choose good, the land whose two kings you dread will be forsaken." *Isaiah 7:14,16*

The Assyrian/Syrian land was laid waste during the Roman-Parthian wars in 60-20 BC. In 20 BC, it was divided, half going to Rome and the other half going to Parthia. The last Samarian/Idumean king, Herod Archelaus, was deposed in AD 6. When Herod Archelaus was deposed, Rome chose to absorb Samaria into a Roman province. Although the people still continued to live there, Syria and Samaria *as nations with armies* ceased to exist. This prophecy was fulfilled within four years of Jesus' Bar Mitzvah!

The Messiah's First Coming

Prophecies surrounding the three-and-a-half-year ministry of Jesus

Date	Prophecy	Prediction	Fulfillment
28	165. John the Baptist is the messenger in the spirit of Elijah	Mal. 3:1; 4:5-6	Matt. 11:7-11; Luke 1:17
	166. John the Baptist cries "Prepare ye the way of the Lord"	Isa. 40:3	Matt. 3:3
	167. The Messiah will be a priest after the order of Melchizedek	Ps. 110:4	Heb. 5:5-6; 6:20; 7:15-17
	168. The Messiah will be anointed with the Holy Spirit	Isa. 11:2	Matt. 3:16
	169. The Messiah will call God, His father	Ps. 89:26	Matt. 11:27
	170. The Father will call the Messiah His firstborn	Ps. 89:26	
	171. The Messiah will be declared to be the Son of God	Ps. 2:7; Prov. 30:4	Matt. 3:16; Heb. 1:5
	172. The Messiah will be a prophet like Moses - a new covenant	Deut. 18:15-18	
	173. The Messiah will start His ministry in Galilee	Isa. 9:1-2	Matt. 4:15
	174. The Messiah will appear as an ordinary man	Isa. 53:2	Phil. 2:7-8
	175. The Messiah will quietly carry out His ministry	Isa. 42:1-4	Matt. 12:15-20
	176. The Messiah will be protected by angels until His crucifixion	Ps. 91:11-12	Luke 4:10-11
	177. The Messiah will speak in riddles so people will not understand	Isa. 6:9-10	Matt. 13:14-15
	178. The Messiah will speak in parables	Ps. 78:1-2	Matt. 13:34-35
	179. The Messiah will preach the Gospel (Good News)	Isa. 61:1-2	
	180. The Messiah will preach to the poor/brokenhearted/captives	Isa. 61:1,2	Matt. 11:5; Luke 4:18-21
	181. The Messiah will heal blind/deaf/lame/dumb	Isa. 35:5-6; Isa. 29:18	Matt. 11:5
	182. Jesus predicts the centurion's servant will be healed	Matt. 8:5-13; Luke 7:1-10	
	183. Synagogue will be hypocritical & devoid of wisdom at His coming	Isa. 29:13-14	Matt. 15:7-9; 1 Cor. 1:18-3
	184. The Messiah will be a stone of stumbling to Israel	Isa. 8:14-17	1 Pet. 2:8
	185. Jesus predicts Korazin, Bethsaida, & Capernaum will be destroyed	Matt. 11:20-24	
	186. Those not believing Jesus' miracles will be condemned	Matt. 12:38-45	
32	187. The Messiah will enter Jerusalem as a king, riding on an ass	Zech. 9:9	Matt. 21:5
	188. The Messiah will come to His Temple before it is destroyed	Hag. 2:6-9; Mal. 3:1	Matt. 21:12-15
	189. The Messiah's zeal for the Temple would be His undoing	Ps. 69:9	John 2:17
	190. Jesus predicts the disciples would fall away	Zech. 13:7	Matt. 26:31-32,56
	191. Jesus predicts Peter would deny Him three times	Matt. 26:34; John 18:12-19:16	
	192. The Messiah will be betrayed by a friend (Judas dipping his hand)	Ps. 41:9; 55:12-14	Matt. 26:21-25
	193. Jesus predicts Judas would betray Him	Matt. 26:21	
	194. Judas will die unforgiven	Ps. 55:15	Matt. 27:3-5
	195. The Messiah will be sold for 30 pieces of silver	Zech. 11:12	Matt. 26:15; Luke 22:5
	196. The 30 pieces of silver will be thrown in the Temple	Zech. 11:13	Matt. 27:5
	197. The 30 pieces of silver will be used to buy a potter's field	Zech. 11:12	Matt. 27:9-10
	198. The Messiah will be conspired against by Jewish leaders	Ps. 2:1,2	Acts 4:25
	199. Rulers will plot to put the Messiah to death	Isa. 28:13	
	200. Leaders will take council to put the Messiah to death	Ps. 31:13	John 11:53
	201. Caiaphas prophesies the Messiah will die for the sins of the Jews	Isa. 53:8	John 11:49-53
	202. Caiaphas, the false priest, will tear his clothes	Lev. 10:6, 21:10	Matt. 26:65
	203. The Messiah will be accused by false witnesses	Ps. 27:12, 35:11	Matt. 26:60
	204. The Messiah will be hated without cause	Ps. 35:19, 69:4	John 15:25
	205. The Messiah will be rejected & despised by His own	Isa. 53:3; Ps. 118:22-23	Matt. 21:42
	206. The Messiah will be silent to accusations	Isa. 53:7	Matt. 27:14

Dates given are AD 28 to 32, Jesus' three-and-a-half-year ministry

AD 28
Messiah's Ministry

Encyclopedia Britannica reports the reign of Tiberius Caesar started on August 19, AD 14. Luke 3:1 says Jesus was baptized and started his ministry in the fifteenth year of Tiberius Caesar, which would be AD 28-29. Three and one half years later, in AD 32, the crucifixion occurred as prophesied.

Ancient Prophecies Revealed

Jesus' ministry began with His baptism by John the Baptist. In Matthew 3:3 John the Baptist identified himself as the one Isaiah prophesied in Isaiah 40:3, to prepare the way of the Lord. He came in the spirit and power of Elijah and turned the hearts of the people toward God as prophesied in Malachi 3:1 and 4:5-6.

> "This is the one about whom it is written, 'BEHOLD, I SEND MY MESSENGER AHEAD OF YOU, WHO WILL PREPARE YOUR WAY BEFORE YOU.' Truly I say to you, among those born of women there has not arisen *anyone* greater than John the Baptist! Yet the one who is least in the kingdom of heaven is greater than he... And if you are willing to accept *it*, John himself is Elijah who was to come." *Matthew 11:10-11,14*

Jesus was sinless and did not need to be baptized for remission of sins. Jesus descended from the tribe of Judah and therefore he was born King of the Jews. John the Baptist came from the tribe of Levi, from which comes the priesthood. In this baptism, recorded in Matthew 3:15-16, King Jesus was baptized by a true descendant of Levi, into the priesthood. This combination of King and priest reestablished the Melchizedekian priesthood as prophesied.

> "The LORD has sworn and will not change His mind, 'You are a priest forever according to the order of Melchizedek.'"
> *Psalm 110:4*

God showed His approval of Jesus' priesthood when He declared audibly that Jesus was His only begotten Son and anointed Him with the Holy Spirit. This event fulfilled *six* more prophecies! Jesus is declared to be the Son of God in Psalm 2:7; Proverbs 30:4; 1 Chronicles 17:13; and Isaiah 42:1. Jesus is declared to be the Firstborn of God in Psalm 89:26.

> "After being baptized, Jesus came up immediately from the water; and behold, the heavens were opened, and he saw the Spirit of God descending as a dove *and* lighting on Him, and behold, a voice out of the heavens said, 'This is My beloved Son, in whom I am well-pleased.'" *Matthew 3:16-17*

Deuteronomy 18:15-18 predicts that another prophet like Moses would arise. Humanity must listen to him. This prophecy refers to Christ, who – like Moses – brought a new covenant to the people that would replace the Mosaic covenant.

Jesus began His ministry in Galilee
Isaiah 53:2 states that Jesus would appear as any another man, no one special. Jesus began His ministry by leaving Nazareth and settling in Galilee. This was predicted in Isaiah 9:1-2. The fulfillment of this prophecy is recorded in Matthew.

> "leaving Nazareth, He came and settled in Capernaum, which is by the sea, in the region of Zebulun and Naphtali. *This was* to fulfill what was spoken through Isaiah the prophet: 'THE LAND OF ZEBULUN AND THE LAND OF NAPHTALI, BY THE WAY OF THE SEA, BEYOND THE JORDAN, GALILEE OF THE GENTILES--THE PEOPLE WHO WERE SITTING IN DARKNESS SAW A GREAT LIGHT, AND THOSE WHO WERE SITTING IN THE LAND AND SHADOW OF DEATH, UPON THEM A LIGHT DAWNED.' From that time Jesus began to preach and say, 'Repent, for the kingdom of heaven is at hand.'"
> *Matthew 4:13-17*

Isaiah 42:1-4 predicted Jesus would also carry out His ministry quietly. Psalm 91:11-12 predicts Jesus would be protected by angels until the time of His crucifixion.

Jesus' Teaching
Jesus spoke in parables so those who would have interfered with destiny would not be able to. Jesus gave the interpretation to those whom He wanted to completely understand. This way, God's design would be carried out and a record of it would be kept. This way of teaching was prophesied in Isaiah 6:9-10, and Psalm 78:1-2 and quoted in Matthew.

> "Jesus answered them... I speak to them in parables; because while seeing they do not see, and while hearing they do not hear, nor do they understand. In their case the prophecy of Isaiah is being fulfilled, which says, 'YOU WILL KEEP ON HEARING, BUT WILL NOT UNDERSTAND; YOU WILL KEEP ON SEEING, BUT WILL NOT PERCEIVE; FOR THE HEART OF THIS PEOPLE HAS BECOME DULL, WITH THEIR EARS THEY SCARCELY HEAR, AND THEY HAVE CLOSED THEIR EYES, OTHERWISE THEY WOULD SEE WITH THEIR EYES, HEAR WITH THEIR EARS, AND UNDERSTAND WITH THEIR HEART AND RETURN, AND I WOULD HEAL THEM... All these things Jesus spoke to the crowds in parables, and He did not speak to them without a

parable. This was to fulfill what was spoken through the prophet: 'I WILL OPEN MY MOUTH IN PARABLES; I WILL UTTER THINGS HIDDEN SINCE THE FOUNDATION OF THE WORLD.'"
Matthew 13:11,13-15, 34-35

Jesus Preached the Gospel
After beginning His ministry, Jesus came to Nazareth and read Isaiah 61:1-2. The fulfillment is recorded in Luke.

"And the book of the prophet Isaiah was handed to Him. And He opened the book and found the place where it was written, 'THE SPIRIT OF THE LORD IS UPON ME, BECAUSE HE ANOINTED ME TO PREACH THE GOSPEL TO THE POOR. HE HAS SENT ME TO PROCLAIM RELEASE TO THE CAPTIVES, AND RECOVERY OF SIGHT TO THE BLIND, TO SET FREE THOSE WHO ARE OPPRESSED, TO PROCLAIM THE FAVORABLE YEAR OF THE LORD.' And He closed the book, gave it back to the attendant and sat down; and the eyes of all in the synagogue were fixed on Him. And He began to say to them, 'Today this Scripture has been fulfilled in your hearing.'" *Luke 4:17-21*

Jesus' Healing Ministry
Jesus proved He was Messiah by healing all kinds of diseases. There are many healings recorded in the New Testament. In Matthew 11, Jesus quoted Isaiah 35:5-6 and 29:13-14. Both prophesy about His healing ministry. Jesus commanded the Roman centurion's servant healed. The healing occurred within the hour, according to Matthew 8:5-13!

"Jesus answered and said to them, 'Go and report to John what you hear and see: *the* BLIND RECEIVE SIGHT and *the* lame walk, *the* lepers are cleansed and *the* deaf hear, *the* dead are raised up, and *the* POOR HAVE THE GOSPEL PREACHED TO THEM.'" *Matthew 11:4-5*

Church/Synagogue at His Coming Would Be Hypocritical & Devoid of Wisdom
The Jews had twisted the teachings of Scripture into man-made doctrine that actually did the opposite of what God intended. Toward the time of the Second Coming, the church will do the exact same thing. See the section on the Apostasy of the Church for further details.

"…you invalidated the word of God for the sake of your tradition. You hypocrites, rightly did Isaiah prophesy of you: 'THIS PEOPLE HONORS ME WITH THEIR LIPS, BUT THEIR HEART IS FAR AWAY FROM ME. BUT IN VAIN DO THEY WORSHIP ME, TEACHING AS DOCTRINES THE PRECEPTS OF MEN.'" *Matthew 15:6-9*

Even though they had the Scriptures and the prophets, Israel still misunderstood and killed their own Messiah. Isaiah 8:14-17 says Jesus would be the stumbling stone that causes Israel to fall. 1 Peter 2:8 references and explains that Jesus is the Stone that the builders rejected.

Cites Permanently Destroyed
Jesus cursed the cities that rejected Him: Chorazin, Bethsaida, and Capernaum. These cities were destroyed and are still in ruins today!

"Then He began to denounce the cities in which most of His miracles were done, because they did not repent. 'Woe to you, Chorazin! Woe to you, Bethsaida! For if the miracles had occurred in Tyre and Sidon which occurred in you, they would have repented long ago in sackcloth and ashes. Nevertheless I say to you, it will be more tolerable for Tyre and Sidon in *the* day of judgment than for you. And you, Capernaum, will not be exalted to heaven, will you? You will descend to Hades; for if the miracles had occurred in Sodom which occurred in you, it would have remained to this day. Nevertheless I say to you that it will be more tolerable for the land of Sodom in the day of judgment, than for you.'" *Matthew 11:20-24*

Those Who Do Not Believe Will Be Damned
The same fate is reserved to all who do not believe in who Jesus is, or acknowledge and obey His teachings. Jesus said:

"The men of Nineveh will stand up with this generation at the judgment, and will condemn it because they repented at the preaching of Jonah; and behold, something greater than Jonah is here. *The* Queen of *the* South will rise up with this

Ancient Prophecies Revealed

generation at the judgment and will condemn it, because she came from the ends of the earth to hear the wisdom of Solomon; and behold, something greater than Solomon is here." *Matthew 12:41-42*

Jesus Enters Jerusalem Riding on a Donkey
Zechariah 9 prophesied that Jesus would ride into Jerusalem on a donkey. The fulfillment is recorded in Matthew 21.

"Shout *in triumph*, O daughter of Jerusalem! Behold, your king is coming to you; He is just and endowed with salvation, humble, and mounted on a donkey, even on a colt, the foal of a donkey." *Zechariah 9:9*

"When they had approached Jerusalem and had come to Bethphage, at the Mount of Olives, then Jesus sent two disciples, saying to them, 'Go into the village opposite you, and immediately you will find a donkey tied *there* and a colt with her; untie *them* and bring *them* to Me. If anyone says anything to you, you shall say, 'The Lord has need of them,' and immediately he will send them.' This took place to fulfill what was spoken through the prophet: 'SAY TO THE DAUGHTER OF ZION, BEHOLD YOUR KING IS COMING TO YOU, GENTLE, AND MOUNTED ON A DONKEY, EVEN ON A COLT, THE FOAL OF A BEAST OF BURDEN.' The disciples went and did just as Jesus had instructed them, and brought the donkey and the colt, and laid their coats on them; and He sat on the coats."
Matthew 21:1-6

Jesus comes to His Temple Before it is Destroyed
Jesus was prophesied to suddenly or unexpectedly come to His Temple. Notice if the Messiah was prophesied to come into the Temple and that Temple was destroyed in AD 70, then the Messiah had to have come *before* AD 70! See also Haggai 2:6-9 and Psalm 118:26.

"Behold, I am going to send My messenger, and he will clear the way before Me. And the Lord, whom you seek, will suddenly come to His temple; and the messenger of the covenant, in whom you delight, behold, He is coming, says the LORD of hosts." *Malachi 3:1*

Zeal for the Temple
The extreme zeal Jesus had for God, His father, and the holy Temple in Jerusalem would be the very thing that the scribes and Pharisees would use to justify putting Jesus to death. It was prophesied that the zeal for the Temple would be His undoing. John quotes this prophecy from Psalm 69:9.

"The Passover of the Jews was near, and Jesus went up to Jerusalem. And He found in the temple those who were selling oxen and sheep and doves, and the money changers seated at their tables. And He made a scourge of cords, and drove *them* all out of the temple, with the sheep and the oxen; and He poured out the coins of the money changers and overturned their tables; and to those who were selling the doves He said, 'Take these things away; stop making My Father's house a place of business.' His disciples remembered that it was written, 'ZEAL FOR YOUR HOUSE WILL CONSUME ME.'" *John 2:13-16*

Jesus Predicts the Disciples Would Fall Away
Jesus quoted Zechariah 13:7 in Matthew. This is a prophecy that was fulfilled when the Romans took Jesus prisoner. The disciples fled and were in hiding until the Holy Spirit fell on them, giving them the boldness to preach the Word. Peter said he would never deny Jesus; but Jesus prophesied that very night Peter would deny Him three times before the cock crowed in the early morning.

"Then Jesus said to them, 'You will all fall away because of Me this night, for it is written, "I WILL STRIKE DOWN THE SHEPHERD, AND THE SHEEP OF THE FLOCK SHALL BE SCATTERED." But after I have been raised, I will go ahead of you to Galilee.' But Peter said to Him, '*Even* though all may fall away because of You, I will never fall away.' Jesus said to him, 'Truly I say to you that this *very* night, before a rooster crows, you will deny Me three times.' …But all this has taken place to fulfill the Scriptures of the prophets. Then all the disciples left Him and fled." *Matthew 26:31-34,56*

The Messiah's First Coming

Judas Iscariot Betrayed Jesus
It was prophesied in Psalm 41:9 that one of the disciples who ate with Jesus would betray Him. John quotes this prophecy:

> "I do not speak of all of you. I know the ones I have chosen; but *it is* that the Scripture may be fulfilled, 'HE WHO EATS MY BREAD HAS LIFTED UP HIS HEEL AGAINST ME.' From now on I am telling you before it comes to pass, so that when it does occur, you may believe that I am *He*." *John 13:18-19*

Judas betrayed Jesus for 30 pieces of silver, recorded in Matthew and prophesied in Zechariah. Later, Judas tried to return the money; but the chief priests would not take it back, because it was blood money. Judas then threw the money at them and left the Temple. The chief priests used the money to buy a potter's field for the burial of unclean dead. This purchase completely fulfilled Zechariah's prophecy.

> "Then one of the twelve, named Judas Iscariot, went to the chief priests and said, 'What are you willing to give me to betray Him to you?' And they weighed out thirty pieces of silver to him." *Matthew 26:14-15*

> "I said to them, 'If it is good in your sight, give *me* my wages; but if not, never mind!' So they weighed out thirty *shekels* of silver as my wages. Then the LORD said to me, 'Throw it to the potter, *that* magnificent price at which I was valued by them.' So I took the thirty *shekels* of silver and threw them to the potter in the house of the LORD." *Zechariah 11:12-13*

> "Judas, who had betrayed Him… threw the pieces of silver into the temple sanctuary and departed; and he went away and hanged himself. The chief priests took the pieces of silver and said, 'It is not lawful to put them into the temple treasury, since it is the price of blood.' And they conferred together and with the money bought the Potter's Field as a burial place for strangers. For this reason that field has been called the Field of Blood to this day. Then that which was spoken through Jeremiah the prophet was fulfilled: 'AND THEY TOOK THE THIRTY PIECES OF SILVER, THE PRICE OF THE ONE WHOSE PRICE HAD BEEN SET by the sons of Israel; AND THEY GAVE THEM FOR THE POTTER'S FIELD, AS THE LORD DIRECTED ME.'" *Matthew 27:3,5-10*

Conspired Against by Jewish leaders
The conspiracy to murder Jesus included the Jewish leaders of the Sanhedrin and the Gentile rulers, including Pilate, Herod, and others. Acts 4 recorded the fulfillment of this prophecy which was given in Psalm 2:1-2. Isaiah 28:13 and Psalm 31:13 also record that the leaders would seek to put the Messiah to death.

> "who by the Holy Spirit, *through* the mouth of our father David Your servant, said, 'WHY DID THE GENTILES RAGE, AND THE PEOPLES DEVISE FUTILE THINGS? THE KINGS OF THE EARTH TOOK THEIR STAND, AND THE RULERS WERE GATHERED TOGETHER AGAINST THE LORD AND AGAINST HIS CHRIST.' For truly in this city there were gathered together against Your holy servant Jesus, whom You anointed, both Herod and Pontius Pilate, along with the Gentiles and the peoples of Israel, to do whatever Your hand and Your purpose predestined to occur." *Acts 4:25-28*

Caiaphas' Prophecy
Caiaphas is a perfect example of a person whose heart is not given to the Messiah. He tried in his own power to decipher the prophecies. Caiaphas misapplied the prophecy from Isaiah 53:8, in which Jesus would die to pay the penalty for the sins of Israel. Caiaphas interpreted it to mean God's judgment would fall on Israel if the Sanhedrin did *not* put Jesus to death for heresy. This prophecy actually says God will judge Israel *for* putting their Messiah to death. See the section on the First Crossover Period for details of how God punished Israel for this act.

> "He was oppressed and He was afflicted, yet He did not open His mouth; like a lamb that is led to slaughter, and like a sheep that is silent before its shearers, so He did not open His mouth. By oppression and judgment He was taken away; and as for His generation, who considered that He was cut off out of the land of the living For the transgression of my people, to whom the stroke *was due*?" *Isaiah 53:7-8*

Ancient Prophecies Revealed

"Therefore the chief priests and the Pharisees convened a council, and were saying, 'What are we doing? For this man is performing many signs. If we let Him *go on* like this, all men will believe in Him, and the Romans will come and take away both our place and our nation.' But one of them, Caiaphas, who was high priest that year, said to them, 'You know nothing at all, nor do you take into account that it is expedient for you that one man die for the people, and that the whole nation not perish.' Now he did not say this on his own initiative, but being high priest that year, he prophesied that Jesus was going to die for the nation, and not for the nation only, but in order that He might also gather together into one the children of God who are scattered abroad. So from that day on they planned together to kill Him." *John 11:47-53*

Caiaphas – False High Priest Tears His Clothes

God cursed the priesthood of Eli to end. This was fulfilled by King Solomon when he dismissed the priest Abiathar, the last of Eli's line. From that time on, all true priests were to come only though the line of Zadok.

"So Solomon dismissed Abiathar from being priest to the LORD, in order to fulfill the word of the LORD, which He had spoken concerning the house of Eli in Shiloh." *1 Kings 2:27*

According to Jewish records (see Jewish Timeline Encyclopedia), the descendants of Zadok retained the role of high priest all the way though the time of the Maccabees. When Onias III was assassinated by Antiochus Epiphanies, usurper Jason was placed in the position of high priest by Antiochus. See Antiochus Epiphanies in the section on Rise of Babylon to the Messiah. We know that the officially-recognized high priest of Jesus' time was Caiaphas. He was a Sadducee (unbeliever) and was placed in that position, not by the Jews, but by the Romans. Caiaphas was not of the linage of Zadok!

"Those who had seized Jesus led Him away to Caiaphas, the high priest… But Jesus kept silent. And the high priest said to Him, 'I adjure You by the living God, that You tell us whether You are the Christ, the Son of God.' Jesus said to him, 'You have said it *yourself*; nevertheless I tell you, hereafter you will see THE SON OF MAN SITTING AT THE RIGHT HAND OF POWER, and COMING ON THE CLOUDS OF HEAVEN.' Then the high priest tore his robes and said, 'He has blasphemed!'" *Matthew 26:57,63-65*

In Leviticus 10:6; 21:10 God forbids a true high priest to tear his clothes as others do. This command is actually a prophecy. In Matthew 26, the usurper high priest Caiaphas, when hearing Jesus say He was the Messiah, tore his clothes, fulfilling this prophecy. John the Baptist's father was Zachariah, of the course of Abijah (Luke 1:5). Zadok's linage comes though Abijah. So we can see John the Baptist, the only true representative of the Levitical/Zadokian priesthood, baptized King Jesus into the priesthood. He thereby recreated the Melchizedian priesthood. For more on the Zadokian priesthood, see the section on the Millennial Reign.

Accused by False Witnesses

The illegal trial that was held to condemn Jesus even had false witnesses, as prophesied in the Psalms. We see this fulfilled in Matthew 27.

"Malicious witnesses rise up; they ask me of things that I do not know." *Psalm 35:11*

"They did not find *any*, even though many false witnesses came forward. But later on two came forward," *Matthew 26:60*

Hated Without Cause

The Jewish rulers would reject Jesus as Messiah – and even hate Him, though He never did anything but good to them.

"But they have done this to fulfill the word that is written in their Law, 'THEY HATED ME WITHOUT A CAUSE.'" *Matthew 15:25*

Rejected and Despised By His Own People

The Messiah was prophesied to be rejected by His own people so He could die for us all. Isaiah 53 shows clearly the Messiah was despised and forsaken. Psalm 118 prophesied that even though Jesus was the cornerstone of the faith, He would be rejected. Matthew 21:42 quotes the Psalm and shows it referred to Jesus. See also Zechariah 12:10.

The Messiah's First Coming

"He was despised and forsaken of men, a man of sorrows and acquainted with grief; And like one from whom men hide their face, He was despised, and we did not esteem Him." *Isaiah 53:3*

"The stone which the builders rejected has become the chief corner *stone*. This is the LORD'S doing; it is marvelous in our eyes." *Psalm 118:22-23*

Jesus Would Be Silent to His Accusers
In the midst of this fixed trial, Jesus would not even respond to His accusers. Instead, He kept silent so the Scriptures would be fulfilled.

"He was oppressed and He was afflicted, yet He did not open His mouth; like a lamb that is led to slaughter, and like a sheep that is silent before its shearers, so He did not open His mouth." *Isaiah 53:7*

"And He did not answer him with regard to even a *single* charge, so the governor was quite amazed." *Matthew 27:14*

Ancient Prophecies Revealed

Prophecies surrounding the crucifixion and resurrection of Jesus

Date	Prophecy	Prediction	Fulfillment
32	207. Jesus predicts He will be in the grave for three days	Matt. 12:38-45; John 2	Matt. 27:50
	208. Jesus' first prediction of His own death	Matt. 16:21-28; Mark 8:31-9:1	Matt. 27:50
	209. Jesus' second prediction of His own death and resurrection	Matt. 20:17-19; Mark 10:32-34	Matt. 27:50
	210. Jesus' third prediction of His own death	Matt. 26:2-5; Mark 14:1-9	Matt. 27:50
	211. The Messiah will be spat upon, smitten, and scourged	Isa. 50:6; 53:5; Mic. 5:1	Matt. 27:26, 30
	212. The Messiah's back beaten and His beard pulled out	Isa. 50:6	Matt. 26:67
	213. The Messiah will hang on a cross	Deut. 21:23	Gal. 3:13
	214. Not one of the Messiah's bones will be broken	Num. 9:12; Ps. 34:20	John 19:31-36
	215. The Messiah's body will be pierced	Zech. 12:10; Ps. 22:16	John 19:34; 20:25, 27
	216. The Messiah will be killed before the Temple is destroyed	Dan. 9:26c	
	217. Crucified 173,880 days after the decree to rebuild Jerusalem	Dan. 9:25	Matt. 27:50
	218. The Messiah's friends & family will stand far off at crucifixion	Ps. 38:11; 88:8	Luke 23:49
	219. Soldiers gambled for the Messiah's garment	Ps. 22:18	Matt. 27:35
	220. The Messiah will be thirsty & given vinegar to drink	Ps. 22:15; 69:21	Matt. 27:34,48
	221. The Messiah's hands and feet pierced	Ps. 22:16	
	222. The Messiah will feel his bones are out of joint	Ps. 22:14	
	223. The Messiah will pray for His enemies	Ps. 109:4	Luke 23:34
	224. The onlookers revile Him and shake their heads	Ps. 22:7	Matt. 27:39
	225. "He trusted in God, let Him deliver him" – ridiculed	Ps. 22:8; 109:25	Matt. 27:43
	226. The Messiah will say "My God, why have you forsaken me?"	Ps. 22:1	Matt. 27:46; Mark 15:34
	227. The Messiah will say "Into thy hands I commit my spirit"	Ps. 31:5	Luke 23:46
	228. Sun darkened and an earthquake will occur at the Messiah's death	Isa. 50:3; Amos 8:8-9	Matt. 27:45
	229. The Messiah will be crucified with criminals	Isa. 53:12	Matt. 27:35
	230. The Messiah will be buried with the rich	Isa. 53:9	Matt. 27:57,60
	231. The Messiah will come to Zion as a redeemer	Isa. 59:20	
	232. The Messiah will die on Mt. Moriah	Gen. 22:8,14	
	233. The Messiah is the Lamb slain	Gen. 22:8	John 1:29
	234. The Messiah's death will not be for Himself, but for us	Dan. 9:26	Matt. 20:28
	235. The Messiah will die for the sins of the world	Dan. 9:26b	Heb. 2:9
	236. God fully satisfied with the Messiah's death for us	Isa. 53:11b	
	237. The Messiah will bear the sins of many	Isa. 53:10-12	Mark 10:45
	238. The Messiah will bear our sicknesses	Isa. 53:4	Matt. 8:16-17
	239. The Messiah will pay for our sins	Isa. 53:4-6	1Pet. 2:24
	240. The Messiah will be wounded for our sins (the world)	Isa. 53:5-12	John 6:51
	241. The Messiah will make an end to sin	Dan. 9:24a	Gal. 1:3-5
	242. The Messiah's death will destroy Satan's/sin's hold on mankind	Gen. 3:15	1 John 3:18
	243. The Messiah will defeat death (where is its sting?)	Hos. 13:14	1 Cor. 15:55-57
	244. The Messiah will be resurrected from the dead	Ps. 16:8-11; 49:15, cmp Ps. 17:15; 30:3; 40:2-5; Acts 13:34; Isa. 55:3; 1 Cor. 15:54; Isa. 25:7-8	John 20:9; Acts 2:25-28; Mark 16:6
	245. The Messiah will ascend to the right hand of God	Ps. 68:18; 110:1	Acts 1:11; 2:35; Luke 24:51

These events were fulfilled in AD 32.

Jesus Dead for Three Days and Nights

Jesus alluded to Jonah 1:17, where God had the prophet Jonah in the belly of a great fish for three days and nights. Jesus identified this event as a cryptic prophecy where Jonah symbolized Jesus being dead in the tomb for three days and nights.

"Then some of the scribes and Pharisees said to Him, 'Teacher, we want to see a sign from You.' But He answered and said to them, 'An evil and adulterous generation craves for a sign; and *yet* no sign will be given to it but the sign of Jonah the prophet; for just as JONAH WAS THREE DAYS AND THREE NIGHTS IN THE BELLY OF THE SEA MONSTER, so will the Son of Man be three days and three nights in the heart of the earth.'" *Matthew 12:38-40*

Jesus' Death
Jesus predicted His own death, knowing the Scriptures well. Jesus knew He would be tried by the Jews, condemned to death, turned over to the Gentiles, mocked, scourged, and crucified. He also repeated His promise to raise from the dead three days after He died. Jesus first predicted His death in Matthew 16:21-28; Mark 8:31-9:1; and Luke 9:21-27. The second time Jesus predicted His death is recorded in Matthew 20:17-19; Mark 10:32-34; and Luke 18:31-34.

> "From that time Jesus began to show His disciples that He must go to Jerusalem, and suffer many things from the elders and chief priests and scribes, and be killed, and be raised up on the third day." *Matthew 16:21*

> "As Jesus was about to go up to Jerusalem, He took the twelve *disciples* aside by themselves, and on the way He said to them, 'Behold, we are going up to Jerusalem; and the Son of Man will be delivered to the chief priests and scribes, and they will condemn Him to death, and will hand Him over to the Gentiles to mock and scourge and crucify *Him*, and on the third day He will be raised up.'" *Matthew 20:17-19*

Spat Upon, Smitten, Scourged, and Beard Pulled Out
Matthew 27 shows Jesus prophesying the same things found in the book of Isaiah.

> "Then he released Barabbas for them; but after having Jesus scourged, he handed Him over to be crucified... They spat on Him, and took the reed and began to beat Him on the head." *Matthew 27:26,30*

> "I gave My back to those who strike *Me*, and My cheeks to those who pluck out the beard; I did not cover My face from humiliation and spitting... But He was pierced through for our transgressions, He was crushed for our iniquities; the chastening for our well-being *fell* upon Him, and by His scourging we are healed." *Isaiah 50:6, 53:5*

Hung Upon a Cross (Crucifixion)
In Galatians 3, Paul quotes Deuteronomy 21 which says God has cursed anyone who is hung on a tree. He adds that the body should not be left hanging on the tree overnight. What is interesting about this prophecy is that the Jews never practiced crucifixion as a form of capital punishment. This was invented by the Persians and perfected by the Romans centuries after Deuteronomy was written. Jesus took the punishment of the curse of "hanging on a tree" for us.

> "Christ redeemed us from the curse of the Law, having become a curse for us--for it is written, 'CURSED IS EVERYONE WHO HANGS ON A TREE'" *Galatians 3:13*

> "his corpse shall not hang all night on the tree, but you shall surely bury him on the same day (for he who is hanged is accursed of God), so that you do not defile your land which the LORD your God gives you as an inheritance." *Deuteronomy 21:23*

In Numbers 21, Moses created a brass serpent and placed it on a pole. Whoever looked to it was healed from poisonious snake bites. Jesus made illusion to this in John 3. The brass serpent was a symbol of Jesus being crucified.

> "As Moses lifted up the serpent in the wilderness, even so must the Son of Man be lifted up;" *John 3:14*

Not One Bone Broken and **They Would Look Upon Him Whom They Pierced**
Normally when Romans wanted to speed up a crucifixion, they would break the legs of the victim in order to cause them to suffocate. With their legs broken they could not push up to breathe. The Jewish leaders were in a hurry to get Jesus off the cross and into a tomb before the start of the high Sabbath (commanded in Deuteronomy 21:33). So they asked the Romans to speed up the deaths; but when they came to Jesus, they saw He was already dead. As a result they did not break any of His bones, but they did pierce His side to make absolutely certain He was dead. This fulfilled the prophecies in Psalm 34:20 and

Ancient Prophecies Revealed

Numbers 9:12, which stated not one bone would be broken, and Zechariah 13:10, which prophesied they would look upon Him whom they had pierced.

"Then the Jews, because it was the day of preparation, so that the bodies would not remain on the cross on the Sabbath (for that Sabbath was a high *day*), asked Pilate that their legs might be broken, and *that* they might be taken away. So the soldiers came, and broke the legs of the first man and of the other who was crucified with Him; but coming to Jesus, when they saw that He was already dead, they did not break His legs. But one of the soldiers pierced His side with a spear, and immediately blood and water came out. And he who has seen has testified, and his testimony is true; and he knows that he is telling the truth, so that you also may believe. For these things came to pass to fulfill the Scripture, 'NOT A BONE OF HIM SHALL BE BROKEN.' And again another Scripture says, 'THEY SHALL LOOK ON HIM WHOM THEY PIERCED.'" *John 19:31-37*

Jesus Killed Before the Temple was Destroyed
Daniel's prophecy clearly shows the Messiah would first come and be killed, *then* the Temple in Jerusalem would be destroyed. Obviously the Messiah had to have come before the destruction of the Temple in AD 70!

"Then after the sixty-two weeks the Messiah will be cut off and have nothing, and the people of the prince who is to come will destroy the city and the sanctuary..." *Daniel 9:26*

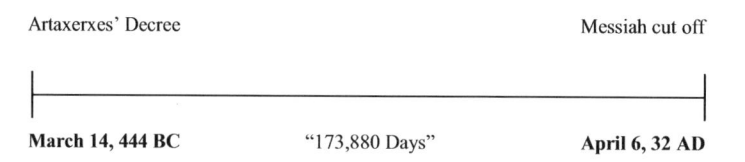

```
AD 32              Artaxerxes' Decree                    Messiah cut off
Messiah's Death    |----------------------------------|
                   March 14, 444 BC   "173,880 Days"   April 6, 32 AD
```

In the ninth chapter of the book of Daniel, the angel Gabriel gave a prophecy about 70 weeks of years, or 490 prophetical years. He said there would be 490 prophetical years between the command to rebuild Jerusalem, to the time when the Messiah would reign bringing in a kingdom of everlasting righteousness. There was to be a gap between the 483 years and the last seven. At the end of the 69th week (or 483 years) the Messiah would die. Then the Temple of Jerusalem would be destroyed (this occurred 40 years later). Eventually the Temple would be rebuilt and the last week, or last seven years, would commence. This gives us the exact date of the Messiah's first coming.

"...from the issuing of a decree to restore and rebuild Jerusalem until Messiah the Prince *there will be* seven weeks and sixty-two weeks; it will be built again, with plaza and moat, even in times of distress. Then after the sixty-two weeks the Messiah will be cut off..." *Daniel 9:25-26*

Nehemiah 2:1 states the decree to restore and rebuild Jerusalem occurred in the month of Nissan in the twentieth year of the reign of the Persian king, Artaxerxes. Encyclopedia Britannica says Artaxerxes Longimanus took the Persian throne in July of 465 BC. So his twentieth year began in July of 445 BC. The month of Nissan following that would have been in March of 444 BC, which was before the twenty-first anniversary of Artaxerxes'

> 69 x 7 = 483 prophetic years; 483 x 360 = 173,880 days
>
> 173,880 days on the modern calendar is 476 yrs & 21 days
> 476 yrs x 365.25 = 173,859; 173,880 – 173,859 = 21 days
>
> March 14, 444 BC + 476 yrs = March 14, AD 31
> Add 1 year (no 0 Year) = AD 32; Add 21 days = April 6, AD 32

reign. The seven weeks, or 49 years, ran from Artaxerxes' decree to the year Jerusalem's wall and moat were finished in the period of Ezra and Nehemiah. From that time another 62 weeks went by until the Messiah was "cut off," a term meaning "put to death."

In the early third century, ancient church father Julius Africanus wrote a book entitled, *"On the Weeks and This Prophecy."* Only fragments remain today; but in fragment 16, he tells us how to calculate the exact date by converting the years to days and changing them from the Jewish prophetical calendar to the Roman calendar used in his day. Julius says that the "70 weeks" prophecy of Daniel 9 started when Artaxerxes gave the decree in his twentieth year. Years later, Sir Robert Anderson

The Messiah's First Coming

recreated the conversion process for our modern calendar as follows: first, the 69 weeks of years ends with the Messiah's death. If we multiply 69 times 7 this gives us the 483 prophetic years between Atrtxerxes' decree and the death of the Messiah.

We convert from the Jewish/prophetic calendar to the Gregorian/Roman calendar this way:
We take the 483 years times 360 days per year (the sacred Jewish calendar) and that comes out to 173,880 days. The 173,880 days on the modern calendar comes out to be 476 years and 21 days (476 x 365.25 = 173859 and 173880-173859 = 21). March fourteenth, 444 BC plus 476 years comes out to be March fourteenth, AD 31. We add one year because there was no "0" year between AD and BC. We then add the 21 days. The final date arrives at April 6, AD 32!

In the section on Modern Israel, we will identify prophecies that date the reestablishment of the nation of Israel on May 14, 1948. We will use the same calculation method for those prophecies.

Rabbinical Quotes Concerning the Death Of the Messiah:
The Talmud relates the tradition that Elijah formed the first "school of the prophets," to teach the sons of the prophets how to correctly interpret the prophecies. One of Elijah's basic teachings was that there would be three distinct periods of time. First, the age of Chaos; second, the age of the Torah, or Mosaic Law; and third, the "days of the Messiah."

> "The school of Elijah taught the world is to exist six thousand years. In the first two thousands years was chaos; two thousand years the Torah flourished; and the next two thousand years are the days of Messiah, but through our many iniquities all these years have been lost" *Talmud, b.Sanhedrin 96a-97b*

History shows the Talmud's teaching that each age would last exactly 2,000 was incorrect. The Years of Chaos were from the Creation (3924 BC) to the Exodus from Egypt (1476 BC), or 2448 years. The Years of Torah were from the Exodus of Egypt to the death of the Messiah (AD 32), or 1509 years. The first two ages totaled 3,957 years. If the days of the Messiah are to be exactly 2,000 years, then they would end before AD 2032. Since the years are off in the first two ages, I really do not think the years of each age were taught by Elijah. I suspect Elijah simply taught the concept of the three ages.

It is clear that we are now living in the "Days of the Messiah." The idea that the "Days of the Messiah" would be the Messiah's reign on earth, instead of the church age, led some Jews to think the Messiah did not come as prophesied in AD 32. When witnessing to Jews today, most will say Daniel's 70 weeks prophecy has nothing to do with the Messiah; but the ancient rabbinical writings, including the Talmud, state the prophecy *does* refer to King Messiah. The ancient rabbis expected the Messiah to come in AD 32! Here are a few quotes:

> "Daniel has elucidated to us the knowledge of the end times. However, since they are secret, the wise [rabbis] have barred the calculation of the days of Messiah's coming so that the untutored populace will not be led astray when they see that the end times have already come but there is no sign of the Messiah."
> *Maimonides: Igeret Teiman, Chapter 3*

> "The anointed King is destined to stand up and restore the Davidic Kingdom to its antiquity, to the first sovereignty. He will build the Temple in Jerusalem and gather the strayed ones of Israel together. All laws will return in his days as they were before: Sacrificial offerings are offered and the Sabbatical years and Jubilees are kept, according to all its precepts that are mentioned in the Torah. Whoever does not believe in him, or whoever does not wait for his coming, not only does he defy the other prophets, but also the Torah and Moses our teacher... Bar Kokhba claimed that he was King Messiah. He and all the Sages of his generation deemed him King Messiah, until he was killed by sins; only since he was killed, they knew that Bar Kokhba was not the Messiah."
> *Maimonides: Mishneh Torah, Hilkhot Melakhim Umilchamoteihem, Chapter 11.*

> "These times (Daniel's 70-Weeks) were over long ago." *Rabbi Judah: Babylonian Talmud, Sanhedrin.*

Ancient Prophecies Revealed

"I have examined and searched all the Holy Scriptures and have not found the time for the coming of Messiah clearly fixed, except in the words of Gabriel to the prophet Daniel, which are written in the 9th chapter of the prophecy of Daniel." *Rabbi Moses Abraham Levi*

"Similarly, one should not try to calculate the appointed time [for the coming of Messiah]. Our Sages declared: [Sanhedrin 97b] 'May the spirits of those who attempt to calculate the final time [of Messiah's coming] expire!' Rather, one should await [his coming] and believe in the general conception of the matter, as we have explained."
Maimonides: Mishneh Torah, Hilkhot Melakhim Umilchamoteihem, Chapter 12

"…all we need is to do teshuva until Messiah comes, for all the predestined dates for the redemption have already passed." *Talmud: Sanhedrin 97b*

"All the time limits for redemption (the coming of Messiah) have passed and the matter now depends only on repentance and good deeds." *Babylonian Talmud: Rabbi Rabh*

Another Jewish history book that identifies that King Messiah is the one spoken of in Daniel 9 is the *Ancient Seder Olam*. The Messiah's death marked the end of the sixty-ninth week and the start of the church age. Later, when the church is removed by the Rapture, the Seventieth Week will begin and fulfill the rest of this prophecy. See the sections on the Rapture and Tribulation for more details. See also the timeline prophecies of AD 1948, and AD 1967 in the section on Modern Israel.

Josephus on Jesus
Historian Josephus describes Jesus Christ in this way:
"Now there was about this time Jesus, a wise man, if it be lawful to call him a man; for he was a doer of wonderful works, a teacher of such men as receive the truth with pleasure. He drew over to him both many of the Jews and many of the Gentiles. He was [the] Christ. And when Pilate, at the suggestion of the principal men amongst us, had condemned him to the cross, those that loved him at the first did not forsake him; for he appeared to them alive again the third day; as the divine prophets had foretold these and ten thousand other wonderful things concerning him. And the tribe of Christians, so named from him, are not extinct at this day." *Josephus Antiquities of the Jews 18.3.3*

Friends and Family Stood Far Off at His Crucifixion
Psalm 88:8 and 38:11 record that the friends and family of Jesus would be at the crucifixion, but stand far off from the cross. The fulfillment is recorded in Luke 23.

"And all His acquaintances and the women who accompanied Him from Galilee were standing at a distance, seeing these things." *Luke 23:49*

"My loved ones and my friends stand aloof from my plague; and my kinsmen stand afar off." *Psalm 38:11*

Soldiers Gambled for His Garment
The cloak Jesus wore was of high quality, so instead of tearing it up the guards gambled for it. This prophecy is recorded in Psalm 22:18 and was fulfilled in Matthew 27.

"And they crucified him, and parted his garments, casting lots: that it might be fulfilled which was spoken by the prophet, they parted my garments among them, and upon my vesture did they cast lots." *Matthew 27:35 KJV*

Thirsty and Given Vinegar
Jesus was thirsty on the cross and was given gall and vinegar to drink. In ancient times gall and vinegar were combined with herbs to ease pain. When Jesus realized what they gave Him, He refused to drink it.

"They gave him vinegar to drink mingled with gall: and when he had tasted thereof, he would not drink." *Matthew 27:34*

"After this, Jesus, knowing that all things had already been accomplished, to fulfill the Scripture, said, 'I am thirsty.'"
John 19:28

The Messiah's First Coming

"They also gave me gall for my food, and for my thirst they gave me vinegar to drink." *Pslam 69:21*

Hands and Feet Pierced and Bones Out Of Joint
Not only was Jesus pierced with a spear in His side, but He was nailed to a cross. Psalm 22:14,16 recorded at Jesus' death not one single bone would be broken, but that His bones would be out of joint.

"I am poured out like water, and all my bones are out of joint; my heart is like wax; it is melted within me… For dogs have surrounded me; a band of evildoers has encompassed me; they pierced my hands and my feet… They look, they stare at me;" *Psalm 22:14,16,17*

Prays For His Enemies
This prophecy is recorded in Psalm 109, while Luke 23 records the fulfillment. Even though Jesus is being ridiculed, He still prays for their salvation. We should do the same when we meet opposition to our faith.

"When they came to the place called The Skull, there they crucified Him and the criminals, one on the right and the other on the left. But Jesus was saying, 'Father, forgive them; for they do not know what they are doing.' And they cast lots, dividing up His garments among themselves. And the people stood by, looking on. And even the rulers were sneering at Him, saying, "He saved others; let Him save Himself if this is the Christ of God, His Chosen One." *Luke 23:33-35*

"In return for my love they act as my accusers; but I am in prayer." *Psalm 109:4*

Reviled and Ridiculed
Psalm 109:25 prophesied they would ridicule Jesus by shaking their heads at Him. Matthew 27 records that they ridiculed Him and quotes Psalm 22:8, using *the exact words* they used when they mocked Jesus on the cross!

"And those passing by were hurling abuse at Him, wagging their heads and saying, 'You who *are going to* destroy the temple and rebuild it in three days, save Yourself! If You are the Son of God, come down from the cross.' In the same way the chief priests also, along with the scribes and elders, were mocking *Him* and saying, 'He saved others; He cannot save Himself. He is the King of Israel; let Him now come down from the cross, and we will believe in Him. 'HE TRUSTS IN GOD; LET GOD RESCUE *Him* now, IF HE DELIGHTS IN HIM; for He said, 'I am the Son of God.'''"
Matthew 27:39-42

My God, My God, Why Have You Forsaken Me?
Psalm 22:1 is quoted in Matthew 27. It is one of the seven sayings Jesus spoke while He was hanging on the cross. Those around Him thought He was calling for Elijah and did not realize He was quoting the Psalm. Here is another instance where people who are not filled with the Holy Spirit were unable to correctly interpret the Scripture.

"About the ninth hour Jesus cried out with a loud voice, saying, 'ELI, ELI, LAMA SABACHTHANI?' that is, 'MY GOD, MY GOD, WHY HAVE YOU FORSAKEN ME?' And some of those who were standing there, when they heard it, began saying, 'This man is calling for Elijah.'" *Matthew 27:46-47*

Into Your Hands I Commit My Spirit
From noon to three in the afternoon darkness fell on the land. At 3:00 PM Jesus cried out to His Father, asking Him to receive His spirit; then He died. Luke 23 records this fulfillment. The original prophecy, using *the exact words* Jesus spoke, is given in Psalm 31.

"It was now about the sixth hour, and darkness fell over the whole land until the ninth hour, because the sun was obscured; and the veil of the temple was torn in two. "And Jesus, crying out with a loud voice, said, 'Father, INTO YOUR HANDS I COMMIT MY SPIRIT.' Having said this, He breathed His last." *Luke 23:44-46*

"Into Your hand I commit my spirit; You have ransomed me, O LORD, God of truth." *Psalm 31:5*

Ancient Prophecies Revealed

Sun Going Dark
The above verse records the darkness occurring between noon and 3:00 PM. Amos prophesied this unexpected darkness.

> "'It will come about in that day,' declares the Lord GOD, 'That I will make the sun go down at noon and make the earth dark in broad daylight." *Amos 8:9*

It is interesting that this darkness occurred on Passover. Passover, the fifteenth of Nissan on the Jewish calendar, always occurs during a full moon. Many have speculated that the darkness was caused by an eclipse of the sun by the moon, but a solar eclipse can only occur at a new moon. At Passover, the moon is on the wrong side of the planet to block the sun's light. We don't know what caused the darkness, but whatever caused it was not an eclipse.

Three Roman historians record a day of darkness occurring between the fifteenth and eighteenth years of the reign of Tiberius Caesar. Two of them, Thallus and Phlegon, remark the darkness could not have been a solar eclipse because it occurred during a full moon!

Messiah Crucified with Criminals but **Buried with the Rich**
The Messiah was to die with criminals and yet be buried with the rich! Even though Jesus was not a criminal, He was crucified between two thieves. Yet at His death, Joseph of Arimathea took His body and laid it in what was to be Joseph's own tomb. Joseph was a wealthy man and a member of the Sanhedrin.

> "At that time two robbers were crucified with Him, one on the right and one on the left." *Matthew 27:38*

> "His grave was assigned with wicked men, yet He was with a rich man in His death" *Isaiah 53:9*

Messiah Comes to Zion as a Redeemer
The prophets wrote that Messiah would come as a redeemer. They also predicted that His redemption would occur on Mount Zion.

> "'A Redeemer will come to Zion, and to those who turn from transgression in Jacob,' declares the LORD." *Isaiah 59:20*

Messiah Would Die on Mount Moriah and **Is the Lamb Slain**
Genesis records God commanded Abraham to sacrifice Isaac. This was a test for Abraham, but also a symbolic prophecy. The Hebrew literally says "God will provide Himself a lamb." The Hebrew can actually be translated as "God will provide Himself as the lamb for the sacrifice." Abraham acknowledged that idea when he said (in verse 14) "on this very mountain it will be seen." The Hebrew word for *provided* can be translated *seen* or *seen to*. So here Abraham is prophesying that the Messiah, who is God incarnate, will sacrifice Himself for our sins on this very mountain, Mount Moriah!

> "Abraham said, 'God will provide for Himself the lamb for the burnt offering, my son.' So the two of them walked on together... Abraham called the name of that place The LORD Will Provide, as it is said to this day, 'In the mount of the LORD it will be provided.'" *Genesis 22:8,14*

> "The next day he saw Jesus coming to him and said, 'Behold, the Lamb of God who takes away the sin of the world!'" *John 1:29*

His Death not for Himself but for **The Sins of the World**
Jesus' death was not because He sinned or did anything wrong; but He died to pay the price for the sins of the whole world. Those who accept the free gift of God's salvation can have eternal life.

> "And after threescore and two weeks shall Messiah be cut off, but not for himself:" *Daniel 9:26 KJV*

> "But we do see Him who was made for a little while lower than the angels, *namely*, Jesus, because of the suffering of death crowned with glory and honor, so that by the grace of God He might taste death for everyone." *Hebrews 2:9*

The Messiah's First Coming

Jesus Died Bearing the Sins of Many and **His Death Satisfied God**
In Isaiah 53 we read that God would be fully satisfied with Jesus' death on the cross as payment for our sins. God, the Father, will not hold anything to our charge; Jesus paid for it all.

> "But the LORD was pleased to crush Him, putting *Him* to grief; if He would render Himself as a guilt offering, He will see *His* offspring, He will prolong *His* days, and the good pleasure of the LORD will prosper in His hand. As a result of the anguish of His soul, He will see *it* and be satisfied; by His knowledge the Righteous One, My Servant, will justify the many, as He will bear their iniquities. Therefore, I will allot Him a portion with the great, and He will divide the booty with the strong; because He poured out Himself to death, and was numbered with the transgressors; yet He Himself bore the sin of many, and interceded for the transgressors." *Isaiah 53:10-12*

Messiah Bore Our Sicknesses and **Paid for Our Sins by Being Wounded**
Jesus, by His wounds, chastisement, and being pierced on the cross, took our sins and sicknesses on Himself. Therefore we are no longer under punishment for our sins.

> "Surely our griefs He Himself bore, and our sorrows He carried; yet we ourselves esteemed Him stricken, smitten of God, and afflicted. But He was pierced through for our transgressions, He was crushed for our iniquities; the chastening for our well-being *fell* upon Him, and by His scourging we are healed. All of us like sheep have gone astray, each of us has turned to his own way; but the LORD has caused the iniquity of us all to fall on Him."
> *Isaiah 53:4-6*

Made an End to Sin
Jesus' death on the cross made an end to the power that sin has over us. This was a once-and-for-all sacrifice that would cover all sins, past, present, and future. You never have to pay for any future sin. All you must do is repent for them. By the time the 70-weeks prophecy is over, sin will be finished. All will be atoned for. Jesus will be reigning on earth as king.

> "Seventy weeks have been decreed for your people and your holy city, to finish the transgression, to make an end of sin, to make atonement for iniquity, to bring in everlasting righteousness, to seal up vision and prophecy and to anoint the most holy place." *Daniel 9:24*

> "Grace to you and peace from God our Father, and the Lord Jesus Christ, who gave Himself for our sins, so that He might rescue us from this present evil age, according to the will of our God and Father, to whom *be* the glory for evermore. Amen." *Galatians 1:3-5*

His Death Destroyed Satan's/Sin's Hold on Mankind
As predicted in Genesis 3, Satan's kingdom – or power over mankind – was broken by the Messiah's death. See the first prophecy in this book for full details. In Hebrews 2, Paul records the fulfillment of this prophecy by saying Jesus' death is what rendered Satan powerless over mankind.

> "And I will put enmity between you and the woman, and between your seed and her seed; He shall bruise you on the head, and you shall bruise him on the heel." *Genesis 3:15*

> "Therefore, since the children share in flesh and blood, He Himself likewise also partook of the same, that through death He might render powerless him who had the power of death, that is, the devil," *Hebrews 2:14*

AD 32
Messiah's Resurrection

Jesus' resurrection from the dead is recorded in many places in the New Testament. The Old Testament Psalms show the Resurrection, too. Also, all the Scriptures about the Messiah doing things after His death prove the Resurrection. Paul in 1

Ancient Prophecies Revealed

Corinthians 15 tells us that to be a *real* Christian, one must believe in the Resurrection. In Acts 2, Paul quotes the resurrection Psalms to show they point to Jesus Christ.

"For You will not abandon my soul to Sheol; nor will You allow Your Holy One to undergo decay." *Psalm 16:10*

"But God will redeem my soul from the power of Sheol, for He will receive me. Selah." *Psalm 49:15*

"But God raised Him up again, putting an end to the agony of death, since it was impossible for Him to be held in its power... Brethren, I may confidently say to you regarding the patriarch David that he both died and was buried, and his tomb is with us to this day. And so, because he was a prophet and knew that GOD HAD SWORN TO HIM WITH AN OATH TO SEAT *one* OF HIS DESCENDANTS ON HIS THRONE, he looked ahead and spoke of the resurrection of the Christ, that HE WAS NEITHER ABANDONED TO HADES, NOR DID His flesh SUFFER DECAY. This Jesus God raised up again, to which we are all witnesses." *Acts 2:24,29-32*

The Resurrection Proves Jesus Defeated Death

Jesus defeated death and resurrected. Because He defeated death for all of us, we too will resurrect (or be raptured). In 1 Corinthians 15, Paul says Hosea 13:14 will be fulfilled when we have our new bodies.

"Behold, I tell you a mystery; we will not all sleep, but we will all be changed, in a moment, in the twinkling of an eye, at the last trumpet; for the trumpet will sound, and the dead will be raised imperishable, and we will be changed. For this perishable must put on the imperishable, and this mortal must put on immortality. But when this perishable will have put on the imperishable, and this mortal will have put on immortality, then will come about the saying that is written, 'DEATH IS SWALLOWED UP' in victory. 'O DEATH, WHERE IS YOUR VICTORY? O DEATH, WHERE IS YOUR STING?' The sting of death is sin, and the power of sin is the law; but thanks be to God, who gives us the victory through our Lord Jesus Christ." *1 Corinthians 15:51-57*

Jesus' Ascension

After Jesus' resurrection, He was prophesied to ascend back to heaven and sit at the right hand of the Father until the time of the Second Coming. Paul quotes Psalm 68 in Ephesians as proof Jesus resurrected, ascended, and gave salvation and other spiritual gifts to men. The historical record of the Ascension is written in Acts 1.

"You have ascended on high, You have led captive *Your* captives; You have received gifts among men, even *among* the rebellious also, that the LORD God may dwell *there*. Blessed be the Lord, who daily bears our burden, the God *who* is our salvation [or our God Yeshua]. Selah. God is to us a God of deliverances; and to GOD the Lord belong escapes from death." *Psalm 68:18-20*

"The LORD says to my Lord: 'Sit at My right hand until I make Your enemies a footstool for Your feet.'" *Psalm 110:1*

"And after He had said these things, He was lifted up while they were looking on, and a cloud received Him out of their sight. And as they were gazing intently into the sky while He was going, behold, two men in white clothing stood beside them. They also said, 'Men of Galilee, why do you stand looking into the sky? This Jesus, who has been taken up from you into heaven, will come in just the same way as you have watched Him go into heaven.'" *Acts 1:9-11*

Spring Festivals

God ordained seven festivals for the Jews to observe, recorded in Leviticus 23. Four occur in the spring and three occur in the fall. The four spring festivals prophetically foreshadow the Messiah's first coming. The three fall festivals prophetically foreshadow the Messiah's second coming. The spring festivals, in order, are: Passover, Unleavened Bread, First Fruits, and Pentecost. Passover occurs on the fourteenth of Nissan; the festival of Unleavened Bread occurs on the fifteenth of Nissan and goes on for one week. First Fruits is the weekly Sabbath after Unleavened Bread. This varies from year to year but on the year the Messiah was crucified, it occurred on the seventeenth of Nissan.

The Passover Seder for Those at Home – Nissan 14
The Passover Seder is the ritual that families observe at home, as apposed to the ritual that took place in the Jerusalem Temple. The Passover Seder commemorates the Exodus from Egypt, but it also teaches about the coming of the Messiah. The Seder starts at 6 PM and must be finished by 12 AM. On the dining table is a special cloth container with three pockets called a Matzah-Tash with a loaf of unleavened bread in each pocket. (This probably symbolizes the Trinity.) The middle loaf of unleavened bread, or Matzah, is taken out and torn in two. The smaller piece is placed back in the pocket between the other two. The father of the household wraps the larger piece in a napkin, and hides it somewhere in the house. (This symbolizes the death and burial of the second person of the Trinity, the Son.) It will be used later for the Afikomen. Then the story of the Exodus from Egypt is told, and the group sings Psalms 113-114. Next, the father brings out the lower peace of Matzah from the Matzah-Tash, blesses it, and each member eats a small peace of the bread. (This symbolizes the Holy Spirit, third person of the Trinity.) Finally, the Passover meal is eaten, which may take several hours.

After the meal, the father sends the children to hunt for hidden Matzah. The Seder can not continue until the Matzah is found and given back to the father. (This symbolizes the resurrection and ascension of the Messiah) The child negotiates what gift the father will give him for returning the Matzah. Then the father gives the child a coin as a down payment for the gift and the matzah is returned and the Seder can continue. This gift of a coin is referred to as "the promise of the father," (symbolizing the giving if the Holy Spirit at Pentecost as an earnest deposit of the gift of eternal life).

Then the father brings out the Matzah that was hidden. Each member is given two pieces of matzah to make the Afikomen. The Afikomen is a sandwich made of two pieces of matzah with the Maror (bitter herbs) on one side and the Charoset (a sweet antidote to the bitter herbs) on the other side. The sandwich is eaten Maror side first, then Charoset. (This symbolizes that the Messiah is the only antidote for sin.) Since it was forbidden to eat the Passover lamb anywhere except Jerusalem (Deuteronomy 16:5), together the group says "I am observing this commandment so I may remember the Passover lamb eaten at the end of the Seder. May the eating of the Afikomen achieve all the spiritual things accomplished by the Passover lamb itself."

During the first Passover at the Exodus, if one placed the blood of the Passover lamb on the door post, the death angel would not kill the firstborn in the house. Salvation was offered only if you believed in the protecting blood of the Passover lamb. Matzah is pierced and has stripes from being cooked unleavened. Isaiah makes allusion to this in Isaiah 53 when he says the Messiah was pierced for us and by His stripes we are healed.

At this point in the Seder, Psalm 126 is sung and they drink the third cup of wine. The first cup of wine is called the "cup of sanctification," the second is the "cup of affliction," the third is the "cup of redemption," the fourth is the "cup of Elijah." Then the fourth cup, the cup of Elijah, is poured. A child is then sent to the door to see if Elijah has come back that year. This shows the fact that Elijah and another witness will appear in the Temple in Jerusalem before the Second Coming of the Messiah. Then they sing the Hallel (which are Psalms 115-118 and Psalm 136).

Meanwhile in the Temple...
In the time of Jesus, the high priest, on the 10th of Nisan, would go to Bethany to get an unblemished lamb and bring it into the Temple to be inspected for four days. As the lamb was brought to the Eastern Gate, pilgrims would line the sides of the road leading to the gate and wave the palm branches and say "Baruch Ha Shem Adonai," quoted from Psalm 118:26-27. At 9 AM on the fourteenth of Nisan, the lamb was tied on one of the horns of the altar. At 3 PM the high priest would slay the lamb while saying the words "it is finished." These words are said at any "shelem" or peace offering.

This ceremony teaches us about the Messiah's death. Jesus left the house of Lazarus in Bethany on Nissan 10 to teach in the Temple. There the scribes asked their hardest questions of Jesus and walked away saying "never a man spoke as this man." So Jesus was without blemish. Jesus was hung on the cross at 9 AM and died at 3:00 PM, or "between the evenings" on Nissan 14. He acted as both priest and sacrifice when He said "it is finished," and then died.

Ancient Prophecies Revealed

The Israelites killed a lamb on the fourteenth (cooking must be done by 6 PM), ate the lamb and left Egypt on the fifteenth (Seder must be done by 12 AM). They crossed the Red Sea on the seventeenth. They brought a lamb to the house on the tenth, killed it "between the evenings," which is 3:00 PM on the fourteenth. The father of the house dipped hyssop in the blood and applied it to each doorpost and the lintel, forming a cross of blood. The lamb was then roasted on a large stick, upright, with a cross piece. Its intestines were roasted too, wrapped around the head and called the crown sacrifice!

Anyone who really believes the prophecies would know the exact day of the Exodus, because of the 430-year prophecy God gave to Abraham. Likewise, they would know the exact time of the crucifixion of the Messiah based on the 70-Weeks prophecy.

Unleavened Bread – Nissan 15
The festival of Unleavened Bread occurred the day after Passover. Leaven represents sin, and unleavened bread represents the Messiah being a sinless sacrifice for us. He was buried on the first day of Unleavened Bread and remained in the grave until He resurrected on First Fruits. This festival of Unleavened Bread also teaches us to remain pure from sin. Paul explained it this way:

> "Clean out the old leaven, so that you may be a new lump, just as you are *in fact* unleavened. For Christ our Passover also has been sacrificed. Therefore let us celebrate the feast, not with old leaven, nor with the leaven of malice and wickedness, but with the unleavened bread of sincerity and truth." *1 Corinthians 5:7-8*

First fruits – Nissan 17
Some rabbis taught First Fruits was at the end of the week of Unleavened Bread. But originally it was the Sabbath after Unleavened Bread. We see this makes up the three days and nights Jesus was in the grave. He was crucified on Passover, buried on Unleavened Bread, and resurrected on the first day of the week, at the end of the Sabbath, on First Fruits!

> "For I delivered to you as of first importance what I also received, that Christ died for our sins according to the Scriptures, and that He was buried, and that He was raised on the third day according to the Scriptures… But now Christ has been raised from the dead, the First Fruits of those who are asleep." *1 Corinthians 15:3-4,20*

Other Historical Events that Occurred on Festivals

10th of Nissan
God commanded Abraham to travel to Moriah and sacrifice Isaac.
Jesus taught in the Temple
Passover lamb put on display

Passover – 14th
The Messiah was sacrificed
Isaac was born
Abraham almost sacrificed Isaac
The Exodus from Egypt occurred
Fall of Massada occurred

First Fruits – 17th
The Messiah's Resurrection (during the fourth watch, 4-6AM)
Noah's Ark came to rest on the 17 of Nisan (Genesis 8:4).
Haman killed (Esther 7:2)
Egyptians drowned in the Red Sea (during the fourth watch, Exodus 14:24)

✡

The Messiah to the Great Dispersion

First Crossover Period, AD 32 to 132 – 36 prophecies in 100 years

Date	Prophecy	Prediction	Fulfillment*
32	246. Holy Spirit will manifest after Jesus returns to the Father	John 16:7-15	Acts 2
	247. Don't leave Jerusalem until the Holy Spirit is given	Acts 1:4-5, 8	Acts 2
	248. Birth of the church on Pentecost	John 14:16-18,20,25-26	Acts 2
	249. The coming of the Holy Spirit	John 7:37-39; 15:26-27; Isa. 44:3	Acts 2
	250. Spiritual gifts will be given to men	Ps. 68:18	Eph. 4:7-16
	251. Peter says Pentecost fulfills Joel's prophecy	Joel 2:28-32	Acts 2:17-21
	252. Gift of tongues – the church's blessing and Israel's destruction	Isa. 28:10-13	Acts 2; 1 Cor. 14
	253. Christians will be given a new nature	Jer. 31	Eph. 4:24
	254. Mosaic Covenant will be replaced	Jer. 31:31-33; Mal. 3:1c; Isa. 42:6	Heb. 8:13
	255. New Covenant will be placed on believers' hearts	Jer. 31:31-33	
	256. Priesthood will be changed	Exod. 25:40	Heb. 8:1; 1 Pet. 2:9
	257. Animal sacrifices will be abolished	Jer. 31	Heb. 10:1-8
	258. Judas' office will be filled by another (Mathias)	Ps. 109:7-8	Acts 1:16-20
	259. Church will grow and gates of hell will not prevail against it	Matt. 16:17-18	
	260. Wolves in sheep's clothing will rise up from within the church	Matt. 7:15	Acts 8:9-22
45	261. Famine predicted by NT prophets	Acts 11:27-30	Acts 11:28
58	262. Agabus predicts Paul will be imprisoned in Rome	Acts 21:10-11	Acts 28:11-31
67	263. Paul predicts his own death	Acts 20:25-27	
70	264. James (Lord's brother) will be slain on Temple Mount	Isa. 3:10 LXX	Eusebius 2:23
	265. Every building on the Temple Mount will be destroyed	Matt. 24:1-2 (no stones remaining)	
	266. Jerusalem will be destroyed	Luke 19:42-44; 21:20-24	
	267. Temple will be destroyed by Titus (the prince)	Dan. 9:26	
	268. Romans will destroy the Jerusalem Temple	Dan. 11:33	
	269. Pharisees that reject Jesus will die in their sins	John 8:12-20	
	270. Jerusalem will be plowed down like a field	Mic. 3:11-12	
	271. After Jesus' crucifixion, the "prince of this world" will come	John 14:28-31	
95	272. Some will not see death until they see Jesus in His kingdom	Matt. 16:28	Rev. 1:9-20
132	273. Jewish kingdom will be be desolated	(Matt. 23:37-38; Luke 13:33-36,)	
	274. Jews will be dispersed by the Romans	Num. 24:23-24; Dan. 11:30,33; Mic. 5:1,3	
	275. Israel will be scattered because of rejecting Messiah	Matt. 26:31-56 (Zech. 13:7d)	
	276. The Jews will accept a false Christ (Simon BarKokhba)	John 5:41-44	
	277. Two-thirds of Israel will be destroyed by the Romans	(Zech. 13:8)	
	278. Israel will be destroyed by Rome (Eagle)	Deut. 28:49-52; Dan. 11:30,33-34	
	279. Israel will be dispersed into all nations	Deut. 28:64; Ezek. 12:15-16; Hos. 9:17	
	280. Land will become a complete desolation (sulfur)	Deut. 29:23; Isa. 6:10-13	
	281. Israel will dwell many days (1816 years) without her land	Hos. 3:4-5; 6:1-3	

*After AD 95 the fulfillments are not recorded in Scripture

AD 32
Pentecost, Birth of the Church

The coming of the Holy Spirit and the birth of the church is recorded in Acts 2. It began this way: before Jesus ascended, He told His disciples to wait in Jerusalem until the Holy Spirit came upon them (Acts 1:4-5, 8). At that time they would be empowered to preach the gospel (Acts 1:8). Jesus also told them this would not occur until He had returned to the Father

Ancient Prophecies Revealed

(John 16:7-15). On the Pentecost of AD 32, 50 days after the Crucifixion, the Holy Spirit came. The apostles were filled with boldness to preach the gospel and given the gift of the ability to speak in other languages.

> "When the day of Pentecost had come, they were all together in one place. And suddenly there came from heaven a noise like a violent rushing wind, and it filled the whole house where they were sitting. And there appeared to them tongues as of fire distributing themselves, and they rested on each one of them. And they were all filled with the Holy Spirit and began to speak with other tongues, as the Spirit was giving them utterance." *Acts 2:1-4*

Gifts of the Spirit

In Ephesians 4:7-16 Paul quotes the prophecy of Psalm 68:18, where he explains after the Resurrection of the Messiah, spiritual gifts would be given to those who believe in the Messiah. There are many gifts, not just speaking in tongues. For a complete list of the gifts, see 1 Corinthians 12:8-10, 29-30; Romans 12:6-8; and Ephesians 4:11.

The festival of Passover foreshadowed the Crucifixion. Pentecost, which occurred when Moses came down from Mount Sinai with the Ten Commandments, foreshadowed the birth of the church and the giving of the Holy Spirit. One Jewish legend says:

> "When God gave the Law on Mt Sinai, he displayed untold marvels to Israel with his voice. What happened? God spoke and the voice reverberated throughout the whole land... it says, the people witnessed the thunderings (Exodus 18:15). Note that it does not say "the thunder," but "the thunderings;" wherefore Rabbi Johanan said that God's voice, as it was uttered, split into 70 languages, so that all the nations should understand." *Exodus Rabbah 5:9*

In another legend, not only does God's voice split into 70 languages, but can be seen visibly as tongues of fire coming upon the carved stones to produce the Ten Commandments. What is interesting about these legends is that about 1500 years later, on another Pentecost, as the Holy Spirit was given at the birth of the church, cloven tongues of fire could be seen resting on the heads of believers. Then the believers spoke in other tongues. Acts 2 lists over 17 different foreign languages, but I believe it was a lot more.

> "And how is it that we each hear *them* in our own language to which we were born? Parthians and Medes and Elamites, and residents of Mesopotamia, Judea and Cappadocia, Pontus and Asia, Phrygia and Pamphylia, Egypt and the districts of Libya around Cyrene, and visitors from Rome, both Jews and proselytes, Cretans and Arabs--we hear them in our *own* tongues speaking of the mighty deeds of God." *Acts 2:8-11*

Peter recorded that all these things were a partial fulfillment of the prophecy given by Joel:

> "but this is what was spoken of through the prophet Joel: 'AND IT SHALL BE IN THE LAST DAYS,' God says, 'THAT I WILL POUR FORTH OF MY SPIRIT ON ALL MANKIND; AND YOUR SONS AND YOUR DAUGHTERS SHALL PROPHESY, AND YOUR YOUNG MEN SHALL SEE VISIONS, AND YOUR OLD MEN SHALL DREAM DREAMS; EVEN ON MY BONDSLAVES, BOTH MEN AND WOMEN, I WILL IN THOSE DAYS POUR FORTH OF MY SPIRIT and they shall prophesy. AND I WILL GRANT WONDERS IN THE SKY ABOVE AND SIGNS ON THE EARTH BELOW, BLOOD, AND FIRE, AND VAPOR OF SMOKE. THE SUN WILL BE TURNED INTO DARKNESS AND THE MOON INTO BLOOD, BEFORE THE GREAT AND GLORIOUS DAY OF THE LORD SHALL COME. AND IT SHALL BE THAT EVERYONE WHO CALLS ON THE NAME OF THE LORD WILL BE SAVED.'" *Acts 2:16-21*

Tongues a Sign at Pentecost

In 1 Corinthians 14:21, Paul quoted a passage from Isaiah to say that the Christian gift of speaking in tongues is a sign that the nation of Israel had corporately rejected Jesus Christ as Messiah and was about to be destroyed. Within 40 years this prophecy was fulfilled. (Notice the same quote is used to denote the Rapture – see section on the Rapture for more details.)

> "To whom would He teach knowledge, and to whom would He interpret the message? Those *just* weaned from milk? Those *just* taken from the breast? For *He says*, 'Order on order, order on order, line on line, line on line, a little here, a little there.' Indeed, He will speak to this people through stammering lips and a foreign tongue, He who said to them, 'Here is rest, give rest to the weary,' and, 'Here is repose,' but they would not listen. So the word of the LORD to them will be, 'Order on order, order on order, line on line, line on line, a little here, a little there,' that they may go and stumble backward, be broken, snared, and taken captive." *Isaiah 28:9-13*

"In the Law it is written, 'BY MEN OF STRANGE TONGUES AND BY THE LIPS OF STRANGERS I WILL SPEAK TO THIS PEOPLE, AND EVEN SO THEY WILL NOT LISTEN TO ME,' says the Lord. So then tongues are for a sign, not to those who believe but to unbelievers; but prophecy is for a sign, not to unbelievers but to those who believe." *1 Corinthians 14:21-22*

Replacement of the Covenant, Sacrifices, and Priesthood
The apostle Paul points out that in the church age we have a different covenant than they had in the Old Testament. He teaches that we have a *different* covenant (Hebrews 8:13), with a *different* priesthood (Hebrews 8:1), where animal sacrifices have been abolished (Heb 10:1-8). The Levitical laws regarding food and observance of the Sabbaths have been abolished (Colossians 2:16). When we become Christian, we receive not only forgiveness and eternal life, but a new nature (Ephesians 4:24). This new nature is specifically mentioned by Jeremiah.

"'Behold, days are coming,' declares the LORD, 'when I will make a new covenant with the house of Israel and with the house of Judah, not like the covenant which I made with their fathers in the day I took them by the hand to bring them out of the land of Egypt, My covenant which they broke, although I was a husband to them,' declares the LORD. 'But this is the covenant which I will make with the house of Israel after those days,' declares the LORD, 'I will put My law within them and on their heart I will write it; and I will be their God, and they shall be My people.'"
Jeremiah 31:31-33

Judas Replaced
Judas Iscariot betrayed our Lord and committed suicide shortly afterwards. According to Acts 1:16-20, the apostles realized that Psalm 109:7-8 was referring to Judas and that they were supposed to pick another person to replace him. They selected a group of men who were both eyewitnesses of the Lord in the flesh and who had a godly reputation. Out of these they picked Mathias.

"Appoint a wicked man over him, and let an accuser stand at his right hand. When he is judged, let him come forth guilty, and let his prayer become sin. Let his days be few; let another take his office." *Psalm 109:6-8*

The True Church Never Destroyed
Matthew 16:17-18 records Jesus' prophecy that nothing, including hell itself, could stop the church. The church has continued over 2000 years and is still here today. See the section on the Apostasy of the Church for more details on the apostasy and the section the Rapture to see the conclusion of the church age.

Rise of the Cults
Jesus said in Matthew 7:15 there would arise false teachers and false prophets much like wolves in sheep's clothing. We see the start of this in Acts 8:9-22. A man named Simon Magus tried to buy the power and gifts of the Holy Spirit. Church history records that he went on to found the first Gnostic cult and started a movement that almost wiped out Christianity by the end of the second century. We will deal with Gnosticism in great detail in the section on the Apostasy of the Church.

The Prophecy of a Famine
About AD 45, the Lord revealed to His church by certain Christian prophets that there would be a famine in the land. Knowing this in advance, they took up a collation so that when the famine hit, the Christians in that area would not be so devastated.

"Now at this time some prophets came down from Jerusalem to Antioch. One of them named Agabus stood up and *began* to indicate by the Spirit that there would certainly be a great famine all over the world. And this took place in the *reign* of Claudius. And in the proportion that any of the disciples had means, each of them determined to send *a contribution* for the relief of the brethren living in Judea. And this they did, sending it in charge of Barnabas and Saul to the elders." *Acts 11:27-30*

Ancient Prophecies Revealed

The Prophecy of Paul's Imprisonment
The Christian prophet Agabas revealed to Paul that if Paul went to Jerusalem, he would be put into prison. Paul decided, however, that this was the will of the Lord for him and went to Jerusalem, anyway. He was put into prison about the year AD 45.

> "As we were staying there for some days, a prophet named Agabus came down from Judea. And coming to us, he took Paul's belt and bound his own feet and hands, and said, 'This is what the Holy Spirit says: 'In this way the Jews at Jerusalem will bind the man who owns this belt and deliver him into the hands of the Gentiles.' When we had heard this, we as well as the local residents began begging him not to go up to Jerusalem. Then Paul answered, 'What are you doing, weeping and breaking my heart? For I am ready not only to be bound, but even to die at Jerusalem for the name of the Lord Jesus.'" *Acts 21:10-13*

Paul Prophesies His Own Death
Paul knew by revelation from God that he would preach the Gospel in Rome and be put to death there. Here in Acts 20, Paul shares this with his brothers at Ephesus, because he knows this will be the last time he will ever see them, until he sees them in the kingdom of heaven.

> "And now, behold, I know that all of you, among whom I went about preaching the kingdom, will no longer see my face… For I did not shrink from declaring to you the whole purpose of God." *Acts 20:25,27*

AD 70
Destruction of the Temple

The destruction of the Temple took place 40 years after the death of the Messiah and the birth of the church. It occurred in the church age. AD 32 to AD 132 is referred to as the First Cross-over Period, the time when the church age had started but apostate Israel had not yet been dispersed as prophesied. See section on modern Israel to see the Second Cross-over Period.

> "Jesus came out from the temple and was going away when His disciples came up to point out the temple buildings to Him. And He said to them, 'Do you not see all these things? Truly I say to you, not one stone here will be left upon another, which will not be torn down.'" *Matthew 24:1-2*

> "But when you see Jerusalem surrounded by armies, then recognize that her desolation is near." *Luke 21:20*

Prince That Is To Come – Titus
In the 70-Weeks prophecy, we have seen that we can calculate the *exact date* for the first coming of the Messiah! After His death, we have a gap, called "the church age," which ends with the 70th Week, also called the Tribulation period. We also see that after the Messiah's death a "prince" will come and destroy the Temple with a flood of people. The Roman general Titus was that prince. The soldiers involved were mainly hired from surrounding nations, mostly Syria. The Temple was destroyed as predicted. Titus and his father, Vespasian, were both Roman generals, neither one was a prince. Together they worked on besieging Jerusalem. During this time the Roman Caesar died. The Roman senate quietly recalled Vaspasian back to Rome to make him the next Caesar before anyone could cause a revolt. Titus did not know, but the day he broke though the walls of Jerusalem and his troops destroyed the Temple, he had become a prince! This occurred in AD 70 as prophesied. The gold in the Temple melted and ran in between the cracks of the stones when the Temple was burned. This is why the Romans tore the temple apart stone by stone – to get the gold.

> "Then after the sixty-two weeks the Messiah will be cut off and have nothing, and the people of the prince who is to come will destroy the city and the sanctuary. And its end *will come* with a flood; even to the end there will be war; desolations are determined." *Daniel 9:26*

The Messiah to the Great Dispersion

"Now I have told you before it happens, so that when it happens, you may believe. I will not speak much more with you, for the ruler (prince) of the world is coming, and he has nothing in Me;" *John 14:29-30*

Those who rejected the Messiah and His teachings did not heed the warnings of the Christian prophets and were destroyed. Many people perished when Titus besieged Jerusalem in AD 70 and many more in the Bar Kokhba Rebellion of AD 132.

"Then He said again to them, 'I go away, and you will seek Me, and will die in your sin; where I am going, you cannot come.'" *John 8:21*

Josephus On The Destruction Of The Temple

Here is Josephus' account of the events that took place before the destruction of the Jerusalem Temple (*Wars of the Jews* 6.5.3,4). Josephus writes that in spite of these events, the Jews attacked and demolished the tower of Antonia. This made the Temple Mount foresquare. They should have known better, because it was written in their sacred oracles that "once the Temple Mount becomes foursquare, then the city of Jerusalem and the holy Temple shall be taken." Instead of looking at this, they turned their eyes to an ambiguous oracle in their sacred writings, which said, "about that time, one from their country should become governor of the habitable earth." They thought this meant the coming of a Jewish Messiah, but the prophecy was fulfilled by Vespasian, who then was governor of Judah. Shortly before the Temple was destroyed, he became the next Caesar. Here are the signs that foretold the city's desolation.

1. Seven years before the destruction, when all was at peace and Jews from all over came to celebrate the feast of Passover, a prophet called Jesus, son of Ananus, walked though the streets crying "woe to Jerusalem." He continued this for seven years until he was slain.
2. The year before the Roman war, during the feast of Unleavened Bread, at 3:00 AM, a great light shown down on the Temple and the altar. It was as bright as day and lasted for half an hour.
3. A star appeared resembling a sword, along with a comet that could be seen every evening for a whole year.
4. The Eastern Gate of the inner court of the Temple opened by itself about 12:00 AM. This brass gate was so heavy it took 20 men to shut it!
5. On Iyar 20, 16 days before Pentecost, just before sunset, everyone could clearly see chariots and armored troops of soldiers in the clouds, not only above the city of Jerusalem but other cites as well.
6. During the festival of Pentecost there was an earthquake and a loud noise. Then the sound of a great multitude of voices cried, "Leave this place!"

The Plowing of Jerusalem

With the Temple destroyed in AD 70, the Romans sought to create a new pagan city on the site of ancient Jerusalem. The very next year in AD 71, the Romans ran a plow through Jerusalem. The prophet Micah predicted this would happen almost 700 years before it took place! The destruction of the Temple occurred on the ninth of Av. It interesting to note that according to the Talmud, the ninth of Av is also when Jerusalem was plowed under by Turnus Rufus, a Roman officer!

"Her leaders pronounce judgment for a bribe, her priests instruct for a price, and her prophets divine for money. Yet they lean on the LORD saying, 'Is not the LORD in our midst? Calamity will not come upon us.' Therefore, on account of you, Zion will be plowed as a field, Jerusalem *will become* a heap of ruins, and the mountain of the temple will become high places of a forest." *Micah 3:11-12*

James Martyred – AD 69 or 70

James, the half-brother of the Lord, was the pastor of the Jerusalem church for over 14 years. He was considered to be so holy he was allowed to pray kneeling in the Temple daily. This gave him the nickname "camel knees" because of calluses he had from praying on the stone. Eusebius records, in his *Ecclesiastical History* 2.23, that James was asked to speak about the Messiah and Jesus of Nazareth at a festival. In his speech he testified that Jesus was indeed the promised Messiah. Immediately he was thrown to the ground from the pinnacle of the Temple, and stoned to death. Eusebius adds that immediately after James' death, Titus attacked Jerusalem, and this fulfilled the prophecy in Isaiah 3:8-10. Quoted below is

Ancient Prophecies Revealed

the Septuagint version Eusebius used. In this prophecy, the killing of James the Just would be the sign that Titus' army would soon destroy the Temple.

> "For Jerusalem is ruined, and Judea has fallen, and their tongues have spoken with iniquity, disobedient as they are towards the Lord. Wherefore now their glory has been brought low, and the shame of their countenance has withstood them, and they have proclaimed their sin as Sodom, and made it manifest. Woe to their soul, for they have devised an evil counsel against themselves, saying against themselves, Let us **bind the just** [author's emphasis], for he is burdensome to us: therefore shall they eat the fruits of their works." *Isaiah 3:8-10 LXX*

Jesus in His Kingdom – AD 95
Jesus prophesied that some of his disciples would not see death until they saw Him in His kingdom. One primary example of this was the apostle John. John was banished to the isle of Patmos to live out the rest of his life in exile. During his stay there in AD 95, he received a vision and wrote it down. This vision was added to the canon of Scripture and is the last book of the Bible, the book of Revelation. In this vision, John saw Jesus in all of his glory or when He had "come into his kingdom." John died about 23 years later in 118 AD.

AD 132
Great Dispersion

In AD 130, the Romans tried to dedicate a temple to Jupiter on the Temple Mount, causing the Bar-Kokhba Rebellion. In AD 132 the Romans crushed the rebellion by destroying over 1000 villages and killing over 500,000 Jews. The remainder of the Jews was dispersed to other countries and the nation of Israel ceased to exist. The Romans renamed the land Syria-Palestine, and Jerusalem was renamed Aelia Capitolina.

> "Jerusalem, Jerusalem, who kills the prophets and stones those who are sent to her! How often I wanted to gather your children together, the way a hen gathers her chicks under her wings, and you were unwilling. Behold, your house is being left to you desolate!" *Matthew 23:37-38*

Daniel speaks about the burning of the Temple and the dispersion of Israel under Rome. "Those who have insight" are Christians who converted many. The "sword" is Massada and the Bar-Kokhba Rebellion. The "flame" is the destruction of the Temple in AD 70 and the "captivity" is the dispersion of AD 132-1948.

> "Those who have insight among the people will give understanding to the many; yet they will fall by sword and by flame, by captivity and by plunder for *many* days. Now when they fall they will be granted a little help, and many will join with them in hypocrisy. Some of those who have insight will fall, in order to refine, purge, and make them pure until the end time; because *it is* still *to come* at the appointed time." *Daniel 11:33-35*

Balaam prophesied in Numbers that Rome (or Kittim) would destroy Eber, the Hebrews. See the section on Jesus' childhood for details on the destruction of Ashur, which was Greek-ruled Syria. Micah said sometime after the siege of Jerusalem, the nation of Israel would be given up (or dispersed) until the appointed time.

> "Then he took up his discourse and said, 'Alas, who can live except God has ordained it?' But ships *shall come* from the coast of Kittim [Rome], and they shall afflict Asshur [Greek-ruled Syria] and will afflict Eber [Israel]; so they also will come to destruction." *Numbers 24:23-34*

> "Now muster yourselves in troops, daughter of troops; they have laid siege against us… Therefore He will give them *up* until the time when she who is in labor has borne a child. Then the remainder of His brethren will return to the sons of Israel." *Micah 5:1,3*

The Messiah to the Great Dispersion

The unbelieving Jews accepted Simon Bar-Kokhba as the Messiah. Jesus said this would happen in the Gospel of John. Bar-Kokhba means "son of the star." By crushing this last rebellion, two-thirds of the Jews in Israel were killed. The rest were scattered among the nations and the nation of Israel ceased to exist.

> "I have come in My Father's name, and you do not receive Me; if another comes in his own name, you will receive him." *John 5:43*

> "'It will come about in all the land,' declares the LORD, 'That two parts in it will be cut off *and* perish; but the third will be left in it.'" *Zechariah 13:8*

Even Moses and Hosea prophesied about this:
> "The LORD will bring a nation against you from afar, from the end of the earth, as the eagle swoops down, a nation whose language you shall not understand, a nation of fierce countenance who will have no respect for the old, nor show favor to the young. Moreover, it shall eat the offspring of your herd and the produce of your ground until you are destroyed, who also leaves you no grain, new wine, or oil, nor the increase of your herd or the young of your flock until they have caused you to perish. It shall besiege you in all your towns until your high and fortified walls in which you trusted come down throughout your land, and it shall besiege you in all your towns throughout your land which the LORD your God has given you… Moreover, the LORD will scatter you among all peoples, from one end of the earth to the other end of the earth…" *Deuteronomy 28:49-52,64*

> "My God will cast them away because they have not listened to Him; and they will be wanderers among the nations." *Hosea 9:17*

Jesus quoted this passage from Isaiah in Matthew 13:15. This shows the destruction was fulfilled by the Romans.

> "'Render the hearts of this people insensitive, their ears dull, and their eyes dim, otherwise they might see with their eyes, hear with their ears, understand with their hearts, and return and be healed.' Then I said, 'Lord, how long?' And He answered, 'Until cities are devastated and without inhabitant, houses are without people, and the land is utterly desolate, the LORD has removed men far away, and the forsaken places are many in the midst of the land. Yet there will be a tenth portion in it, and it will again be *subject* to burning, like a terebinth or an oak whose stump remains when it is felled. The holy seed is its stump.'" *Isaiah 6:10-13*

1816-year Desolation – AD 132-1948

Deuteronomy described that the land would become a complete desolation – a desert wilderness with no trees, plant life, or animals. There were 1816 years from the dispersion of the nation of Israel to its return (AD 132-1948). There were 1,897 years between the time when the Jews lost Jerusalem until the time they received it back in full (AD 70-1967). Hosea referred to this by saying the Jews would be raised up "on the third day," meaning at the end of almost 2000 years of dispersion. In 2 Peter 3:8 we are told that in terms of some of the prophecies "day is like a thousand years." If we apply this to Hosea we will have 2,000 years of dispersion. On the "third day," or after 2,000 years, Israel will be raised up.

> "Come, let us return to the LORD. For He has torn *us*, but He will heal *us*; He has wounded us, but He will bandage us. He will revive us after two days; He will raise us up on the third day, that we may live before Him. So let us know, let us press on to know the LORD. His going forth is as certain as the dawn; and He will come to us like the rain, like the spring rain [Later Rain] watering the earth." *Hosea 6:1-3*

Hoesa continued and described during those 2,000 years what they would *not* have. The sacrifice, sacred pillar, and ephod will be restored when the third Temple is build and its services restored. The taraphim, or idol that speaks, will be placed in the Temple by the Antichrist in the middle of the Tribulation. The King or prince will be restored at the Second Coming of the Messiah!

Ancient Prophecies Revealed

"For the sons of Israel will remain for many days without king or prince, without sacrifice or *sacred* pillar and without ephod or household idols [Taraphim]. Afterward the sons of Israel will return and seek the LORD their God and David their king; and they will come trembling to the LORD and to His goodness in the last days." *Hosea 3:4-5*

"Now the generation to come, your sons who rise up after you and the foreigner who comes from a distant land, when they see the plagues of the land and the diseases with which the LORD has afflicted it, will say, All its land is brimstone and salt, a burning waste, unsown and unproductive, and no grass grows in it, like the overthrow of Sodom and Gomorrah, Admah and Zeboiim, which the LORD overthrew in His anger and in His wrath. All the nations will say, 'Why has the LORD done thus to this land? Why this great outburst of anger?' Then men will say, 'Because they forsook the covenant of the LORD, the God of their fathers, which He made with them when He brought them out of the land of Egypt. They went and served other gods and worshiped them, gods whom they have not known and whom He had not allotted to them. Therefore, the anger of the LORD burned against that land, to bring upon it every curse which is written in this book; and the LORD uprooted them from their land in anger and in fury and in great wrath, and cast them into another land, as it is this day." *Deuteronomy 29:22-28*

✡

The Great Dispersion
AD 132 to 1948 – 24 prophecies in 1816 years

Date	Prophecy	From Scripture	From Other Sources
350	282. Pagan temple of Serapis destroyed		Socrates EH 5.17
395	283. Roman Empire will divide into parts, Eastern and Western	Dan. 2	Esdras Apocalypse 11
476	284. The old Roman Empire will fall		Esdras Apocalypse 11
	285. Papal Rome will arise		Esdras Apocalypse 11
625	286. Edom/Petra will become desolate	Isa. 34:5-10	
1056	287. The East (including Russia) will break away from Papal Rome		Esdras Apocalypse 11
1090	288. The Martyrs of York		Tisha B'Av
1095	289. First Crusade		Tisha B'Av
1290	290. All Jews expelled from England		Tisha B'Av
1492	291. All Jews expelled from Spain		Tisha B'Av
1517	292. Eastern Gate sealed	Ezek. 44:1-2	
1523	293. The West (including Germany) will break away from Papal Rome		Esdras Apocalypse 11
1929	294. Greece will become independent	Dan. 8:22-23	
1880s	295. Jews will buy back their land (1880's-1920's)	Jer. 32:44	
1914	296. World War I		Tisha B'Av
1917	297. Residue of Roman Caesars in Russia and Germany destroyed		Esdras Apocalypse 11
	298. Balfour Declaration will be made (Tarshish)	Isa. 60:9	
1920s	299. Land of Israel will be partitioned by the nations	Joel 3:2	
1922	300. Egypt will become independent	Dan. 8:22-23	
1929	301. Turkey will become independent	Dan. 8:22-23	
1942	302. Deportation of Jews to death camps start		Tisha B'Av
1944	303. Syria will become independent	Dan. 8:22-23	
1945	304. Nazi Holocaust will occur	Dan. 8:22-24; Deut. 28:64-6	
	305. Russia will conquer East Germany (WWII ends)		Esdras Apocalypse 11

In this section we will deal with the prophecies from the Bible and the ancient church fathers first. Then we will look at the patterns from the seven Jewish festivals, specifically Tisha B'Av. Finally, we will reveal some prophecies from an extra-biblical source referring to the Roman Empire.

Great Serapian Temple Destroyed
By the year AD 350, the Roman Empire had officially embraced Christianity as its religion for over 25 years. At this time Caesar decreed that the pagan temples be torn down. One of the last temples to be destroyed was the Great Temple of Serapis in Egypt. Christian Historian Socrates recorded this event, saying:

> "When the Temple of Serapis was torn down and laid bare, there were found in it, engraven on stones, certain characters which they call hieroglyphics, having the forms of crosses. After the hieroglyphics had been deciphered it was found that it contained a prediction that 'When the cross should appear,'—for this was 'life to come,'—'the Temple of Serapis would be destroyed,' a very great number of the pagans embraced Christianity, and confessing their sins, were baptized ..." *Socrates, Ecclesiastical History 5.17*

Who was Serapis and how was he able to accurately prophesy? The ancient church fathers relate that Serapis was one of the Egyptian names given to Joseph, son of Jacob. Joseph knew that in time the Egyptians would worship him as they did most of the ancestral kings. So he built a library to house the oracles of the one true God of the Hebrews, and carved the prophecy into the stone walls of the library. In time it was perverted into a pagan temple, and Sarapis became synonymous with the god Osiris. When worshiped under the figure of a bull, he is called Apis.

Ancient Prophecies Revealed

Because of Joseph's prophecy, the worshipers of the pagan gods were looking for a new religion to replace their own. The symbol of that religion was a cross and its coming would be marked by the destruction of their temple. A Socrates states that's the reason scores of pagans instantly became believers when the hieroglyphics were read. This should tell us that if there is anything true in paganism, it came from a real Hebrew prophet. Most myths have a basis in historical fact, and when there is something supernatural about them, they always come from the one true God.

Division of the Old Roman Empire – AD 395
The first prophecy of this section concerns the division of the Roman Empire. Daniel recorded that the Roman Empire would first be divided; then, in the last days, revive in the form of ten nations. We will see this again later in this section.

> "In that you saw the feet and toes, partly of potter's clay and partly of iron, it will be a divided kingdom; but it will have in it the toughness of iron, inasmuch as you saw the iron mixed with common clay." *Daniel 2:41*

Edom's Desolation – AD 625
The remnant of Esau left Edom and migrated into Israel shortly after Babylon captured Judah. It is thought that these Edomite descendants are modern Palestinians. After the migration, the Nabateans conquered Edom and Petra. By AD 625, all the rivers and streams had completely dried up and Petra, the capital of the ancient Edom, became a ghost town. About this time Islam was born.

> "For My sword is satiated in heaven, behold it shall descend for judgment upon Edom…For the LORD has a day of vengeance, a year of recompense for the cause of Zion. Its streams will be turned into pitch, and its loose earth into brimstone, and its land will become burning pitch. It will not be quenched night or day; its smoke will go up forever from generation to generation it will be desolate; none will pass through it forever and ever." *Isaiah 34:5,8-10*

Eastern Gate Sealed – AD 1517
Ezekiel 40-48 describes the future millennial Temple in great detail. Although the second Temple was destroyed, the outer structure, including the Western Wall and the Eastern Gate, has remained. Ezekiel writes that sometime before the millennial Temple is built (which is in the church age) the Eastern Gate would be sealed up because the "glory of the Lord" (or the Messiah) had entered through it. This refers to the Triumphal Entry of Jesus in AD 32.

> "Then He brought me back by the way of the outer gate of the sanctuary, which faces the east; and it was shut. The LORD said to me, This gate shall be shut; it shall not be opened, and no one shall enter by it, for the LORD God of Israel has entered by it; therefore it shall be shut." *Ezekiel 44:1-2*

In AD 1517, Suleiman the Magnificent, the tenth Sultan of the Ottoman Empire, annexed Jerusalem. He commanded the city with its walls to be rebuilt, and in the process the Eastern Gate was sealed. No official record explains why he did this, but one legend states the Jews believed that Ezekiel 44:1-2 referred to the Messiah coming from the east to conquer all non-Jews and rebuild the kingdom of David. The Christians of his time stated Jesus would return to the Mount of Olives, based on Acts 1:10-12 and Zechariah 14, then come though the Eastern Gate, based on Ezekiel 44:1-2. So Suleiman ordered the eastern gate closed and a cemetery put right outside the gate, believing no Jewish holy man would walk though a Muslim cemetery. He also did this to prevent anyone from using these beliefs to start an uprising.

The gate continued untouched until December 9, 1917. On that day, with British General Allenby's army approaching, the Grand Mufti of Jerusalem ordered the open Jerusalem gates sealed and the sealed Eastern Gate opened for defensive purposes. As the workmen picked up their sledgehammers, Allenby's airplanes flew over the city dropping leaflets ordering the Arabs to flee. Since there was a Muslim legend that said they would never leave the city until a prophet of Allah told them to and since "allenby" in Arabic can be translated "prophet of Allah," the workers put down their hammers and left – along with all the Muslim soldiers. Jerusalem came into British hands without a single shot being fired in the Holy City. This was just one month after the Balfour Declaration was signed, giving the Jews the right to their ancient homeland!

In 1967, Jordan's King Hussein wanted to unseal the Eastern Gate for Muslim pilgrimages to the El Aksa Mosque. The opening of the gate was set to commence on June 5, 1967. This was the very day the Six Day-War began. At the end of the

The Great Dispersion

war the Jews controlled the Old City and would not let the gate be opened until the advent of the Messiah. Today the gate remains sealed, and will continue to be sealed until the return of Jesus, the Messiah.

Greece, Syria, Egypt, and Turkey
Alexander the Great's Empire broke into these four nations: Greece, Syria, Egypt, and Turkey. Turkey created the great Ottoman Empire and conquered Syria, Egypt, Greece, and many other nations. Since Daniel states in the later days when the Antichrist rises to power these four nations will be ruling, the Ottoman Empire had to be dissolved and these ancient nations recreated and given their independence. The Ottoman Empire came to an end in WWI. After WWI, Syria, Egypt, and Turkey were recreated by the League of Nations. Egypt became autonomous in 1922, Turkey in 1929, and Syria in 1944. Greece was conquered by the Ottoman Empire in AD 1453, but managed to break away, gaining its independence in 1829. Over the next century it regained its former islands, but was conquered again by the Nazis in WWII. After WWII the nationals and communists waged a civil war. By 1975 a democratic government was firmly in place and continues to this day. See the Ten Nations in the section on Post-2008 for more details.

> "The broken *horn* and the four *horns that* arose in its place *represent* four kingdoms *which* will arise from *his* nation, although not with his power. In the latter period of their rule, when the transgressors have run *their course*, a king will arise, insolent and skilled in intrigue." *Daniel 8:22-23*

Jews Buy Back Their Land
Jeremiah prophesied that in the last times, before Israel would become a nation, Jews would begin to return to the land and buy back parcels of it. These purchases began to occur in the late 1880's and continued through 1948.

> "'Men will buy fields for money, sign and seal deeds, and call in witnesses in the land of Benjamin, in the environs of Jerusalem, in the cities of Judah, in the cities of the hill country, in the cities of the lowland and in the cities of the Negev; for I will restore their fortunes,' declares the LORD." *Jeremiah 32:44*

Balfour Declaration - 1917
Isaiah states Tarshish (Britain) would be the first to bring the Jews back to their land. After WWI, Great Britain was given the mandate by the League of Nations to create a homeland for the Jews. See the section on Modern Israel for more details. They began to carve out a Jewish homeland, but before it was finished they divided the land into two main parts, one for Israel and the other for the Palestinians. The Palestinian partition was called Trans-Jordan. The division of the land of Israel always angers God, and Great Britain lost her empire as a result.

> "Surely the coastlands will wait for Me; and the ships of Tarshish *will come* first, to bring your sons from afar, their silver and their gold with them, for the name of the LORD your God, and for the Holy One of Israel because He has glorified you. Foreigners will build up your walls, and their kings will minister to you; for in My wrath I struck you, and in My favor I have had compassion on you." *Isaiah 60:9-10*

> "For behold, in those days and at that time, when I restore the fortunes of Judah and Jerusalem, I will gather all the nations and bring them down to the valley of Jehoshaphat. Then I will enter into judgment with them there on behalf of My people and My inheritance, Israel, whom they have scattered among the nations; and they have divided up My land." *Joel 3:1-2*

The Holocaust
Daniel prophesied the four kingdoms that came out of Alexander the Great's Empire (Greece, Turkey, Syria, and Egypt) would continue to exist and rule in the latter times. This *might* indicate that these four nations are part of the ten nations ruling in the last days. Whether or not they are part of the ruling ten nations, their rule and the rise of Antichrist occurs after the time when 'the transgressors have run their course.' I believe this refers to the persecution of the Jews during the great dispersion, which ended with the greatest persecution up to that time, the Holocaust. To date, this has been the worst catastrophe the Jews have ever faced, including the destruction of the Temple in AD 70. We can safely say to preterists the Tribulation did not occur in AD 70.

Ancient Prophecies Revealed

"The broken *horn* and the four *horns that* arose in its place *represent* four kingdoms *which* will arise from *his* nation, although not with his power. In the latter period of their rule, when the transgressors have run *their course*, a king will arise…" *Daniel 8:22-23*

In response to Hitler's "Jewish problem," nations like the USA and Britain kept asking Hitler to find a nation that German Jews could move to. At point during Hitler's reign in Germany, Hitler actually stated he would be willing to *sell* the Jews to any nation that would pay for them. Since no one took him up on his offer, the extermination camps were opened.

"Moreover, the LORD will scatter you among all peoples, from one end of the earth to the other end of the earth; and there you shall serve other gods, wood and stone, which you or your fathers have not known. Among those nations you shall find no rest, and there will be no resting place for the sole of your foot; but there the LORD will give you a trembling heart, failing of eyes, and despair of soul. So your life shall hang in doubt before you; and you will be in dread night and day, and shall have no assurance of your life. In the morning you shall say, 'Would that it were evening!' And at evening you shall say, 'Would that it were morning!' because of the dread of your heart which you dread, and for the sight of your eyes which you will see. The LORD will bring you back to Egypt in ships, by the way about which I spoke to you, 'You will never see it again!' And there you will offer yourselves for sale to your enemies as male and female slaves, but there will be no buyer." *Deuteronomy 28:64-68*

Jeremiah wrote that before God brought Israel back (1948) he would first "fish" for them. The "fishers" were all those groups that tried to get Jews to go back to their ancient homeland with financial promises and other incentives. This was back in the earlier part of the twentieth century. After this time God would send "hunters" to force them to go home. This is most likely a reference to the Nazi Holocaust and other European pogroms.

"but, 'As the LORD lives, who brought up the sons of Israel from the land of the north and from all the countries where He had banished them.' For I will restore them to their own land which I gave to their fathers. 'Behold, I am going to send for many fishermen,' declares the LORD, 'and they will fish for them; and afterwards I will send for many hunters, and they will hunt them from every mountain and every hill and from the clefts of the rocks.'"
Jeremiah 16:15-16

Even today we still see the hunters and fishers being used by God to cause more and more Jews to return to Israel.

Jewish Festivals
We have identified many of the prophecies that were fulfilled on the festivals of Passover and Pentecost. So we can be certain that the rituals done on these festivals have embedded prophecy in them. In addition to the seven festivals, there are certain dates on the Jewish calendar that seem to be prophetic. The ninth of the month of Av is one such date. It varies each year but always occurs in July or August on our calendar. Both Temples were destroyed on the Ninth of Av, called Tisha B'Av on the Hebrew calendar. If we examine this date we will see many prophetical occurrences during the time of the Great Dispersion. The following chart lists some of the historical events on various years on Tisha B'Av.

The Great Dispersion

Tisha B'Av

Date	Prophecy	References
1453 BC	1. Twelve Spies return and the 40-year wandering in the wilderness begins. (Num 14:1-10)	Ta'anit 29a
	2. Temple of Solomon desecrated with Asharah poles	
July 29, 587 BC	3. Temple of Solomon burned by the Babylonians	
Aug 4, 70 AD	4. Second Temple burned by the Romans	
July 25, 71 AD	5. The Roman army, under Turnus Rufus, plowed the site of the Temple with salt. Romans began to build the pagan city of Aelia Capitolina on the site of Jerusalem.	
Aug 5, 132 AD	6. Bar Kokhba rebellion occurs in which 1,000,000 die	
July 14, 1090 AD	7. The Martyrs of York - 500 Jews died as a result of a mob storming a castle in York England.	
July 14, 1095 AD	8. First Crusade declared by Pope Urban II. 10,000 Jews killed in first month of Crusade. Whole Jewish communities in Rhineland and France totally obliterated.	
July 18, 1290 AD	9. All Jews expelled from England	
August 2, 1492 AD	10. All Jews expelled from Spain	
August 1, 1914 AD	11. World War I is declared on the Ninth of Av, August 1st	
August 1, 1914 AD	12. Russia mobilized for World War I and launched persecutions against the Jews in Eastern Russia.	
July 10, 1942 AD	13. On July 10, 1942, the Germans began a systematic liquidation of the Warsaw Ghetto, deporting Jews to extermination camps at the rate of six to ten thousand per day. Deportation started on Av 9, and by autumn there were only 40,000 Jews left in Warsaw.	
	14. Antichrist Born? A Jewish tradition says the Messiah would be born on Tisha B'Av and he would build the Third Temple. The true Messiah, Jesus, was not born on the Av 9 but probably on Tishrei 15 (Tabernacles)	

Ancient Prophecies Revealed

Remains of the Old Roman Empire
We will now trace the Roman Empire from its pagan times up through the end times. Church father Irenaeus wrote, in AD 178, that the Roman Empire would first be divided into two parts. Then it would be dissolved (*Against Heresies 5.26*). Then, much later, ten kings would arise out of what used to be the territory of the old Roman Empire. We will see in the section on the Apostasy of the Church, the early church fathers were pre-millennial; that is, they all believed in the future fall of Rome, the seven-year Tribulation, a rebuilt Temple on the Temple Mount in Jerusalem, and a Second Coming of Jesus in the flesh where He would reign for 1000 years from the city of Jerusalem. But here, Irenaeus gives us some new information. The Roman Empire would first be divided. This occurred 217 years after he gave this prediction. Then he said after it was divided, it would be dissolved. This happened 298 years after he gave this prediction. We know from the book of Daniel that it would be divided and later the ten kings would arise, but how did he know about its division and then its destruction? And how did he have them in the right order?

The Scroll
As we will detail in the section on the Apostasy of the Church, first-century cults created fake documents to further their cause. Sometimes they took *real* history and *real* words of knowledge from ancient church fathers and combined them with their heretical teachings. The *Apocalypse of Esdras* appears to be that sort of hybrid work, which reports to be visions from the same Ezra who authored the biblical book of Ezra. The *Apocalypse of Esdras* has existed from the second century AD and was included in the original 1611 King James Verson Bible. It has never been included in the Roman Catholic or Eastern Orthodox apocrypha. It does contain errors and contradictions, which is why it was eventually removed from the 1611 KJV. The Anglicans originally included it in the 1611 KJV because it was so anti-Roman Catholic in doctrine. This is also why it will never be in a Roman Catholic or Eastern Orthodox Bible. The *Apocalypse of Esdras 11-12* contains a prophecy dealing with the rise of Papal Rome and Eastern Orthodoxy which predicts their doom. Therefore I conclude that the *majority* of the work is fake; but the section on the prophecy of the three-headed eagle is probably a word of knowledge from an ancient church father. It fits with what occurred in history up to AD 1945 and the premillennial and pretribulational biblical teachings. If anyone wants to be contentious about a prophecy outside of the Scriptures they may skip over this section as it has absolutely no baring on the rest of the biblical prophecies contained in this book.

This prophecy is divided into six sections:
1. The fall of Rome in 476
2. The fall of Constantinople in 476
3. The rise and fall of Papal Rome from 476-1523
4. The rise and fall of the Holy Roman Empire from 800 to 1917
5. The rise of Russia in 1945
6. The end times – Rapture, Great Tribulation, and Second Coming

I have broken up the order so you can see each part's vision, the angel's interpretation, and fulfilled history before going on to the next section.

The Great Dispersion

AD 395-476
Fall of Rome

Apocalypse of Esdras 11 & 12

Vision (11:1-19)

"I dreamed an eagle came up from the sea, which had **twelve feathers** sticking up on one wing, and **three heads**. I saw she spread her wings over all the earth, and all the winds of the air blew on her, and clouds were gathered around her. Out of her feathers there grew opposing feathers; and they became little, puny feathers. But her heads were asleep: the middle head was greater than the other heads, but it was asleep also. Then the eagle flew with her wings and reigned over the earth and all those who dwell therein. All things under heaven were subject unto her, and no one spoke against her, not a single creature upon earth.

The Voice
Then the eagle rose upon her talons, and spoke to her feathers, saying, 'Do not watch not all at once: let each sleep in his own place, and watch by course: But let the **heads be preserved** for the **last**. And I beheld, the voice did not come out of her heads, but from the middle of her body.'

Eight Opposing Feathers
I counted her opposing feathers and there were eight of them.

First of the Twelve
On the right side there arose one feather, and reigned over all the earth; after a time his reign came to an end, and he disappeared so that even his place was no longer seen.

Second of the Twelve
The next feather stood up and reigned a long time; while he was reigning his end came also, and he disappeared like the first.

Then a voice said to it, 'Listen you who have ruled over the earth so long: this I say to you, before you disappear, after you no feather shall rule as long as you have ruled, not even half as long.'

Third of the Twelve
Then arose the third feather, and reigned as the others before, and disappeared also. So went it with the rest of the feathers reigning one after the other, and never seen again."

Interpretation (12:10-18)

"And he said unto me, 'this is the interpretation of the vision: the eagle, that you saw come up from the sea, is the **fourth kingdom** which apeared in the vision to your brother **Daniel**. But it was not explained to him, therefore I will now declare it to you. The days will come when a kingdom will arise on the earth, and it shall be more terrifying than all the kingdoms that were before it.

The Twelve
Twelve kings reign in it, one after another. The second that begins to reign shall reign longer than any of the other twelve. This is the interpretation of the twelve feathers that you saw in the vision.

The Voice
As for the voice which you heard speak, and that came not from the heads but from the middle of the body; this is the interpretation: that after the time of that kingdom there shall arise great struggles. It shall be in danger of failing: nevertheless it shall not fall then, but it shall begin again.'"

Historical Fulfillment

This first part of the vision of the three-headed eagle is a picture of the division of the Roman Empire.

The Roman Empire was in danger of collapsing, so the empire was split into two and the Caesars moved to the new capital of Constantinople in AD 395.

From that point, there were 12 rulers on the western side until the fall of the empire in AD 476. The first ruled 25 years. The second, Valentian III, ruled 30 years (2 Ezra 12:15). None of the rest ruled for even half of that time. To verify this, see World Book Encyclopedia 1985 Vol. 16 Q-R under Roman Empire p. 393.

Western Roman Empire	
Honorius	395-421 (25)
Valentian III	425-455 (30)
Petronius Maximus	455
Avitus	455-456 (1)
Majorian	457-461 (4)
Libius Severus	461-465 (4)
Anthimus	467-472 (5)
Olybrius	472
Glyceruis	473-474 (1)
Julius Nepos	474-475 (1)
Romulus Augustulus	475-476 (1)
Odacer	476

From that explanation notice that both the eastern and western divisions of the old Roman Empire appeared on the right side of the eagle. Since the middle head symbolizes Rome itself, all these rulers would be on the eastern side. The western side will be the Holy Roman Empire later in time.

85

Ancient Prophecies Revealed

AD 476
Fall of Constantinople

Apocalypse of Esdras 11 & 12

Vision (11:20-27)

"Then I beheld in process of time the feathers that followed stood up upon the **right side**, that they might rule also; and some of them ruled, but within a while they also disappeared for some of them started to reign, but could not hold on to the rule. After this I looked, and the **twelve feathers** and the **two little feathers** disappeared. Nothing remained on the eagle's body except the three heads and the six opposing feathers.

Last Two Opposing Feathers
Then I saw that two little feathers also separated themselves from the six, but remained under the head that was upon the right side: for the four continued in their place.

I beheld the feathers that were under the wing thought to set up themselves and to have the rule. And I beheld, there was one set up, but it suddenly disappeared. The second disappeared more quickly than the first."

Interpretation (12:19-21)

Eight Feathers
"As for you seeing the eight opposing feathers sticking to her wings, this is the interpretation: eight kings will arise in her; their reigns shall be short and swift. The first two will perish in the middle of her time: the middle four shall be kept until the time of her end: but two shall be kept unto the end."

Historical Fulfillment

This second set of feathers represents the rulers of the Eastern Roman Empire from its division in AD 395 to its fall in AD 476. As prophesied, the first two ruled to the middle of the 81 years. The middle four made it close to the end of the empire. The last two survived the fall of the Roman Empire. Their descendants fled north to Russia under Nicolas I, after the rise of the Muslim Ottoman Empire.

Eastern Roman Empire	
Arcadius	395-408 (13)
Theodosius II	408-450 (42)
Marcian	450-457 (7)
Leo I	457-474 (17)
Leo II	474
Zeno	474-475 (1)
Flavius Basiliscus	475-476 (1)
Zeno restored	476

AD 476-1423
Rise of Papal Rome

Apocalypse of Esdras 11 & 12

Vision - Interpretation (11:28-32)

Middle Head – Papal Rome
"I beheld the two [heads] that remained planned to reign together. While they were making plans, one of the sleeping heads – the middle one – suddenly awoke. It was greater than the other two heads. Then I saw that the two other heads joined with the middle one. And all three heads turned and ate up the two puny feathers under the wing that were planning to reign. The middle head frightened the entire earth.

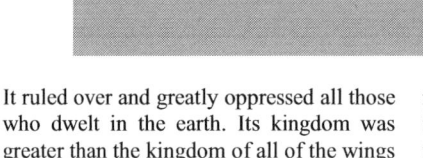

It ruled over and greatly oppressed all those who dwelt in the earth. Its kingdom was greater than the kingdom of all of the wings that were before it."

Historical Fulfillment
First Stage – Middle Head
Papal Rome   AD 476-1523

The three stages of the heads started with the rise of Papal Rome. At the height of its power, it controlled all of Europe and the East. But its power was different; it did not reign with an army, but by religion. Under its rule the Holy Roman Empire was formed. The H.R.E. moved from Spain to France and towards its end, to Germany. The last of the Caesars moved to Russia intermarrying with the Czars (Czar means Caesar). In AD 1056, the Eastern Orthodox Church (including Russia) broke away from Rome. In 1523, Germany, under Martin Luther, broke away from Rome. From this point on Papal Rome's power continued to diminish.

The Great Dispersion

AD 1423 to 1917 Rise of Germany

Apocalypse of Esdras 11 & 12

Vision (11:33-34)

Middle Head Disappears 1056, 1523
"After this, I beheld the middle head suddenly disappeared, just like the wings had done before it. The two heads still remained, which in the same manner ruled over the earth and over all those that dwelt in the earth."

Interpretation (12:22-26)

Three Heads
"As for you, seeing the three sleeping heads resting, this is the interpretation: in her **last days** the Most High will raise up three kingdoms, and renew many things with her; and they shall have dominion over the earth, and greatly oppress all those who dwell in the earth, much more than all who were before them. This is why they are called the heads of the eagle. These three will finish all the wickedness and perform the eagle's last actions.

Middle Heads Disappearance
As for you, seeing that the large middle head disappeared; this means one of them will die in bed, but in pain."

Historical Fulfillment
Second Stage – Left Head
Germany AD 1423-1945

The second stage started with the Holy Roman Empire ruling in Europe under the control of Rome. Rome's power waned and Germany became Protestant under Martin Luther. Then, from 1523 to 1917, the great German empire controlled most of Europe.

The Holy Roman Empire was crushed by Napoleon in the 1800's, although the Kaisers continued to rule until the end of WWI.

In the 1930's, Adolph Hitler tried to create a third Roman Empire (Reich) in which the "final solution" was to destroy the Jewish race completely. After WWII, this led the United Nations to recognize Israel's right to be a state in their ancient homeland.

This would be the start of the next section of our history, "Modern Israel."

AD 1917 to 1945 Rise of Russia

Apocalypse of Esdras 11 & 12

Vision (11:35)

WWII
"Then I beheld the head on the right side devour the head that was on the left side."

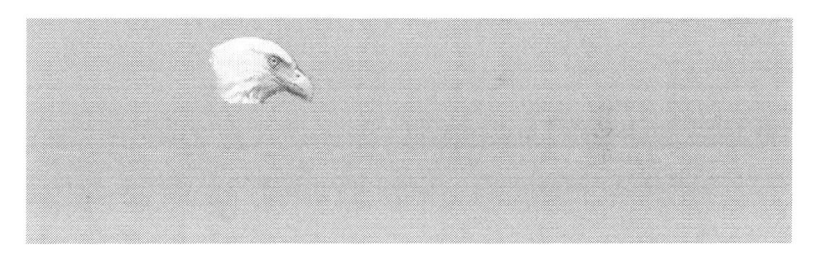

Interpretation (12:22-26)

"The two that remain shall be slain with the sword. For the sword of the one shall devour the other: but in **the last days** shall he fall by the sword himself.

Two Little Wings
As for you, seeing the two puny feathers under the wings **passing over** to the head that is on the **right side**; this is the interpretation: these are the ones that the Most High has kept for the eagle's end. This kingdom's reign was brief and full of trouble, as you have seen."

Historical Fulfillment
Third Stage – Right Head
Russia AD 1945-Second Coming

The third stage starts with the demise of Germany. Russia became a world power and captured East Germany. This sets the stage for the Gog-Magog invasion of Israel. Ezekiel shows Germany reunited but as an ally to Russia, not a Russian slave state, during that future invasion.

Ancient Prophecies Revealed

Rapture, Tribulation, and the Second Coming

Apocalypse of Esdras 11 & 12

Vision (11:36-12:3)

A Lion Roused From the Forest
"Then I heard a voice saying, 'Look before you, and consider what you see.' I beheld; what appears to be a roaring lion roused from the forest. It spoke in a man's voice to the eagle saying, 'Listen now and I will speak with you. The Most High says to you "Aren't you what is left of the four beasts I made to reign in My world, that the End Times might come though them? You, the fourth beast, overcame all the beasts that came before you; and you have ruled the word with terror and oppression. For so long you have lived on the earth with deceit. You have not judged the earth with truth. You have afflicted the meek and hurt the peaceable. You have loved liars, and destroyed the homes of those who brought forth fruit and broke down the walls of those who never harmed you. Therefore your insolence has been judged by the Most High, and your pride judged by the Mighty One. The Most High has also seen your proud times, and ended them, and the eagle's abominations are complete. Therefore eagle, disappear! You and your horrible wings, wicked feathers, malicious heads, hurtful claws, and your entire vain body: so that all the earth may be refreshed, and return, being delivered from your violence, and that she may hope for the judgment and mercy of him that made her.'" It came to pass, while the lion spoke these words unto the eagle, I saw the remaining head and the four wings disappear and the two that went under it and set themselves up to reign, whose kingdom was small, and full of uproar, also disappeared. The whole body of the eagle was burnt and the earth was in great fear. Then I woke from the dream, but my mind was troubled."

Interpretation (12:31-35)

The Messiah
"The lion whom you saw coming up out of the forest, roaring and speaking to the eagle, and rebuking her for her unrighteousness with all the words which you have heard: this is the Messiah, whom the Most High has kept for them and for their wickedness in the end of days. The Messiah shall reprove them and shall upbraid them for their cruelty.

Great Tribulation
First they will be placed before His judgment seat. They will be rebuked and then destroyed.

Rapture
Because of His mercy, He will deliver the **remnant of my people**, those who have been saved throughout my borders, and he will make them joyful **until** the coming of the **day of judgment**, of which I have spoken unto you from the beginning. This is the dream that you saw, and these are the interpretations."

Historical Fulfillment
The End – The Lion's Judgment
The Great Tribulation

This last part of this vision has the Lion of the Tribe of Judah returning and passing judgment on the nations. This is the Great Tribulation.

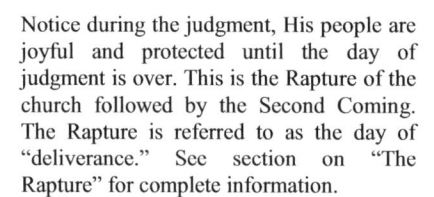

Notice during the judgment, His people are joyful and protected until the day of judgment is over. This is the Rapture of the church followed by the Second Coming. The Rapture is referred to as the day of "deliverance." See section on "The Rapture" for complete information.

Notice the eagle has claws, not talons. The wording is just like the claws of Daniel's fourth beast, probably numbering ten claws.

For other translations of the Apocalypse of Esdras 11 &12 see the 1611 KJV and the NRSV.

1945-1989 Cold War
Russia enslaved other countries and used their resources to become a super power. Then the USSR collapsed, freeing those states. Ezekiel 38:7-8a refers to these events as "the gathering together and preparing." This is also represented here in the *Apocalypse of Esdras* as the left head (Germany) being eaten up.

The fall of the Berlin Wall set the stage for the Gog-Magog invasion. Since 1989, with Ezekiel 38:7-8a fulfilled, God can draw Russia (Rosh) with its –
allies – not slave states, as they were before the Wall fell.

See section on Modern Israel for more details.

Modern Israel

Second Crossover Period, AD 1948 to 2008 – 53 prophecies in 60 years

Date	Prophecy	References
1948	306. Israel will be reestablished as a nation	Isa. 11:11
	307. British ships will be the first to bring the Jewish people home	Isa. 60:9
	308. Israel will come back as one nation, not two	Hosea 1:11; Ezek. 37:18,19,22
	309. The nation of Israel will be born in a day	Isa. 66:8
	310. Israel will be reestablished by a leader named David	Hosea 3:5
	311. The revived state will be named "Israel"	Ezek. 37:11
	312. The Star of David will be on the Israeli flag	Isa. 11:10
	313. The nation will be reestablished in the ancient land of Canaan	Jer. 30:2,3; Ezek. 37:12
	314. Israel will no longer speak of being freed from Egypt	Jer 16:14,15
	315. Israel will not be restored as a monarchy	Mic 5:5
	316. Israel will be established on the date predicted	Dan 4; Ezek. 4:4-6
	317. The Hebrew language will be revived in Israel	Jer. 31:23
	318. Jerusalem will be divided	Zech. 14:1-3
	319. Jordan will occupy the West Bank	Zeph. 2:8; Zech. 12:1-7
	320. Israel will be initially restored without Jerusalem	Zech. 12:1-7
	321. Israel will have a fierce military (firepot)	Zech. 12:1-7; Isa. 41
	322. Dead Sea Scrolls will be found	Isa. 29:1-4
	323. Israel will be reestablished by the fourth craftsman	Zech 1:18-21
	324. The Jewish people will come back in unbelief	Ezek. 37:7-8,11
	325. First Shepherd will arise	Mic. 5:5-8
1949	326. Yemenite Jews will return	Isa. 43:3-7
1951	327. Israel will control Ashkelon	Zech. 9:1-8
1953	328. Egypt will no longer have kings (Suez crises)	Zech. 10:9-11
1967	329. Second Shepherd will arise	Mic. 5:5-8
	330. The 1967 war will occur on the date predicted	Dan. 5
	331. Five Egyptian cities will be conquered by the Israelis	Isa. 19:16-18
	332. Jordan will give up the West Bank	Zech. 12:6
	333. West Bank Jews will go home to Jerusalem	Zech. 12:6
1968	334. Israel will control Ashdod	Zech. 9:1-8
1973	335. Yom Kippur War will occur	Mic. 5:5-8
	336. Jerusalem will be a burden to all nations	Zech. 12:2,3
1980	337. The shekel will be revived as Israeli currency	Ezek. 45:1,2
1981	338. Third Shepherd will arise	Mic. 5:5-8
	339. Israel will attack Iraqi (Nuclear) facility	Mic. 5:5-8
1982	340. Israel will give back the Sinai peninsula	Zech. 10:6
	341. First Lebanese War will occur (firepot)	Zech. 12:6
1989	342. The Berlin Wall will fall	Ezek. 38:4-6
1990	343. Ethiopian Jews will be brought to Israel	Isa. 18:1-7
~2000	344. Cities will be restored and Israel will have non-Jewish farmers	Isa. 61:4,5; Zeph. 2
	345. Jerusalem will grow beyond its old walls	Zech. 2:4,5
	346. Land of Israel will be divided by its rivers and by Muslims	Isa. 18:1-7
	347. Tourists will fly in and support Israel	Isa. 60:8-10; Isa. 61
	348. There will be constant planting and reaping (crops)	Amos 9:13-15
	349. Forests will reappear in Israel (cedar, etc)	Isa. 41:18-20
	350. Desolate land and cities will be restored	Ezek. 36:33-36
	351. Five cities will stay desolate	Matt. 11:20-24

Ancient Prophecies Revealed

Date	Prophecy	References
	352. Muslims will not "reckon Israel among nations"	Num. 23:9
	353. Israel will inherit remnant of Edom/Palestinians	Amos 9:12
	354. Satellite-Television Communication Systems Invented	Rev. 17:8
2004	355. Sanhedrin will be reestablished	Matt. 24:15,20
2005	356. Palestinians will want Jerusalem as their capital	Ezek. 36:2,7,10-11
	357. Gaza will be forsaken	Zeph. 2:4
	358. Russia and Iran will sign a military defense pact	Ezek. 38:3-8
2006	359. Second Lebanese War will occur	Psalm 83:1-18

Introduction

In this section we will deal with the time period from the rebirth of modern Israel since it was recognized by the U.N. in AD 1948, to the present. It is interesting to note that the period from the birth of the Messiah's church, in AD 32, to the dispersion of the unbelieving nation of Israel, in AD 132, was exactly 100 years. That generation saw the death of the Messiah, the birth of His church, the destruction of the Jerusalem Temple by the Romans, and the failure of the Simon Bar-Kokba rebellion, which resulted in the dispersion of the Jews into the Gentile nations.

That 100-year-period is known as the First Crossover Period. The church had already been instituted, but unbelieving Israel had not yet been removed. We are now living in the Second Crossover Period, which began 1,816 years after the dispersion. The Jewish people have returned to their land as a nation *exactly on the date prophesied*, but, as of AD 2008, the Rapture has not yet taken place. The church is living on borrowed time. As of AD 2008, Israel has existed as a nation for 60 years. Within the next 40 years all these prophecies *might* be fulfilled, including the Rapture!

```
●AD 32, Birth of the Church                         Rapture of the Church●
       ┊                                                       ┊
       ┊    AD 132, Israel removed    AD 1948, Israel Reborn   ┊
◄──────┊──────────●────────────────────────●──────────────────┊──────►
       ┊                                                       ┊
  1st Crossover Period                              2nd Crossover Period
      100 years                                         100 years?
```

In the First Crossover Period the nation of Israel was in apostasy, having rejected her messiah. In the last years of the Second Crossover Period, the church will be in her apostasy. See the section on the Apostasy of the Church for a complete description of the state of the end time church. In these last 60 years there have been many ancient prophecies fulfilled. Let's start by looking at the prophecies about the Jewish people coming back into their land and the two prophecies that give the *exact date* of the birth of modern Israel.

As long as there is a sun and moon, the Jewish people will continue to exist as a specific people. Even during the 1816-year-dispersion, they have remained an identifiable ethnic group and are now a nation once again.

> "Thus says the LORD, Who gives the sun for light by day and the fixed order of the moon and the stars for light by night, Who stirs up the sea so that its waves roar; The LORD of hosts is His name: 'If this fixed order departs from before Me,' declares the LORD, 'Then the offspring of Israel also will cease from being a nation before Me forever.'"
> *Jeremiah 31:35*

The nation of Israel was dispersed for the first time in 606 BC by the Babylonians. There are several prophecies about Israel's return from "the land of the north," which was their return from Babylon in 536 BC. After this first return to their land, they were dispersed again by the Romans for 1,816 years (AD 132 to AD 1948). The Jewish people began returning to their homeland in the mid 1800's and in AD 1948 the modern nation of Israel was born. This return from all nations, or from the four corners of the earth, is referred to as the *second return* by Isaiah the prophet.

Modern Israel

"Then it will happen on that day that the Lord will again recover the second time with His hand the remnant of His people, who will remain, from Assyria, Egypt, Pathros, Cush, Elam, Shinar, Hamath, and from the islands of the sea. And He will lift up a standard for the nations and assemble the banished ones of Israel, and will gather the dispersed of Judah from the four corners of the earth." *Isaiah 11:11-12*

Return from "all nations"
Isaiah 11:11-12; 43:5-7
Jeremiah 16:14-15; 23:8; 24:6; 29:14; 3:18; 30:3, 10-11; 31:1; 32:37-38; 33:7
Ezekiel 28:25; 34:11-12
Zechariah 10:6,
Deut 4:25-27, 30

There is no mention of a *third* return to the land. In fact, Amos says that after this second return, Israel will never be dispersed again. Jeremiah 24:6 also records this.

"'I will also plant them on their land, and they will not again be rooted out from their land which I have given them,' says the LORD your God." *Amos 9:15*

The following prophecies deal with the return from *all* nations – the second return – so we know the fulfillments occur sometime after AD 1948.

British Ships First to Bring the Jewish People Home
The prophets predicted the second return would begin with Great Britain bringing the Jewish people back to their ancient homeland by ship. This took place during the first half of the twentieth century. The ancient name of England/Great Britain was Tarshish. She is also mentioned in the prophecy of the Gog-Magog invasion.

"Surely the coastlands will wait for Me; and the ships of Tarshish will come first, to bring your sons from afar, their silver and their gold with them, for the name of the LORD your God" *Isaiah 60:9*

The Ottoman Empire (Muslim Turkey) ruled over the Holy Land from AD 1290 to AD 1918. After Germany started WWI, the Ottoman Empire entered the war on Germany's side. General Edmund Allenby (pictured to the right) was assigned commander in chief of the Egyptian Expeditionary Force in 1917. He led an offensive against the Turkish armies in the Middle East, capturing Jerusalem without firing a shot on December 10, 1917. Allenby refused to ride horseback into the conquered city because Jesus had entered it that way. His crowning victory was at Megiddo (also called Armageddon) in September 1918. When Germany lost the war, the Ottoman Empire was divided into smaller states. In 1920 the Mandate over Palestine (both sides of the Jordan River) was given to England by the allied Council. Britain took control of the territory that was the Ottoman Empire, dividing it into small states. Iraq became independent in 1932, and Kuwait in 1961. The remaining territory was to be split in two. Jordan was artificially created by Britain in 1920 to be a homeland for Palestinians; and the ancient land of Israel was to be restored to the Jews. On November 2, 1917, Lord James Balfour (pictured to the left), Foreign Secretary of the British government, wrote to Lord Rothschild, chairman of the British Zionist Federation, stating:

"His Majesty's Government view with favour the establishment in Palestine of a home for the Jewish people. And will use their best endeavors to facilitate the achievement of this object. It being clearly understood that nothing shall be done which may prejudice the civil and religious rights of the existing non-Jewish communities in Palestine. Or the rights and political status enjoyed by Jews in any other country. I should be grateful if you would bring this declaration to the knowledge of the Zionist Federation."

This document became known as "The Balfour Declaration." In 1922 the British mandate over Palestine was ratified by the new League of Nations. England then divided Palestine (46,049 sq. miles) at the Jordan River. The eastern part was named Transjordan (77% of the land). It was created to be a Palestinian Arab state. The western part retained the name of Palestine (23% of the land). It was created to be a homeland for the Jewish people. In AD 1939-1945 Hitler, in his final solution to the world's problems, tried to destroy the Jewish people. By the end of the war over 6,000,000 Jews were dead. At the end of WWII Britain relinquished the mandate to the United Nations. Within three years the United Nations made a proclamation recognizing the modern state of Israel. Many prophecies were fulfilled on that single day.

91

Ancient Prophecies Revealed

Jewish People Return as One Nation, Not Two
"Yet the number of the sons of Israel will be like the sand of the sea, which cannot be measured or numbered; and in the place where it is said to them, 'You are not My people,' it will be said to them, 'you are the sons of the living God.' And the sons of Judah and the sons of Israel will be gathered together, and they will appoint for themselves one leader, and they will go up from the land, for great will be the day of Jezreel." *Hosea 1:10-11*

Israel Born In a Single Day
When the United Nations made the decree, the nation of Israel, which did not exist a moment before, became a sovereign nation.

"Who has heard such a thing? Who has seen such things? Can a land be born in one day? Can a nation be brought forth all at once? As soon as Zion travailed, she also brought forth her sons." *Isaiah 66:8*

Israel Reborn Under David
Hosea said Israel would be reborn under the leadership of a man named after King David. This prophecy was fulfilled in 1948 when the nation was reborn under the leadership of David BenGurion. BenGurion also fulfilled portions of the seven-shepherds prophecy and the four-craftsmen prophecy. These will be discussed later on in this chapter.

"For the sons of Israel will remain for many days without king or prince, without sacrifice or sacred pillar and without ephod or household idols. Afterward the sons of Israel will return and seek the LORD their God and David their king; and they will come trembling to the LORD and to His goodness in the last days." *Hosea 3:4-5*

"It shall come about on that day,' declares the LORD of hosts, 'that I will break his yoke from off their neck and will tear off their bonds; and strangers will no longer make them their slaves. But they shall serve the LORD their God and David their king, whom I will raise up for them. Fear not, O Jacob My servant,' declares the LORD, 'And do not be dismayed, O Israel; for behold, I will save you from afar and your offspring from the land of their captivity and Jacob will return and will be quiet and at ease, and no one will make him afraid." *Jeremiah 30:8-10*

New State Will Be Named Israel
The revived state will consist of the *whole* house of Israel, both Judah and Israel. At the time of the modern Return, the land will be named "Israel," not Samaria or Judah.

"Then He said to me, 'Son of man, these bones are the whole house of Israel; behold, they say, 'Our bones are dried up and our hope has perished. We are completely cut off.' Therefore prophesy and say to them, 'Thus says the Lord GOD, Behold, I will open your graves and cause you to come up out of your graves, My people; and I will bring you into the land of Israel.'" *Ezekiel 37:11-12*

"…Thus says the Lord GOD, 'I will gather you from the peoples and assemble you out of the countries among which you have been scattered, and I will give you the land of Israel.' …that they may walk in My statutes and keep My ordinances and do them. Then they will be My people, and I shall be their God." *Ezekiel 11:17,20*

Star of David Prophesied to Be On the Israeli Flag
Isaiah prophesied the Israeli flag will have the symbol of the root of Jesse, or King David's star, on it. Jesse was the father of King David. The crest, or symbol, of his household was the six pointed star. Today this is known as the Star of David. The Star of David is the symbol for the nation of Israel and is the symbol on the modern Israeli flag.

"Then in that day the nations will resort to the root of Jesse, who will stand as a signal for the peoples; and His resting place will be glorious." *Isaiah 11:10*

The Nation of Israel Will Be Planted In the Ancient Land of Canaan, Nowhere Else
The restored nation of Israel would be placed back in its old land, not resettled somewhere else. Jeremiah and Ezekiel foretold this in Jeremiah 30:3; Jeremiah 16:15 (see below); and Ezekiel 37.

Modern Israel

"'For behold, days are coming,' declares the LORD, 'when I will restore the fortunes of My people Israel and Judah.' The LORD says, 'I will also bring them back to the land that I gave to their forefathers, and they shall possess it.'"
Jeremiah 30:3

Israel Will No Longer Speak of Being Freed From Egypt

Although at Passover the Exodus from Egypt is always remembered, today all Jews agree that God fulfilled His promise by bringing them back to their land in 1948. Great numbers of European and Russian Jews have migrated back into Israel.

"Therefore behold, days are coming, declares the LORD, when it will no longer be said, 'As the LORD lives, who brought up the sons of Israel out of the land of Egypt,' but, 'As the LORD lives, who brought up the sons of Israel from the land of the north and from all the countries where He had banished them.' For I will restore them to their own land which I gave to their fathers. Behold, I am going to send for many fishermen, declares the LORD, and they will fish for them; and afterwards I will send for many hunters, and they will hunt them from every mountain and every hill and from the clefts of the rocks." *Jeremiah 16:14-16*

"Then I Myself will gather the remnant of My flock out of all the countries where I have driven them and bring them back to their pasture, and they will be fruitful and multiply. I will also raise up shepherds over them and they will tend them; and they will not be afraid any longer, nor be terrified, nor will any be missing,' declares the LORD. 'Behold, the days are coming,' declares the LORD, 'When I will raise up for David a righteous Branch; and He will reign as king and act wisely and do justice and righteousness in the land. In His days Judah will be saved, and Israel will dwell securely; and this is His name by which He will be called, 'The LORD our righteousness.' 'Therefore behold, the days are coming,' declares the LORD, 'when they will no longer say, 'As the LORD lives, who brought up the sons of Israel from the land of Egypt,' but, 'As the LORD lives, who brought up and led back the descendants of the household of Israel from the north land and from all the countries where I had driven them.' Then they will live on their own soil." *Jeremiah 23:3-8*

Restored Israel Will Not Be a Monarchy

In the Seven-Shepherds prophecy (see Micah 5:5), there will not be eight *kings* but eight *principle leaders*. This shows that modern-day Israel would not have kings, but leaders with different titles and powers. This means they had to create a republic or a democracy; they could not have created a dictatorship or monarchy.

AD 1948 The Rebirth of Israel	Cyrus' Decree — "907,200 Days" — War of Independence
	August 3, 537 BC — **May 14, 1948 AD**

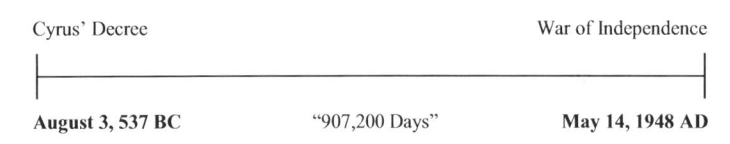

Psalm 102 predicts God will arise and build up Zion at the appointed time. The phrase "the appointed time" occurs several times in Scripture. It means God has predestined an event to occur on a specific date. God predestined the *exact day* Israel would be restored as a nation. Both Daniel and Ezekiel foretold *the exact date* of the reestablishment of Israel.

"You will arise and have compassion on Zion; for it is time to be gracious to her, for the appointed time has come… For the LORD has built up Zion…" *Psalm 102:13,16*

In the section on the Messiah's death, we saw the time the Messiah was "cut off" occurred on the *exact date* prophesied. We saw that once the dates were converted to our calendar, the death of the Messiah occurred on April 6, 32 AD. Similarly, there are two Timeline Prophecies that arrive at the date of May 14, 1948 as the *exact date* the Israelis would return to their land for the second time and become a nation!

"As for you, lie down on your left side and lay the iniquity of the house of Israel on it; you shall bear their iniquity for the number of days that you lie on it. For I have assigned you a number of days corresponding to the years of their iniquity, three hundred and ninety days; thus you shall bear the iniquity of the house of Israel. When you have

Ancient Prophecies Revealed

completed these, you shall lie down a second time, but on your right side and bear the iniquity of the house of Judah; I have assigned it to you for forty days, a day for each year." *Ezekiel 4:4-6*

In this passage the sin of Israel and Judah was 390 years and 40 years. To symbolize this, Ezekiel had to lie on his left side for 390 days, a day for each year of Israel's sin, and 40 days on his right side, a day for each year of Judah's sin. The total time then was 430 years of sin. The Babylonian captivity took up 70 years of this punishment, leaving 360 years.

> "But if you do not obey Me and do not carry out all these commandments, if, instead, you reject My statutes, and if your soul abhors My ordinances so as not to carry out all My commandments, and so break My covenant… I will set My face against you so that you will be struck down before your enemies; and those who hate you will rule over you, and you will flee when no one is pursuing you. If also after these things you do not obey Me, then I will punish you seven times more for your sins." *Leviticus 26:14-18*

Here God declares that if Israel does not repent after the Babylonian captivity, when Cyrus freed Israel, then the remaining time would be multiplied sevenfold. If you multiply 360 years by seven, you get 2520 prophetical years. The Prophet Daniel predicted this same time period in another way.

```
360 x 7 = 2,520 prophetic years; 2,520 x 360 = 907,220 days
907,220 days on the modern calendar is 2,483 yrs & 285 days
2,483 yrs x 365.25 = 906915; 907200 – 906915 = 285 days

August 3, 537 BC + 2,483 yrs = August 3, AD 1946
Add 1 year (no 0 Year) = AD 1947; Add 285 days = May 14, AD 1948
```

In Daniel 4, God punished King Nebuchadnezzar with insanity for seven years, in order to humble him. God had Nebuchadnezzar *act out* a prophecy, just as Ezekiel acted out his 430-day prophecy by lying on his side. In Nebuchadnezzar's case, the restoration of his kingdom after seven years is also a symbolic prophecy that illustrates that the Children of Israel would be restored a second time to *their* land after seven *years* of days. Since the prophetic calendar uses a 360-day year, if you mutiply Nebuchadnezzar's seven years by the 360-day calendar, you get 2,520 years – just like Ezekiel's prophecy. (For more details on calculating prophetic dates see the section on the Messiah's death.)

From these two prophets we are told the time of the second return of Israel. To see this we must first convert the Jewish years to Roman years so we can see the outcome on our modern calendar. 2,520 Jewish years times 360 days per year is 907,200 days. Cyrus issued his decree freeing the Jews and declaring the state of Israel to exist again on August 3, 537 BC. This date plus 907,200 days (plus one year changing from BC to AD) brings us to May 14, 1948. This was the very day that the UN declared Israel to be a sovereign state. (To see the complete pattern for timeline prophecies see the Death of the Messiah in the section on the Messiah's First Coming.)

Note: Any time you are counting the years and switch from BC to AD you must add one year, because there is no zero year.

Hebrew Language Restored in Israel

Zephaniah 3 predicts that when the Messiah returns to earth He will undo what He did at the tower of Babel. He will "return to all peoples the pure language." Someday we will *all* be speaking ancient Hebrew! But the prelude to that time is when the nation of Israel comes into existence in the latter times, or 1948, it would revive the Hebrew language for itself as the national language. Notice also the phrase "in the cities thereof." This implies that Israel will restore the original Hebrew names to those cities.

> "Thus saith the LORD of hosts, the God of Israel; as yet they shall use this speech in the land of Judah and in the cities thereof, when I shall bring again their captivity; the LORD bless thee, O habitation of justice, and mountain of holiness."
> *Jeremiah 31:23 KJV*

Eliezer Ben-Yehuda was the key figure in reviving the Hebrew language in Israel. The League of Nations officially recognized Hebrew to be the language of Jews in Palestine in AD 1922. When Israel became a state, Hebrew was automatically accepted as the language of the new nation.

Modern Israel

Jerusalem Divided
Zechariah prophesied about the war in which half of the city of Jerusalem would be captured and its Jewish population exiled. The prophet added the Lord would later return this half of the city to the Israelis. At the end of the War of Independence, the nation of Israel controlled half of the city of Jerusalem and Jordan controlled the other half. Jordan retained control of half of Jerusalem until the Six Day War – a total of 19 years.

> "Behold, a day is coming for the LORD when the spoil taken from you will be divided among you. For I will gather all the nations against Jerusalem to battle, and the city will be captured, the houses plundered, the women ravished and half of the city exiled, but the rest of the people will not be cut off from the city. Then the LORD will go forth and fight against those nations, as when He fights on a day of battle." *Zechariah 14:1-3*

Jordan Occupied the West Bank
When Israel was declared a state, Jordan immediately occupied the West Bank and secured half of Jerusalem, including the Temple Mount. Zephaniah states that ancient Moab (present day Jordan), would be greedy for land and attack. Zechariah 12 doesn't mention Jordan (Moab) by name, but does speak about the besiegement. See the section on Ashdod and Askalon and the Zechariah quote at the bottom of the page for more detail. When Jordan captured the West Bank in 1948, they destroyed all the synagogues, trying to wipe out any trace of the Jewish presence.

Israel Reborn Without Jerusalem and Israel a Supreme Military Force
The surrounding Muslim nations reel in fear of Israel. Today the IDF is the fourth most powerful military force next to the three superpowers: USA, Russia, and China. In the War of Independence, the Six Day War, and in the Yom Kippur War, Israel is described as a "firepot among the nations." After the Yom Kippur War, the Arabs decreed that any nation that recognized that Jerusalem was the capital of Israel would pay four times the normal amount for barrels of oil. To this day no nation has moved their embassy from Tel Aviv to Jerusalem.

The Lord says He would first create the nation of Israel without Jerusalem so the Muslims will know the God of Israel is the Lord. Jordan besieged half of Jerusalem and the citizens were displaced from their homes for 19 years. After the Six Day War they were allowed to go back to their homes in East Jerusalem. Isaiah 41 also predicts Israel would have a fierce military.

> "Behold, I am going to make Jerusalem a cup that causes reeling to all the peoples around; and when the siege is against Jerusalem, it will also be against Judah. It will come about in that day that I will make Jerusalem a heavy stone for all the peoples; all who lift it will be severely injured. And all the nations of the earth will be gathered against it. 'In that day,' declares the LORD, 'I will strike every horse with bewilderment and his rider with madness. But I will watch over the house of Judah, while I strike every horse of the peoples with blindness. Then the clans of Judah will say in their hearts, "A strong support for us are the inhabitants of Jerusalem through the LORD of hosts, their God." In that day I will make the clans of Judah like a firepot among pieces of wood and a flaming torch among sheaves, so they will consume on the right hand and on the left all the surrounding peoples, while the inhabitants of Jerusalem again dwell on their own sites in Jerusalem. The LORD also will save the tents of Judah first, so that the glory of the house of David and the glory of the inhabitants of Jerusalem will not be magnified above Judah.'" *Zechariah 12:1-7*

> "If you walk in My statutes and keep My commandments so as to carry them out… I shall also grant peace in the land, so that you may lie down with no one making you tremble. I shall also eliminate harmful beasts from the land, and no sword will pass through your land. But you will chase your enemies and they will fall before you by the sword; five of you will chase a hundred, and a hundred of you will chase ten thousand, and your enemies will fall before you by the sword." *Leviticus 26:3,6-8*

Discovery of the Dead Sea Scrolls
This prophecy states that when Israel is brought back as a nation, Jerusalem, or Ariel, will be besieged. Then the old ones will speak "out of the ground." The *very day* the War of Independence started, Jordan besieged Jerusalem as predicted in Zechariah 12 and *that same day* the Dead Sea Scrolls fell into Jewish hands. The Isaiah scroll was one of the first discovered. I wonder if Isaiah realized that when he wrote the following:

Ancient Prophecies Revealed

"Woe to you, Ariel, Ariel, the city where David settled! Add year to year and let your cycle of festivals go on. Yet I will besiege Ariel; she will mourn and lament, she will be to me like an altar hearth. I will encamp against you all around; I will encircle you with towers and set up my siege works against you. Brought low, you will speak from the ground; your speech will mumble out of the dust. Your voice will come ghostlike from the earth; out of the dust your speech will whisper." *Isaiah 29:1-4*

```
AD 1948
The Four Craftsmen
```

In Zechariah's second vision he sees four horns or kingdoms that scatter/enslave the nation of Israel.

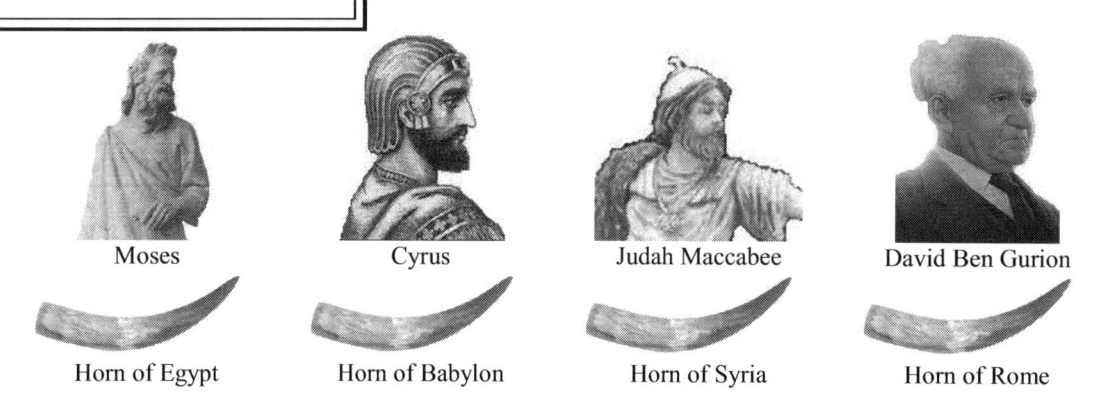

Moses	Cyrus	Judah Maccabee	David Ben Gurion
Horn of Egypt	Horn of Babylon	Horn of Syria	Horn of Rome

"Then I lifted up my eyes and looked, and behold, there were four horns. So I said to the angel who was speaking with me, 'What are these?' And he answered me, 'These are the horns which have scattered Judah, Israel and Jerusalem.' Then the LORD showed me four craftsmen. I said, "What are these coming to do?" And he said, "These are the horns which have scattered Judah so that no man lifts up his head; but these craftsmen have come to terrify them, to throw down the horns of the nations who have lifted up their horns against the land of Judah in order to scatter it." *Zechariah 1:18-21*

First Horn and Craftsman
The first great horn was Egypt which enslaved Israel. Moses was the first craftsman who destroyed Egypt and delivered Israel by leading the Exodus in 1453 BC.

Second Horn and Craftsman
The second great horn was Nebuchadnezzar's Babylonian Empire which destroyed Solomon's Temple and held the Jews captive for 70 years, from 607 to 537 BC. The second craftsman was King Cyrus of Persia who destroyed the Babylonian Empire and freed the Jews. Cyrus gave them permission to go back and rebuild the Temple in Jerusalem in 536 BC.

Third Horn and Craftsman
The third great horn was Antiochus Epiphanies' Seleucid Empire which captured Jerusalem and desecrated the Temple, banning the Jews from Jerusalem from 168 BC to 165 BC. The third craftsman was Judas Maccabee who pushed out Antiochus' forces and re-dedicated the Temple in 165 BC.

Fourth Horn and Craftsman
The last great horn was Rome, which destroyed the Second Temple and scattered the Jews throughout the world in AD 132 shortly after the Bar-Kokhba rebellion. The fourth and last craftsman was David Ben-Gurion, who became the first great leader of the newly established state of Israel in AD 1948 and led the nation in its first War.

Jews Come Back in Unbelief
Today, the Jewish people believe in the God of Abraham, but not that Jesus Christ is the Messiah. Ezekiel prophesied their unbelief in his vision when they would be regathered as a nation. In his vision they re-assemble as a nation but have no

Modern Israel

"breath" in them. The breath would be true spirituality or a belief in the true Messiah. This will happen during the Tribulation.

"So I prophesied as I was commanded; and as I prophesied, there was a noise, and behold, a rattling; and the bones came together, bone to its bone. And I looked, and behold, sinews were on them, and flesh grew and skin covered them; but there was no breath in them… these bones are the whole house of Israel" *Ezekiel 37:7-8,11*

**AD 1948-1981
Seven Shepherds**

The map to the right shows the ancient land of Bashan, now called the Golan Heights. This is the focus point for the Israeli-Syrian Wars.

Occupying Syrian Land

The prophet Micah recorded an incredible prophecy about seven shepherds in the last days. In Chapter 5 he begins by predicting the Messiah will be rejected by the Jewish people and handed over to the Romans. This part of the prophecy, fulfilled in AD 32, is referenced in Matthew 27:30 and Mark 15:19. In reaction to the Jewish leaders rejecting the Messiah and handing Him over to the Romans, God handed Jerusalem over to the Romans to be besieged and destroyed. This was fulfilled in AD 70.

"Now muster yourselves in troops, daughter of troops; they have laid siege against us; with a rod they will smite the judge of Israel on the cheek." *Micah 5:1*

"They kept beating His head with a reed, and spitting on Him, and kneeling and bowing before Him." *Mark 15:19*

Bethlehem would be spared Roman besiegement and destruction because the Messiah (the Eternal One) was born there. Jesus Christ fulfilled part of this prophecy when He was born in 2 BC. This part of the prophecy is quoted in Matthew 2:4-6.

"Gathering together all the chief priests and scribes of the people, he inquired of them where the Messiah was to be born. They said to him, 'In Bethlehem of Judea; for this is what has been written by the prophet: 'AND YOU, BETHLEHEM, LAND OF JUDAH, ARE BY NO MEANS LEAST AMONG THE LEADERS OF JUDAH; FOR OUT OF YOU SHALL COME FORTH A RULER WHO WILL SHEPHERD MY PEOPLE ISRAEL.''" *Matthew 2:4-6*

"But as for you, Bethlehem Ephrathah, too little to be among the clans of Judah, from you One will go forth for Me to be ruler in Israel. His goings forth are from long ago, from the days of eternity." *Micah 5:2*

God allowed the Romans to dissolve the nation of Israel and disperse the Jewish people throughout the rest of the world. At the appointed time, God planned for the Jewish people to return and reestablish the nation of Israel. This was fulfilled in AD 1948 when Israel was reestablished as a nation. Sometime after this, the Messiah will return and set up His millennial reign that will extend to "the ends of the earth."

"Therefore He will give them *up* until the time when she who is in labor has borne a child. Then the remainder of His brethren will return to the sons of Israel. And He will arise and shepherd *His flock* in the strength of the LORD, in the majesty of the name of the LORD His God. And they will remain, because at that time He will be great to the ends of the earth." *Micah 5:3-5*

In Balaam's last oracle, Numbers 24:24, he prophesied that the Romans (Kittim) would destroy Assyria (Ashur), then Israel (Eber). Back in the section entitled Babylon to the Messiah, we learned that Kittim is Rome. Eber was an ancestor of Abraham and it is from his name that we get the word "Hebrew." Ashur was a son of Shem and the founder of the Assyrians. Balaam predicted that Rome would attack and destroy the land of Assyria and *then* the land of Israel. See the section on the

Ancient Prophecies Revealed

Messiah's birth for full details on this prophecy. When this prophecy was fulfilled, the land of Ashur had been renamed Syria and was ruled by Greeks. This prophecy's fulfillment proves that ancient prophecies that mention Assyria refer to present-day Syria.

> "But ships shall come from the coast of Kittim, and they shall afflict Asshur and will afflict Eber; so they also will come to destruction." *Numbers 24:24*

The Seven Shepherds – 1948, 1967, 1973, 1982

One of the main keys to understanding end time prophecy is understanding the Seven Shepherds Prophecy in Micah 5:5-8. The time period from the rebirth of Israel in 1948 to the Second Coming of the Messiah will be the time of the Seven Shepherds. Micah describes the Messiah as the one born in Bethlehem, and the one who will be "our peace" when He destroys the final "Assyrian" and sets up a kingdom that will extend "to the ends of the earth." Micah's prophecy refers to the Prince of Peace destroying the Antichrist at the Second Coming. According to the prophet Micah, between 1948 and the Second Coming there will be **eight leaders** and **seven shepherds** over Israel.

> "This One will be our peace. When the Assyrian invades our land, when he tramples on our citadels, then we will raise against him **seven shepherds** and **eight leaders** of men. They will shepherd the land of Assyria with the sword, the land of Nimrod at its entrances; and He will deliver us from the Assyrian when he attacks our land and when he tramples our territory. Then the remnant of Jacob will be among many peoples like dew from the LORD, like showers on vegetation which do not wait for man or delay for the sons of men. The remnant of Jacob will be among the nations, among many peoples like a lion among the beasts of the forest, like a young lion among flocks of sheep, which, if he passes through, tramples down and tears, and there is none to rescue." *Micah 5:5-8*

In Israel the position of a principle leader is called a "Prime Minister" and the one who "shepherds with the sword" is called a "Defense Minister." The key to identifying the leaders and shepherds is that they must be the Prime Minster and Defense Minister at a time *when Israel enters a war with Syria and occupies territory that is considered Syrian land at the time of the war*. This area between Israel and Syria was called Bashan in ancient times; but today is called the Golan Heights. It was part of Israel over 2,000 years ago but was not given back to Israel in 1948. Syria controlled this area until the War of Independence.

1st Leader	2nd Leader	3rd Leader	4th Leader
David Ben-Gurion 1948	Levi Eshkol 1967	Golda Meir 1973	Menachem Begin 1981

1st Shepherd	2nd Shepherd	3rd Shepherd
David Ben-Gurion War of Independence	Moshe Dayan Six Day War & Yom Kippur War	Ariel Sharon Golan Annexation

Modern Israel

War of Independence – 1948 – First Shepherd and First Leader
In 1948, on the very day the UN declared Israel to be a sovereign state, the Muslim nations surrounding her attacked. Syria attacked from the north. David Ben-Gurion ordered Israeli troops to push Syria back into Syrian territory. Since Israel began as a brand new state, it had no Prime Minister yet, but David Ben-Gurion acted as Defense Minster. Shortly after the war he was elected Israel's very first Prime Minster. David Ben-Gurion functioned as both Prime Minister and Defense Minister in the War of Independence. He was the First Leader *and* the First Shepherd! On July 20, 1949, Israel and Syria signed the Israel-Syria Armistice Agreement. Syria withdrew its forces from *most* of the Golan Heights, which became a demilitarized zone. Israel occupied its border.

Six Day War – 1967 – Second Shepherd and Second Leader
At the Beginning of the Six Day War, Syria again invaded from the north and Egypt from the south. By the end of the war Israel had captured the Golan Heights. Israel used the Golan Heights as a buffer zone between herself and Syria. Levi Eshkol was the second leader (Prime Minster) that ordered the attack on Syria. Moshe Dayan was the second shepherd (Defense Minister) and he captured the Golan Heights. Part of the Golan Heights was given back to Syria right before the Yom Kippur War.

Yom Kippur War – 1973 – Second Shepherd and Third Leader
In the Yom Kippur War Syria attacked again. The third leader, Golda Meir, ordered the response to this Syrian aggression on Israeli soil. The second shepherd, Moshe Dayan, who was still Defense Minister at that time, took control of the war effort. He pushed Syria back and recaptured the Golan Heights. He was the shepherd for two different leaders. Now you know why there are *eight* leaders but only *seven* shepherds. As of 2008, the Golan Heights still remains in Israeli hands.

Golan Annexation – 1981 – Third Shepherd and Fourth Leader
On December 14, 1981, Israel ratified the Golan Heights Law, which applied Israeli law to the area of the Golan controlled by Israel. Fourth leader, Menachem Begin, directed third shepherd, Ariel Sharon, to annex all of the Golan and start Jewish settlements in the area. A very small amount of land was returned to Syria and another section of Golan land was incorporated along with the land the Israelis already possessed. The very next year was the First Lebanese War.

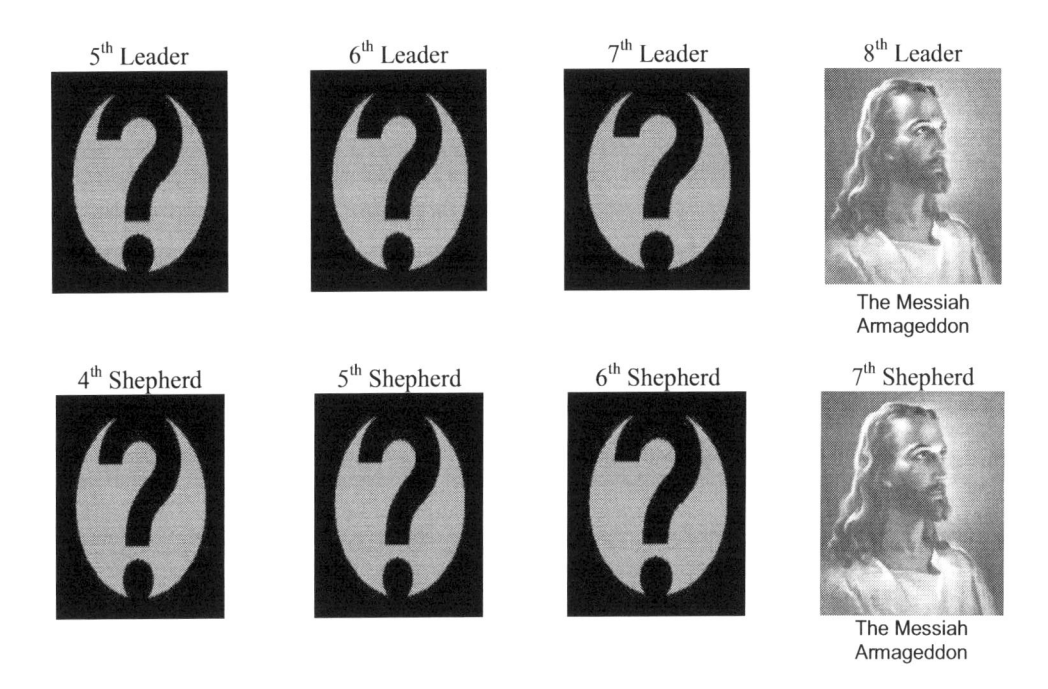

5th Leader	6th Leader	7th Leader	8th Leader
?	?	?	The Messiah — Armageddon

4th Shepherd	5th Shepherd	6th Shepherd	7th Shepherd
?	?	?	The Messiah — Armageddon

Ancient Prophecies Revealed

Since 1981

In 1981 Israel bombed an Iraqi nuclear facility. In 1982 Israel led a full-scale invasion of Lebanon. Syria entered the war in support of Lebanon. Still, nearly 80 Syrian MiGs and 19 missile batteries in the Bekaa Valley were destroyed without the loss of a single Israeli plane. By the end of June, Israel had captured most of southern Lebanon and besieged PLO and Syrian forces in West Beirut. Begin and Sharon were still in power during those events. These events, then, would all be counted under the fourth leader and third shepherd. Syria stopped occupying Lebanon in 2005.

In the 2006 Lebanese War there was fighting in the Galilee/Golan Heights area but this land was still occupied by Israel at that time. Shepherds four through seven will likewise control Israeli troops on Syrian land. One such war will be "even to the entrance of Nimrod's land" or Iraq.

The fifth, sixth, and seventh leaders and the fourth, fifth, and sixth shepherds are yet future. Just as David Ben-Gurion was the first leader and shepherd, so Jesus Christ, at His Second Coming, will be the eighth leader and the seventh shepherd.

To the right is a list of all the Israeli Prime Ministers since AD 1948, compared with Micah's prophecy of the seven shepherds. As of AD 2008, there have been twelve separate people occupying sixteen terms as Prime Minster.

	Name	Leader	Major Events
1	David Ben-Gurion 1948-1953	First	1948 – War of Independence
2	Moshe Sharett 1953-1955		
3	*David Ben-Gurion* 1955-1963		1956 – Suez Crisis
4	Levi Eshkol 1963-1969	Second	1967 – Six Day War
5	Golda Meir 1969-1974		1969 – War of Attrition
		Third	1973 – Yom Kippur War
6	Yitzhak Rabin 1974-1976		
7	Menachem Begin 1977-1983	Fourth	
8	Yitzhak Shamir 1983-1984		1982 – First Lebanese War
9	Shimon Peres 1984-1986		
10	*Yitzhak Shamir* 1986-1992		1992 – Intifada
11	*Yitzhak Rabin* 1992-1995		
12	*Shimon Peres* 1995-1996		
13	Benjamin Netanyahu 1996-1999		
14	Ehud Barak 1999-2001		
15	Ariel Sharon 2001-2006		2005 – Gaza pullout
16	Ehud Olmert 2006- Present		2006 – Second Lebanese War
		Fifth	
		Sixth	
		Seventh	
	Jesus the Messiah	Eighth	Armageddon

Names *italicized* are men in their second terms as Prime Minster.

AD 1949
Yemenite Jews Return

"For I am the LORD your God, the Holy One of Israel, your Savior; I have given Egypt as your ransom, Cush and Seba in your place. Since you are precious in My sight, *since* you are honored and I love you, I will give *other* men in your place and *other* peoples in exchange for your life. Do not fear, for I am with you; I will bring your offspring from the **east**, and gather you from the **west**. **I will say to the north, 'Give *them* up!'** And to the **south**, 'Do not hold *them* back.' Bring My sons from afar, and My daughters from the **ends of the earth**, everyone who is called by My name, and whom I have created for My glory, whom I have formed, even whom I have made." Isaiah 43:3-7

Here, in Isaiah 43, we have a prophecy that tells us that after the return of the nation of Israel, God would begin to gather Jews from all the nations back into their land. What is unique about this passage is that the word used for south is not the usual word for south in Hebrew. Instead of the normal word "Negev," Isaiah uses the word "Teman." The word Teman is sometimes used for the word "south." It also means a region in ancient Ideuma, and is the modern Hebrew word for the

100

county of Yemen. When the Yemenite Jews heard that God had restored the nation of Israel and there was a new "king" ruling Israel by the name of David, they immediately looked at this passage as a call to go home to Israel. Yemen did not "hold them back." Within one year more than 50,000 Yemenite Jews moved to Israel!

Egypt Becomes a Republic - 1953
This prophecy is about a future time when the Antichrist will destory Egypt and the Nile River will go dry. This is detailed in Isaiah 19:1-7. This is a future propehcy, but it indicates that it will occur after the Jews return to their land (1948), the "scepter departs from Egypt" (1953), and they are brought back from "Egypt and Assyria" (the withdrawl from the Golan in 1972 and the Sinai in 1979). Egypt has always had pharoahs and kings until the last king was deposed in 1953 by Nasser. Egypt then became a republic. The Antichrist's attack on Egypt must occur sometime after AD 1953. See the section on post-2008 prophecies for more informatin on the unfulfilled parts of this prophecy.

"When I scatter them among the peoples, they will remember Me in far countries, and they with their children will live and come back. I will bring them back from the land of Egypt and gather them from Assyria; and I will bring them into the land of Gilead and Lebanon until no room can be found for them. And they will pass through the sea of distress, and He will strike the waves in the sea, so that all the depths of the Nile will dry up; and the pride of Assyria will be brought down and the scepter of Egypt will depart." *Zechariah 10:9-11*

AD 1951-2005
Ashdod, Ashkalon, and Gaza

"The burden of the word of the LORD is against the land of Hadrach, with Damascus as its resting place (for the eyes of men, especially of all the tribes of Israel, are toward the LORD), and Hamath also, which borders on it; Tyre and Sidon, though they are very wise. For Tyre built herself a fortress and piled up silver like dust, and gold like the mire of the streets. Behold, the Lord will dispossess her and cast her wealth into the sea; and she will be consumed with fire. Ashkelon will see it and be afraid. Gaza too will writhe in great pain; also Ekron, for her expectation has been confounded. Moreover, the **king will perish from Gaza**, and Ashkelon will not be inhabited. And **a mongrel race will dwell in Ashdod**, and I will cut off the pride of the Philistines. And I will remove their blood from their mouth, and their detestable things from between their teeth. Then they also will be a remnant for our God, and be like a clan in Judah, and Ekron like a Jebusite. But I will camp around My house because of an army, because of him who passes by and returns; and no oppressor will pass over them anymore," *Zechariah 9:1-8*

Alexander the Great fulfilled this prophecy by destroying Tyre and throwing all of her rubble into the sea (See Tyre in the section on Babylon to the Messiah for full details).

According to the historian Josephus, after Alexander destroyed Tyre he went on to wipe out the rest of the Philistines. He attacked and destroyed Ashkelon and Ekron. Ashdod was conquered and made into a port city for Alexander's fleet. This afforded him a way to protect and re-supply his troops before he proceeded to conquer Babylon. The Greeks left the Philistine temple of Dagon in Ashdod untouched. It was not destroyed until

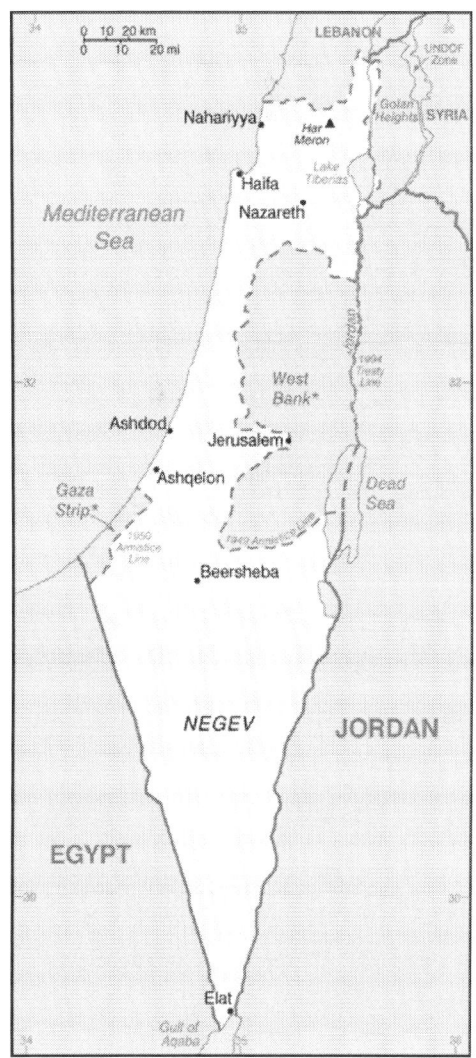

Ancient Prophecies Revealed

the time of the Maccabees. Notice Ekron will be like the Jebusite, utterly destroyed. Ekron to this day remains in ruins, completely uninhabited.

"Gather yourselves together, yes, gather, O nation without shame, before the decree takes effect-- the day passes like the chaff-- before the burning anger of the LORD comes upon you, before the day of the LORD'S anger comes upon you. Seek the LORD, all you humble of the earth who have carried out His ordinances; seek righteousness, seek humility. **Perhaps you will be hidden in the day of the LORD'S anger**. For Gaza will be abandoned and Ashkelon a desolation; Ashdod will be driven out at noon and Ekron will be uprooted. Woe to the inhabitants of the seacoast, the nation of the Cherethites! The word of the LORD is against you, O Canaan, land of the Philistines; and I will destroy you so that there will be no inhabitant. So the seacoast will be pastures, with caves for shepherds and folds for flocks. And the coast will be for the remnant of the house of Judah, they will pasture on it. In the houses of Ashkelon they will lie down at evening; for the LORD their God will care for them and restore their fortune. I have heard the taunting of Moab and the revilings of the sons of Ammon, with which they have taunted My people and become arrogant against their territory. 'Therefore, as I live,' declares the LORD of hosts, the God of Israel, 'Surely Moab will be like Sodom and the sons of Ammon like Gomorrah-- a place possessed by nettles and salt pits, and a perpetual desolation. The remnant of My people will plunder them and the remainder of My nation will inherit them.'" *Zephaniah 2:1-9*

In this prophecy, God promises the humble (the humble heed the prophecies and become Christians) that they "will be hidden in the day of the Lord's anger." This means they will be raptured (see section on the Rapture). Zephaniah then predicts that prior to the Rapture Gaza would be abandoned.

Gaza and Gaza City have been conquered many times in war but never just handed away to an enemy. Then, in AD 2005, Ariel Sharon forsook all of Gaza by handing it over to Hamas. How do we know this prophecy is pointing to the Last Days?

We have already seen the destruction of the Philistines and Ashkelon and the Greek occupation of Ashdod (323 BC). In the Middle Ages Ashkelon and Ashdod became uninhabited pasture land. In AD 1948, Israel's War of Independence occurred. Jordan (ancient Moab and Ammon) invaded the new country of Israel and captured the West Bank, being "arrogant against Israeli territory." Jordan continued the occupation until the Six Day War in 1967. The cities were then under the control of the "remnant of the house of Judah." Modern Ashkelon, founded in 1951 after the Israelis captured territory in the War of Independence, grew to be the eighth largest city in Israel by 2005. Modern Ashdod, founded in 1968, after the Six Day War, grew to become the fifth largest city in Israel by 2005. Ekron, as predicted by Zephaniah, still lies in ruins. Jordan captured the West Bank in AD 1948 but they relinquished it after the Six Day War in 1967, having controlled it for 19 years. By the year AD 2000, the old city parts of Ashkelon and Ashdod were "restored to their original fortune" by archeology and are now tourist attractions. Jeremiah 47 also prophesies Ashdod will be rebuilt.

Modern Timeline
1948 Israel reborn
1948 Jordan takes West Bank
1951 Ashkelon founded
1967 Six Day War
1968 Ashdod founded
2000 Ancient sites made public
2005 Gaza forsaken
after 2005 the Rapture

What will happen to Jordan? See Isaiah 15!

**AD 1967
The Temple Mount Taken**

Darius Decree — "907,200 Days" — Six Day War
August 25, 518 BC — June 7, 1967 AD

In the section on the Messiah's death, we dealt with the timeline prophecy showing the Messiah's death would occur in AD 32. Then in the section on the rebirth of Israel, we dealt with the prophecy showing the modern nation if Israel would be reborn in AD 1948. Here we will show the Israelis were destined to capture the Temple Mount in the year AD 1967.

Modern Israel

In Daniel 5, we read of the account of the handwriting on the wall. This handwriting is an inscription prophecy with a double fulfillment. Daniel leaves out the first mene in this riddle and interprets the words Mene, Tekel, and Pharsin as Hebrew verbs which literally read "numbered," "weighed," and "divided." Daniel tells Belshazzer that the words of the handwriting on that wall mean he personally has been weighed and found to be godless. Therefore, the days of his kingdom have been numbered and have come to an end. His kingdom will be divided and given to the Medes and Persians.

"Now this is the inscription that was written out: 'MENE, MENE, TEKEL, UPHARSIN.'" *Daniel 5:25*

The double fulfillment is for the latter days. First, notice that Mene is stated twice. If we take these words as *nouns* instead of *verbs,* a different meaning becomes clear. If we decipher them as nouns they turn out to be names for weights/money. A Mene is 1000 Garahs (A garah is a base unit of weight like our penny), a Tekel is 20 garahs, and a Peres is half a mena. "Upharsin" is the Hebrew way of saying "and Peres." So the inscription reads 2,520 garahs or 2,520 periods of time. On this night the control of the temple vessels passed to the children of Israel. Real control of the Temple Mount would be given later by Darius. The actual building of the Temple would be much later.

Mene	1,000	garahs
Mene	+1,000	garahs
Tekel	+ 20	garahs
Peres	+ 500	garahs
	2,520	garahs

```
2,520 garahs/prophetic years; 2,520 x 360 = 907,220 days

907,220 days on the modern calendar is 2,483 yrs & 285 days
2,483 yrs x 365.25 = 906915; 907200 – 906915 = 285 days

August 25, 518 BC + 2,483 yrs = August 25, AD 1965
Add 1 year (no 0 Year) = AD 1966;
Add 285 days = June 7, AD 1967
```

This prophecy tells us that from the decree Darius would give granting full control of the Temple Mount plus 2,520 Jewish years, the children of Israel would again be granted control of the Temple Mount – but not build the Temple itself. We will calculate this in the same way we did the death of the Messiah in AD 32, and the birth of Israel in AD 1948. Since the prophetic calendar uses a 360-day year, if you mutiply the 2,520 Jewish years by the 360-day calendar, you get 907,200 days.

Darius's decree to grant the Jews control of the Temple Mount was August 25, 518 BC. This date plus 907,200 days (plus one year changing from BC to AD) brings us to June 7, 1967. *On this exact date* the Israelis again gained control of the Temple Mount during the Six Day War!

For more information on timeline prophecies, see the sections on AD 32, and AD 1967.

AD 1967
The Five Cities

"In that day the Egyptians will be like women. They will shudder with fear at the uplifted hand that the LORD Almighty raises against them. And the land of Judah will bring terror to the Egyptians; everyone to whom Judah is mentioned will be terrified, because of what the LORD Almighty is planning against them. In that day five cities in Egypt will speak the language of Canaan and swear allegiance to the LORD Almighty. One of them will be called the City of Destruction."
Isaiah 19:16-18

The Six Day War brought us the second leader and second shepherd from the Micah 5 prophecy. It also brought us the fulfillment of the Isaiah 19 prophecy. In this war Syria attacked Israel on the north and Egypt attacked Israel from the south. Israel responded immediately and pushed Egypt back beyond her original border and captured the Sinai Peninsula.
With blazing speed Israel strategically captured five cities which caused the whole Peninsula to fall under their control. Most important to this prophecy is a city called El Arish. Located on the Mediterranean coast, it would allow Israeli ships to port and control the northern section. The Hebrew word for "destruction" is "arish." So El Arish literally is the "City of destruction." When controlled by Egypt, these cities spoke Arabic, but now controlled by Israel would speak Hebrew (the

Ancient Prophecies Revealed

language of Canaan), and swear allegiance to the LORD and Israel. Israel controlled El Arish from the Six Day War until it was retuned to Egypt in 1979, 12 years later.

Yom Kippur War – 1973
This war is part of the seven shepherds prophecy of Micah 5 and also shows Israel being a firepot among the nations. This also started the "trouble" nations would get into by recognizing Jerusalem as Israel's capital.

Revival of the Shekel – 1980
The shekel was revived as the basic monetary unit for the nation of Israel in 1980. It was recommissioned as the "New Shekel" in 1985. It is currently abbreviated as NIS for "New Israeli Shekel." Ezekiel writes that before the new Temple is built, the Shekel would be revived along with the bath, homer, and ephah. In 45:21,25 and 46:2,17 we are also told of the revival of the New Moon, Seven Festivals, including Passover and Tabernacles, worship at the Eastern Gate and the return of the Jubilee years.

The New Israeli Shekel

"The shekel shall be twenty gerahs; twenty shekels, twenty-five shekels, and fifteen shekels shall be your maneh."
Ezekiel 45:12

First Lebanese War - 1982
In 1982 Israel invaded Lebanon to stop Hezbollah terrorists. In a matter of days Israel advanced all the way to Beirut, the capital of Lebanon. This again shows Israel's military would be a "firepot among the nations" as foretold in Zechariah 12.

AD 1989
Fall of the Berlin Wall

As we have seen in the section on the Great Dispersion, Germany was prophesied to be divided and its greater part swallowed up by Russia. This happened in 1945, at the end of World War II. In Ezekiel 38, Germany was prophesied to be reunited.

"I will turn you about and put hooks into your jaws, and I will bring you out, and all your army, horses and horsemen, all of them splendidly attired, a great company with buckler and shield, all of them wielding swords; Persia, Ethiopia and Put with them, all of them with shield and helmet; Gomer with all its troops; Beth-togarmah from the remote parts of the north with all its troops--many peoples with you." *Ezekiel 38:4-6*

In this passage, Ezekiel is prophesying a future war in which Russia and its allies attack Israel. In the above passage, Gomer, which is modern Germany, is mentioned as fighting in the war. Germany was involved in both World War I and World War II. The exact phrase here is "Gomer with all its bands." At the end of WWII, Germany was divided and half was swallowed up by Russia. So between 1945 and the Gog-Magog War, Germany must be reunited with all its parts. With the fall of the Berlin wall in 1989, East and West Germany were reunited. Sometime in the future, Austria will rejoin Germany and all of Gomer's parts will be back together as in the days of the Holy Roman Empire. Then it will be ready to start this war. Gomer was the son of Japheth and grandson of Noah. Gomer's son was Ashkenaz. The descendants of Ashkenaz settled in the area today named Germany. Even today the Hebrew word for Germany is Ashkenaz and German Jews are known as Ashkenazic Jews. One other theory has Ashkenaz as Germany and Gomer as its parent. If this view is correct, then Gomer's bands may have *already* united in the form of Germany and Austria joining the European Common Market.

Modern Israel

AD 1990
Ethiopian Jews Fly Home

Pictured here is the Hercules C-130 cargo plane used in Operation Solomon to free the Ethiopian Jews.

Ancient History of Ethiopia
About 2000 BC Ham, the son of Noah, gave the land we call Ethiopia to his son, Cush. After the Flood the continent that would become known as Africa was given to the third son of Noah, Ham. Ham gave what would become Egypt to his son Mizraim. He gave the land to the south of Egypt to his son Cush. Cush is the Hebrew name for Ethiopia. The "River of Ethiopia" ran through the midst of this land, but eventually there was a war. The land split into two countries, Sudan and Ethiopia. Isaiah prophesied about the land that is beyond the rivers of Ethiopia, which is a riddle. What country is beyond its own border? The prophet wanted us to understand he was referring to a future-day Ethiopia.

A Jewish Dynasty
Both the Talmud and the Ethiopian Chronicles (haggadic Ethiopian Kebra Negast) tell the story of Menelik I, who was the son of King Solomon of Israel and Makida, the Queen of Sheba. At the age of ten or twelve he accepted Judaism and took priests and relics to Ethiopia from Israel. The dynasty he started was the longest lasting dynasty in history. It ranged from 1000 BC to AD 1974, when the communists took over Ethiopia. The Talmud states that among the relics was a copy of the Ark of the Covenant. According to the Ethiopian Chronicle, because his father Solomon was in apostasy, the copy was switched with the original and Menelik took the original back to Ethiopia with him.

Christianity
In AD 32 Philip converted the Ethiopian eunuch by explaining Isaiah 53 to him. This is recorded in Acts 8. Being an official in the court of Queen Candice, he went back to Ethiopia with the Good News and the Ethiopian Coptic Church was born. The church would control the relics from that point onward, until the Second Coming of the Messiah.

> "For then I will return to the peoples a pure language, which they may call on the name of the LORD, to serve Him shoulder to shoulder. From beyond the rivers of Ethiopia My worshipers, the daughter of my dispersed ones, will bring my present." *Zephaniah 3:9-10* (Hebrew)

God caused a division of the nations at the tower of Babel by creating multiple languages. In this Zephaniah prophecy, the Messiah returns and undoes what he did at the tower of Babel, causing all the peoples or nations to once again speak the "pure language." When this happens, we will see the "dispersed ones," (Falasha Jews) have already been back in the land of Israel since AD 1990. Only their "daughter," the Ethiopian Coptic Church, is left. Since she still has control of the relics, it is the Coptic Church that will bring the "present" back to Mount Zion and present it directly to the Messiah. This may or may not include the Ark of the Covenant. So how did the Ethiopian Jews get back to Israel?

> "Alas, oh land of noisy wings which lies beyond the rivers of Cush, [Ethiopia] which sends envoys by the sea, even in **papyrus** vessels *on* the surface of the waters. Go, swift messengers, to a nation scattered and fearful, to a people awesome or terrible from their beginning onward to the present, a nation partitioned out and trodden down whose land the rivers divide. All you inhabitants of the world and dwellers on earth, as soon as a banner is raised on the mountains, you will see it, and as soon as the trumpet is blown, you will hear it. For thus the LORD said to me, 'I will take my rest and look from My dwelling place like clear heat over light, like a cloud of dew in the heat of harvest.' For before the harvest, as soon as the bud blossoms and the ripening grape flowers out, then He will cut off the sprigs with pruning knives and remove and cut away the spreading branches. They will be left together for mountain birds of prey, and for the beasts of the earth; and the birds of prey will spend the summer feeding on them, and all the beasts of the earth will winter on them. At that time a gift of homage will be brought to the LORD of hosts [originally] from a people scattered and fearful, even from a people awesome or terrible from their beginning onward to the present, a nation partitioned out

Ancient Prophecies Revealed

and trodden down, whose land the rivers divide— [back] to the place of the name of the LORD of hosts, even Mount Zion." *Isaiah 18:1-7* (Hebrew)

The key to understanding this obscure passage is that envoys come on "papyrus vessels." The Hebrew word used here for papyrus is גמא, which, as a noun, means paper or papyrus. Since it would not be possible to send a large amount of people anywhere in paper boats, it must be translated as a verb. The word גמא, as a verb, means "to drink," much like paper drinks up spilled water. So the envoys travel in ships that drink some form of liquid fuel, and make a lot of noise with their wings as they travel over the Red Sea, from Ethiopia to Israel. These ships are modern airplanes. This occurred in AD 1990.

So the "land of whirring wings" is Ethiopia, but how do we know they go to Israel? At the time this prophecy was fulfilled, Israel was a land "scattered and divided" by the Palestinians. In many cases rivers divide Islamic territory from the land of Israel. The Jordan River divides Israel from Trans-Jordan. The Palestinian areas of the West Bank, Golan Heights, and the Gaza Strip are divided from the rest of Israel. Even when the Lord is on Israel's side and they are a nation "terrible from its beginning to the present time," they still are a nation partitioned and trodden down by Muslim peoples.

Israeli Rivers
Belus
Ga'aton
Jordan
Kishon
Lachish
Yarmouk
Yarqon

Isaiah 18 is divided into four parts. Verse 3 refers to two events. First, the world sees the return of Israel as a nation (1948). Second, "as soon as the trumpet is blown" refers to the Rapture. Verses 4-6 describe the Lord's view of the Great Tribulation. Zephaniah 3:9-10 proves verse 7 refers to the millennium. That leaves verses 1-2 to refer to our time.

The end of Menelik's dynasty came with the Communist revolution of 1974. By the 1980's, communists, under the control of Colonel Mengistu Haile Mariam (1982-1990), forbade the practice of Judaism. Even learning the Hebrew language was illegal. Some Falasha (Ethiopian Jews) started migrating to Sudan to be taken to Israel, but when other Muslim nations put pressure on Sudan, the migrations stopped. In 1990 another revolution occurred. The extreme persecution caused the Falasha to flee from Gonder to Addis Ababa. Israel was greatly concerned that the remaining Falasha Jews would be annihilated. A joint effort was undertaken by Israel and the USA to get them out.

Israel carried out Operation Solomon, in which Hercules C-130 cargo planes (liquid fuel drinking ships that make a buzzing sound while flying) were used to secretly fly out the remaining Jews before they were put to death. The planes flew the refugees from Ethiopia to Israel by flying *over* the Red Sea.

AD 2000 Multiple Points

In this section we want to list prophecies that were fulfilled by the end of the Twentieth Century but occurred in stages, rather than on specific dates during that time.

Archeologically Restored Cities and Palestinian Farmers
In the Twentieth Century we saw the growth of archeology in Israel and with it, the rebuilding of modern Israeli cities on the actual sites of former ancient cities. Not just Ashdod and Ashkalon, as described in Zephaniah 2, but many ancient cities are now tourist attractions. Palestinians (foreigners) will be hired for some jobs in Israel.

> "Then they will rebuild the ancient ruins, They will raise up the former devastations; and they will repair the ruined cities, the desolations of many generations. Strangers will stand and pasture your flocks, and foreigners will be your farmers and your vinedressers." *Isaiah 61:4,5*

City of Jerusalem Grows Beyond Its Old Walls
Jerusalem would expand so much that it would grow outside its ancient walls because of the multitude of people and cattle. Jerusalem finally became this "city without walls" in the last century. As prophesied, it occurred after they came back from "all nations" – or in 1948. Notice also that in the future the LORD will protect it by being a wall of fire around it. Compare this to when Alexander came to Jerusalem. See Alexander the Great in the Section on Babylon to the Messiah.

Modern Israel

"...Jerusalem will be inhabited without walls because of the multitude of men and cattle within it. 'For I,' declares the LORD, 'will be a wall of fire around her, and I will be the glory in her midst.' Ho there! 'Flee from the land of the north,' declares the LORD, 'for I have dispersed you as the four winds of the heavens,' declares the LORD."
Zechariah 2:4-6

Tourists Fly In and Support Israel
Isaiah prophesied that some would "fly… like doves…" In the Twentieth and Twenty-first centuries, millions of people have flown into Israel and supported the nation though tourism. Most are Christians who want to see where "the name of the Lord" – or Jesus – walked, lived, died, and resurrected. Since Israel is not "reckoned among the nations" by her Muslim neighbors, for much of Israel's history tourists couldn't cross directly into Israel from bordering countries. Instead most tourists flew in from places like Amsterdam and Paris. While refugees usually come with little more than the clothes on their backs, tourism is one of the top five industries supporting the nation. Tourists come with their "silver and gold."

"Who are these who fly like a cloud and like the doves to their lattices? … Their silver and their gold with them, for the name of the LORD your God, and for the Holy One of Israel because He has glorified you. Foreigners will build up your walls, and their kings will minister to you; for in My wrath I struck you, and in My favor I have had compassion on you." *Isaiah 60:8,10*

Constant Planting and Reaping In Israel
With the blessing of the Lord, the once desolate land now has constant crop rotation. It truly has become like the Garden of Eden. Today Israel sends her superior fruit all over the world. This prophecy would be fulfilled after the return of 1948. God promised Israel will *NEVER* be uprooted again. Isaiah 27:6 also says they would "fill the world with fruit."

"'Behold, days are coming,' declares the LORD, 'When the plowman will overtake the reaper and the treader of grapes him who sows seed; when the mountains will drip sweet wine and all the hills will be dissolved. Also I will restore the captivity of My people Israel, and they will rebuild the ruined cities and live in them; they will also plant vineyards and drink their wine, and make gardens and eat their fruit. I will also plant them on their land, and they will not again be rooted out from their land which I have given them,' says the LORD your God." *Amos 9:13-15*

Forests Reappear In Israel
Along with the water and crops, Isaiah said after Israel's second return she would be reforested with cedar, acacia, myrtle, olive, juniper, box tree, and cypress trees. This should not be simply dismissed. Understand is it a move of God!

"I will open rivers on the bare heights and springs in the midst of the valleys; I will make the wilderness a pool of water and the dry land fountains of water. I will put the cedar in the wilderness, the acacia and the myrtle and the olive tree; I will place the juniper in the desert together with the box tree and the cypress, that they may see and recognize, and consider and gain insight as well, that the hand of the LORD has done this, and the Holy One of Israel has created it."
Isaiah 41:18-20

Desolate Cities Restored
The ancient cities would be restored and renamed their original Hebrew names. This name restoration of ancient cities should be a sign to everyone that the LORD is doing this! After AD 132 the land of Israel was completely desolated. See Deuteronomy 29:23 for details. (The desert blooming like a rose will occur before the Antichrist's appearance: see Isaiah 35:1 & Psalm 67:6)

"Thus says the Lord GOD, 'On the day that I cleanse you from all your iniquities, I will cause the cities to be inhabited, and the waste places will be rebuilt. The desolate land will be cultivated instead of being a desolation in the sight of everyone who passes by.' They will say, 'This desolate land has become like the Garden of Eden; and the waste, desolate and ruined cities are fortified and inhabited.' Then the nations that are left round about you will know that I, the LORD, have rebuilt the ruined places and planted that which was desolate; I, the LORD, have spoken and will do it."
Ezekiel 36:33-36

Ancient Prophecies Revealed

"Those from among you will rebuild the ancient ruins; you will raise up the age-old foundations; and you will be called the repairer of the breach, the restorer of the streets in which to dwell." *Isaiah 58:12*

Sites That Will Remain In Ruin For All Time
In Matthew 11:20-24, Jesus stated that Chorazin, Bethsaida, and Capernaum would be left desolate. Also to be desolate for all time are Ekron according to Zephaniah 2, and Phoenician Tyre according to Ezekiel 26. Alexander the Great destroyed Tyre in 336 BC and shortly after that he destroyed Ekron. Chorazin, Bethsaida, and Capernaum were destroyed by the Romans after Jesus' first advent. Today these cities remain in ruins. The ruins of Chorazin and Bethsaida are tourist attractions.

Israel Not Reckoned Among the Muslim Nations:
From 1948 to the present (2008), no Islamic country has Israel on their maps. They refuse to reckon Israel as a real nation. In Numbers 23:9 Moses prophesied in the later days Israel would "not be reckoned among the nations."

"…Behold, a people who dwells apart, And will not be reckoned among the nations." *Numbers 23:9*

Israel To Possess the Remnant of Edom (Palestinians)
With the return of the state of Israel, the local people would be incorporated into the society. Many of these would be peaceful but many would try to start wars. The remnant of the people from ancient Edom and the surrounding nations to day are called "Palestinians" and live mainly in Jordan and Israel.

"'In that day I will raise up the fallen booth of David, and wall up its breaches; I will also raise up its ruins and rebuild it as in the days of old; that they may possess the remnant of Edom and all the nations who are called by My name,' declares the LORD who does this." *Amos 9:11-12*

Satellite-Television Communication Systems Invented
Revelation 11:9-10 describes all the world watching the two witnesses die and resurrect. Revelation 17:8 depicts all nations looking at the beast after it is resurrected. Only through satellites, television, and the internet could this have been made possible.

AD 2004
The Sanhedrin Reestablished

Left: Rabbi Yoel Swartz.
Vice-Chairman of the Sanhedrin.
Head of the Court for Bnei Noach.

Right: Rabbi Adin Steinsaltz
Sanhedrin President, Nassi

"Therefore when you see the ABOMINATION OF DESOLATION which was spoken of through Daniel the prophet, standing in the holy place (let the reader understand), then those who are in Judea must flee to the mountains… But pray that your flight will not be in the winter, or on a Sabbath." *Matthew 24:15,20*

Here Jesus warns those during the Tribulation who see the abomination of desolation, described by Daniel, being placed in the new Temple, to flee immediately, because it is a sign that war is imminent. Jesus told them to pray that it does not occur on a Sabbath. If the ancient Sabbath laws were in place in the entire land of Israel, it would be impossible to flee by bus, car, train, plane, or ship. The adopting of the Sabbath law would never happen in a secular state. Since Jesus Himself warned us of this, we can see that by the time the Antichrist desecrates the newly built Temple, the Sabbath laws will be in effect in Israel.

For the Sabbath laws to be reinstituted, first there must be a reestablishment of the ancient religious ruling body known as the Sanhedrin. Then they must grow in power to the point of being able to enforce religious laws on everyone in the whole nation of Israel. This has started to come to pass. The Sanhedrin is a group of 71 rabbis who form the religious Jewish government,

Modern Israel

a kind of Supreme Court. After the destruction of the Temple in AD 70, the ancient Sanhedrin moved from Jerusalem to Tiberias where it continued to exist until about the year AD 425 when it was officially disbanded. Then in AD 2004, over 1500 years later, the Sanhedrin was officially reestablished in Israel according to the laws as passed down by Maimonides.

The marking of bodies described in Ezekiel 39 may happen because the religious laws have been reinstituted by the Sanhedrin.

> "As those who pass through the land pass through and anyone sees a man's bone, then he will set up a marker by it until the buriers have buried it in the valley of Hamon-gog." *Ezekiel 39:15*

AD 2005 Palestinians Claim Jerusalem

Ezekiel prophesied that the local enemies of God (today's Palestinian Muslims) would claim that Jerusalem and other holy sites (the high places) have always been theirs. But the restored land and cities proves the land, including Jerusalem, belongs to the Jews. Notice the cities are restored 'after their own estates' or, in other words, have their old Hebrew names back, not the Palestinian, Arabic names.

> "Thus saith the Lord GOD; because the enemy hath said against you, aha, even the ancient high places are ours in possession... Therefore thus saith the Lord GOD; I have lifted up mine hand, surely the heathen that are about you, they shall bear their shame... and the cities shall be inhabited, and the wastes shall be builded: and I will multiply upon you man and beast; and they shall increase and bring fruit: and I will settle you after your old estates, and will do better unto you than at your beginnings: and ye shall know that I am the LORD." *Ezekiel 36:2, 7,10-11*

The dome of the rock was constructed on the Temple Mount in AD 691 by Abd-al-Malik. Legend holds Abraham began to offer Isaac on the rock in the center of the mosque. It was not until the 1920's that the Mufti of Jerusalem, Haj Amin al-Husseini invented the idea that it was *also* the rock from which Mohammad ascended into heaven. This idea was kept alive by the Mufi's nephew, Yassar Arafat. This was done in order to aid the Palestinians in their effort to claim Jerusalem for themselves. Today the Palestinian Muslims claim there never was a Temple or a King David or a Jewish state in the land of Israel! (Regardless of archeological evidence to the contrary!)

Gaza Forsaken - 2005
As mentioned earlier, Gaza has been occupied many times by different people over the centuries, but never *given away* until AD 2005 by Ariel Sharon. Joel wrote that God hates *anyone* who would divide or try to give away His land. As a result, Ariel Sharon suffered a stroke and to this day is still in a coma. For details, see the section on Ashdod, Ashkalon, and Gaza.

> "For behold, in those days and at that time, when I restore the fortunes of Judah and Jerusalem, I will gather all the nations and bring them down to the valley of Jehoshaphat. Then I will enter into judgment with them there on behalf of My people and My inheritance, Israel, whom they have scattered among the nations; and they have divided up My land." *Joel 3:1-2*

Russian-Iranian Military Pact - 2005
The future Gog-Magog invasion will consist of Russia (Rosh) and Iran (Persia). These two nations have never had military ties in the past. In February 2005, a military agreement was signed; if either is attacked the other will come to their aid. This sets the stage for the future invasion. Notice that in verse 7 Russia was to prepare herself. This took place during the Cold War of 1945 to 1989. Russia used the resources of her slave states to become a super power. Then, with the fall of the Berlin Wall, the slave states became separate powers. So in the future, Russia and her *allies*, not *satellite states* will invade Israel. See the section about the Gog-Magog invasion for more details.

Ancient Prophecies Revealed

"Thus says the Lord GOD, "Behold, I am against you, O Gog, prince of Rosh (Russia), Meshech (Moscaw) and Tubal (Tubolsk). I will turn you about and put hooks into your jaws, and I will bring you out, and all your army, horses and horsemen, all of them splendidly attired, a great company *with* buckler and shield, all of them wielding swords; Persia (Iran), Ethiopia and Put (Lybia) with them, all of them *with* shield and helmet; Gomer (Germany) with all its troops; Beth-togarmah (Turkey) *from* the remote parts of the north with all its troops--many peoples with you. Be prepared, and prepare yourself, you and all your companies that are assembled about you, and be a guard for them. After many days you will be summoned; in the latter years you will come into the land that is restored from the sword, *whose inhabitants* have been gathered from many nations to the mountains of Israel which had been a continual waste; but its people were brought out from the nations, and they are living securely, all of them." *Ezekiel 38:3-8*

```
AD 2006
Second Lebanese War
```

On July 20, 2006, during the Second Lebanese War, an ancient Bible was found in a bog in Ireland. It was approximately 1200 years old and was sealed *open* to Psalm 83. The Psalm accurately described who and why Israel was being attacked in the 2006 war. The Rabbis took this as sign and had Psalm 83 read on Israeli National Radio every day at six PM, followed by a prayer for deliverance. This continued until the war ended.

"O God, do not remain quiet; do not be silent and, O God, do not be still. For behold, Your enemies make an uproar, And those who hate You have exalted themselves. They make shrewd plans against Your people, and conspire together against Your treasured ones. They have said, "Come, and let us wipe them out as a nation, that the name of Israel be remembered no more." For they have conspired together with one mind; against You they make a covenant… The tents of Edom (southern Jordan, northern Saudi Arabia) and the Ishmaelites (Arabs), Moab (Jordan) and the Hagrites; Gebal and Ammon and Amalek, Philistia (Lebanon) with the inhabitants of Tyre; Assyria (Syria) also has joined with them; they have become a help to the children of Lot. Selah." *Psalm 83:1-5, 6-8*

So far we have presented most of the prophecies recently fulfilled. Now let us proceed into the future and look as the prophecies that will be fulfilled after AD 2008.

✡

Future Events – Post 2008

AD 2008 to the Tribulation – 15 prophecies in _____ years

This section deals with those prophecies that have not yet happened but seem to happen before the Tribulation starts. This is still in the time of the Second Crossover Period. Since these will occur sometime after AD 2008, we will be guessing about the order in which they will occur. The dates for each of the nine are left blank. As you see them come to pass, write in the dates in the space provided at the left on the chart below.

Date	Prophecy	References
2008		
	360. An independent state will be created out of the West Bank	Dan. 11:45
	361. Fourth Shepherd's Syrian war will occur	Mic. 5:1-8
	362. Fifth Shepherd's Syrian war will occur	Mic. 5:1-8
	363. Lebanon-Jordan war will occur	Zech. 10-11; Obad. 1:19
	364. Sephardic Jews will return to Israel, & populate the Negev	Obad. 1:20
	365. Sixth Shepherd's Syrian war will occur	Mic. 5:1-8
	366. Damascus will be destroyed	Isa. 17:1
	367. Gog-Magog War will occur immediately after Israel wins another war	Ezek. 38
	368. Rise of the ten nations occurs after the Gog-Magog War	Dan. 8,11
	369. Increased understanding of prophecies will occur	Dan. 12:4
	370. Children will be rebellious and society will be materialistic	Mark 13:12; 1 Tim. 3:2-3
	371. Jesus' words will never be forgotten	Luke 21:33; Mat. 24:15; 1 Pet. 1:25
	372. Christians will be hated for Jesus' Name's sake	Luke 21:17
	373. The apostasy of the church will fully form	See Section on the Apostasy of the Church
	374. The Rapture of the believing church will occur	See Section on the Rapture
Tribulation Begins		

4, 5, & 6 Shepherds

We have seen that there would be eight leaders (Prime Ministers) and seven shepherds (Defense Ministers) rise up in Israel between 1948 and the Second Coming that go to war with, and take territory from, Syria. As of AD 2008, we are still waiting for the fourth shepherd to arise and battle with Syria. Since the seventh shepherd will be the Messiah at the Battle of Armageddon, we only need to look for the fourth though the sixth shepherds.

Based on what we know, my guess is the following scenario:
1. Sometime after 2008, a war will occur between Israel and Syria. The Israeli defense minister will be the fourth shepherd. This may be a short-lived war. It may occur because Israel once again gives back the Golan Heights.
2. The fifth shepherd, or Israeli defense minister, will again fight with Syria. This time, with Hezbollah in Lebanon and other terrorists in Jordan, Zechariah's prophecy about the destruction of part of Jordan and Lebanon will occur. The Israelis will permanently occupy part of Lebanon and all of ancient Gilead, (which is NW Jordan.)
3. The sixth shepherd, or Israeli defense minister, will attack Syria and destroy the capital of Damascus. Russia will decide that the best time to attack will be immediately after this war. This will be the war that triggers the Gog-Magog invasion.
4. The Gog-Magog invasion will occur resulting in only 1/6 of each of those attacking nations surviving. Therefore, they have no strength. This vacuum of power in the Middle East immediately causes the next event to occur.
5. Ten nations will rise up and form a confederacy.
6. The Church will be Raptured.
7. The Antichrist will arise, and confirm the "peace covenant," which starts the Tribulation period.

Ancient Prophecies Revealed

West Bank Becomes a Sovereign State

In Daniel 11:45 we are told that the Antichrist plants his headquarters between the two seas and the holy mountain. Today the area between the Mediterranean Sea, Sea of Galilee, and mount Zion, where Jerusalem sits, is called the West Bank. Today it is controlled by the state of Israel. In the future we will see the West Bank become a sovereign state. I have no guess as to what its name will be. Then the stage will be set for the Antichrist to start his rise to power.

Lebanese-Jordanian War

The details on how this war begins and its outcome are given in two sections. Zechariah 11:1-3 gives a general outline of wars prior to this Lebanese-Jordanian War. Then Zechariah 10:6-12 gives the details surrounding this war.

> "Open your doors, O Lebanon, that a fire may feed on your cedars. Wail, O cypress, for the cedar has fallen, because the glorious trees have been destroyed; wail, O oaks of Bashan, for the impenetrable forest has come down. There is a sound of the shepherds' wail, for their glory is ruined; there is a sound of the young lions' roar, for the pride of the Jordan is ruined."
> *Zechariah 11:1-3*

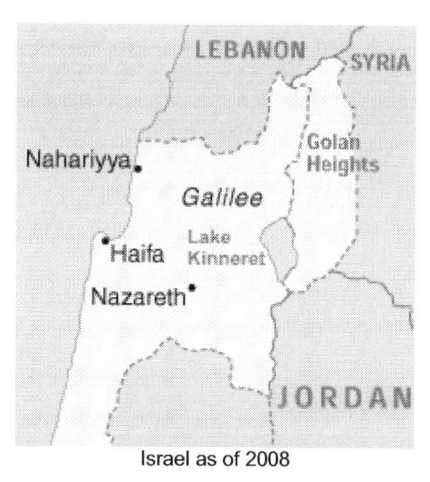

Israel as of 2008

In this prophecy we see a time when Israel invades and occupies Lebanon and Bashan. Today the ancient area that was called Bashan is now called the Golan Heights. Zechariah 11:1-3 took place after Israel came back in 1948. The first Lebanese War occurred in 1981. Israel occupied Lebanon until 2000. The Golan Heights (or Bashan) was occupied in the Six-Day War and annexed in 1981. It is still held by Israel today. Zechariah 11:2 says the destruction of Bashan occurred by the shepherds' wail. This same event was also prophesied in Micah 5 in the prophecy about the seven shepherds. See the "Seven Shepherds" in the section on Modern Israel for more details. The "Pride of the Jordan (river)" was to lie in ruins. The pride of the Jordan River could be referring to where the Jordan River starts, which is the area of Lebanon and the Golan. Today the demilitarized zone at the border of the Golan and Syria still lies in ruins. The taking of Jordan's pride could also be referring to the taking of Gilead, see below.

> "'I will bring them back from the land of Egypt and gather them from Assyria; and I will bring them into the land of Gilead and Lebanon until no room can be found for them. And they will pass through the sea of distress and He will strike the waves in the sea, so that all the depths of the Nile will dry up; and the pride of Assyria will be brought down and the scepter of Egypt will depart. And I will strengthen them in the LORD, and in His name they will walk,' declares the LORD." *Zechariah 10:6-12*

In this section we first see Israel being drawn back from Lebanon and Assyria (the Syrian Golan Heights). In the Six Day War, Israel captured the Sinai Peninsula. This was a fulfillment of Isaiah's prophecy. See the "Five Cities" in the section on Modern Israel for full details. Israel gave back the Sinai in stages, starting in 1979 and ending in 1982. The Israelis took the Golan, (called Bashan in this prophecy) in 1967 and returned it to Syria in 1973. Syria along with other Muslim nations attacked Israel again within six months of their giving back the

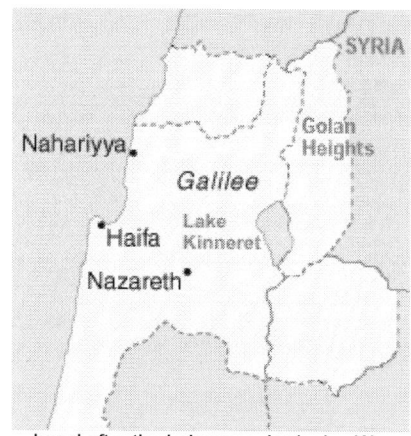

Israel after the Lebanese-Jordanian War

112

Future Events – Post 2008

Golan. The Israelis took back the Golan a second time. For more information on the Bashan/Golan wars see the "Seven Shepherds" in the section on Modern Israel. As of today, Israel still controls the Golan but does not control Gilead. Israel will take Gilead and Southern Lebanon sometime after 1982. Exactly where is Gilead?

The country we know as Jordan was artificially created by the British in 1922 and given full independence in 1946. It never existed before. It was created out of the ancient biblical lands of Gilead, Ammon, Moab, and Edom, running from north to south on the east of the Jordan River.

Sections of Zechariah's Prophecy	
1948	10:6-9 The return
1953	10:11 Egyptian scepter departs
1967	11:2-3 Capture of Golan & Sinai
1967	11:2 Capture of Golan/Bashan
1973	10:10 Brief return of Golan/Bashan
1982	11:1 Conquest of Lebanon
1982	10:10 Return of Sinai Peninsula
	11:10 Settling in Gilead & Lebanon
	10:11 Antichrist conquers Egypt
	10:11 Nile dries up
	11:4-9 Antichrist taking 3 of the 10

"He will also enter the Beautiful Land, and many countries will fall; but these will be rescued out of his hand: Edom, Moab and the foremost of the sons of Ammon." *Daniel 11:41*

Notice that Daniel 11:41 predicts that Edom, Moab, and the chiefest part of Ammon will escape out of the Antichrist's hands. Apparently Gilead does not escape. That means in the near future a war will occur in which Israel will capture Gilead, the tip of Jordan, right under the Golan Heights and north of ancient Ammon and Moab.

After WWI the countries that made up the Muslim-ruled Ottoman Empire were recreated. Their borders were redrawn and governments put in place by the French and British under mandates given to them by the League of Nations. Later the countries were given their autonomy: Egypt in 1922; Turkey in 1923; Saudi Arabia in 1927; Syria in 1944; Lebanon in 1946; Jordan in 1946; and Israel in 1948.

"The broken horn and the four horns that arose in its place represent four kingdoms which will arise from his nation, although not with his power. In the latter period of their rule, when the transgressors have run their course, a king will arise, insolent and skilled in intrigue." *Daniel 8:22-23*

These ancient countries had to be recreated and given independence because the prophecy in Daniel 8:22-23 predicts that the four states that made up the ancient empire of Alexander the Great would be ruling independently in the last days. These four counties were Greece, Turkey, Syria, and Egypt. For details see the section on the Great Dispersion.

In the near future, probably during the fifth shepherd war, Lebanon and Gilead (northwestern Jordan) will be occupied by Israelis. The "fire feeding in Lebanon" could be referring to the 1982-2000 occupation or it could be a future event. Note: Israel still controls the Shebaa farms region, which lies at the border of Lebanon and the Golan.

"Thus says the LORD my God, 'Pasture the flock doomed to slaughter. Those who buy them slay them and go unpunished, and each of those who sell them says, "Blessed be the LORD, for I have become rich!" And their own shepherds have no pity on them. For I will no longer have pity on the inhabitants of the land,' declares the LORD; 'but behold, I will cause the men to fall, each into another's power and into the power of his king; and they will strike the land, and I will not deliver them from their power.' So I pastured the flock doomed to slaughter, hence the afflicted of the flock and I took for myself two staffs: the one I called Favor and the other I called Union; so I pastured the flock. Then I annihilated the three shepherds in one month, for my soul was impatient with them, and their soul also was weary of me. Then I said, 'I will not pasture you. What is to die, let it die, and what is to be annihilated, let it be annihilated; and let those who are left eat one another's flesh.' I took my staff Favor and cut it in pieces, to break my covenant which I had made with all the peoples." *Zechariah 11:4-10*

"'Moreover, I will deliver the Egyptians into the hand of a cruel master, and a mighty king will rule over them,' declares the Lord GOD of hosts. 'The waters from the sea will dry up, and the river will be parched and dry. The canals will emit a stench, the streams of Egypt will thin out and dry up; the reeds and rushes will rot away. The bulrushes by the Nile, by the edge of the Nile and all the sown fields by the Nile will become dry, be driven away, and be no more. And the fishermen will lament, and all those who cast a line into the Nile will mourn, and those who spread nets on the waters

Ancient Prophecies Revealed

will pine away. Moreover, the manufacturers of linen made from combed flax and the weavers of white cloth will be utterly dejected. And the pillars of Egypt will be crushed'" *Isaiah 19:4-10*

"And the LORD will utterly destroy the tongue of the Sea of Egypt; and He will wave His hand over the River with His scorching wind; and He will strike it into seven streams and make men walk over dry-shod." *Isaiah 11:15*

Zechariah 11:10b and 11:4-9 refer to the Antichrist conquering three nations of the ten-nation confederacy. One of those countries will be Egypt. At that time the Nile River will be dried up and plagues will begin. The drying up of the Nile is prophesied in Isaiah 19:4-10 & 11:15. Notice in Isaiah 19:4, this takes place after the Antichrist arises and attacks Egypt. This verse also states the Antichrist's attack will occur "after the scepter departs from Egypt" or after Egypt changes its government from a monarchy to a republic. This occurred in 1953 when the last king of Egypt, Farouk I, was deposed and Nasser took office, forming a republic. The Antichrist's attack on Egypt must take place sometime after 1953!

Isaiah 29:17 seems to indicate that Lebanon will be a fruitful field after the Second Coming. If this is true, it may be made desolate before that time.

"Is it not yet just a little while before Lebanon will be turned into a fertile field, and the fertile field will be considered as a forest?" *Isaiah 29:17*

Jordanian Cities
Ar
Kir
Dibon
Nebo
Medeba
Heshbon
Elealeh
Jahaz
Zoar
Eglath-shelishiyah
Horonaim
Waters of Nimrim
Eglaim
Beer-elim
Waters of Dimon

One interesting note is found in Isaiah 15, which talks about the destruction of "Moab." Some prophecy scholars think this was fulfilled long ago; others think it is yet future. If it *is* future, it could be connected to this Lebanese-Jordanian war. The problem with determining if this is past or future is that most of the names of the destroyed cities are not known to currently exist, nor is there any record of them existing in the past. There does not seem to be any ruins that would fit. If they were completely destroyed long ago we might never know about them.

The cities from Isaiah 15 are listed on the chart to the right. If this is a future destruction, then we should see new cities created in Jordan in the next few years with these names. These may be the Hebrew equivalent of the Arabic names, so some translations may apply.

Sephardic Jews Return

In 1948, at the time of the second return, the Muslims living in the Negev fled to Jordan. Those in the area of ancient Judah fled to the Gaza strip and the West Bank. At the same time, the newly created state of Israel was born in the ancient land of Judah. Obadiah writes the Benjaminites will posses ancient Gilead and Israel will control southern Lebanon up to Sarafand, which is between Tyre and Sidon. This will be the result of the Lebanese-Jordanian war. After this happens, the Sephardic Jews (the descendants of those 80,000 Jews exiled to Spain by the Romans) will return and populate the Negev desert. It has been estimated that to date there may be millions of Bnai Anusim that have yet to return to Israel. Notice Obadiah records this will take place during the time of the "saviors," which are the seven shepherds of Micah 5.

"For the day of the LORD is near upon all the heathen… they of the south [Negev] shall possess the mount of Esau [Petra]; and they of the plain the Philistines [Gaza strip]: and they shall possess the fields of Ephraim, and the fields of Samaria [West Bank]: and Benjamin shall possess Gilead. And the captivity of this host of the children of Israel shall possess that of the Canaanites, even unto Zarephath [Sarafand, Lebanon]; and the captivity of Jerusalem, which is in Sepharad [Spain], shall possess the cities of the south [Negev]. And saviours shall come up on mount Zion to judge the mount of Esau; and the kingdom shall be the LORD's." *Obadiah 15,19-21 KJV*

The trigger for the Lebanese-Jordanian war will probably be when Hezbollah terrorists attack from southern Lebanon with long range missiles that have accurate guidance systems. That would mean Hezbollah missiles will hit their targets most of the time. This will be an unacceptable risk to the nation of Israel. They will have to capture and permanently hold on to southern Lebanon for national security reasons. After this war Hezbollah will no longer be a problem for Israel. Prime Minister and shepherd, Ariel Sharon, started making plans before his stroke to settle the entire Negev desert for future Jews to migrate there. First, the problem of a need for more water must be solved. Many desalination plants have begun this quest from the Dead Sea and Mediterranean Sea. It is hoped that more settlements could begin by AD 2010 and by AD 2025 the complete settlement of the Negev would be finished. Then the Negev would bloom like a rose. Notice Obadiah 15 shows all this occurs before the Day of the Lord.

If your Spanish ancestors converted to Roman Catholicism all those centuries ago, then you know the truth about the Messiah. The Holy Spirit may be leading you to convert to Messianic Judaism and to begin plans for Aliyah, permanently settling in the land of Israel. You personally may be part of the fulfillment of this prophecy.

Destruction of Damascus, Syria

Isaiah said:
"The oracle concerning Damascus. Behold, Damascus is about to be removed from being a city, and will become a fallen ruin." *Isaiah 17:1*

Some have theorized that the destruction of Damascus, Syria, has already occurred. Tiglath-Pileser III of Assyria is said to have captured and destroyed the city about 732 BC. It lost its independence for hundreds of years, until it was restored in 537 BC when the Persians, under Cyrus, captured the city and made it the capital of the Persian province of Syria. The problem with that view is that Damascus did not permanently "cease from being a city" in 732 BC. Obviously, Damascus is still here today and is the capital of the modern nation of Syria. So I believe Damascus will be destroyed during the sixth war Israel has with Syria. The result of the sixth Shepherd War will cause Russia to attack Israel. This is known as the Gog-Magog War. Ezekiel gives us this clue by saying the Gog-Magog war is triggered by the nation of Israel just returning from a small war. If Russia has a military pact with Syria, and Syria's capital is wiped out, that would definitely cause Russia to respond. Of Russia, Ezekiel says:

"In the distant future you will swoop down on the land of Israel, which will be enjoying peace after recovering from war..." *Ezekiel 38:8 NLT*

First Gog-Magog War

We have traced the Roman Empire through these prophesied stages:
- The fall of the old Roman Empire in AD 476.
- The rise of Papal Rome and the Holy Roman Empire.
- The last of the Caesars intermingling with the Czars of Russia.
- The end of the remnant of the Holy Roman Empire under the Kaisers by 1917.
- The demise of the Czars in Russia by 1917.
- The rise and fall of Germany, which set up the return of the nation of Israel.
- Germany split in two and half swallowed up by Russia in 1945.

The time between 1945 and 1989 was called the Cold War and is referred to in Ezekiel 38. Russia prepared itself by swallowing up – not only East Germany – but many nations

Against Israel	
Rosh	Russia
Meshech	Moscow / Scythians
Tubal	Tobolsk
Magog	Southern Russian states
Gog	Ruler of Russia
Persia	Iran
Cush	Sudan / Ethiopia
Put	Libya
Gomer	Germany
Togarmah	Balkan states
Uppermost North	Russia
Neutral or for Israel	
Sheba & Dedan	Saudi Arabia
Tarshish	Britain
Young lions	USA, Canada, South Africa, poss Spain

Ancient Prophecies Revealed

with her. Using those resources, Russia became the third superpower, next to the USA and China.

> "Be prepared, and prepare yourself, you and all your companies that are assembled about you, and be a guard for them. After many days you will be summoned;" *Ezekiel 38:7*

In 1989 Russia appeared to be broken, and the Berlin Wall came down. This allowed Germany, called "Gomer" in Ezekiel 38:6, to come back together with all of her bands. It also allowed the states previously held by Russia to gain their freedom. Now the stage is set for Russia –with Germany and her other *allies* – not slave states, to attack Israel.

To understand this war, we need to see the big picture. Ezekiel 39 shows the outline of events and chapter 38 shows the details.

Ezekiel 39:1-8
Notice in 39:1-8 we see in order: the Gog-Magog invasion, the Lord destroys most of the invaders, while one sixth of them survive and return to their countries to fight again another day, followed by the Day of the Lord. Revelation 20 shows another Gog-Magog war will occur at the end of the millennium.

Ezekiel 39:9-29
Then in 39:9-29 we are given another order: after the Gog-Magog war, Israel will burn the weapons of the fallen troups for fuel for seven years, then the Lord's sacrifice occurs (where the birds eat the flesh of the invaders). This would refer to Armageddon. Then the gathering occurs. This is at the time of the Second Coming (see Matthew 24), then the millennial reign where the Lord no longer hides his face (see 1 Corinthians 13).

Isaiah 66:15-19 states after the fire judgment, where God destroys five sixths of the Gog-Magog invaders, the survivors flee to Tarshish (Great Britain), Meshak and Tubal (Russia), Put (Libya), Lud (Lydia and Media), and Javan (Greece).

Ezekiel 38:1-13
As seen above, Ezekiel 38:7-8a has already been fulfilled. In Febuary of 2005, Iran (ancient Persia) *for the first time ever* established ties with Russia and signed a mutual defense pact. So, the Gog-Magog invasion will occur sometime after AD 2005! Israel will be dwelling in safety with her villages unwalled. This is in

Sections of the Gog-Magog Prophecy	
38:1-6	List of nations against Israel
38:7-8a	1945-1989
	2005 Russian/Persian alliance formed
38:8b-9	Invasion when they "dwell in safety"
38:10-12	Unwalled villages – 21st century (Zech 2)
38:13	List of nations for/neutral toward Israel
38:14-15	God is glorified through this
38:17	The one prophesied (Antichrist) comes
38:18-23	God's wrath of hailfire, brimstone, sword against themselves, great earthquake in Israel
39:2	1/6 left alive to fight again (KJV)
39:3-8	Invaders & coastlands destroyed by fire, birds eat flesh – this is the "day" the Lord spoke of
39:9-10	Israel burns weapons for 7 years - Tribulation
39:11-16	7 months burying the dead
39:17-20	Birds eat the Lord's sacrifice - Armageddon
39:26	Gathering after the Second Coming
39:29	Lord no longer hides his face – 1000 years

reference to the prophecy in Zechariah 3 of Jerusalem growing beyond her own walls, which was fulfilled by the end of the twentieth century. When the invasion occurs, Britain (Tarshish), with its cubs (or the nations she founded) including the USA, South Africa, and others, who are allies of Israel now, will somehow be neutralized. They will not help her, but simply say to Russia "you shouldn't do that." After this war the "one prophesied of old," the Antichrist, appears on the scene and God's wrath is poured out (compare this to the sixth trumpet of Revelation).

To pull all of this together: we have the Gog-Magog invasion when God supernaturally destroys five sixths of the attacking nations, leaving one sixth to return to their respective homelands. Then the Antichrist will arise and the seven-year

Gog-Magog War	Armageddon
1. Starts a seven year period	1. Ends a seven year period
2. Some nations are for Israel	2. All nations are against Israel
3. The purpose is to take spoil	3. The purpose is to annihilate the Jews
4. 5/6 of the attackers are destroyed by fire	4. All attackers destroyed by the Lord
5. Israel dwelling in safety in their land	5. Israel has fled and is in hiding (Petra)

Tribulation will begin, including God's wrath, then the Second Coming will occur with the gathering, and the Thousand-Year Reign of Jesus Christ. This chart shows five contrasting points that prove the Gog-Magog war could not be the battle of Armageddon.

Future Events – Post 2008

Ezekiel 37 - Fulfilled	Ezekiel 37 - Unfulfilled
Nation of Israel established in their land	Reestablishing of the ordnances
No more idols	Accept the Messiah
Majority of Jews in Israel - 2004	Messiah reigns over them forevermore.

Ezekiel 37 gives us more information. The scattered bones represent the great 1816-year dispersion of the Jewish people from AD 132-1948. The whole house of Israel came back into their land as one nation, without idols in 1948. Currently, they have no breath in them, or in other words, they have not accepted Jesus as their Messiah. By the year AD 2004, there were more Jews in the nation of Israel than any other country and the Sanhedrin was reestablished. The Sanhedrin will bring about the return of the religious ordnances in the near future.

Ancient Prophecies Revealed

Ten Kingdoms Arise

Daniel predicts that ten nations will arise out of what was once the old Roman Empire. The map on the right shows the extent of that Empire. The first thing we need to do is list the names of those nations that now exist where the Roman Empire was. That list of 49 nations is given below.

Since the 10 nations hate the whore (the apostate church) they may be Muslim (Shiites and Sunnis who do not hold together, see Dan. 2:41). Therefore it seems likely that ten Muslim states will turn against the apostate Christian church after they rise to power. They will then give that kingdom to the Antichrist.

49 Modern Nations
Greece, Turkey, Syria, Egypt

European
Portugal, Spain
United Kingdom
France, Monaco
Luxembourg
Belgium, Andorra
Netherlands
Switzerland
Liechtenstein
Italy, San Marino
Vatican City
Malta,

Russian states
Slovenia, Croatia
Bosnia-Herzegovina
Hungary, Serbia,
Montenegro,
Albania, Azerbaijan,
FYR Macedonia
Romania, Bulgaria
Georgia, Armenia,

Middle East
Iraq, Kuwait, Cyprus,
Lebanon, Jordan,
Israel, *West Bank,*
Gaza Strip

African
Tunisia, Libya

Small Parts of:
Germany, Austria
Czech Republic
Slovakia,
Saudi Arabia
Sudan

- Daniel 11:41 predicts that Jordan (ancient Moab, Amman, and Edom) will escape out of the Antichrist's hand. Therefore Jordan *will not* be one of the ten nations.
- Daniel 8:22-23 predicts that the four nations that broke out of what was the Grecian Empire, under Alexander the Great, will be ruling in the last days. Therefore Greece, Turkey, Syria, and Egypt *will* be part of the ten nations.
- Daniel 11:38 predicts Egypt will be attacked by the Antichrist. Therefore, Egypt must be one of the three nations he destroys.
- If the nations that attack Israel in the Ezekiel 38 Gog-Magog war only have one sixth survivors, then they will not have enough manpower to be one of the ten ruling nations. Therefore, Russia (Moscow & Tubolsk, or Siberia), the Southern Russian states (the Stans), Iran, Germany, Sudan/Ethiopia, Libya, and the Balkan states (non-Turkey Togarmah) could not be a part of the ten nations.
- Daniel 11:45 predicts the Antichrist will set his royal palace "between the seas and the holy mountain" (the Sea of Galilee, Mediterranean Sea, and Mount Moriah, where Jerusalem sits). Today this area is called the West Bank. By then it will become a sovereign state.
- Ezekiel 38 predicts Saudi Arabia (ancient Sheba and Dedan) will side with Jordan and Britain (Tarshish) and the nations spawned by Britain (cubs of Tarshish). Therefore, Saudi Arabia is not one of the nations destroyed in the Gog-Magog invasion. It *could* be one of the ten nations.
- If one of the three nations the Antichrist destroys is NE of Israel, then Syria or Iraq or both may be part of the ten nations.
- The Antichrist claims to be God incarnate, which is blasphemy in most Muslim theologies. The exception is Syrian Islam, called Alawis, which teaches the Imams were incarnations of Allah. Therefore Syria could gladly accept the Antichrist, whether he is from Syria or not. Syria is most likely *not* a nation attacked by the Antichrist.

Antichrist attacks
1. Egypt
2. ?
3. ?

11 Nations/Horns
1. Egypt
2. Greece
3. Turkey
4. Syria
5. ?
6. ?
7. ?
8. ?
9. ?
10. ?
11. West Bank

Using the information above, we can deduce two theories.
1. The ten nations are a combination of European and Middle East nations
2. The ten nations are all Middle East nations

We know Greece, Turkey, Syria, and a yet-to-be-created West Bank State will be under the control of the Antichrist.

Future Events – Post 2008

Listed on the previous page are the charts listing what we know to be three of the ten nations that the Antichrist attacks and the 11 nations (the ten nations plus the nation that the Antichrist comes from).

Miscellaneous Points

In this section we will deal with a few minor points that I believe will occur before the Tribulation period.

Increased Understanding of Prophecies
The knowledge of God and the understanding of prophecies will increase in the last days. See Dan 12:4 and Isaiah 11:9. The more prophecies we see fulfilled, the more we will know about all of them as a whole.

> "But as for you, Daniel, conceal these words and seal up the book until the end of time; many will go back and forth, and knowledge will increase." *Daniel 12:4*

Ancient church father Irenaeus understood Daniel to mean that after the second return of the Jewish people to Israel all the prophecies would begin to be understood. His version of Daniel 12:4 reads this way:

> "Daniel the prophet says 'Shut up the words, and seal the book even to the time of consummation, until many learn, and knowledge be completed. For at that time, when the dispersion shall be accomplished, they shall know all these things.'" *Irenaeus Against Heresies 4.26*

Children Rebellious and Society Materialistic
> "Brother will betray brother to death, and a father his child; and children will rise up against parents and have them put to death." *Mark 13:12*

> "For men will be lovers of self, lovers of money, boastful, arrogant, revilers, disobedient to parents, ungrateful, unholy, unloving, irreconcilable, malicious gossips, without self-control, brutal, haters of good" *1 Timothy 3:2-3*

> "End times will manifest: abortion, euthanasia, children carrying weapons, winter and summer will be confused, years months and days will be shortened," *Lactantius Epitome of Divine Institutes 71*

Words of Jesus Will Never be Forgotten
Jesus' words will never pass away and God's word will endure forever.

> "Heaven and earth will pass away, but My words will not pass away." *Luke 21:33*

> "'BUT THE WORD OF THE LORD ENDURES FOREVER' And this is the word which was preached to you." *1 Peter 1:25*

Jesus says, in Matthew 24, "let the reader understand." From this one phrase we can see the words of Jesus would be written down (this formed the basis for the New Testament). During the Tribulation, when the Antichrist is in power, Israelis will be literate and have Jesus' words (the New Testament) in their native language of Hebrew.

> "Therefore when you see the ABOMINATION OF DESOLATION which was spoken of through Daniel the prophet, standing in the holy place (let the reader understand)…" *Matthew 24:15*

Christians Hated for Jesus' Name Sake
We have already seen the banning of public prayer, nativities, the Ten Commandments, etc. Many Christians are martyred every year in many countries. See Revelation 6:9-11; 20:4.

Ancient Prophecies Revealed

"and you will be hated by all because of My name." Luke 21:17

"When the Lamb broke the fifth seal, I saw underneath the altar the souls of those who had been slain because of the word of God, and because of the testimony which they had maintained; and they cried out with a loud voice, saying, 'How long, O Lord, holy and true, will You refrain from judging and avenging our blood on those who dwell on the earth?' And there was given to each of them a white robe; and they were told that they should rest for a little while longer, until the number of their fellow servants and their brethren who were to be killed even as they had been, would be completed also." *Revelation 6:9-11*

"Then I saw thrones, and they sat on them, and judgment was given to them. And I saw the souls of those who had been beheaded because of their testimony of Jesus and because of the word of God, and those who had not worshiped the beast or his image, and had not received the mark on their forehead and on their hand; and they came to life and reigned with Christ for a thousand years." *Revelation 20:4*

The Birth Pangs

Before the Tribulation – 12 prophecies

The Birth Pangs	References
375. Many false Christs will come	Matt. 24:4
376. Wars and rumors of wars will occur	Matt. 24:6
377. Famines, earthquakes, pestilences will occur	Matt. 24:7
378. Plagues will be widespread	Luke 21:11
379. Fearful events and signs from heaven will be seen	Luke 21:11
380. Religious persecution will occur	Matt. 24:9
381. Discord among churches	Matt. 24:10
382. The falling away will occur	Matt. 24:10
383. False prophets will arise	Matt. 24:11
384. Lawlessness will increase	Matt. 24:12
385. The love of many will grow cold	Matt. 24:12
386. Severe ocean activity will occur – hurricanes	Luke 21:25; Jer. 25:32

In Matthew 24, Luke 21, and Mark 13, Jesus lists the "birth pangs." The KJV calls it the "beginning of sorrows." Jesus is referring to the signs that occur before the end of time.

In Matthew 24 He mentions the beginning of the end starts with the "abomination of desolation" being set up. Before this are the birth pangs. These occur over time and are in full swing before the middle of the seven-year tribulation.

"You will be hearing of wars and rumors of wars. See that you are not frightened, for those things must take place, but that is not yet the end. For nation will rise against nation, and kingdom against kingdom, and in various places there will be famines and earthquakes. But all these things are merely the beginning of **birth pangs**." *Matthew 24:6-8*

We don't know all the details to these prophecies. These begin before the seven-year Tribulation starts, and continue during its first half. Jesus adds that the "gospel will be preached to all nations." We have this added in the chart of the first 3.5 years of the Tribulation. Today Christianity is divided into over 158 denominations so we definitely have discord among the churches!

Hurricane Judgments We Should Expect
Towards the end time we should expect earthquakes, hurricanes and tsunamis. The waves of the sea will become very unpredictable.

> "There will be signs in sun and moon and stars, and on the earth dismay among nations, in perplexity at the roaring of the sea and the waves, men fainting from fear and the expectation of the things which are coming upon the world; for the powers of the heavens will be shaken." *Luke 21:25-26*

In Jeremiah we are told one of the major judgments from God will be a huge hurricane that bounces from cost to cost destroying whole cities. This seems to take place during the tribulation, but may begin before the start of the seven years. This gives us reason to believe that hurricanes today may be small judgments of God for how nations treat Israel. This judgment may occur when the angels stop holding back the four winds after the 144,000 have been sealed. If this huge hurricane makes it impossible to navigate the ocean (or even fly over it), it could explain why Israel's allies do nothing during the Gog-Magog invasion of Israel.

> "And all the mingled people, and all the kings of the land of Uz, and all the kings of the land of the Philistines, and Ashkelon, and Azzah, and Ekron, and the remnant of Ashdod, Edom, and Moab, and the children of Ammon, and all the kings of Tyrus, and all the kings of Zidon, and the kings of the isles which are beyond the sea, Dedan, and Tema, and Buz, and all that are in the utmost corners, And all the kings of Arabia, and all the kings of the mingled people that dwell in the desert, And all the kings of Zimri, and all the kings of Elam, and all the kings of the Medes, and all the kings of the north, far and near, one with another, and all the kingdoms of the world, which are upon the face of the earth: and the king of Sheshach shall drink after them… Thus saith the LORD of hosts, behold, evil shall go forth from nation to nation, and a ***great whirlwind*** shall be raised up from the coasts of the earth. And the slain of the LORD shall be at that day from one end of the earth even unto the other end of the earth: they shall not be lamented, neither gathered, nor buried; they shall be dung upon the ground." *Jeremiah 25:20-26,32-33*

Jewish Version of the Birth Pangs
The Talmud, the official writings of the Jews from AD 800, records the Jewish version of what the birth pangs will entail. Remember this is from apostate Jews who have rejected Jesus as the true Messiah.

Talmud Sanhedrin 97b gives ten signs that are called the birth-pangs of the Messiah. These are supposed to occur before the Gog-Magog War and the coming of the Messiah.

- The world will be in a state of complete degradation
- Truth will decrease and lies will prevail
- Inflation will be out of control
- The Jews will return to their biblical homeland and the desert will bloom
- There will be fewer and fewer wise and righteous people
- Many Jews will give up the hope of redemption
- The young will treat the old with disrespect
- Learning will be rejected because people will desire a life of ease.
- The whole world will turn against Israel
- The Jews will fight each other (the secular against religious)

Ancient Prophecies Revealed

The Apostasy of the Church

AD 32-Present
Seven Church Ages

יהושע ה נצרי

Yehshua Ha Natzari

Joshua My Branch

Jesus the Nazarene

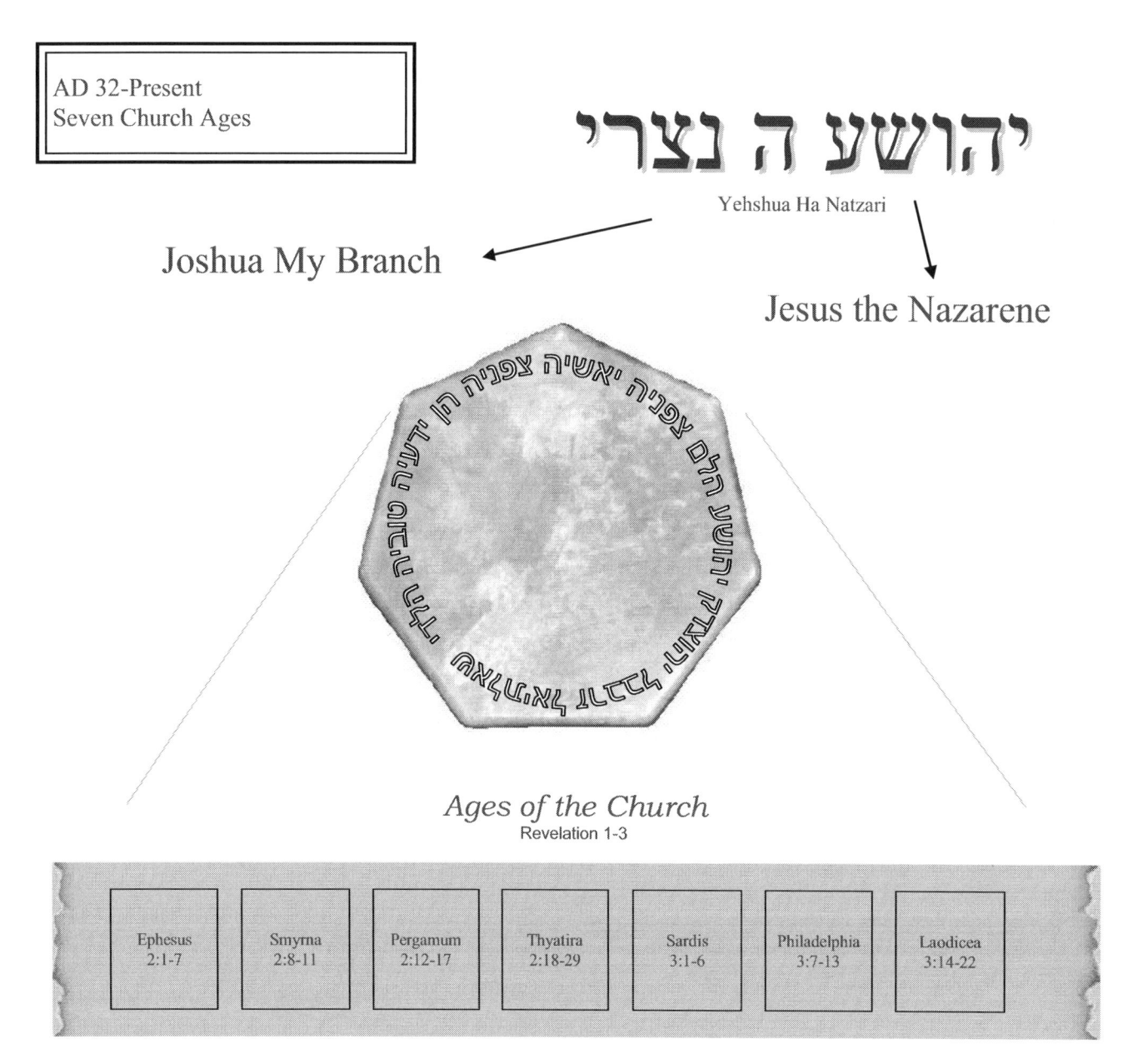

Ages of the Church
Revelation 1-3

| Ephesus 2:1-7 | Smyrna 2:8-11 | Pergamum 2:12-17 | Thyatira 2:18-29 | Sardis 3:1-6 | Philadelphia 3:7-13 | Laodicea 3:14-22 |

Introduction:
In this section we will look at both the teachings of Scripture and the Ancient Church Fathers to see exactly how prophecies describe the apostasy of the church toward the end of the church age. At the end of this section we will compile all the information into a master list so we can see what is still to come.

We begin the church age by looking at this amazing prophecy from Zechariah 3:8-10. Here Joshua the high priest is made to play the part of the Messiah. His name is Joshua, or Yehshua, which translated through the Greek into English, becomes

Apostasy of the Church

Jesus. God also calls him "my branch." One of the Hebrew words for branch is "Nazar" and the Hebrew way of saying *my branch* would be "Nazari." So his full title is "Jesus the Nazarene." This is the prophecy referred to in Matthew 2:23 that says Jesus would be called a Nazarene. In this first part, the prophecy pictures the First Coming of Jesus. Verse 10 refers to the millennial reign where everyone knows the Messiah and sits under his own fig tree. So between the First and Second Comings of the Messiah, we see Jesus of Nazareth sitting on a throne. In front of him is a seven-sided stone with an inscription engraved on it. If we read the inscription, we will know what the stone represents. But how do we find the inscription so that we can read it?

"'Now listen, Joshua the high priest, you and your friends who are sitting in front of you--indeed they are men who are a **symbol**, for behold, I am going to bring in My servant the Branch. For behold, the stone that I have set before Joshua; on one stone are seven eyes. Behold, I will engrave an **inscription** on it,' declares the LORD of hosts, 'and I will remove the iniquity of that land in one day. In that day,' declares the LORD of hosts, 'every one of you will invite his neighbor to sit under his vine and under his fig tree.'" *Zechariah 3:8-10*

The prophet expects the reader to connect the fact that Joshua and his friends (more than one) are collectively, the symbol. This symbol somehow is the inscription. So first we must discover the number of people who are included in the friends of Joshua. We know that Zerubbabel is one friend. Then Zechariah declares that a total of *seven* people are the friends of Zerubbabel and will be glad to see him complete the construction of the Second Temple.

"The hands of Zerubbabel have laid the foundation of this house, and his hands will finish it. Then you will know that the LORD of hosts has sent me to you. For who has despised the day of small things? But these **seven** will be glad when they see the plumb line in the hand of Zerubbabel--these are the eyes of the LORD which range to and fro throughout the earth." *Zechariah 4:9-10*

So if Joshua has seven friends and Zerubbabel is one of them, we need to find the other six friends. Then we must figure out how they are "the symbol." It is interesting to note that in Zechariah 6:9-15 exactly *six* other returnees are mentioned by name. No others are mentioned in the entire book of Zechariah. Zechariah also tells us that the Messiah will be a king-priest, or a Melchizedekian priest.

"The word of the LORD also came to me, saying, 'Take an offering from the exiles, from **Heldai**, **Tobijah** and **Jedaiah**; and you go the same day and enter the house of **Josiah** the **son of Zephaniah**, where they have arrived from Babylon. Take silver and gold, make an ornate crown and set it on the head of **Joshua** the **son of Jehozadak**, the high priest.' Then say to him, 'Thus says the LORD of hosts, Behold, a man whose name is **Branch**, for He will branch out from where He is; and He will build the temple of the LORD. Yes, it is He who will build the temple of the LORD, and He who will bear the honor and sit and rule on His throne. Thus, He will be a priest on His throne, and the counsel of peace will be between the two offices.' Now the crown will become a reminder in the temple of the LORD to **Helem**, Tobijah, Jedaiah and **Hen** the **son of Zephaniah**. Those who are far off will come and build the temple of the LORD. Then you will know that the LORD of hosts has sent me to you. And it will take place if you completely obey the LORD your God." *Zechariah 6:9-15*

Since we know nothing about the seven friends except their names, we must conclude that their *names* are the inscription. Their names, in the order they are found, form a sentence in Hebrew. This sentence is the inscription written on the stone. Some Hebrew words can have more than one meaning, so it is important that we get the right meaning in order to properly understand the inscription. Provided here are the names in order, in English and Hebrew, then their meanings, so one can double check this in Strong's or another Hebrew lexicon. Finally, you can read the complete inscription.

Ancient Prophecies Revealed

English:	Heldi	Tobijah	Jedaiah	Hen	Zephaniah	Josiah	Zephaniah	Helem	Joshua	Jehozedek	Zerubabbal	Shialtiel
Hebrew:	הלדי	טוביה	ידעיה	הן	צפניה	יאשיה	צפניה	הלם	יהושע	יהוצדק	זרבבל	שאלתיאל
Strong's:	age	good	news	grace	Yahweh prepared	foundation	Yahweh has hidden	pierced one	salvation	cleanses	The Lord overflows or infills	God's charge laid up
Inscription:	Yahweh has prepared the age of the Gospel (good news) of grace, hidden from the foundation of the world, that by the pierced one's salvation, we should be cleansed from the charge God laid up against us and infilled with the Lord's (spirit).											

Note, we have added Zerubabbal's last name. We did not know that his last name was Shialtiel. It is not given in the book of Zechariah, but we find it in the second chapter of the book of Haggai. We can see, then, that the seven-sided stone represents the church age. But why is it divided into seven sections? Because the church age, itself, will be divided into seven periods of time. This information was hidden until the Apostle John wrote Revelation chapters two and three.

The seven churches of Revelation are indeed seven literal churches. Their problems were problems we need to identify in our churches today. We can find representatives of each church in our world today. But these also show a pattern for seven ages of church history. In the early days of the church, cultic groups, called Gnostics, brought errors into the church. Revelation 2 and 3 will explain what the major problems were in each age of the church. Using these two chapters and the church fathers, we will build a list of errors that the apostate church will accept toward the end of the church age. We will then add to that list what Paul and John says, in the New Testament, will be errors in the last days. This will give us a master chart of 101 points.

Ages of the Church

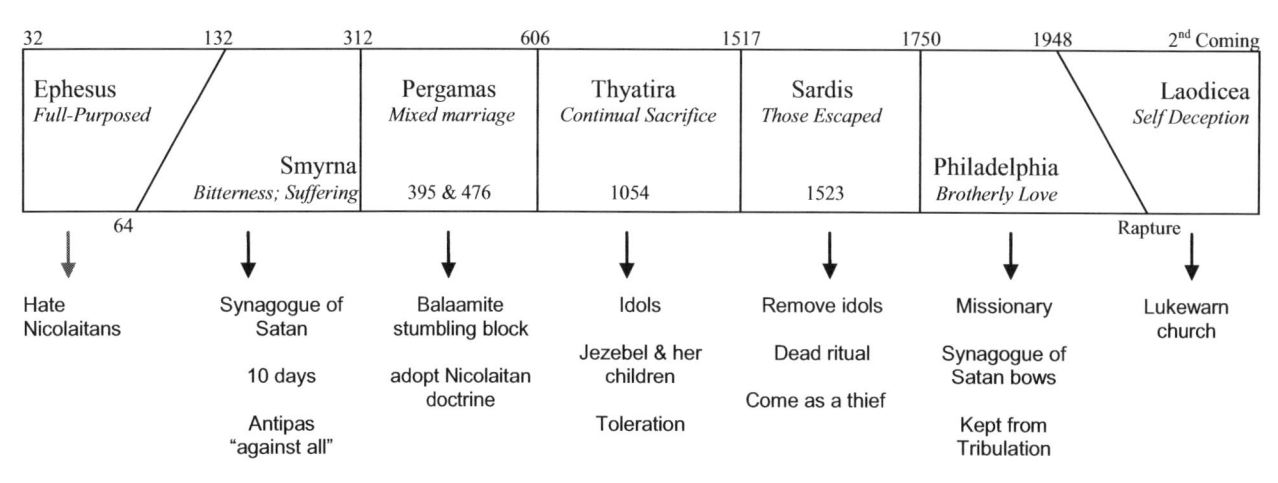

32	132	312	606	1517	1750	1948	2nd Coming
Ephesus *Full-Purposed*	Smyrna *Bitterness; Suffering* (64)	Pergamas *Mixed marriage* 395 & 476	Thyatira *Continual Sacrifice* 1054	Sardis *Those Escaped* 1523	Philadelphia *Brotherly Love*		Laodicea *Self Deception* Rapture

| Hate Nicolaitans | Synagogue of Satan 10 days Antipas "against all" | Balaamite stumbling block adopt Nicolaitan doctrine | Idols Jezebel & her children Toleration | Remove idols Dead ritual Come as a thief | Missionary Synagogue of Satan bows Kept from Tribulation | Lukewarm church |

The chart above shows the seven churches from the second and third chapters of the book of Revelation. Each church age is listed by name with the Greek meaning listed under the name in *italics*. The dates are also given showing when that age of the church took place. The heresies of each age are listed underneath so we can begin to see the major points of the apostasy as they happened.

Please carefully study Revelation chapters two and three. The first thing we want to notice is Antipas is the faithful servant of God in Smyrna. The word "Antipas" is made up of two Greek words, "anti" meaning "against" and "pas" meaning "all." So Antipas reminds us that a faithful servant of God will be against *all* the heresies mentioned in the seven churches. We will list these as the major points of the apostasy of the church. Lets look at each problem one by one.

Apostasy of the Church

AD 32 Ephesus – The Nicolaitans

This is the apostolic age of the church dating from its creation in AD 32 through the death of the apostle John in AD 120. It concluded at the Bar Kokhba rebellion in 132. Notice this age overlaps with the second age and corresponds to the First Crossover Period. The First Crossover Period is the period of the church age when Israel still existed as a nation. This spans the time between AD 32 and AD 132.

Nicolaitan Error
Fornication
Adultery
Homosexuality
Chambering
Weekly confession
Participate in Pagan rituals
Christian demon possession
Use of Idols
Tolerance/Ecumenicism

The Ephesus church hated the Nicolaitans and got rid of the false apostles who started the Gnostic cults, but in the process they lost their first love. It is important for the church to be intolerant of sin and hunt down and excommunicate heretics; but other things are equally important. The church fathers teach Nicolaitan characteristics include: fornication (both heterosexual and homosexual) practiced, then forgiven in a confession ritual on a weekly basis (on the eighth day). Nicolaitans used idols and participated in pagan rituals, which also means they tolerated ungodly things. The idea that food had to be exorcised before it was eaten was based on the idea that a Christian could be demon possessed. They taught they had a special way of exorcizing meat offered to idols so that if a Christian ate it they would not become demon-possessed. In other words, they believed Christains could be possessed by demons, which is an error.

> "This sect took its name after Nicolas one of the seven deacons of Acts (although Nicolas had nothing to do with them). Influenced by the Gnostics they began practicing adultery and eating meat offered to idols in order to prove they had conquered their flesh." *Eusebieus 3.29; Ireneaus, Against All Heresies, 3:11*

> "The works of the Nicolaitans were in that time false and troublesome men, who, as ministers under the name of Nicolas, had made for themselves a heresy, to the effect that what had been offered to idols might be exorcised and eaten, and that whoever should have committed fornication might receive peace on the eighth day."
> *Victorinus Commentary on the Apocalypse 2.6*

AD 64 Smyrna – The Synagogue of Satan

This second age dates from AD 64 to AD 312. Notice this time period overlaps with the first church age, the time of the apostles. Smyrna would be under persecution ten days (or periods of time). This predicts that in the second church age there would be ten major persecutions. These are listed on the next page, for your convenience. This proves the Smyrnan age existed from AD 64 to 312. Therefore, the Ephesian age overlapped it, spanning from AD 32 to 132. So what was the Synagogue of Satan? You might be surprised to find out there are two types of the Synagogue of Satan. They are the ones that "say they are Jews but are not." The Synagogue of Satan always tries to say that the church has replaced Israel. This was done in two ways.

Ten Persecutions	
1.	Nero 64-68
2.	Domitian 95-96
3.	Trajan 100-115
4.	Aurelius 168-177
5.	Severus 203-210
6.	Maxinin 235-237
7.	Decius 250-255
8.	Valerian 257-260
9.	Aurelian 276
10.	Diocletian 303-310

Judaizing Christians – Legalism/Ebionites

The Judaizers said that since the church has replaced Israel, the church has to observe the Mosaic Law. We call this "legalism" or "Judaising." This type insisted that believers must be circumcised, not eat pork, and keep the Sabbath. Paul, in Titus 1:10-11, stated that people who teach this kind of theology "must be silenced!" These are the ones that forced the formation of the first Jerusalem Council, recorded in Acts 15, to create a decree that the Mosaic Law has nothing to do with salvation.

Replacement Theology

By the third century the Jewish form of legalism had long vanished. All that was left was Replacement Theology. The church began to think they did not have to observe the Mosaic Law, but since it had replaced Israel, it inherited all of her blessings. The prophecies that would have been fulfilled by Israel were now thought to be fulfilled by the church. If it was not possible for the church to fulfill the prophecies, then they were spiritualized away. This doctrine denies that God would bring Israel back in the last days and completely opposes the pre-millennial teaching of the First and Second Century Church Fathers. See Pergamos below for a full discussion on Amillennialism.

Ancient Prophecies Revealed

Ebionites

After the Jerusalem Council, in Acts 15, some broke away refusing to accept the resolution of the council. They claimed Jesus was Messiah, but taught the following: (Eusebius' Church History, 6:17 and Ireneaus' Against All Heresies, 1:26, 3:11, & 5:1)

1. Denied the divinity and virgin birth of Jesus. Taught Mary and Joseph were Jesus' physical parents.
2. Jesus was not the Son of God.
3. Observance of the ceremonial law was altogether necessary for salvation.
4. One couldn't be saved by faith in Christ alone.
5. Practiced circumcision, and observed the Law of Moses, and the Judaic style of life.
6. Refused to acknowledge that Jesus pre-existed.
7. Strictly observed all the points of the Mosaic Law.
8. Reproached Christians for eating unclean meats.
9. They used only the so-called Gospel according to the Hebrews (some say the Hebrew version of Matthew). Rarely made use of the other Gospels.
10. Rejected all the Epistles of the apostle Paul, whom they called an apostate from the law.
11. Stated Isaiah's prophecy that a "virgin" would conceive should be translated "young woman."

Synagogue of Satan
Jesus not God
Jesus not Son of God
Jesus not virgin born
Salvation by good works
Must keep Sabbath
Must keep food laws
Must be circumcised
Reject some Scripture
Vegetarianism
Church Replaced Israel
Baptismal Regeneration
Oaths of poverty

The Apostle John would not even enter a bathhouse when the Gnostic Cerinthus was inside because Cerinthus taught Jesus was just a man, born of Joseph and Mary. (Ireneaus' Against All Heresies, 3:11) Eusebius says their doctrines were spawned by evil demons. Those who believe Ebionite doctrine are not Christians. Ignatius, in Smyraeans 7, said those who don't believe the Passover refers to Jesus' death on the cross are not Christians and we should not even speak to them.

A subgroup developed that added these doctrines to the above:
1. Did not deny that the Lord was born of a virgin and of the Holy Spirit, but they did deny the divinity of Jesus.
2. They observed the Sabbath and the rest of the Jewish lifestyle, but also celebrated the Lord's Day as a memorial of the Resurrection of the Savior.
3. Some also practiced oaths of poverty and vegetarianism.

Later a full Gnostic sect developed that: (Ireneaus' Against All Heresies, 1:26, 3:11, & 5:1 and the Pseudo-Clementines)
1. Rejected any distinction between Jehovah the Demiurge, and the supreme good God.
2. Taught matter is eternal, and an emanation of the Deity
3. Taught the Son of God or Christ is a middle-being between God and creation, not a creature, yet not equal to, nor even to be compared with, the Father
4. Taught that man is saved by knowledge (gnosis), by believing in God the Teacher, and by being baptized unto remission of sins.
5. This system is Pantheism, Persian Dualism, Judaism, and Christianity fused together.

Tertullian states the founder of the Ebionite sect was named Ebion. Epipanius traces their origin to the Christians who fled to Pella after the destruction of the Temple at Jerusalem in 69-70AD. He also adds that some of them held the belief that Adam was an incarnation of Jesus. Ebionites were found all over Israel and the surrounding region, Cyprus, Asia Minor and even a far away as Rome. Ebionites seemed to have died out about the fifth century. In reaction to these kinds of Gnostics the Third and Fourth Century Church Fathers (early catholic fathers) fully developed "Replacement Theology" which completely goes against the pre-millennial teachings of the First and Second Century Fathers.

The following references list the sources from where we get our information on the Ebionites:
1. Irenaeus Against Heresies 1.26
2. Irenaeus Against Heresies 4.21
3. Irenaeus Against Heresies 5.1
4. Tertullian Against Marcion 1.33
5. Hippolytus Against Heresies 7.22
6. Origen Comm. Matthew 6.12
7. Origen Cel. 5.61
8. Origen Cel. 5.65
9. Irenaeus Against Heresies 3.11

Apostasy of the Church

AD 312 Pergamos – Balaam's Stumbling Block
Balak promised gold to Balaam if he cursed Israel. God would not curse Israel. So Balaam devised a plan to get the Moabite women to seduce the Israeli men with their religious prostitution. In this way God would be angered and have to curse Israel because of idolatry. It's not *what* Balaam did (manipulation) or *why* he did it (greed) that is the point here, but *how* he did it. Balaam did whatever it took to get the job done. That attitude of "whatever it takes," operated under the idea of "anything for the sake of unity." Today this is manifested as ecumenicism. This attitude will allow *anything*, including paganism, into the church to stop division. In this and the next period, paganism crept into the church. Examples are Halloween/all soul's day, elves at Christmas, rabbits and eggs at Easter.

If Satan planned to corrupt the church, three things had to become a reality before true Christians would allow that to happen. First, pre-millennialism would have to be replaced by amillennialism so that the warning about the harlot church would be thought of as events long since passed into history. Second, the church would have to teach that the gifts of the Spirit had ceased, otherwise true prophets would turn the people back to following the Bible alone. But now a *true* prophet would be simply regarded as a demonic *false* prophet. Third, Christians were taught not to read the Scripture for themselves, but rely on priests to interpret it for them. Church "tradition" now became equal with the teaching of Scripture. These changes were done deliberately to create a church-state religion and these three changes are Balaam's stumbling block.

In this period of church history, churches also started accepting Nicolaitan doctrine, which consisted of pieces of Gnostic doctrine with the extreme paganism removed. We will see the in-depth explanation from the ancient church fathers in the next section on Thyatira. So with the false doctrines of amillennialism, cessationism (the teaching that spiritual gifts ceased), and papal authority (tradition on par with Scripture) firmly in place, the medieval church was free to slide further into apostasy. Let's look at each one of these in detail and see exactly how this happened.

Balaam's Stumbling Block
Amillennialism
Cessationism
Forsaking the Scripture
Man-made Tradition
Papal Authority
Halloween
Ecumenicism

Amillennialism
The doctrine called Amillennialism began to be taught in the early fourth century. Amillennialism teaches that the millennium, or 1000-year-reign of Christ, is symbolic of the church age itself. The "1000 years" started with Christ and continues today. The change from pre-millennialism to amillennialism took place in what was called the Schism of Nepos. First, let's look at what the early church fathers taught; then we can see how it was twisted.

Church Fathers on the End Times
The Church Fathers taught pre-millennialism in the first three centuries. Here are the pre-millennial teachings from the Fathers in their order:

1. The Roman Empire would split in two. (This took place in AD 395.)
2. The Roman Empire would fall apart. (This took place in AD 476.)
3. Out of what was the Roman Empire, ten nations would spring up. These are the ten toes/horns of Daniel's prophecies.
4. A literal demon-possessed man, called the Antichrist, will ascend to power.
5. The Antichrist's name, if spelled out in Greek, will add up to 666.
6. The Antichrist will sign a peace treaty between the Jews in Israel and the local non-believers there. This treaty will last seven years.
7. This seven-year treaty is the last seven years of the "sets of sevens" prophecy in Daniel 9.
8. At the end of the seven years, Jesus will return to earth, destroy the Antichrist, and establish reign of peace that will last for a literal 1000 years.
9. They wrote they were taught these things by the apostles. They also wrote that anyone who rises up in the church and begins to say any of these things are symbolic, are immature Christians that can't rightly divide the word of God, and should not be listened too. (Today these beliefs are included in the doctrines of most of, but not all of, the Reformed, Presbyterian, Lutheran, Eastern Orthodox, and Roman Catholic churches!)

Here are some of the references from the early church fathers on the End Times:

Ancient Prophecies Revealed

"After the resurrection of the dead, Jesus will personally reign for 1000 years. He was taught this by the apostle John himself." *Papias Fragment 6*

"The man of Sin, spoken of by Daniel, will rule two (three) times and a half, before the Second Advent... There will be a literal 1000 year reign of Christ... The man of apostasy, who speaks strange things against the Most High, shall venture to do unlawful deeds on the earth against us, the believers." *Justin Martyr Dialogue 32,81,110*

"In 2 Thessalonians, the "falling away" is an apostasy of faith and there will be a literal rebuilt Temple. In Matthew 24 the "abomination spoken by Daniel" is the Antichrist sitting in the Temple as if he were Christ. The abomination will start in the middle of Daniel's 70th week and last for a literal three years and six months. The little (11th) horn is the Antichrist... The Roman Empire will first be divided and then be dissolved. Ten kings will arise from what used to be the Roman Empire. The Antichrist slays three of the kings and is then the eighth king among them. The kings will destroy Babylon, then give the Babylonian kingdom to the Beast and put believers to flight. After that the ten nations and the Beast will be destroyed by the coming of the Lord. Daniel's horns are the same as the ten toes. The toes being part of iron and clay mean some will be active and strong, while others weak and inactive and the kings will not agree with each other... The name of the Antichrist equals 666 if spelled out in Greek. Do not even try to find out the name until the ten kings arise. The fourth kingdom seen by Daniel is Rome. The rebuilt Temple will be in Jerusalem... These are all literal things, and Christians who allegorize them are immature Christians." *Irenaeus Against Heresies 5.25,26,30,35*

"There will be a 1000-year-reign of Jesus Christ... the millennial reign, Resurrection, and the New Jerusalem are literal. In the Resurrection we shall then be changed in a moment into a substance like the angels... The Anti-Christ will be a man who sits in a real temple. *Tertullian Marcion 3.5,25; 5:16*

"Paul mentions the Antichrist, as a literal person who works false miracles... There is a literal future Antichrist coming... The prophecies in 1 Thessalonians and Daniel are real prophecies about the end of the world. There will be a literal rebuilt Temple." *Origen Against Celsus 2:49; 6:45,46*

"There will be a future 1000-year-reign of Christ." *Lactantius Epitome of Divine Institutes 72*

Justin Martyr and Irenaeus studied under Pollycarp. Polycarp worked with the apostle John for over 20 years in ministry. Irenaeus also testifies that he occasionally saw the apostle John himself.

We can see pre-millennialism was the standard teaching by the church fathers, and ranges from about AD 70 with Papias to Lactantius about AD 285. Back in Egypt, however, the amillennial heresy was beginning to develop. About the year 190, Clement of Alexandria, Egypt, started teaching that some prophesies were fulfilled at the destruction of the Temple in AD 70. This later led to the development of the amillennial view.

The Schism of Nepos

If the teaching of pre-millennialism was so clearly taught, complete with eyewitness testimony and warnings that wolves would arise in the church and change these teachings, then how did the change take place?

Since the 1000 years is mentioned only in the book of Revelation, the focus is on how Revelation should be properly interpreted. Most of the older denominations do not believe the teachings in Revelation are literal, or at least never talk about it. The Eastern Orthodox Church, for instance, teaches that the book of Revelation was added to the canon of Scripture only on the condition that it would never be read in a public service. This supposedly happened just prior to the Council of Constantinople in 381. This is the same council that supposedly condemned pre-millennialism. The problem with teaching this is that the "Tome and Anathemas," which described what happened, no longer exists. So no one really knows what took place in the Council of Constantinople.

About 200 years earlier, in AD 170, a document was written detailing what should be included in the New Testament canon and why. This document is called the Muratorian Canon Fragment, because only a portion of it still exists. It clearly states "We receive the Apocalypses of John and Peter only. Some of us do not wish the Apocalypse of Peter to be read in church."

Apostasy of the Church

We can see from very early times the book of Revelation was accepted and read in church. Either the Orthodox legend is a complete myth, or it is mixed up with the statement that some did not like the spurious "Apocalypse of Peter" to be read in church. In either case, the book of the Revelation, written by John, has always been accepted and taken very literally.

Eusebius wrote his "Ecclesiastical History" in AD 325. In EH 3.39 he records Papias' testimony that the apostle John taught him that Jesus would literally come back in the flesh and reign for 1000 years. The apostle John had many enemies, but his arch-rival was the Gnostic, Cerinthus. In Eusebius's Ecclesiastical History 7.24-25 we learn in the apostle John's time when everyone still believed in the literal interpretation of the book of Revelation, Cerinthus added the teaching that the millennium would be for the gratifying of the sensual appetites such as food, drink, and sex. (One can see where the Muslims get the idea that martyrs go to a paradise with all the food and wine they want and their 72 virgins!)

Most of the Christians simply ignored the ravings of Cerinthus the Gnostic; but these perverse teachings lead some early Christians to either reject the book of Revelation or accept it, but view the 1000 years as symbolic. When the allegorical interpretation started really gaining ground about AD 290, an Egyptian Bishop named Nepos wrote a book entitled "Refutation of the Allegorists." This book no longer exists, but Eusebius states it had many of the quotes of the fathers we have given above, plus a lot of history behind the Gnostics. The movement for amillennialism misused his book to convince many he was secretly trying to revive the heretical teaching of Cerinthus. This caused even more Christians to switch to the amillennial view and most of the remaining Christians decided to avoid the issue all together.

By the fourth century amillennialism was the standard and the legend that book of Revelation was never originally designed to be read or studied by the average Christian was firmly in place. It is an interesting note that Eusebius, in AD 325, takes the amillennial position. He may have had to "officially" accept the party line in order to write his church history, but buried deep within his history is the complete story of how it happened!

The Schism Nepos and the millennium are also mentioned by Dionysius, in his "Promises" ECF 6.81. Victorinus' commentary on Revelation, in chapter 22, also mentions Cerinthus.

Cessationism

Most Denominations today that state the gifts ceased in at the end of the apostolic age, use 1 Corinthians 13 as a proof text. Paul, in speaking of the gifts of prophecy and tongues, says "when that which is perfect is come, that which is in part will be done away." A cessationist will say the New Testament is "that which is perfect," so the gifts ceased at the end of the apostolic age. Church father Irenaeus stated clearly that the apostles taught the Second Coming of Jesus was "that which is perfect" and so the gifts would continue until our Lord comes for His Church. To prove this is correct, Irenaeus' quote is given below, followed by numerous quotes showing the gifts were active in many churches at least into the 5th century.

Dates each gift is mentioned as still functioning					
Gifts (in general)	165			240	280
Prophetical	165	177	200	240	280
Exorcism	165	177			
Dead Raised		177			
Foreknowledge		177			
Languages		177			280
Healing		177		240	
Miracles				240	

"In 1 Corinthians 13, 'that which is perfect' and 'face to face' refer to the Second Coming." *Irenaeus Against Heresies 4.9*

"The prophetical gifts are only manifested among Christians and still continue… Jewish exorcists make use of craft when they exorcise, even as the Gentiles do, employing fumigations and incantations… Jewish prophets ceased after John." *Justin Martyr Dialogue 82,85,51&52*

"Christians still heal the blind, deaf, and chase away all sorts of demons. Occasionally the dead are raised. Gnostics and other non-Christians can't chase away demons - except those demons that are sent into others by themselves, if they can even do so much as this… Some Christians do certainly and truly drive out devils, so that those who have thus been cleansed from evil spirits frequently both believe in Christ, and join themselves to the Church. Others have foreknowledge of things to come: they see visions, and utter prophetic expressions. Others still heal the sick by laying their hands upon them, and they are made whole. Yea, moreover, as I have said, the dead even have been raised up, and remained among us for many years. The Church does not perform anything by means of angelic invocations, or

Ancient Prophecies Revealed

incantations, or by any other wicked curious art; but, directing her prayers to the Lord... Those who are 'perfect' are those who have received the Spirit of God, and who through the Spirit of God do speak in all languages, as he, Himself, used also to speak. In like manner we do also hear many brethren in the Church, who possess prophetic gifts, and who through the Spirit speak all kinds of languages, and bring to light for the general benefit the hidden things of men, and declare the mysteries of God, whom also the apostle terms "spiritual," they being spiritual because they partake of the Spirit, and seek spiritual understanding to become purely spiritual." *Irenaeus Against Heresies 2.31,32; 5.6*

"The wicked spirit, bidden to speak by a follower of Christ, will as readily make the truthful confession that he is a demon... The whole power of demons and kindred spirits is subject to us... The arts of astrologers, soothsayers, augurs, and magicians were made known by the angels who sinned, and are forbidden by God." *Tertullian Apology 27, 35*

"Christians still expel demons and heal the sick... Christians still do miracles and prophesy... A true prophet under the control of the Holy Spirit does not fall in to ecstasy or madness like the pagans do... Prophets become clearer of mind. Every Christian, even new converts, has no problem casting out demons... Since the time of Christ there have been no Jewish prophets, only Christian ones... The spirits speaking through the pagan prophets claim to be God, but their speech is 'strange, fanatical, and quite unintelligible words, of which no rational person can find the meaning: for so dark are they, as to have no meaning at all; but they give occasion to every fool or impostor to apply them to suit his own purposes.' ...True prophets speak the plain truth and sometimes in parables and enigmas, but spiritual Christians can always figure out the riddles. Satan will counterfeit with riddles that have no real meaning."
Origen Against Celsus - 1:67; 2.8; 7.4,8,9,10

"The gifts still operate, prophecies, tongues (all the languages of the world) etc." *Archelaus Acts of Manes 37; ECF 6.179*

In addition to 1 Corinthians 13, telling us that the gifts continue until the Second Coming, Isaiah says something similar. In 1 Corinthians 14 Paul quotes Isaiah 28:11. There God speaks by "Men of stammering lips and another tongue." In Isaiah this first refers to the Assyrian invasion of the ten tribes. In 1 Corinthians 14, Paul quotes this as a prophecy about Pentecost. Christians speaking in another language are a sign of the impending destruction coming on Jerusalem for their rejection of the Messiah. Later in Isaiah 33, the prophet talks about the Antichrist's reign and asks: "where are the 'people of stammering lips and another tongue?'" They are hidden until the "King" returns to Mount Zion. This not only shows a pre-tribulational Rapture, but also the gifts (specifically tongues) continueing until the Rapture. Apparently, no one can be found who speaks in tongues during the reign of the Antichrist.

Church Tradition

The third part of Balaam's stumbling block is making church tradition equal to Scripture. In reality tradition supersedes Scripture. For example, if someone notices a contradiction, they are informed they just do not understand correctly, and they need to put the Bible down and follow church tradition. The ancient church fathers clearly taught if a later document or tradition contradicts the teaching of Scripture, it is to be ignored. And if the new tradition is not mentioned in Scripture, it is only opinion and anyone trying to force you to believe/do something that is opinion is sinning against Jesus by dividing His church.

"Heretics allege truth was delivered, not by written documents, but by oral tradition. Without this oral tradition, you can't properly interpret the Scriptures... The Apostles did not pass down any hidden wisdom, just the Scriptures. If an older written document contradicts the newer written document, we believe the older.... Obey the presbyters who are in the Church,--those who possess the succession from the apostles; together with the succession of the episcopate, who have received the certain gift of truth. But it is also incumbent to hold in suspicion others who depart from the primitive succession. Avoid all who do not hold to the doctrine of the Apostles, including presbyters... The doctrine of the apostles has been guarded and preserved without any forging of Scriptures, as a very complete system of doctrine. Neither receive addition to or suffer curtailment from its truths. Read the Word of God without falsification, lawfully and diligently explaining the Old Testament in harmony with the rest of the Scriptures."
Irenaeus Against Heresies 3.2,3; 4.26,33

"There never was any secret doctrine handed down by the apostles, just the Scriptures. Only the heretics say there is secret doctrine from the apostles which you must know to correctly understand the Scripture... To be true, a thing must

Apostasy of the Church

be proven scientifically, by comparison and testing… True Christians do not divide the body of Christ, but heretics try to… Do not accept any teaching that is not clearly taught in the Scriptures. It must be proven logically and completely from the Scriptures, or it is just an opinion. Anyone who divides the body of Christ with opinions is sinning against the body of Christ." *Clement of Alexandria Stromata 2.4,17; 4:15,16*

"The apostles did not keep any secret doctrine, but taught everything openly. Only heretics teach a secret gospel or letter or teaching… The apostles did not give special information to favorite friends."
Tertullian Prescription against heretics 1.25,26

AD 606 Thyatira – Jezebel, Depths of Satan

Jezebel's Idolatry
The Mass
Praying to Saints
Transubstantiation
Consubstantiation
Mariolatry
Statues/Idols
Deny Scripture's Inspiration

Thyatira means "continual sacrifice." This period ranged from AD 606-1517. Those who hold to the false doctrine of Jezebel, her children, or the other depths of Satan will not be Raptured out before the Great Tribulation (Rev. 2:22). Three errors are mentioned here. First, Jezebel teaches "eating food sacrificed to an idol." It was in this time period that the idea of the Mass began, which is a continual sacrifice of the wine and the wafer from an image of a sunburst, called a "monstrance." The false doctrine of transubstantiation/consubstantiation came into the church at this same time. When a priest blesses the wafer in prayer to God, Jesus, Mary and the saints and declares it to have physically changed into human flesh and blood he makes an idol out of it. Even in the case of consubstantiation, which says it does not *physically* change but God is *spiritually present* in the wafer, it is still an idol. The idea of God entering the communion bread came about from a Gnostic heretic named Marcus in the first century. Marcus taught that when he blessed the cup of wine, the Holy Spirit would enter the cup and anyone who drank from it would be filled with the Holy Spirit. In this case, the transmuted communion would impart the Holy Spirit. Today the idea is that the transmuted communion will impart a grace that forgives some sins. About transubstantiation, ancient church father Irenaeus said clearly:

"Pretending to consecrate cups mixed with wine, he contrives to give them a purple and reddish colour, so that Charis [the Holy Spirit], should be thought to drop her own blood into that cup through means of his invocation… the church has never taught such a thing… all who follow such a demonic teaching are crack-brained."
Irenaeus Against Heresies 1.13

Notice in this stage they "tolerate" Jezebel. This compromise, or tolerance of error, today will manifest in ecumenicism and a denial of the verbal inspiration of Scripture.

The second part of this prophecy concerns the children of Jezebel. They are later movements that introduce other forms of idolatry, ranging from praying to saints and angels to having prayer idols of saints and angels (usually the prayer of asking the saint/angel to pray for you). Today this is commonplace, but in ancient times the Church Fathers said:

"The Church does not perform anything by means of angelic invocations, or incantations, or by any other wicked curious art; but, directing her prayers to the Lord." *Irenaeus Against Heresies 2.32*

"Mature Christians pray only to God, without thought for bodily position or set time. (eg. sunrise prayers or on their knees) and their prayers are not selfish." *Clement of Alexandria, Stromata book 7.7*

"Those who make prayers to the dead will suffer for their impiety and rebellion against God since this is an unforgivable rite and a violation of sacred law." *Lactantius 7.67*

Clement of Alexandria, Stromata 3:431, and Tertullian, A.E. 3, mention the Gnostic sect, Carpocrates, who committed a unique kind of sin in that they used small idols of Jesus, Aristotle, Pythagoras, other people and angels, which they said were a means to contact the pure God. They would adorn the idols with wreaths, garlands, and in other ways to honor them. Today many Christians see nothing wrong with honoring statues of saints or praying to them. Tertullian states the book of Jude was written specifically against these Carpocratian Gnostics.

The third part of this prophecy concerns the other "depths of Satan." Other things similar to transubstantiation, idols, and secret scriptures were pulled from the Gnostic cults of the first century with the obvious paganism removed, and added one

Ancient Prophecies Revealed

by one to normal church doctrine. The following is a partial list of Gnostic groups and their teachings that the ancient church fathers exposed:

Gnosticism

The father of Gnosticism was Simon Magus (Acts 8). After trying to buy the Holy Spirit and being sent away by the apostle Peter, Simon went on to form the first of the Gnostic cults. Two major schools had developed by 150 AD, the followers of Valentinus and the followers of Basilides. Our knowledge of Gnostics comes mainly from the early church father Irenaeus, who wrote the five volume set "Against Heresies" and the Gnostic literature itself found at Nag Hammadi, Egypt in 1945. Irenaeus states that Gnostics derived their teachings from the heathen, namely Homer, Plato, Aristotle, the Pythagoreans and others.[16] John the Apostle would not enter a bathhouse where Cerinthus was, and Polycarp said Marcion was the first-born of Satan.[18]

The basic teachings of Gnosticism that the church called heresy are:
1. There are 30 Aeons (Gods) that exist in the Pleroma, outside of time and space.[1]
2. The goddess Sophia created the Demiurge, a creator angel (the God of the Old Testament) who was a tyrant; and being unaware of the Aeons, thought he was the only God. He created man, but Sophia gave man a spirit.[2]
3. Some may be saved if they do enough good works, but some are predestined to go to hell.[4] (works salvation)
4. Gnostics have spirits that are emanations from Sophia. This makes them predestined to be saved. It is imposable for them to loose their salvation. It does not matter if they act good or evil. So the most "perfect" of them addict themselves to evil deeds and are in a habit of defiling the women they convert.[3]
5. Eventually all matter will be destroyed, being evil and not capable of salvation.[9, 6]
6. Gnostics will become spirits and will marry the angels.[9]
7. Christ descended upon Jesus at His baptism and left before Jesus went before Pilot. Sophia would not allow Christ to suffer.[9] (Adoptionism)
8. They utter mantras to effect nature.[10] (Hindu mantra and Kabalistic letter magic, Gramera, and emanations)
9. Souls reincarnate.[32]
10. Perfect knowledge is obtained by baptism, spiritual marriage and last rites.[5] (sacramentalism)
11. Sophia sent the serpent (the angel Michael or Samael) into the Garden of Eden to free Eve and Adam. By eating of the tree, they attained true Gnosis and were set free.[15]
12. Sophia saved Noah from the flood of the evil Demiurge.[15]
13. The Demiurge forced Eve into sexual intercourse many times. She gave birth to evil creator angels.[15] (serpent seed)
14. At death, some souls enter an intermediate state to be purged of the animal nature before going into the Pleroma.[17] (Purgatory)

Later, other Gnostics would add or change some points and found their own schools.

Simon Magus
- Feigned faith, and used exorcisms and incantations, love-potions, and charms, as well as those beings who are called "Paredri" (familiars) and "Oniropompi" (dream-senders).[6]
- He allegorized much Scripture to support his teachings,[44] especially Genesis.[45]

Menander
- By means of magic, one may overcome the angels that made the world. Only if you are baptized into Menander will you obtain the resurrection and never die again, having eternal youth.[6]

Ebionites
- God created the world and Jesus was just a man. They used only the Gospel of Matthew, said Paul was an apostate, and followed the Jewish customs.[12, 38]
- Founded by Ebion.[38]

Apostasy of the Church

Nicolaitans
- Practiced adultery, and ate things sacrificed to idols.[12]
- Became very obscene and Gnostic.[37]

The Carpocrates
- Say Nicolas and Mathias taught fornication is no longer wrong.[24]
- Taught humans are imprisoned in a cycle of reincarnation by evil creator angels, but will eventually break the cycle and be saved.[8]
- Was a magician and a fornicator.[40]
- Carpocrates practiced magical arts, incantations, and spells and had voluptuous feasts. And they are in the habit of invoking the aid of subordinate demons and dream-senders.[49]

Cerinthus
- Taught Jesus was just a man and "the Christ" descended on Him at His baptism and departed before He suffered on the cross.[12] (Adoptionism)

Saturninus[7]
- Saturninus, himself, was a creator angel.[7]
- Jesus did not have a physical body.[7]
- Jesus came to destroy the god of the Jews.[7]
- Sex, marriage, and reproduction are sinful.[7,14]
- Saturninus and his school were vegetarians. They practiced asceticism.[48]

Marcus
- Taught that the Holy Spirit put a drop of her blood into the wine when Marcus blessed it. Upon drinking it, you would understand mysteries and prophesy. (transubstantiation)[11]
- If anything bad begins to happen to them, they pray to the mother goddess who will then Rapture them.[11]
- Marcus said his cup imparted grace.[46]
- Marcus taught a second baptism (of redemption). This was done by a laying on of hands and a word or phrase given by the bishop Marcus. He did this only when the disciple was ready to go on to the higher mysteries, or when the disciple was dying. They were taught to keep secret the word and even deny that is exists. (last rites)[47]

Marcion
- Rejected the Old Testament and used cut up versions of Luke and some of Paul's Epistles. Taught the God of the Old Testament and his prophets are evil and will be destroyed.[13]
- God is the author of sin.[27]
- There are two equal and opposite gods: one good and one evil.[28]
- Strongly addicted to astrology.[29]
- There is no resurrection. The saved should not marry.[31]
- Removed references in his gospel that Christ was Creator[33]
- Jesus was a phantom (no physical body)[34]
- The Law and The Gospel being so contradictory proves two different gods exist.[30]

Depths of Satan
All religions are the same
To say there is only one way is intolerant
Calvinism - Pelegianism
Unconditional election
Double predestination
Born sinless
Sin doesn't really matter
God is the author of sin
Morality is legalism
No original sin
Abortion
Common law marriages
Orgies
Lying is ok
Homosexuality / fornication
Jesus is not the Christ
Adoptionism
Didn't have a physical body
Doesn't currently have a body
Did not die on the cross
Jesus was just a man
Jesus is not the only creator
Tri-theism
Deny Holy Spirit exists
God and Satan are equal
Deny some Scriptures
Parts are man-made
Parts were cultural
Parts are only allegory
Gospel of Thomas, Judas
Bible codes
Reject Textus Receptus
(cut up the text)
Purgatory
Last rites
Baptismal regeneration
Transubstantiation
Consubstantiation
Vegetarianism
Monastic asceticism
Penance
Cardinal and venial sins
Anti-Israel spirit
Circumcision
Serpent seed doctrine
Christians can be possessed
Sex & marriage are evil
Reproduction is evil
Soul sleep
Female angels

Ancient Prophecies Revealed

Titian
- Adam was not saved.[19]
- Drinking wine is a sin.[22]
- The soul is not eternal; it dissolves with the body.[20] (soul sleep)
- Medicine is demonic. Instead of using medicine we should rely on God alone.[21]
- Created the Diatessaron (harmony of the gospels) in which he cut out all references to Christ's divinity and pre-existance.

Depths of Satan
Sorcery (contemplative prayer)
Incantations
Use of illicit drugs
Precognition
Emanations
Magical arts
Astrology
Use of altered states of consciousness
Mantras & meditation
Karma
Reincarnation
No physical resurrection

Ophites - Worshiped the serpent as primary Eon (brazen).[38]

Cainites - Worship Cain, the brother of Abel, as primary Eon.[38]

Cerdo – Was the first to introduce dualism.[39] (Dualism says there are two gods)

Apelles - Agrees Jesus came in the flesh, but after the Resurrection He disintegrated His flesh.[50]

Calistus - Formed a school (commune) that allowed fornication, common law marriages, the use of drugs for producing sterility, and abortions (called murder by him). No true Christian does these things.[51]

Alcibiades (Elchasai) - Formed the Elchasaites who taught there are female angels and a new remission of sins (based on the teachings of his book). Alcibiades' teachings were similar to the teachings of Callistus. They included the use of incantations, circumcision, Christ was born only a man, reincarnation, astrology.[52]

Elchasaites – They taught Jesus incarnated many times. They use to incantations and baptisms in their confession of elements (communion). They also occupy themselves in regard of astrological and mathematical science (Bible codes), and of the arts of sorcery. They allege themselves to have powers of prescience (precognition instead of a Word of Knowledge- a "self" power instead of a spiritual gift)[53]

Naasseni – They worship the serpent and teach their order was started by James, the Lord's brother. They use the Gospel According to Thomas and teach Adam was a hermaphrodite. They take some of their teachings from the Mysteries of Isis and from the Mysteries of the Assyrians, and they practice orgies.[41]

Peratae
- Teach a kind of tri-theism.[42] (A belief in three gods instead of a trinity)
- There is a separate branch of the Peratae who teach Jesus the Son is the serpent.[43]

Basilides
- Taught reincarnation with karma[25]
- Man can grow up and be sinless all of his life.[25] (Born without original sin)
- Spirits (sometimes animal spirits) latch on to us and force us to sin.[23]
- Saving faith is intellectual ascent. All humans are born with the ability.[23] (Pelegianism)
- After baptism, God forgives involuntary sins but you must pay for all voluntary sins in order to be purged from them.[26] (penance, purgatory, cardinal and venial sins)
- Jesus was transformed to look like Simon of Cyrene and Simon like Jesus. Simon was crucified in the place of Jesus.[7, 37]
- The supreme god is named Abraxas.[37]

Valentinus
- Saving faith comes from your spirit (The Holy Spirit is really your human sprit, compare with the teachings of The Way International), if you are one of the chosen.[23] (born saved)
- Only those whose spirit is an emanation from Sophia, are predestined to be saved. All others are predestined to hell.[23] (double predestination)

Apostasy of the Church

- Those not predestined to be saved or predestined for hell might be saved through good works.[35]
- Those predestined for salvation do not need to practice good works.[36]

"When they are called Phrygians, Novatians, Valentinians, Marcionites, Anthropians, or Arians they have ceased to be Christians." *Lactantius Divine Institutes 4.30*

1.	Irenaeus, Against Heresies 1.1-3	19.	Irenaeus, Against Heresies 3.23	37.	Tertullian, Heresies 1.1
2.	Irenaeus, Against Heresies 1.5	20.	Titian, Greeks 13	38.	Tertullian, Heresies 1.2
3.	Irenaeus, Against Heresies 1.6	21.	Titian, Greeks 18	39.	Tertullian, Heresies 1.6
4.	Irenaeus, Against Heresies 1.7; 4.37	22.	Clement of Alexandria, Instructor 2.2	40.	Tertullian, Treatise of the Soul 1.35
5.	Irenaeus, Against Heresies 1.21	23.	Clement of Alexandria, Stromata 2.3,20; 4.13	41.	Hipolytus, Heresies 5.1
6.	Irenaeus, Against Heresies 1.23	24.	Clement of Alexandria, Stromata 3.4	42.	Hipolytus, Heresies 5.7
7.	Irenaeus, Against Heresies 1.24	25.	Clement of Alexandria, Stromata 4.12	43.	Hipolytus, Heresies 5.12
8.	Irenaeus, Against Heresies 1.25	26.	Clement of Alexandria, Stromata 4.24	44.	Hipolytus, Heresies 6.5-9
9.	Irenaeus, Against Heresies 1.7	27.	Clement of Alexandria, Against Heresies 4.29	45.	Hipolytus, Heresies 6.10
10.	Irenaeus, Against Heresies 1.14-15	28.	Tertullian, Against Marcion 1.2	46.	Hipolytus, Heresies 6.34-35
11.	Irenaeus, Against Heresies 1.13	29.	Tertullian, Against Marcion 1.18	47.	Hipolytus, Heresies 6.36-37
12.	Irenaeus, Against Heresies 1.26; 5.1	30.	Tertullian, Against Marcion 1.19-20	48.	Hipolytus, Heresies 7.16
13.	Irenaeus, Against Heresies 1.27	31.	Tertullian, Against Marcion 1.24	49.	Hipolytus, Heresies 7.20
14.	Irenaeus, Against Heresies 1.28	32.	Tertullian, Against Heresies 2.33	50.	Hipolytus, Heresies 7.26
15.	Irenaeus, Against Heresies 1.30	33.	Tertullian, Marcion 2.17	51.	Hipolytus, Heresies 9.7
16.	Irenaeus, Against Heresies 2.14	34.	Tertullian, Marcion 3.8, 4.8	52.	Hipolytus, Heresies 9.8-9
17.	Irenaeus, Against Heresies 2.29	35.	Tertullian, Valentians 1.29	53.	Hipolytus, Heresies 10.25
18.	Irenaeus, Against Heresies 3.3	36.	Tertullian, Valintians 1.30		

Sardis – Dead Ritual

Sardis means "those escaped." This period of church history dates from the Protestant Reformation, AD 1517, to the time when the great revivals / Great Awakenings started, about AD 1750.

The Reformation churches did well to remove idols, prayer to saints and angels, and transubstantiation. They even did away with "tradition is equal with Scripture." They coined the phrase "Sola Scriptura," meaning "by scripture alone," with no added tradition. But they did not go far enough. They replaced transubstantiation with consubstantiation and kept the false doctrines of amillennialism, cessationism, and replacement theology.

The Sardis church would "soil their garments" by adding Augustinian Calvinism to their doctrine. Calvinism would teach true Christians are chosen by God and are destined to heaven and no one, including the pope, could reverse that. So the threats of the pope could safely be ignored. The Sardis church, now fully believing that doctrine, would have no fear of Rome taking away their salvation. Even though we should not fear Rome sending us to hell, Augustinian Calvinism was considered a Valentian Gnostic heresy by the ancient church fathers. See the Gnostic list above for details.

AD 1750 Philadelphia – Missionary Church

This is the period of Missionary activity, AD 1750 to AD 1948. Notice this period overlaps with Laodicea. Jesus said nothing bad about this church. The Philadelphian Church restored the remaining doctrines forgotten by Sardis. They recognized pre-millennialism and that the gifts still function. They rejected Calvinism in favor of true missionary activity. This period saw the reestablishment of the nation of Israel. Anyone who thought the church had replaced Israel completely, once seeing the restoration in AD 1948 would leave the Synagogue of Satan, also called replacement theology, and come and bow at the feet of this church. The Lord promised that this church would be kept from the hour of (Jacob's) Trouble.

AD 1948 Laodicea – Lukewarm Church

In contrast to the Philadelphia church, Laodicea, which overlaps it in time, is the lukewarm church. Neither hot nor cold, Laodicea accepts any doctrine for the sake of compromise. This is the ecumenical spirit going too far by allowing back all those Gnostic ideas from the past. It requires, first of all, a denial of the verbal inspiration of Scripture. Otherwise, we would all have to agree exactly with what God requires of us. The Laodicean Church believes your interpretation is as good as mine. It is interesting to note that the city of Laodicea was named after Laodice, the wife of the Antiochus of Daniel 11. Antiochus replaced Laodice with Bernice, a true loving wife.

Laodicea
Denies
Pre-millennialism
Gifts of the Spirit
Inspiration of Scripture
Israel's right to exist
Allows
Idols
Calvinism
Abortion
Euthanasia
Multiple Interpretations of Scripture

Ancient Prophecies Revealed

Laodice then sought to kill the righteous bride with her child, poison Antiochus, and put her own child on the throne. Laodice is a perfect picture of the apostate church.

At the end of this section we will create a grand list of the facets of the apostasy from the seven churches, other Scripture, and the ancient church fathers that will manifest in the Laodicean church before the Rapture of the true church.

We have already seen the major steps of the apostasy from the seven churches and in so doing we have also looked at the teaching of the ancient church fathers on this subject. Before we build our master list, we want to look at a few other Scriptures and quotes from the fathers to be as complete as we can. Then we can see how far we have to go to reach the worst and thereby how close we might be to the Rapture of the church.

Unsound Doctrines of Demons

This section comes from the New Testament Epistles. The obvious ones are just listed and referenced but some require a bit of explanation:

Doctrines of Demons
Mantra – Matt. 6:7
Meditation – Matt. 6:7
Reincarnation – 1 Cor 15:13
Celibacy – 1 Tim 4:3
Vegetarianism – 1 Tim 4:3
Observe Jewish festivals – Col 2
Resurrection had already occurred
Jesus is a sinner
No future resurrection
There is a Christ consciousness
Homosexuality acceptable – Rom 1, 1 Cor 6
Evolution – 2 Pet 3
Reject Inspiration – 2 Pet 3
Reject virgin birth
Reject miracles
Reject resurrection
Reject prophecies
Reject the Rapture
Word faith movement – 1 Tim 6
Prosperity doctrine – 1 Tim 6
Psychology
Women clergy – 1 Tim 2 & 3

Mantras & Meditation

In Matthew 6:7, Jesus said not to pray like the heathen do, using "vain repetitions." This is done in the form of mantras. A mantra is a word or phrase repeated over and over until one enters an altered state of consciousness. This is also done by breathing techniques, also called "breath prayers." Any form of eastern meditation that creates an altered state of conciseness would be praying like the heathen do.

> "And when you are praying, do not use meaningless repetition as the Gentiles do, for they suppose that they will be heard for their many words." *Matthew 6:7*

Reincarnation

Paul states, in 1 Corinthians 15, that to be a Christian one must believe in the *physical* resurrection of the body. This is impossible if you believe in reincarnation.

> "But if there is no resurrection of the dead, not even Christ has been raised; and if Christ has not been raised, then our preaching is vain, your faith also is vain." *1 Corinthians 15:13-14*

Celibacy, Vegetarianism, & Jewish Festivals

> "But the Spirit explicitly says that in later times some will fall away from the faith, paying attention to deceitful spirits and doctrines of demons… men who forbid marriage and advocate abstaining from foods…" *1 Timothy 4:1,3*

> "Therefore no one is to act as your judge in regard to food or drink or in respect to a festival or a new moon or a Sabbath day" *Colossians 2:16*

Resurrection, Idolatry, and the Christ Consciousness

The ancient church identified several individuals who left the true faith and had to be excommunicated. In 2 Timothy 2:17, Paul wrote Hymenaeus and Philetus taught the resurrection had already occurred. Tertullian wrote in *Flesh of Christ 16*, that Alexander left the true faith and joined a subgroup of the Ebionites who followed several heresies: that Jesus was just a man with a sin nature, that there is no physical resurrection and that people can become sinless by obtaining the Christ Consciousness. Hypolytus wrote in *The 70 Disciples* that Demas forsook the true faith and became a priest of idols. (Propbably a Carpocratian Gnostic.) Lastly, Tertullian wrote in *On the Resurrection* that Phygellus and Hermogenes denied there would be a resurrection of the physical body. Instead, they taught the Gnostic teaching of reincarnation.

Homosexuality & Sorcery

Romans 1:22-28 and 1 Corinthians 6:9 describe the sin of homosexuality. In Revelation, John writes when the two witnesses are killed in the holy city of Jerusalem, it will be a time when Jerusalem will be known for two things: sorcery, widely practiced in Egypt, and homosexuality, widely practiced in Sodom.

"And their dead bodies will lie in the street of the great city which mystically is called Sodom and Egypt, where also their Lord was crucified." *Revelation 11:8*

Evolution & Rejection of Inspiration of Scripture
Peter wrote in 2 Peter 3 that scoffers would arise in the last days that would believe Noah's Flood and the book of Genesis are both myths. This shows they no longer believe in the verbal inspiration of Scripture and, in place of Creationism, they hold to the doctrine of evolution. They also no longer believe in the prophecies about the promise of His coming, which is the Rapture.

"Know this first of all, that in the last days mockers will come… saying, 'Where is the promise of His coming? For ever since the fathers fell asleep, all continues just as it was from the beginning of creation.' For when they maintain this, it escapes their notice that by the word of God the heavens existed long ago and the earth was formed out of water and by water, through which the world at that time was destroyed, being flooded with water." *2 Peter 3:3-6*

Word Faith Movement
In 1 Timothy 6, Paul says it is an error to assume godliness is a means of financial gain. Today this manifests as the "Word Faith Movement" and the "Prosperity Doctrine."

"…men of depraved mind and deprived of the truth, who suppose that godliness is a means of gain." *1 Timothy 6:5*

Received Text
We have been told by the ancient church fathers that several heretics cut out parts of Scripture they did not like, for example the Scriptures attesting to the divinity of Jesus. Today the KJV and NKJV Bibles are based on the received text, while all other English Bibles are based on the critical text. I believe that in the Middle Ages, scribes who forgot about the history of the heretics, found some of the original cut-up texts of those heretics. They then compiled the two into one, creating the critical text. This is evident because the critical text is missing *some* of the Scriptures about Jesus' divinity, but most are still there. Therefore the critical text can't be the original texts from the heretics. This is why today it does not matter if your favorite Bible uses the received text or the critical text because no doctrine has changed.

But, since the ancient church fathers described heretics cutting out some of the Scriptures, it will become a point of The Apostasy. I believe later, maybe right after the Rapture, some archeologist will dig up one of the original heretical texts. When the received, critical, and heretical texts are all compared, a decision will be made by the harlot church that Jesus was not really God at all. This will allow the harlot church to be conquered by the Muslim world, and in turn, destroyed by them.

Psychology
Modern science has never found any evidence that even suggests there might be an "unconscious mind." It is just a Freudian theory. Freudian psychology is based on ideas from Aristotle and Pythagoras. The Carpocratian Gnostics combined the teachings of Aristotle and Pythagoras with Christianity and were classified as a cult for it. Today we see the self-esteem movement, instead of true repentance; and tolerance instead of true conversion. These forms of psychology are alluded to as the "myths" in 2 Timothy 4:3-4. In 1 Timothy 3:13 evil deceivers will wax worse and worse deceiving and being deceived.

Victorinus wrote about the seven churches in *Commentary on Revelation*. He stated in the end times there would be "Christians" who are Christians in name only. They would not confront sin under a pretext of mercy. If you want to avoid the subject of repentance from sin while trying to be merciful to someone asking for help, the only other option is modern Psychology. Even if they study Scripture, they refuse to do God's work. Victorinus says if they do not start teaching repentance, they will be judged.

"to those who, under the pretext of mercy, do unlawful sins in the Church, and make them manifest to be done by others; and to those that are at ease in the Church, who are negligent, Christians in name only; and to those who study the

Ancient Prophecies Revealed

Scriptures, and labour to know the mysteries of their announcement, but are unwilling to do God's work: to all he urges repentance, or to all he declares judgment." *Victorinus' Commentary on Revelation Ch 1*

Women Clergy

One of the requirements of a pastor is to be the "husband of one wife," according to 1 Timothy 3:2. No mention is made of the possibility of a pastor being the wife of only one husband. In fact, 1 Timothy 2:12 says women can not "usurp authority over a man" in regard to ruling a church. None of the ancient church fathers ordained women ministers and many stated that was forbidden. The only ones ordaining women were heretics, like Marcus, and the pagan religions. Isaiah prophesied about the end time church allowing the ordination of women:

"O My people! Their oppressors are children, and women rule over them. O My people! Those who guide you lead you astray and confuse the direction of your paths." *Isaiah 3:12*

Abortion and Euthanasia

Church father Lactantius wrote in the fourth century that the end time church would be known for allowing abortion and euthanasia. In America, abortion became legal in 1973 and most of the higher churches accept abortion. Euthanasia seems to be an upcoming issue.

"End times will manifest: abortion, euthanasia, children carrying weapons, winter and summer will be confused, years months and days will be shortened," *Lactantius Epitome of Divine Institutes 71*

Denial of the Doctrine of Christ

Peter prophesied that false prophets would rise up in the church and deny the "master that bought them." Jesus is our master and to deny Him means to deny what He is and what He did. The first and second epistles of John teach the Doctrine of Christ. This is what you must believe about Jesus in order to be a Christian. In the end times the church will deny these:

"But false prophets also arose among the people, just as there will also be false teachers among you, who will secretly introduce destructive heresies, even denying the Master who bought them, bringing swift destruction upon themselves." *2 Peter 2:1*

Doctrine of Christ
1. Jesus is the one and only Christ (1 Jn 2:22)
2. Jesus is from the beginning, eternal. (1 Jn 2:13; Mic 5:2)
3. Jesus had no sin. (1 Jn 3:5)
4. Jesus came in the flesh (Jn 1:14; 1 Jn 4:2; 5:1,5; 2 Jn 7)
5. He resurrected in the flesh (Jn 20:26-29; Lk 24:39)
6. Jesus is the Son of God (1 Jn 5:1,5)
7. Jesus will come back in the flesh (2 Jn 7; Acts 1:9-11)
8. Jesus is the one and only begotten Son of God (1 Jn 4:15)
9. Jesus is God incarnate (Jn 1:1-3; 5:17-18; 8:24; 8:56-59; 10:30-33; 8:24; 20:26-29)

False Prophets

Deuteronomy 18:20-22; Jeremiah 23:16-40; and Ezekiel 13:1-14:9 demand that a true prophet of God must be 100% accurate. In the last days false prophets would arise and even admit they are not 100% accurate, because they are just developing their powers. This amounts to sorcery. The ancient church fathers taught that a true prophet becomes clearer of mind when the Holy Spirit comes upon him. In contrast, a false prophet falls into "ecstasy." Ecstasy is defined as using a technique to fall into a trance to see visions or hear voices. It was called sorcery in ancient times. See Eusebius' *Ecclesiastical History 5.17*. Victorinus, in his commentary on Revelation, wrote the church will again adopt sorcery and call it a "new form of prophesying." Those who allow this new form of prophesying will bring upon themselves many "sorrows and dangers."

"The fourth class intimates the nobility of the faithful, who labour daily, and do greater works. But even among them also He shows that there are men of an easy disposition to grant unlawful peace, and to listen to new forms of prophesying; and He reproves and warns the others to whom this is not pleasing, who know the wickedness opposed to them: for which evils He purposes to bring upon the head of the faithful both sorrows and dangers"
Victorinus' *Commentary on the Apocalypse 2*

Apostasy of the Church

A Word of Knowledge from the Ancient Church
The ancient church fathers show there were many cults (Gnostic groups) that created fake documents in order to give some credibility to their heretical doctrines. A common tactic was to combine three types of documents into one. They would typically find an ancient church father who was named after one of the Old Testament prophets and who had given a real word of knowledge on some subject. Then they would research the history of the Old Testament prophet, what he did and how he died, for example, and create a false document under the name of the Old Testament prophet. Then they would add their corrupt teaching to it. So these fake works were composed of three parts: a real history of an Old Testament prophet, a real word of knowledge from an ancient church father, and a heretical teaching. This method accomplished two things: at first it caused people to assume the heretical teachings were truly given by the Old Testament prophets, which caused the cults to spread quickly. But later, after the cults were crushed, the *real* words of knowledge embedded in the *fake* works were discarded as fake as well.

In this book we will look at two of these fake works. Under the guidance of the ancient church fathers, we will regain what we have lost. The first book we will look at is entitled the "Ascension of Isaiah." This one is easy to dissect. The first part contains the history of the prophet Isaiah, how he prophesied and how he was put to death by Manasseh, king of Judah. Manasseh had him put inside a hollow log and sawn in two. The apostle Paul makes allusion to this in Hebrews 11:37. The middle section contains a word of knowledge from an ancient church father who was named after the prophet Isaiah. This is a word of knowledge about the state of the end time church, which the cult tried to apply to itself. It is obvious from the text that *this* Isaiah was from the first century AD and knew the twelve apostles. He could not have been the Old Testament prophet. The last part is obviously false doctrine as it contradicts Scripture. Reproduced here is the word of knowledge from the ancient church father, Isaiah. Notice that he speaks of the setting aside of the prophecies, which starts with amillennialism, and mentions that the gifts are still functioning in the last days:

"...when the Messiah's coming is at hand, his disciples will forsake the teaching of the twelve apostles and their faith, their love and their purity, and there will arise much contention about his coming and his appearing. And in those days there will be many who will love office though they are devoid of wisdom, and many elders will be lawless and violent shepherds to their sheep and will become ravagers of the sheep, since they have no holy shepherds. And many will exchange the glory of the garment of the saints for the garment of the covetous, and respect for persons will be common in those days, and such as love the honor of this world. And there will be much slandering and boasting at the approach of the Lord and the Holy Spirit will depart from many. And in those days there will not be many prophets nor such as speak reliable words, except a few here and there, on account of the spirit of error, of fornication, of boasting and of covetousness which shall be in those who yet will be called his servants and who receive him. Great discord will arise among them, between shepherds and elders. For great jealousy will prevail in the last days, for each will say what seems pleasing in his own eyes. And they will set aside the prophecies of the prophets, which were before me and also pay no attention to these my visions, in order to speak forth from the torrent of their heart..."

Compare this with the apostle Paul:
"But realize this, that in the last days difficult times will come. For men will be lovers of self, lovers of money, boastful, arrogant, revilers, disobedient to parents, ungrateful, unholy, unloving, irreconcilable, malicious gossips, without self-control, brutal, haters of good, treacherous, reckless, conceited, lovers of pleasure rather than lovers of God, holding to a form of godliness, although they have **denied its power**; Avoid such men as these… But evil men and impostors will proceed from bad to worse, deceiving and being deceived." *1 Timothy 3:1-5,13*

Hippolytus, a disciple of Irenaeus, about AD 210 wrote what he was taught about the state of the end time church:
"The temples of God will be like houses, and there will be overturnings of the churches everywhere. The Scriptures will be despised, and everywhere they will sing the songs of the adversary. Fornications, and adulteries, and perjuries will fill the land; sorceries, and incantations, and divinations will follow after these with all force and zeal. And, on the whole, from among those who profess to be Christians will rise up then false prophets, false apostles, impostors, mischief-makers, evil-doers, liars against each other, adulterers, fornicators, robbers, thieves, perjurers, deceivers who do not recognize the inspiration of Scripture, haters of one another. The shepherds will be like wolves, embracing falsehood, and lusting after the things of the world."

Ancient Prophecies Revealed

State of the End Time Church

The church age ends with the Laodecian church being so liberal/lukewarm that they no longer seriously believe in the pre-tribulation Rapture. They are not looking for it and it catches them off guard (Luke 17:26-36). The Rapture of believers may not be much of a shock if shortly after the Rapture takes place, one quarter of the world's population dies in various events: earthquake, famine, plague etc. They may simply assume those Raptured were killed in some similar catastrophe. Those who lost their first love will not be looking for Jesus to Rapture them but look for the church to conquer. At the First Coming, the Jews wanted a Messiah to rule and reign so they *spiritualized* the prophecies of the suffering Messiah. Before the Second Coming, the church will *spiritualize* the Tribulation and Millennial reign because they want to be the ones who take over the earth.

If we compile all the information from the seven churches, demonic doctrines from the New Testament and what the ancient church fathers taught on the New Testament demonic doctrines and the Gnostic cults of their day, we come up with the master chart of facets of the Great Apostasy of the church.

> "Be watchful for your life; don't let your lamps go out or be caught unprepared, but be ready; for you know not the hour when our Lord will come. Gather together often to seek what benefits your souls; for the whole time of your faith will not profit you, if you aren't found perfect at the last time. For in the last days the false prophets and corrupters shall be multiplied, and the sheep will be turned into wolves, and love will be turned into hate. For as lawlessness increases, they shall hate and persecute and betray one another. And then the world-deceiver will appear as a son of God; and shall work signs and wonders, and the earth shall be delivered into his hands; and he will do unholy things, which have never been since the world began. Then all created mankind will pass into the fiery trial, and many will fall away and perish; but those that endure in their faith will be saved by the Curse itself. Then the signs of the truth will appear. First a sign of a rift in the heaven, then a sign of a voice of a trumpet, and third a resurrection of the dead; but not of all, but as it was said: 'The Lord shall come and all His saints with Him.' Then the world will see the Lord coming upon the clouds of heaven." *Didiche 16*

This ancient church document warns us to hold onto a pure faith. The deception will grow great right before the advent of the Antichrist. It also gives us a timetable of events: first the rift is seen, then the Rapture (voice of the trumpet), and finally the resurrection of believers will occur. Now, let's look at the details of the Rapture of the church.

✡

Facets of the Apostasy
Master Chart

From Revelation 2 & 3 — the major steps

Nicolatian Error
1. Fornication, adultery, homosexuality, chambering
2. Belief in a weekly confession for forgiveness of sins
3. Participating in pagan rituals
4. Belief that demons can possess Christians
5. Use of idols in ritual form

Synagogue of Satan
6. Replacement theology
7. Jesus is not God, the Son of God, or virgin born
8. Take oaths of poverty
9. Reject some Scripture
10. Works salvation
    a. Must keep the weekly Sabbath
    b. Must be circumcised
    c. Must keep Mosaic food laws
    d. Must be a vegetarian
    e. Belief in baptismal regeneration

Balaam's Stumbling Block
11. Amillennialism - 'Kingdom Now' theology
    a. Reject teaching on the Rapture
12. Cessationism (gifts of the Spirit ceased)
13. Forsaking the Scripture
    a. Man-made tradition greater than Scripture
    b. Papal authority
14. Halloween / All Souls Day (pagan holidays)

Jezebel's Idolatry
15. The Mass
16. Praying to saints/angels
17. Transubstantiation / Consubstantiation
18. Mariolatry (Queen of Heaven)
    a. Catholic miracles from Mary and the sacraments – Matthew 7:21-23
19. Statues/idols
20. Deny inspiration of Scripture

Antipas (against all these errors)
21. Against Tolerance or Ecumenicism
    a. Sincerity – (Matthew) Jesus says "I never knew you."
22. Standing against immorality and the occult will cause persecution – 2 Tim 3:12
23. Another gospel, Jesus, and Holy Spirit – 2 Cor 11

From Revelation 2 & 3 — the major steps

Jezebel's Idolatry
24. The Mass
25. Praying to saints/angels
26. Transubstantiation / Consubstantiation
27. Mariolatry (Queen of Heaven)
    a. Catholic miracles from Mary and the sacraments – Matthew 7:21-23
28. Statues/idols
29. Deny inspiration of Scripture

Antipas (against all these errors)
30. Against Tolerance or Ecumenicism
    a. Sincerity – (Matthew) Jesus says "I never knew you."
31. Standing against immorality and the occult will cause persecution – 2 Tim 3:12
32. Another gospel, Jesus, and Holy Spirit – 2 Cor 11

Unsound Doctrines of Demons — Timothy, Titus, NT teaching
33. Mantra/Meditation – Contemplative prayer
    a. Sorceries- prayer to saints or gods – Isaiah 47:9-10
34. Reincarnation, no future physical resurrection
35. Celibacy & vegetarianism – 1 Timothy
36. Must observe Jewish Rituals/ Festivals-Sabbaths
37. There is a Christ consciousness
38. Homosexuality – Romans 1
39. Evolution – 2 Peter 3:1-3
40. Reject Inspiration of Scripture
    b. Reject virgin birth, miracles, the Resurrection
    c. Reject the prophecies & the Rapture of the Church
41. Word faith movement
42. Prosperity doctrine
43. Psychology

Denying the Doctrine of Christ – John's epistles
44. Jesus did not physically resurrect
45. Jesus was not sinless
46. Jesus is not God, the son of God, or divine
47. Deny physical return of Jesus – 2 John
48. Jesus/Christians do not resurrect in the flesh
49. Jesus not a descendant of David

Ancient Prophecies Revealed

Facets of the Apostasy
Master Chart

Early Church Fathers — Gnostic depths of Satan
Tolerance/Ecumenicism
50. All religions are the same
51. To say there is only one way is intolerant
Calvinism-Pelegianism
52. Born sinless
53. Unconditional election, double predestination, man does not have free will
Sin no longer matters
54. God is the author of sin
55. Morality is legalism
56. There is no original sin
57. Common law marriages, fornication, homosexuality, orgies, abortion, euthanasia, & lying are ok
Jesus is not the Christ
58. Taught adoptionism (Jesus is not the Christ)
59. Jesus did not die on the cross
60. Jesus did not have a physical body
61. Jesus does not currently have a physical body
62. Jesus was only a man
63. Jesus was not the only creator
64. Jesus was not the Christ or the only Christ
65. Taught tri-theism & dualism
66. Deny the Holy Spirit exists
67. God and Satan are equal
68. Jesus was not the only emanation of God the Father
Deny Scripture
69. Parts were man-made, cultural, or only an allegory
70. Gospel of Thomas, Judas, & others equal to Scripture
71. Use of Bible codes
72. Reject Textus Receptus
73. Tradition is equal to Scripture

Early Church Fathers — Gnostic depths of Satan
Sorcery
74. Use of incantations
75. Use of illicit drugs
76. Taught astrology & fate are real
77. Use of magic
78. Use of statues of angels and saints
79. Taught we evolve into gods
80. Taught we become angels after death
81. Taught prophets need not be 100% accurate
82. Taught prophets make use of "the ecstasy"
Works Salvation
83. Last rites
84. Baptismal regeneration
85. Transubstantiation
86. Monastic asceticism
87. Penance
88. Cardinal and venial sins
89. Purgatory
90. Salvation is by faith in Christ plus something else
91. Multiple baptisms to remove recent sins
92. Taught the Sacraments impart some form of grace
Other Points
93. Anti-Israel
94. Christians can be demon possessed
95. Taught serpent seed doctrine
96. Taught soul sleep / the soul is not eternal
97. Taught there were female angels
98. Medicine is demonic
99. Allow women clergy
100. Drinking wine is a sin
101. Satan will eventually be saved

The ancient church fathers describe all the errors listed in the previous page. For the sake of space I have not listed any error twice.

The Rapture of the Church

First; we want to see *what* the Rapture is and then show *when* it occurs.

What is the Rapture?
A rapture is when God supernaturally takes someone from one place to another. There are various raptures in Scripture. Philip was raptured to another place on earth in order to witness to an Ethiopian. Enoch was changed and raptured to heaven. The word "rapture" is found in the Latin Bible. English Bibles translate it as the "catching up" or the "snatching away." In Greek, the word is "harpizo;" but in the Latin is it called "raptus." The Rapture of the church is the event recorded in 1 Thessalonians 4:15-18. Paul describes the future Rapture of the church in this way:

Various Raptures:
Paul caught up to third heaven – 2 Corinthians 12:2,4
The Church Rapture – 1 Thessalonians 4:17
Philip caught away by the spirit – Acts 8:39
Man child caught away – Revelation 12:5
Two witnesses caught up – Revelation 11:12
Enoch taken – Hebrews 11:5

> "For this we say to you by the word of the Lord, that we who are alive and remain until the coming of the Lord, will not precede those who have fallen asleep. For the Lord Himself will descend from heaven with a shout, with the voice of the archangel and with the trumpet of God, and the dead in Christ will rise first. Then we who are alive and remain will be *caught up* together with them in the clouds to meet the Lord in the air, and so we shall always be with the Lord. Therefore comfort one another with these words." *1 Thessalonians 4:15-18*

At the time of the Rapture, the living believers in Christ will be instantly changed from having a mortal body into having an immortal one. We will no longer have physical problems or a sin nature. This is referred to in Scripture as the time when we receive that "blessed hope" we have been waiting for, the redemption of our bodies. Listed, to the right, are the names for the Rapture given in Scripture.

Names for the Rapture of the Church in Scripture
The Appearing – Hebrews 9:28
The Blessed Hope of the "the appearing" – Titus 2:13
The Catching away – 1 Thessalonians 4:17
The Changing – 1 Corinthians 15:52
The Entering the bridal chamber – Isaiah 26:19-21
The Gathering – 2 Thessalonians 2:1
The Manifesting of the Sons of God – Romans 8:18-25
The Mercy – Jude 21
The Receiving – John 14:3
The Redemption of our Bodies – Romans 8:18-25
The Rescue/Deliverance from "the wrath" – 1 Thessalonians 1:10
The Rescue – Daniel 12:1-2
The Revelation of Jesus Christ – 1 Corinthians 1:7; 1 Peter 1:13
The Transformation – Philippians 3:20-21

When is the Rapture?
The key to identifying the Rapture in Scripture is understanding the 70 weeks prophecy of Daniel 9. Sixty-nine weeks of years spanned the time between Artexerxes' decree to rebuild the Temple to the death of the Messiah. According to Daniel 9:26, this gap between the 69th and 70th weeks contains the Messiah's death, the birth of the church, Titus destroying the Temple, and the great Dispersion. When we realize that the church age is the gap, we see that the Rapture occurs prior to the seven-year Tribulation.

```
69 weeks         Church Age              70th week
                   "Gap"
   AD 32                         Rapture           2nd Coming
```

During the 70th week, God will pour out His wrath and we are told by Scripture, 1 Thessalonians 1:9-10, and the ancient church fathers that the church will be Raptured out before His wrath is poured out. Notice the order that Paul gives for these events:

> "…with regard to the coming of our Lord Jesus Christ and our gathering together to Him… that you not be quickly shaken… that the day of the Lord has come… for it will not come unless the apostasy comes first, and the man of lawlessness is revealed… And you know what restrains him now, so that in his time he will be revealed. For the mystery of lawlessness is already at work; only he who now restrains will do so until he is taken out of the way."
> *1 Thessalonians 2:2-7*

Ancient Prophecies Revealed

Here Paul is giving the order of the end times. He first refers to the Second Coming and "our gathering together to him" which is the Rapture. First, he shows the order of events as they happen on earth. The church begins to become apostate, *then* the Antichrist is revealed, *then* the Day of the Lord comes, and *then* the Second Coming occurs resulting in the destruction of the Antichrist. But when does the Rapture happen? He teaches that the Rapture of the church, the gathering, is what restrains the Antichrist. The only reason they would be shaken by thinking the Day of the Lord had come is because that would mean they missed a pre-tribulation Rapture.

The last part of verse 7 literally says, in Greek, "it will restrain until it is taken out of the midst." Note: the Greek in this verse can be it/he/she. So if the Antichrist is held back the until the restrainer is "taken out of the midst" then what does the phrase "taken out of the midst" mean? This phrase only occurs once in the entire Bible. Here are a few quotes from the ancient church fathers that show how they interpreted this passage.

> "The sky being split apart like a scroll is the *church being taken away*." (Revelation 6:14)
> *Victorinus Commentary on Revelation 6:14 - AD 240*

> "And I saw another great and wonderful sign, seven angels having the seven last plagues; for in them is completed the Wrath of God. (Revelation 15:1) and these shall be in the last time, when the *Church shall have gone out of the midst*."
> (2 Thessalonians 2:7)   *Commentary on the Apocalypse 15.1 - Victorinus AD 240*

So when the true believers are taken out of the midst of the earth in the Rapture/gathering, *then* the deluding influence of the apostasy can take full effect and the Antichrist can be revealed. The apostasy is the sign that the restrainer is about to be "taken out of the midst." The Scriptures also teach that the church will not be subject to the "wrath" of the Tribulation. Luke 21:23 says the "wrath" is for His people Israel. The church is not appointed to wrath, οργην (1 Thessalonians 5:9) and will be kept from the hour of trial (Revelation 3:10) because the gates of hell will not prevail against the church (Matthew 16:18). Here are a few more comments from the ancient church fathers on the Rapture.

Famous Pre-Trib Raptureists
Shepherd, AD 150
Victorinus, AD 240
Cyprian, AD 250
Ephraim the Syrian, AD 373

The Shepherd of Hermas was written about AD 150. It describes a dream and gives the interpretation of it. The church (bride clothed in white) escapes the Great Tribulation because of the promise of the Lord. This is not to be considered Scripture, but it does show that many second century Christians believed in a pre-tribulational Rapture.

> "Go therefore and declare to the Elect of the Lord His mighty deeds and say to them that this beast is a type of **the great tribulation** which is to come. If ye therefore prepare yourselves and with your whole heart turn to the Lord in repentance, then shall ye **be able to escape it**, if your heart is **pure and blameless**… the golden color stands for you who have escaped from this world… Now ye know the symbol of the **great tribulation** to come. But **if ye are willing, it shall be nothing**." *Shepard AD 150*

Cyprian was bishop of Carthage about AD 250. Notice he did not teach we must endure the time of the Antichrist but we will be "delivered" from it. He tells his readers that the coming resurrection was the hope of the Christian, and points out that the Rapture should motivate us as we see the last days approaching.

> "we who see that terrible things have begun, and know that still more terrible things are imminent, may regard it as the **greatest advantage to depart** from it as quickly as possible. Do you not give God thanks, do you not congratulate yourself, that by an **early departure you are taken away**, **and delivered** from the shipwrecks and disasters that are imminent? Let us greet the day which assigns each of us to his own home, which **snatches us hence**, and sets us free from the snares of the world, and **restores** us to paradise and the kingdom" *Treatises of Cyprian – 21 to 26*

> "The Antichrist is coming, but above him comes Christ also. The enemy goes about and rages, but immediately the Lord follows to avenge our suffering and our wounds. The adversary is enraged and threatens, but there is One who can **deliver us** from his hands." *Epistle 55 – Cyprian AD 250*

Rapture of the Church

This next quote is from a work entitled pseudo-Ephraim. It has the title pseudo, not because anyone doubted the sermon, but because when quoted later, two historians said it was Ephraim the Syrian who wrote it, and one historian said it was Isadore of Seville. Whether this was written by Isadore or Ephraim, the sermon was always accepted as genuine. It clearly shows a Rapture before the Tribulation occurs.

> "...because all saints and the elect of the LORD are gathered together **before the Tribulation** which is about to come and be taken to the LORD..." *On The Last Times 2 – Ephraim the Syrian AD 373*

First Trump, Last Trump, and the Great Trump

When we look at the seven festivals that God instructed the Jews to celebrate every year, we find they are prophetic. The first four, as we have seen, teach about the First Coming of the Messiah. Jesus was crucified on Passover, resurrected on First Fruits, and the church was born on Pentecost. There are many names for each festival. Each name describes something about the prophecy. Pentecost is called the Festival of the "First Trump." In the fall the last three festivals occur. These prophetically teach about the Second Coming of the Messiah, and will be discussed in their entirety in the next section on the Tribulation period. The Festival of Trumpets is called the Festival of "The Awakening Blast" and the "Last Trump." In contrast with this, the festival of the Day of Atonement is called the Festival of the "Great Trump." This helps us organize the prophecies in Scripture. Whenever we see "last trump" in Scripture, we know it is referring to the time of the Rapture/Resurrection of believers. Whenever we see the "great trump" we know it is referring to the Second Coming. To verify the different festival names, look them up in the Encyclopedia Judaica.

> "Behold, I tell you a mystery; we will not all sleep, but we will all be changed, in a moment, in the twinkling of an eye, at the last trumpet; for the trumpet will sound, and the dead will be raised imperishable, and we will be changed."
> *I Corinthians 15:50-52*

Jewish Festivals

The chart at the right shows the outline of this time period with the fall festivals. The New Year starts with Rosh HaShannah (RHS). This is a two-day festival occurring on the first and second of Tishrei. Tishrei occurs during our September/October. This festival is also called Yom Teruah, which means the "day of the awakening blast." Jewish tradition says this is the day when the Resurrection will occur. Paul tells us the Resurrection and the Rapture will occur on the same day in the twinkling of an eye.

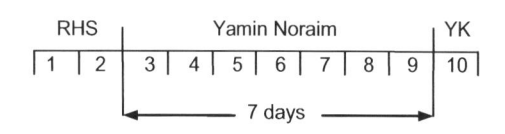

The tenth of Tishrei is the festival of Yom Kippur (YK), which means the "Day of Atonement." The ritual preformed on Yom Kippur teaches about the destruction of the Antichrist and the Second Coming of the Messiah. (See the section on the Tribulation for more details). The time between Rosh HaShannah and Yom Kippur are called the Yomin Noraim, which means the "days of awe" or the terrible days. The ancient rabbi's took this name from Joel 2:11, which refers to the Day of the Lord. Notice, the Yomin Noraim are the seven days/years that occur between the Rapture/Resurrection and the Second Coming! This gives a perfect picture of the pre-tribulational Rapture of the Church.

> "The LORD utters His voice before His army; surely His camp is very great, for strong is he who carries out His word. The day of the LORD is indeed great and very awesome [Nora], and who can endure it?" *Joel 2:11*

Daniel On the Rapture

Daniel describes the "time of distress," which is that seven-year period prior to the start of the Messiah's one thousand-year reign, saying that it starts with all believers being rescued. The "rescue" is one of the names for the Rapture; see the chart at the beginning of this section. This will also include believers who have died. The unbelieving dead will resurrect later.

> "Now at that time Michael, the great prince who stands guard over the sons of your people, will arise. And there will be a time of distress such as never occurred since there was a nation until that time; and at that time your people, everyone who is found written in the book, will be rescued. Many of those who sleep in the dust of the ground will awake, these to everlasting life, but the others to disgrace and everlasting contempt." *Daniel 12:1-2*

Ancient Prophecies Revealed

Isaiah On the Rapture:
The prophet Isaiah spoke of the time right before the time of the Lord's Indignation (also called the Great Tribulation), when His people would be hidden in their bridal chamber. The church is always referred to as the bride of Christ. The Rapture/Resurrection occurs before the wrath is poured out.

> "Your dead will live; their corpses will rise. You who lie in the dust, awake and shout for joy, for your dew is as the dew of the dawn, and the earth will give birth to the departed spirits. Come, my people, enter into your rooms [chedar, or wedding chamber], and close your doors behind you; hide for a little while until indignation runs its course. For behold, the LORD is about to come out from His place to punish the inhabitants of the earth for their iniquity; and the earth will reveal her bloodshed, and will no longer cover her slain." *Isaiah 26:19-21*

Removal Of the Gift of Tongues a Sign the Rapture Has Occurred
Paul quotes Isaiah 28:9-13 in 1 Corinthians 14:21. Paul interprets this as a prophecy that the gift of speaking in tongues by the Christians is a sign that the nation of Israel, which had corporately rejected Jesus Christ as Messiah, was about to be destroyed. Within 40 years Jerusalem was destroyed by the Romans. This same phrase "speak to this people through stammering lips and a foreign tongue" is used in Isaiah 33. This prophecy states those in the Tribulation will no longer see the church, those who speak in tongues. It asks "where did they go?" They went to a far distant land with the King of beauty; while they are gone the people who remain will be in terror. But when the appointed feast is fulfilled, those who survive will see the king and the church return.

> "Your eyes will see the King in His beauty; they will behold a far-distant land. Your heart will meditate on terror: 'Where is he who counts? Where is he who weighs? Where is he who counts the towers?' You will no longer see a fierce people, a people of unintelligible speech which no one comprehends, of a stammering tongue which no one understands. Look upon Zion, the city of our appointed feasts; your eyes will see Jerusalem, an undisturbed habitation, a tent which will not be folded; its stakes will never be pulled up, nor any of its cords be torn apart." *Isaiah 33:17-20*

The apostle Paul said the same thing in 1 Corinthians. Love would continue forever but prophecy would come to an end when they are all fulfilled. Tongues would not be seen any longer when "that which is perfect comes." Ancient church father Irenaeus, in *Against Heresies 4.9*, stated that the spiritual gifts will continue to manifest in the church until "that which is perfect" has come and we see Him "face to face." In quoting these phrases from 1 Corinthians 13, Irenaeus teaches the gifts will continue until the Rapture.

Zephaniah On the Rapture
We have seen in previous sections Zephaniah 2:1-4 prophesied a series of events ending with the Rapture. True believers will be "hidden in the day of the LORD'S anger." Before this occurs, Gaza would be forsaken. Gaza has been conquered several times but never just given away until Israel under Ariel Sharon handed it over to the Palestinians in AD 2005. See the section on Modern Israel for full details. So the Rapture of the Church must occur sometime after AD 2005!

Other Notes
In 1 Thessalonians 4:15-18, the Lord comes and takes the saints with him into the clouds. In John 14:1-3, Jesus said that He would return and immediately receive us and take us with Him to the mansions of heaven. In 1 Thessalonians 3:13 and 4:14 Jesus brings the saints back with Him at the Second Coming. 1 Thessalonians 5:2 shows the Day of the Lord comes as a "thief in the night." This means the Day of the Lord begins with Jesus stealing away His church in the Rapture. That will be completely unexpected by the apostate church which no longer believes in the prophecies of the Rapture and the coming wrath.

As we have seen, the Rapture begins the Day of the Lord. One characteristic of the unbelievers who will be left behind when the Rapture takes place, is that they were not really expecting the Rapture to occur. We see this today in the Kingdom Now movement and Amillennialism. Instead of realizing things get worse with the coming of the Antichrist, they think we are dwelling in "peace and safety" and the church will eventually take over the world for Jesus. This same thing occurred in Daniel 11:14. Even though the prophecies were very clear as to what would happen and who would win the war, a false prophet arose and convinced some of the Jews they were to arise and fight and take the kingdom for God. The result is they were all slaughtered. Today those in the church who believe in Amillennialism and Kingdom Now theology don't want to wait for the Lord, but think they are supposed to take the world by force. They may suffer a similar fate.

In Matthew 24:48, Jesus said the *evil servant* says the Lord delays His coming; this is exactly what the amillennial position does. Jesus also said the *good servant* looks for his master's coming. This is the pre-millennial and pre-tribulational Rapture positions. In 1 John 3:2-3, John says all who look forward to the Rapture purify themselves. If you believe you must endure the Antichrist's reign before the Rapture, you will not be looking forward to it. So your doctrine is not pure.

> "and to wait for His Son from heaven, whom He raised from the dead, that is Jesus, who **rescues** us from the wrath to come." *1 Thesalonains 1:10*

Ancient Prophecies Revealed

The Tribulation
Rapture to the Second Coming – 82 prophecies in seven years

Prophecies concerning the first half of the Tribulation	References
387. Apostasy comes – See section on the Apostasy of the Church	
388. Restrainer leaves – See section on the Rapture of the Church	2 Thess. 2:6-7
389. Antichrist revealed when he ratifies the peace covenant	Dan. 9:27; 2 Thess. 2:3
390. The Tribulation (Daniel's 70th week) will begin a seven-year period with a signed peace covenant	Dan. 9:27
391. New Jerusalem Temple built	2 Thess. 2:4; Dan. 9:27
392. Temple Mount divided	Ezek. 43; Rev. 12
393. Gospel preached to all nations	Matt. 24:14
394. Elijah returns and preaches against the Antichrist for 3.5 years	Mal. 4:5-6
The Antichrist's rise to power	
395. He will be revealed when the ten nations are in power	Dan. 7:24
396. He will be different from the ten (previous) kings	Dan. 7:24
397. He will rise to power by trickery like Antiochus Epiphanes did	Dan. 11:21-24
398. He will give great honor to those who acknowledge him and cause them to rule over many, and will parcel out land for a price	Dan. 11:39
The Antichrist's identifying characteristics	
399. The letters of his name will equal 666 if spelled out in Greek	Rev. 13:16-17
400. Antichrist's right eye and one arm damaged	Zech. 11:17
The wars fought by the Antichrist in his rise to power	
401. He will subdue three kings (of the ten) then ten kings will be given into his hand for 42 months	Dan. 7:8,24,25
402. Egypt, the King of the south, will attack the Antichrist	Dan. 11:40
403. Egypt and many other countries will fall to him.	Dan. 11:42
404. Syria, the King of the North, will attack the Antichrist	Dan. 11:40
405. Many other nations will be destroyed by the Antichrist	Dan. 11:40
406. He will destroy to an extraordinary degree	Dan. 8:24
407. He will destroy many while they are at ease (at peace)	Dan. 8:25
408. The Libyans and Ethiopians will follow at his heels	Dan. 11:43
409. Rumors from the east and north will disturb him and he will annihilate many	Dan. 11:44
410. One-fourth of the world's population will be destroyed under his "leadership"	Rev. 6:8
411. Animals attack	Amos 5:18; Rev. 6:8
Antichrist rules supreme	
412. The remaining seven nations will willingly accept his leadership	Rev. 17:12-13
413. He will pitch the tent of his royal pavilion between the seas and the holy mountain.	Dan. 11:45

First 3.5 years of the Tribulation

Introduction - The 70 Weeks
To begin to draw a good picture of the Tribulation period we must start by identifying it with the 70th week of Daniel, a period of 2,520 days or two sets of 1260 days. In Daniel Chapter 9, the angel Gabriel explains that at the end of the 70 weeks of years (490 Jewish years) all would be fulfilled, meaning the Second Coming would occur and Jesus would be anointed king and start His millennial reign.

> "Seventy weeks have been decreed for your people and your holy city, to finish the transgression, to make an end of sin, to make atonement for iniquity, to bring in everlasting righteousness, to seal up vision and prophecy and to anoint the most holy. [Jesus Christ]" *Daniel 9:24*

The Tribulation

As we saw in the section on the Messiah's First Coming, Jesus died at the end of the 69th week, which occurred in AD 32. His death and resurection began the church age, which fills the gap in the 70-weeks prophecy. About this gap Daniel says:

> "the people of the prince who is to come will destroy the city and the sanctuary. And its end will come with a flood; even to the end there will be war; desolations are determined." *Daniel 9:26*

Here, Daniel describes the period when Titus came and destroyed the Temple. Of this destruction, Jesus prophesied that not one stone would be left upon another. This was fulfilled in AD 70. The last part of verse 26 predicts that the nation of Israel would become desolate. This desolation, or dispersion, took place in stages beginning with the destruction of the Temple in AD 70. The nation was completely dissolved by AD 132. The period of desolation ended when the nation of Israel was reestablished in 1948. So, verse 27 is speaking of the Antichrist during the Tribulation period which occurs sometime after AD 1948.

> "And **he** will make a firm covenant with the many for one week, but in the middle of the week he will put a stop to sacrifice and grain offering; and on the wing of abominations will come one who makes desolate, even until a complete destruction, one that is decreed, is poured out on the one who makes desolate." *Daniel 9:27*

In verse 27, the "he" who stops the Temple sacrifices is the Antichrist. Since Jesus returns at the end of the last seven year period we know this was not fulfilled by Titus. In order for the Antichrist to *stop* the Temple sacrifices they must be started up again. In order for the sacrifices to be started, the Jerusalem Temple must be rebuilt. As of AD 2008, this has not occurred. So some time in the future the Antichrist will confirm, or enforce, a peace covenant with the Jews and Palestinians for a period of seven years. Part of the agreement will permit the Jews to rebuild their Temple.

To this we add the information from 2 Thessalonians 2. Paul here describes the order in which the prophecies will be fulfilled. First, the apostasy comes, then the restrainer leaves, then the Antichrist is revealed by enforcing the peace plan, and finally, the Day of the Lord occurs.

> "Now we request you, brethren, with regard to the coming of our Lord Jesus Christ and our gathering together to Him, that you not be quickly shaken from your composure or be disturbed either by a spirit or a message or a letter as if from us, to the effect that the day of the Lord has come. Let no one in any way deceive you, for it will not come unless the apostasy comes first, and the man of lawlessness is revealed, the son of destruction, who opposes and exalts himself above every so-called god or object of worship, so that he takes his seat in the temple of God, displaying himself as being God... For the mystery of lawlessness is already at work; only he who now restrains will do so until he is taken out of the way. Then that lawless one will be revealed whom the Lord will slay with the breath of His mouth and bring to an end by the appearance of His coming." *2 Thessalonians 2:1-4,7-8*

The chart at the right shows the outline of the Tribulation from Daniel 9 and 2 Thessalonians 2.

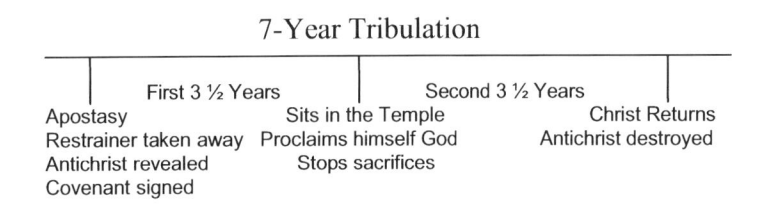

7-Year Tribulation

First 3 ½ Years	Second 3 ½ Years
Apostasy	Sits in the Temple
Restrainer taken away	Proclaims himself God
Antichrist revealed	Stops sacrifices
Covenant signed	
	Christ Returns
	Antichrist destroyed

The Day Of the Lord

This seven-year Tribulation is also known as the "Day of the Lord" and the "indignation." When some prophets describe the Day of the Lord, they focus on the great battle, Armageddon, at the Second Coming. Still other prophets focus on events in the last half of the seven-year period when the wrath of God is poured out. These descriptions have led some to think the Day of the Lord is actually only the second half of the seven-year period. A few prophets describe events that occur in the Day of the Lord that occur during the *first* half of the seven-year period. That proves the Day of the Lord covers the *entire* seven-year period.

Names for the Tribulation
Daniel's 70th Week
Day of the LORD – Amos 5:18
The Indignation – Daniel 8:19

Ancient Prophecies Revealed

Daniel describes the period of the indignation as the rise and fall of the Antichrist.

> "He said, "Behold, I am going to let you know what will occur at the final period of the indignation, for it pertains to the appointed time of the end… A king will arise, insolent and skilled in intrigue… He will even oppose the Prince of princes, but he will be broken without human agency." *Daniel 8:19,23,25*

Amos describes the Day of the Lord as the time when the animals attack. As we will see, Revelation has the animals' attack in the Fourth Seal. This occurs after the rise of the Antichrist in the First Seal but before the persecution of the martyrs in the Fifth Seal, which occurs in the middle of the Tribulation.

> "…the day of the LORD, …It will be darkness and not light; as when a man flees from a lion, and a bear meets him, or goes home, leans his hand against the wall, and a snake bites him." *Amos 5:18-19*

> "When the Lamb broke the fourth seal… Authority was given to them over a fourth of the earth, to kill with sword and with famine and with pestilence and by the wild beasts of the earth." *Revelation 6:7-8*

Paul clearly teaches that when the restrainer leaves, *then* the Antichrist is revealed. His revelation begins the Day of the Lord.

> "…only he who now restrains will do so until he is taken out of the way. Then that lawless one will be revealed whom the Lord will slay…" *2 Thessalonians 2:7-8*

> "… to the effect that the day of the Lord has come. Let no one in any way deceive you, for it will not come unless the apostasy comes first, and the man of lawlessness is revealed, the son of destruction," *2 Thessalonians 2:2-3*

Day of the Lord
Isaiah 2:12; 13:6-9
Ezekiel 13:5; 30:3
Joel 1:15; 2:1,11,31; 3:14
Amos 5:18,20
Obadiah 15
Zephaniah 1:7, 14-18
Zechariah 14:1
Malachi 4:5
Acts 2:20
1 Thessalonians 5:2
2 Thessalonians 2:2
2 Peter 3:10

The Apostasy

Toward the end of the church age a great apostasy (or falling away from the faith) will occur. In the section on the Apostasy of the Church we listed 92 points describing this apostasy. Of these 92 points, only about five have yet to be fulfilled! See the section on the Apostasy of the Church for complete details.

The Rapture

In the section on the Rapture, we saw several Old and New Testament Scriptures that chronicle the Rapture of the Church. Paul writes that the Antichrist can not be revealed until "the restrainer" is taken from the midst of the earth. We saw in the section on the Rapture, the ancient church fathers taught the restrainer was the church itself. This means the Antichrist will be revealed *after* the Rapture of the church. See the section on the Rapture for complete details.

> "And you know what restrains him now, so that in his time he will be revealed. For the mystery of lawlessness is already at work; only he who now restrains will do so until he is taken out of the way." *2 Thessalonians 2:6-7*

Antichrist Revealed

As seen above, the Antichrist is revealed after the Rapture of the Church. The Antichrist will be identified when he enforces a peace covenant with Israel. This "peace covenant" will start the seven-year Tribulation, which is identical with the last week of Daniel's 70-Weeks prophecy. 2 Thessalonians tells us the revelation of the Antichrist initiates the "Day of the Lord," which is another name for the Tribulation.

> "And he will make a firm covenant with the many for one week, but in the middle of the week he will put a stop to sacrifice and grain offering; and on the wing of abominations will come one who makes desolate, even until a complete destruction, one that is decreed, is poured out on the one who makes desolate." *Daniel 9:27*

> "that you not be quickly shaken from your composure or be disturbed either by a spirit or a message or a letter as if from us, to the effect that the day of the Lord has come. Let no one in any way deceive you, for it will not come unless the apostasy comes first, and the man of lawlessness is revealed, the son of destruction," *2 Thessalonians 2:2-3*

The Tribulation

The first Seal in the book of Revelation shows the Antichrist on a white horse conquering with a bow that has no arrows. This symbolizes the Antichrist will be revealed when he enforces the peace covenant. A bow with no arrows is not a weapon of war.

> "I looked, and behold, a white horse, and he who sat on it had a bow; and a crown was given to him, and he went out conquering and to conquer." *First Seal – Revelation 6:2*

New Temple Built on the Jerusalem Temple Mount

Paul describes the Antichrist will sit in the Temple and proclaim himself to be God. He can not sit in the Temple until one is built on the Temple Mount in Jerusalem!

> "who opposes and exalts himself above every so-called god or object of worship, so that he takes his seat in the temple of God, displaying himself as being God." *2 Thessalonians 2:4*

The ancient church fathers understood this verse to mean that a Jewish Temple will be rebuilt on the Temple Mount in Jerusalem. In *Marcion* 5.16, Tertullian wrote that the Temple will be rebuilt. Irenaeus, in *Against Heresies* 5.25, says the apostle Paul proves there will be a literal rebuilt Temple (in 2 Thessalonians). Irenaeus goes on to say when Jesus spoke about Daniel's Abomination of Desolation (in Matthew 24), He was referring to the Antichrist sitting in a rebuilt Temple. Origen, in *Against Celsus* 6:46, asserts the prophecies in 1 Thessalonians and Daniel are *real* prophesies about the end of the world and that there will be a literal rebuilt Temple.

Tribulation Temple/Peace Plan

> "And he shall confirm the covenant with many for one week: and in the midst of the week he shall cause the sacrifice and the oblation to cease, and for the overspreading of abominations he shall make it desolate, even until the consummation, and that determined shall be poured upon the desolate." *Daniel 9:27 KJV*

Notice that the Antichrist does not make up the points of the Peace Plan all by himself. He "confirms" or *ratifies one already in place*. The chart at the right shows the proposed Peace Plans between 1947 and 2007. The heart of each of these plans includes Israel trading land for peace. An independent state will be created out of the West Bank. Daniel 11:45 states the Antichrist will build his headquarters "between the seas and the holy mountain." This describes

Date	Peace Agreements	Details
1947	UN Resolution 181	Jerusalem to be an international city, not belonging to Jews
1978	Camp David Accords	Gaza Strip & West Bank become autonomous; Israel withdraws from Sinai
1991	Madrid Conference	Exchange land for peace
1993	Oslo Accords	Withdraw from parts of West Bank & Gaza and allow them limited self rule
1996	Israel-Jordan treaty	Jordan River water rights and some land went back to Jordan
2000	Camp-David Summit	Israel returns land from the 67 war, Palestinian state in West Bank & Gaza
2007	Annapolis Conference	Independent Palestinian State, Jerusalem to be divided

the current area of the West Bank. It lies between the seas of Galilee and Mediterranean and mount Zion in Jerusalem. The Antichrist is not originally from the West Bank; but after the war with Egypt, he will build his palace there.

The "many" peoples will include: Israel, Syria, Egypt, possibly the ten nations, and others. Egypt and two other nations will not agree with the peace plan and the Antichrist will attack and conquer them.

The main points of the Peace Plan will be the reshaping of the Israeli borders, the creation of an independent Palestinian State in the West Bank with full autonomy, and possibly an independent state of Gaza. The most interesting part of the plan will be to allow the Temple Mount to be divided between the Jews and the Muslims. The Dome of the Rock will be left untouched and the Jews will rebuild their Temple *without the outer Gentile court*. This will leave enough space between the two structures that a wall will be built between the holy Temple and the "profane" Dome of the Rock, according to the prophet

Ancient Prophecies Revealed

Ezekiel. The wall will be 500 cubits by 500 cubits and can be seen in the diagram to the right. This will allow both Jews and Muslims to keep their sacred sites, much like today's Jerusalem is divided into four quarters: Catholic, Orthodox, Armenian, and Jewish. This Peace Plan and the division of the Temple Mount will only last for 42 months. Then the Antichrist will assume control of all the land of Israel.

> "Leave out the court which is outside the temple and do not measure it, for it has been given to the nations; and they will tread under foot the holy city for forty-two months." *Revelation 11:2*

> "He measured it on the four sides; it had a wall all around, the length five hundred and the width five hundred, to divide between the holy and the profane. *Ezekiel 42:20*

If the Temple Mount is divided, then Antichrist's Peace Plan may also divid Jerusalem, possibly as part of the new nation in the West Bank. This might account for the prophecy in Zechariah 14 and Isaiah 13.

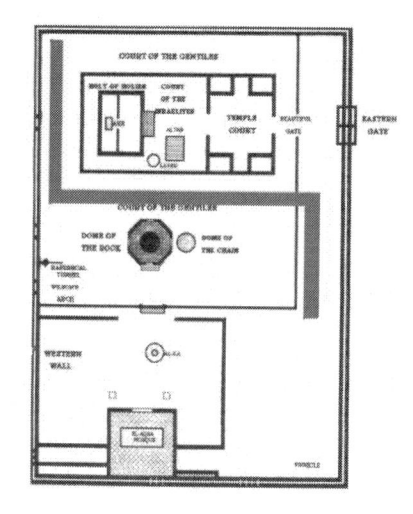

> "For I will gather all the nations against Jerusalem to battle, and the city will be captured, the houses plundered, the women ravished and *half of the city exiled* [my emphasis], but the rest of the people will not be cut off from the city." *Zechariah 14:2*

Many Jews today think the Temple can only be rebuilt by the coming of the Messiah; this prepares them for the delusion of the Antichrist.

Gospel Preached To All Nations
In Matthew 24:14, Jesus said the Gospel will be preached to all nations before the Great Tribulation. This will be accomplished by the two witnesses of Revelation 11 and the 144,000 Jewish witnesses of Revelation 7.

Elijah the Prophet
Malachi recorded a prophecy that said God will send Elijah the prophet back before the Day of the Lord begins. Given below is the quote from the Scriptures and a paraphrase showing how the ancient church interpreted it.

> "Behold, I am going to send you Elijah the prophet before the coming of the great and terrible day of the LORD. He will restore the hearts of the fathers to their children and the hearts of the children to their fathers, so that I will not come and smite the land with a curse." *Malachi 4:5-6*

> "It is a matter of course that His forerunners must appear first, as He says by Malachi and the angel, 'I will send to you Elias the Tishbite before the day of the Lord, the great and notable day, comes; and he shall turn the hearts of the fathers to the children, and the disobedient to the wisdom of the just, lest I come and smite the earth utterly.' These, then, shall come and proclaim the manifestation of Christ that is to be from heaven; and they shall also perform signs and wonders, in order that men may be put to shame and turned to repentance for their surpassing wickedness and impiety."
> Hipolytus *Treatise on Christ and Antichrist 46*

The Antichrist's Rise To Power
Through his deceit and trickery, the Antichrist will deceive the world rulers into recognizing him. This is the same way Antiochus Epiphanes manipulated his way into power. (Please study Daniel 11 in detail to see Antiochus' example.) This will occur while the ten nations are in power. The Antichrist, however, will be different from the rulers of the ten nations. He will not be a rightful king. His claim to power will be religious instead of secular.

"As for the ten horns, out of this kingdom ten kings will arise; and another will arise after them, and he will be different from the previous ones and will subdue three kings." *Daniel 7:24*

Jesus made the connection between the abomination that Antiochus Epiphanes set up in the Temple and what the Antichrist will do; so we know Antiochus Epiphanes is a type of the Antichrist. In Daniel 11 Antiochus Epiphanes deceived the Roman Empire into thinking he was the rightful king of Syria. Likewise, the Antichrist will come into power through trickery. Antiochus placed an idol of his god in the Jerusalem Temple. He tried to force all the Jews to sacrifice to his god. Likewise the Antichrist will try to do the same thing. Since Antiochus tricked the Roman Empire, could that mean the Antichrist will trick Papal Rome into recognizing his power?

"...a despicable person will arise, on whom the honor of kingship has not been conferred, but he will come in a time of tranquility and seize the kingdom by intrigue. The overflowing forces will be flooded away before him and shattered, and also the prince of the covenant. After an alliance is made with him he will practice deception, and he will go up and gain power with a small force of people. In a time of tranquility he will enter the richest parts of the realm, and he will accomplish what his fathers never did, nor his ancestors; he will distribute plunder, booty and possessions among them, and he will devise his schemes against strongholds, but only for a time." *Daniel 11:21-24*

"...he will give great honor to those who acknowledge him and will cause them to rule over the many, and will parcel out land for a price." *Daniel 11:39b*

The Name of the Antichrist – 666

The Antichrist will cause all under his authority to receive a mark on their hand or forehead. <u>Those who take this mark will be damned.</u> This is why no Christian will allow an identification mark or

Geek Numerals								
α 1	β 2	γ 3	δ 4	ε 5	ς 6	ζ 7	η 8	θ 9
ι 10	κ 20	λ 30	μ 40	ν 50	ξ 60	ο 70	π 80	ϙ 90
ρ 100	σ 200	τ 300	υ 400	φ 500	χ 600	ψ 700	ω 800	ϡ 900

computer chip to be implanted in them! Those who receive the mark will either take the number or the name of the Antichrist. This probably means that there will be two types of mark: one mark for his government and military, and another for citizens. Revelation 13 recorded the number of his name is 666. In the Greek and Hebrew languages, the symbols for numbers are the same as their letters. Using the chart at the right we can decipher names. I'll use my name, Ken, as an example. If my name is spelled the same way in Greek, then "K" is 20, "e" is 5, and "n" is 50. Therefore, my name, "Ken," equals 75. Interestingly enough, Ken spelled out in Hebrew and converted into a number also comes out to be 75. I'm glad it does, because if it came out to 666, you might be a little worried about having me teach you prophecy!

"And he causes all, the small and the great, and the rich and the poor, and the free men and the slaves, to be given a mark on their right hand or on their forehead, and *he provides* that no one will be able to buy or to sell, except the one who has the mark, *either* the name of the beast or the number of his name. Here is wisdom. Let him who has understanding calculate the number of the beast, for the number is that of a man; and his number is six hundred and sixty-six. [χξς´]" *Revelation 13:16-17*

Ancient church father Irenaeus recorded a conversation with Polycarp in his *Against Heresies* 5.30. Irenaeus asked Polycarp how to interpret the 666 passage in Revelation. Polycarp responded that he did not understand the Antichrist's mark, at first, either, so he asked the Apostle John how to interpret it. Polycarp stated that shortly after the death of the apostle John, which occurred towards the end of Domitian's reign, a copyist mistakenly, replaced the ξ with ι. So a variant manuscript of the Scripture developed that stated the antichrist's number was 616. Even today, some Study Bibles will have a note on the 666 passage that says "some ancient manuscripts read 616." Polycarp stated we need first to know the number is 666 or else we *will* be counted along with the false prophets! Polycarp said John explained it this way:

Names that match 666
Titan (Teitan)
Evanthas (Euanqas)
Lateinos (Lateinos)

(Greek spelling)

"But, knowing the sure number declared by Scripture, that is, six hundred sixty and six, let them await, in the first place, the division of the kingdom into ten; then, in the next place, when these kings are reigning, and beginning to set their affairs in order, and advance their kingdom, [let them learn] to acknowledge that he who shall come claiming the kingdom for himself, and shall terrify those men of whom we have been speaking, having a name

Ancient Prophecies Revealed

containing the aforesaid number, is truly the abomination of desolation." Irenaeus' *Against Heresies* 5.30

To summarize, Polycarp is relating to us that the Apostle John's instructions were not to try to figure out the name until you see ten kingdoms arise from what used to be the Roman Empire! When the ten nations form a confederacy then another person will arise and claim the kingdom for himself. His name will total 666.

"It is therefore more certain, and less hazardous, to await the fulfillment of the prophecy, than to be making surmises... We will not, however, incur the risk of pronouncing positively as to the name of Antichrist; for if it were necessary that his name should be distinctly revealed in this present time, it would have been announced... But John indicates the number of the name now, that when this man comes we may avoid him, being aware who he is... But when this Antichrist shall have devastated all things in this world, he will reign for three years and six months, and sit in the temple at Jerusalem; and then the Lord will come from heaven in the clouds, in the glory of the Father, sending this man and those who follow him into the lake of fire." Irenaeus' *Against Heresies* 5.30

Polycap seems to be saying we should covert the name into a number using Greek, but he does not come right out and say that. Just in case we were supposed to be using the Hebrew language for conversion, I have included the Hebrew numerals to the right. Notice most of the numbers correspond to the same sounds, except, 6, 9, 90, 100-400, 600-900. Hippolytus, a disciple of Irenaeus, recorded this same information, in chapter 50 of his book his book *Treatise on Christ and Antichrist*.

Hebrew Numerals								
א 1	ב 2	ג 3	ד 4	ה 5	ו 6	ז 7	ח 8	ט 9
י 10	כ 20	ל 30	מ 40	נ 50	ס 60	ע 70	פ 80	צ 90
ק 100	ר 200	ש 300	ת 400	ך 500	ם 600	ן 700	ף 800	ץ 900

The final form of Hebrew (500 though 900) was not used in their number system until modern times.

Those who could not have been the Antichrist		
Ariel (242) *146*	Sharon (621) *421*	Total (863) *587*
Ehud (16) *417*	Olmert (286) *540*	Total (302) *957*
Adolf (605) *905*	Hitler (243) *453*	Total (848) *1358*
Saddam (179) *250*	Hussein (261) *823*	Total (410) *1073*
Mahmoud (155) *551*	Ahmadinejad (126) *134*	Total (681) *685*
Bashar (504) *304*	al-Assad (167) *437*	Total (671) *741*

(Greek) *Hebrew* Total

Revelation 16:2, which records the first bowl judgment, describes how those who have taken the mark receive a plague of sores. This could be a direct result of a chip implanted under the skin reacting to something in the human body.

"So the first angel went and poured out his bowl on the earth; and it became a loathsome and malignant sore on the people who had the mark of the beast and who worshiped his image." *Revelation 16:2*

Antichrist's Eye and Arm

Zechariah describes the Antichrist as a worthless shepherd. Zechariah predicted that he will destroy three of the ten nations (three shepherds), break his covenant, then divide the Jews and start the persecution. After describing this, Zechariah says this about the Antichrist:

"Woe to the worthless shepherd who leaves the flock! A sword will be on his arm and on his right eye! His arm will be totally withered and his right eye will be blind." *Zechariah 11:17*

This had led many to assume the Antichrist will be wounded in one of the wars he fights. Although this could be describing weakness, it seems more likely that he will become blind in his right eye and loose mobility in one arm.

The Southern War – Egypt

As we have seen in Daniel 7:24, when the Antichrist makes a move for dominance over the ten nations, three of them rebel. Daniel goes on to tell us he will be attacked by the kingdom of the north and the south. Thoughout the rest of Daniel 11, the southern kingdom was Egypt and the northern kingdom was Syria. Daniel 8:24-25 describes these events as the Antichrist

The Tribulation

destroying to an "extraordinary degree" while the "many" are "at peace." These events take place in the first three and a half years of the Tribulation.

> "As for the ten horns, out of this kingdom ten kings will arise; and another will arise after them, and he will be different from the previous ones and will subdue three kings. He will speak out against the Most High and wear down the saints of the Highest One, and he will intend to make alterations in times and in law; and they will be given into his hand for a time, times, and half a time." *Daniel 7:24-25*

> "And another, a red horse, went out; and to him who sat on it, it was granted to take peace from the earth, and that men would slay one another; and a great sword was given to him." *Second Seal – Revelation 6:4*

> "At the end time the king of the South will collide with him, and the king of the North will storm against him with chariots, with horsemen and with many ships; and he will enter countries, overflow them and pass through. He will also enter the Beautiful Land, and many countries will fall; but these will be rescued out of his hand: Edom, Moab and the foremost of the sons of Ammon. Then he will stretch out his hand against other countries, and the land of Egypt will not escape. But he will gain control over the hidden treasures of gold and silver and over all the precious things of Egypt; and Libyans and Ethiopians will follow at his heels." *Daniel 11:40-43*

As a result of this war, the Antichrist will conquer Egypt, Israel, and many other countries. Present day Jordan is comprised of the ancient lands of Edom, Moab, and Ammon. Jordan, then, is the one country in that region that will escape the Antichrist. As a result of this war and the judgment of God, Egypt will be totally devastated.

The Northern War – Syria
After he has conquered Egypt, the Antichrist goes back north and east to attack another country. We are not sure which country is referred to here. If it is *one* country, it must be NE of Egypt. If it is *two* countries, they lay north and east of Egypt. We do know three of the ten nations attack the Antichrist.

> "But rumors from the East and from the North will disturb him, and he will go forth with great wrath to destroy and annihilate many." *Daniel 11:44*

We do not know for sure what nation the Antichrist originates from, but ancient church father, Lactantius, in his *Divine Institutes 7:14* states the Antichrist comes from "the extreme North Country." He also speculated in *Divine Institutes 7:17*, the north country might be Syria.

One Quarter of the World's Population Dies
In the aftermath of the Antichrist's war and rise to power, over one quarter of the population of the earth dies! The war causes famine. As a result of the famine, many people will die from hunger; others will die from other people (the sword) and wild animals (beasts) killing them to get any food they might have. If that does not kill them, they will die of disease (death) from all the dead lying around. Amos calls this time when the animals attack, the Day of the Lord and Revelation shows the animals attacking in the first half of the Tribulation. This proves the Day of the Lord is the whole seven-year period, not just the last half.

> "…an ashen horse; and he who sat on it had the name Death; and Hades was following with him. Authority was given to them over a fourth of the earth, to kill with sword and with famine and with pestilence and by the wild beasts of the earth." *Fourth Seal – Revelation 6:8*

> "Alas, you who are longing for the day of the LORD, for what purpose *will* the day of the LORD *be* to you? It *will be* darkness and not light; as when a man flees from a lion, and a bear meets him, or goes home, leans his hand against the wall, and a snake bites him." *Amos 5:18-19*

Ancient Prophecies Revealed

Antichrist Elected Supreme Ruler

When the Antichrist wins the war with the three nations, the remaining seven nations will elect him as their head. At this point his power will be complete. He will rule for 42 months, until the Messiah returns and destroys him.

> "The ten horns which you saw are ten kings who have not yet received a kingdom, but they receive authority as kings with the beast for one hour. These have one purpose, and they give their power and authority to the beast."
> Revelation 17:12-13

The Book of Revelation confirms the Antichrist's rise to power through the war with three of the ten nations will happen in the first half of the seven-year period.

1. Revelation 12:6 tells us Israel flees into the wilderness to avoid the beast's persecution, remaining there for 3.5 years
2. Revelation 12:3 adds when the dragon pursues fleeing Israel, he only has *seven* crowns on his ten horns
3. Revelation 13:1 explains that when the dragon starts his climb to power, he has *ten* crowns on his ten horns.

So the Antichrist's kingdom must start out with ten sovereign nations. Three kingdoms rebel against him. He wins the war with them, stripping the three rebel nations of their governments. This leaves ten nations with seven rulers. These are the ten horns with only seven crowns. This all happens *before* the three and one half years when Israel goes into hiding.

The Antichrist Selects His Headquarters

After the wars the Antichrist will select a place to create his new headquarters and palace. This will be in the capital of the new nation created out of what is now called the West Bank. It lies north of Jerusalem and lies between the Mediterranean Sea and the Sea of Galilee. The largest city in the West Bank is Nablus, which anciently housed the Samaritan Temple on Mount Gerizim. Ramallah is the psudo-capital of the region right now. My guess is that either Ramallah or Nablus will be the headquarters for the Antichrist!

> "He will pitch the tents of his royal pavilion between the seas and the beautiful Holy Mountain; yet he will come to his end, and no one will help him." Daniel 11:45

At this point, the Antichrist will look toward the Jerusalem Temple and will break the seven-year peace covenant.

The Tribulation

The Person of the Antichrist	**References**
414. He will be a man and the king/ruler of a nation	Dan. 8:23
415. He will be insolent and skilled in intrigue	Dan. 8:23
416. His power will be mighty, but not by his own power (demonic power)	Dan. 8:24
417. He will prosper and perform his will	Dan. 8:24
418. Through shrewdness, he will cause deceit to succeed	Dan. 8:25
419. He will magnify himself in his heart	Dan. 8:25
420. He will do as he pleases	Dan. 11:36
421. He will fling truth to the ground and perform his will and prosper	Dan. 8:12
The Religion of the Antichrist	
422. He will speak out against the Most High	Dan. 7:25
423. He will intend to make alterations in the times and laws	Dan. 7:25
424. He will exalt himself above every known god	Dan. 11:36; 2 Thess. 2:4
425. He will speak monstrous things against the God of gods	Dan. 11:36
426. He will show no regard for the god of his fathers	Dan. 11:37
427. He will worship a strange god that his ancestors never knew	Dan. 11:38
428. He will honor a strange god of forces	Dan. 11:38
429. He will not regard the desire of women	Dan. 11:37
430. He will magnify himself to be equal with the Commander of the Host (Jesus)	Dan. 8:11
431. He will oppose the Prince of princes	Dan. 8:25
432. He will deny the Father and Son	1 John 2:22
433. He will deny Jesus is the Son of God	1 John 4:15
434. He will deny Jesus is *the* Christ	1 John 2:22
435. He will deny Jesus came in the flesh	1 John 4:3
436. He will deny Jesus will come back in the flesh	2 John 7
The Invasion of Israel	
437. He will take action against the strongest of fortresses with the help of a foreign god (the strange god)	Dan. 11:39
438. Armies surround Jerusalem	Luke 21:20
439. The Jewish people will be expelled from their half of Jerusalem	Zech. 14:2
440. Antichrist's kingdom grows exceedingly great toward the south, east, and toward Israel	Dan. 8:9
441. He will destroy mighty men and the holy people	Dan. 8:24
442. He enters the beautiful land and many countries will fall	Dan. 11:41
443. Jordan will escape out of his hand	Dan. 11:41
The Abomination of Desolation	
444. He takes his seat in the temple of God, displaying himself as God	2 Thess. 2:4
445. He opposes and exalts himself above every so-called god or object of worship	2 Thess. 2:4
446. God will send upon non Christians a deluding influence so that they will believe *the* lie	2 Thess. 2:11
447. Antichrist places the Teraphim in the new Temple	Rev. 13:14-18
448. He grows in power and causes some of the host to fall	Dan. 8:10
449. The place of God's sanctuary is thrown down	Dan. 8:11
450. He removes the regular sacrifice from God	Dan. 8:11
451. On account of transgression, the host (idol or army) will be given over to the horn along with the regular sacrifice	Dan. 8:12

The Middle of the Tribulation

The ancient church fathers stated that the Antichrist is referred to as the "little horn" in Daniel 7:8,11,20-28 and 8:9-14, the "arising king" in Daniel 8:23-26, the "willful king" in Daniel 11:36-45, the "son of perdition" in 2 Thessalonians 2, and the "beast" of Revelation 13. (See Amillennialism in the section on the Apostasy of the Church for quotes and full details.) So if we take all these passages together, we have the following information on the Antichrist:

Ancient Prophecies Revealed

The Person of the Antichrist
The Antichrist will be the king of a nation. He can't be stopped by mankind because his power is demonic. He is described as insolent, shrewd, deceitful.

> "In the latter period of their rule, when the transgressors have run *their* course, a king will arise, insolent and skilled in intrigue. His power will be mighty, but not by his *own* power, and he will destroy to an extraordinary degree and prosper and perform *his will*; he will destroy mighty men and the holy people. And through his shrewdness he will cause deceit to succeed by his influence; and he will magnify *himself* in his heart, and he will destroy many while *they are* at ease. He will even oppose the Prince of princes, but he will be broken without human agency." Daniel 8:23-25

> "And on account of transgression the host will be given over to *the horn* along with the regular sacrifice; and it will fling truth to the ground and perform *its will* and prosper." Daniel 8:12

Through his influence he will cause deceit to flourish and fling truth to the ground by his "strange" religion.

The Religion Of the Antichrist
The Antichrist will blaspheme the Jews. He will try to change the "times and laws." This refers to the seven Jewish festivals that teach us about prophecy. He will play down those and in their place reinstitute the ancient pagan festivals.

> "He will speak out against the Most High and wear down the saints of the Highest One, and he will intend to make alterations in times and in law; and they will be given into his hand for a time, times, and half a time." Daniel 7:25

The Strange God Of the Antichrist
Daniel 11 predicts the Antichrist will consider himself a god to be worshiped above all other known gods of the religions of the world. He, however, will worship a "god of forces" his fathers did not know, honoring it with gold and silver. This strange god was completely unknown in Israel during the time of Cyrus (Isaiah 43:12). The Antichrist will take action against the strongest of fortresses with the help of this foreign (strange) god. At this time, the strongest fortress will be Jerusalem with its Temple, which is protected by the two witnesses and the Israeli army.

> "Then the king will do as he pleases, and he will exalt and magnify himself above every god and will speak monstrous things against the God of gods; and he will prosper until the indignation is finished, for that which is decreed will be done. He will show no regard for the gods of his fathers or for the desire of women, nor will he show regard for any *other* god; for he will magnify himself above *them* all. But instead he will honor a god of fortresses, a god whom his fathers did not know; he will honor *him* with gold, silver, costly stones and treasures. He will take action against the strongest of fortresses with *the help of* a foreign god (Heb. Strange God)" Daniel 11:36-39

> "'It is I who have declared and saved and proclaimed, and there was no strange *god* among you; so you are My witnesses,' declares the LORD, 'and I am God.'" Isaiah 43:12

Not regarding the "god (Elohim Heb.) of his fathers" means the Antichrist will not be a typical Jew, Christian, Buddhist, or Hindu.

A "god which his fathers knew not" could mean a strange combination of paganism mixed with the worship of the God of Abraham. The "Allah" of the Muslims is just that, a mixture of the pagan Moon God "Allah" and the God of Abraham. Since it is a god of "forces" or energy, this new Islam will be combined with the ancient paganism that taught mankind contains what is left of what was the original God. The Antichrist will pass himself off as the most advanced, or godlike human. Compare this with the Syrian form of Islam where the Imams can be Allah incarnate. In Revelation 13, a speaking image is set up in the temple. This kind of idol was called a Teraphim, in ancient times.

The Tribulation

Not regarding the "desire of women" could mean he appears to be either a homosexual or celibate. This characteristic is put with all the others that speak of his religion. Therefore, it more likely refers to what women desire in the form of religion. In ancient times, all Hebrew women wanted to be the mother of the Messiah, so this may mean he has no regard for the Messiah. It could also mean that his religion is more chauvinistic and degrades women.

Cults like Unity and Religious Mind already say Jesus is not *the* Christ, but He had the Christ Consciousness in Him. This idea is what the Antichrist will use to mislead people to think he is evolving into a god. He will do miracles in the sight of men to try to deceive them into believing it.

Doctrine of the Antichrist
He is the supreme god on earth
He honors a god of energy
His god is impersonal
Jesus was not God
Jesus was not a son of a god
Jesus was not the *only* Christ
He has the Christ consciousness
Jesus will not come back to earth
Jesus was not raised in the flesh
There is no resurrection

Antichrist Denies Jesus
The apostle John, in his first epistle, informs us the Antichrist will teach the following: Jesus was not God when He was on earth; Jesus was not the only son of God (1 John 2:22). He was just a man who had the Christ consciousness. The true Christ never came in the flesh (1 John 4:3). He will say Jesus will not return in the flesh because He did not resurrect in the flesh (2 John 7).

The Invasion Of Israel
After the Antichrist establishes complete control of the ten nations and moves his headquarters north of Jerusalem, he will break the seven-year covenant and conquer all of Jerusalem, the "strongest of fortresses." Being recognized both as Messiah by the Jews and the Madhi by the Muslims, the Antichrist will command Muslim armies to enter Jerusalem and take by force the Jewish part of Jerusalem and the Temple Mount. The Muslim side of the city will be left alone, but there will be a severe slaughter on the Jewish side.

> "But when you see Jerusalem surrounded by armies, then recognize that her desolation is near. Then those who are in Judea must flee to the mountains, and those who are in the midst of the city must leave, and those who are in the country must not enter the city; because these are days of vengeance, so that all things which are written will be fulfilled... and they will fall by the edge of the sword, and will be led captive into all the nations; and Jerusalem will be trampled under foot by the Gentiles until the times of the Gentiles are fulfilled." *Luke 21:20-22,24*

> "He will take action against the strongest of fortresses with *the help of* a foreign god... He will also enter the Beautiful Land, and many *countries* will fall; but these will be rescued out of his hand: Edom, Moab and the foremost of the sons of Ammon." *Daniel 11:39,41*

> "For I will gather all the nations against Jerusalem to battle, and the city will be captured, the houses plundered, the women ravished and half of the city exiled, but the rest of the people will not be cut off from the city." *Zechariah 14:2*

Notice, by this time, Israel has possession of Gilead. This was Jordanian territory in AD 2008, but now Jordan (which consists of only Moab, Ammon, and Edom) escapes from the Antichrist's hand.

The Desolating Abomination

As the Muslim armies surround Jerusalem, the Antichrist will enter the Holy Temple and proclaim himself to be God. This is called the abomination of desolation.

> "who opposes and exalts himself above every so-called god or object of worship, so that he takes his seat in the temple of God, displaying himself as being God." *2 Thessalonians 2:4*

> "Forces from him will arise, desecrate the sanctuary fortress, and do away with the regular sacrifice. And they will set up the abomination of desolation. By smooth *words* he will turn to godlessness those who act wickedly toward the covenant..." *Daniel 11:31-32*

Ancient Prophecies Revealed

"The 'Abomination spoken by Daniel' (Matthew 24) is the Antichrist sitting in the temple as if he were Christ. The abomination will start in the middle of Daniel's 70th week and last for a literal three years and six months. After that they will be destroyed by the coming of the Lord." *Irenaeus Against Heresies 5.26 - 178 AD*

The Strong Delusion

Paul taught God will send a "strong delusion" upon those people who "do not have a love for the truth," so they will believe "the Lie." The lie Paul wrote about here is that the Antichrist is God. The truth they won't love are the Bible prophecies. Anyone who believed the prophecies about the Antichrist and the Tribulation will not fall for the lie.

"…because they did not receive the love of the truth so as to be saved. For this reason God will send upon them a deluding influence so that they will believe what is false, in order that they all may be judged who did not believe the truth, but took pleasure in wickedness." *2 Thessalonians 2:10b-12*

Teraphim Set Up and the Mark Instituted

The prophet Hosea, speaking of the time when Israel would return to their land in 1948, after the "many days" of the great dispersion, said:

"For the sons of Israel will remain for many days without king or prince, without sacrifice or *sacred* pillar and without ephod or household idols." *Hosea 3:4*

By the middle of the Tribulation, Israel has their Temple with the sacrifices and ephod reinstituted, but they do not use the "household idols," Hosea described. The literal Hebrew word used here for "household Idols" is "teraphim." The teraphim were supposed to be idols that actually spoke and gave direction to their people. The Antichrist has an idol/teraphim in the Temple. It speaks and causes those who do not worship the Antichrist to be hunted down and killed. It also implements the mark of the beast.

"And he deceives those who dwell on the earth because of the signs which it was given him to perform in the presence of the beast, telling those who dwell on the earth to make an image to the beast who had the wound of the sword and has come to life. And it was given to him to give breath to the image of the beast, so that the image of the beast would even speak and cause as many as do not worship the image of the beast to be killed. And he causes all, the small and the great, and the rich and the poor, and the free men and the slaves, to be given a mark on their right hand or on their forehead, and *he provides* that no one will be able to buy or to sell, except the one who has the mark, *either* the name of the beast or the number of his name. Here is wisdom. Let him who has understanding calculate the number of the beast, for the number is that of a man; and his number is six hundred and sixty-six." *Revelation 13:14-18*

The ancient Jewish history book, Jasher, gives the only known description of a teraphim.

"And Rachel stole her father's images [teraphim], and she took them and she concealed them upon the camel upon which she sat, and she went on. And this is the manner of the images; in taking a man who is the first born and slaying him and taking the hair off his head, and taking salt and salting the head and anointing it in oil, then taking a small tablet of copper or a tablet of gold and writing the name upon it, and placing the tablet under his tongue, and taking the head with the tablet under the tongue and putting it in the house, and lighting up lights before it and bowing down to it. And at the time when they bow down to it, it speaketh to them in all matters that they ask of it, through the power of the name which is written in it. And some make them in the figures of men, of gold and silver, and go to them in times known to them, and the figures receive the influence of the stars, and tell them future things, and in this manner were the images which Rachel stole from her father." *Jasher 31:40-43*

Temple Sacrifices Stop

The Antichrist stops all the daily sacrifices in the Temple. With this and the teraphim, the truth of God is cast down. This incident begins the Antichrist's three and a half year rule.

The Tribulation

"It grew up to the host of heaven and caused some of the host and some of the stars to fall to the earth, and it trampled them down. It even magnified *itself* to be equal with the Commander of the host; and it removed the regular sacrifice from Him, and the place of His sanctuary was thrown down. And on account of transgression the host will be given over *to the horn* along with the regular sacrifice; and it will fling truth to the ground and perform *its will* and prosper."
Daniel 8:10-12

Prophecies concerning the second half of the Tribulation	References
452. Peace covenant will be broken	Zech; Dan; 2 Thess. 2
453. 2300 days will start	Dan. 8:13-14
454. 1290 days will start	Dan. 12:11-12
455. 1335 days will start	Dan. 12:11-12
The Persecution	
456. He will wage war with the saints and overpower them	Dan. 7:21
457. He will wear down the saints of the Highest One	Dan. 7:25
458. The saints of the Highest One will be given into his hands for a time, times, and half a time	Dan. 7:25
459. Antichrist will persecute Messianic Jews	Rev. 12:17
460. 1260 days will start	Dan. 12:6-7
461. Some of the Jews will flee to Petra/Bozrah	Rev. 12:6
The Wrath	
462. The sign of the sun and moon going dark will occur	Joel 2:30-32; Rev. 6:12-17
463. The wrath of God will begin	Rev. 6:16-17
464. Days will be shortened	Matt. 24:22
465. The wrath of God will end	Rev. 15:1
The Antichrist's Destruction	
466. He will be broken without human agency (by Christ)	Dan. 8:25
467. He will prosper until the indignation is finished (until the Second Coming)	Dan. 11:36
468. He will be destroyed and thrown into the fire	Dan. 7:11; 2 Thess. 2

The Second 3.5 Years

1260, 1290, 1335, & 2300 Days

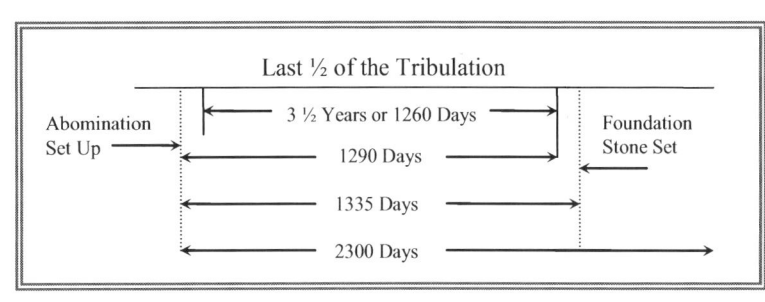

In the chart at the right we can see the last half of the seven-year Tribulation. The first line shows 1260 days from the Antichrist taking full control and starting the major persecution in the middle of the Tribulation to the Second Coming. The second line of 1290 days is the interval between the setting up of the desolating abomination to the Second Coming. The third line of 1335 days describes the period from the stopping of the sacrifices and setting up of the abomination to the cleansing of the Temple Mount and the beginning of the construction of the Millennial Temple. The fourth line of 2300 days indicates the days between the abomination to the rededication of the new Millennial Temple. The 2300 days begins at the same time as the 1290 days. If we subtract 1290 days from 2300 days, we come to 1010 days or another 33 months and 20 days. This means the new Temple will be dedicated two years, nine months and 20 days after the Second Coming.

"'How long *will it be* until the end of *these* wonders?' I heard the man dressed in linen, who was above the waters of the river, as he raised his right hand and his left toward heaven, and swore by Him who lives forever that it would be for a **time**, **times**, and **half** *a time*; and as soon as they finish shattering the power of the holy people, all these *events* will be completed." *Daniel 12:6-7*

Ancient Prophecies Revealed

"From the time that the regular sacrifice is abolished and the abomination of desolation is set up, *there will be* 1,290 days. How blessed is he who keeps waiting and attains to the 1,335 days!" *Daniel 12:11-12*

"Then I heard a holy one speaking, and another holy one said to that particular one who was speaking, 'How long will the vision *about* the regular sacrifice apply, while the transgression causes horror, so as to allow both the holy place and the host to be trampled?' He said to me, 'For 2,300 evenings *and* mornings; then the holy place will be properly restored.'" *Daniel 8:13-14*

The Middle Month
What takes place between the setting up of the abomination and the Antichrist's full control? And why does it take a full thirty days to implement?

The Daniel 12 quote above defines the start with "regular sacrifice abolished and the abomination set up." The Daniel 8 quote above has that start with "both the holy place and the host to be trampled." So that one month starts with the setting up of the abomination in the Holy Place and ends with the host (Israeli people) completely trampled down.

In other words, inside that one month the abomination is set up, the Temple sacrifices are stopped, believing Israel flees into Petra, and the Antichrist starts the worst persecution ever on Israeli citizens. The slaughter will continue until the sun goes dark.

The Great Tribulation
Jesus said when you see the abomination in the Temple, and then the time of the Great Tribulation will occur. This is the worst time ever. The Great Tribulation happens the second half of the seven-year period. It starts with the extreme persecution of the Jewish people by the Antichrist. Then God pours out His wrath on the earth.

"Therefore when you see the ABOMINATION OF DESOLATION which was spoken of through Daniel the prophet, standing in the holy place (let the reader understand), then those who are in Judea must flee to the mountains... For then there will be a **great tribulation**, such as has not occurred since the beginning of the world until now, nor ever will. Unless those days had been cut short, no life would have been saved; but for the sake of the elect those days will be cut short." *Matthew 24:15-16,17-22*

The Antichrist's Persecution of Believers
After the city of Jerusalem and the Temple Mount has been divided for almost three and a half years, the Antichrist will break the peace agreement and invade the Jewish part of the city. First, the Antichrist will capture the Temple Mount and set up the abomination, then he will start the persecution of Israeli citizens. Those who will not believe the warning, and understand what the abomination means, will suffer the Antichrist's persecution. Those who heed the warning flee into the wilderness and will be protected for the remaining three and a half years.

"When the Lamb broke the fifth seal, I saw underneath the altar the souls of those who had been slain because of the word of God, and because of the testimony which they had maintained; and they cried out with a loud voice, saying, 'How long, O Lord, holy and true, will You refrain from judging and avenging our blood on those who dwell on the earth?' And there was given to each of them a white robe; and they were told that they should rest for a little while longer, until *the number of* their fellow servants and their brethren who were to be killed even as they had been, would be completed also." *Fifth Seal – Revelation 6:9-11*

"Behold, the day of the LORD is coming... Anyone who is found will be thrust through, and anyone who is captured will fall by the sword. Their little ones also will be dashed to pieces before their eyes; their houses will be plundered and their wives ravished." *Isaiah 13:9,15-16*

"Antichrist will also enwrap righteous men with the books of the prophets, and thus burn them."
Lactantius Divine Institutes 7:17

The Tribulation

The Purging/Refining
One reason for the Tribulation is to purge or refine Israel. Ezekiel 20:33-38 predicts after the Jews are regathered to the land (1948) then the nation will be purged of non-believers by His wrath. Ezekiel 22:17-22 predicts after the Jewish people are regathered to Jerusalem (1967) then they will be melted and refined by the fire of His wrath. Jeremiah 30;6,7,11,22,24 records the result of this chastisement is the conversion of the nation of Israel. Zechariah 13:8,9 predicts after two-parts of land is cut off, then the third left will be bought through the fire to be refined. Other verses that mention the purging/refining are Daniel 12:1,9,10; Isaiah 1:22,25; 48:10; Jeremiah 6:27-30; 9:7; and Malachi 3:2-3.

Once Israel is refined they will corporately accept Jesus Christ, the Messiah of Israel. Passages that predict this are: Hosea 6:1-2; Romans 11:25-27; Zechariah 9:11; 12:10-13:9; Joel 2:28-32; Ezekiel 11;19-20, 16:60-63, 34:25-26, 37:21-28; Isaiah 53:1-9, 59:20-21, 61:8-9, 64;1-12; and Psalm 79:1-13, 80:1-19.

Jesus will not return to earth until Israel has accepted Him as the Messiah. See: Hosea 5:15; Zechariah 12:10; Jeremiah 3:11-18; Lev 26:40-42; Matthew 23:37-39; and Acts 3:19-21.

The Start of the Day of Wrath
God will respond to the Antichrist's extreme persecution of believers. When He begins to pour out His wrath, there will be a visible sign that this has begun. The sun will go dark and the moon will turn blood red.

> "But immediately after the tribulation of those days [the first half of the seven-year period] the sun will be darkened, and the moon will not give its light, and the stars will fall from the sky, and the powers of the heavens will be shaken. And then the sign of the Son of Man will appear in the sky, and then all the tribes of the earth will mourn, and they will see the son of man coming on the clouds of the sky with power and great glory."
> *Matthew 24:29-30*

> "I looked when He broke the **sixth seal**, and there was a great earthquake; and the sun became black as sackcloth *made* of hair, and the whole moon became like blood; and the stars of the sky fell to the earth, as a fig tree casts its unripe figs when shaken by a great wind. The sky was split apart like a scroll when it is rolled up, and every mountain and island were moved out of their places. Then the kings of the earth and the great men and the commanders and the rich and the strong and every slave and free man hid themselves in the caves and among the rocks of the mountains; and they said to the mountains and to the rocks, 'Fall on us and hide us from the presence of Him who sits on the throne, and from **the wrath of the Lamb**; for **the great day** of their wrath has come, and who is able to stand?'"
> *Sixth Seal – Revelation 6:12-17*

> "I will display wonders in the sky and on the earth, blood, fire and columns of smoke. The sun will be turned into darkness, and the moon into blood, before the great and awesome day of the LORD comes. And it will come about that whoever calls on the name of the LORD will be **delivered**; for on Mount Zion and in Jerusalem there will be those who escape, as the LORD has said, even among the survivors (remnant) whom the LORD calls." *Joel 2:30-32*

> "Behold, the day of the LORD is coming, cruel, with fury and burning anger, to make the land a desolation; and He will exterminate its sinners from it. For the stars of heaven and their constellations will not flash forth their light; the sun will be dark when it rises, and the moon will not shed its light." *Isaiah 13:9-10*

> "I kept looking, and that horn was waging war with the saints and overpowering them until the Ancient of Days came and judgment was passed in favor of the saints of the Highest One, and the time arrived when the saints took possession of the kingdom. Thus he said: 'The fourth beast will be a fourth kingdom on the earth, which will be different from all the *other* kingdoms and will devour the whole earth and tread it down and crush it. As for the ten horns, out of this kingdom ten kings will arise; and another will arise after them, and he will be different from the previous ones and will subdue three kings. He will speak out against the Most High and wear down the saints of the Highest One, and he will intend to make alterations in times and in law; and they will be given into his hand for a time, times, and half a time."
> *Daniel 7:21-25*

> "It grew up to the host of heaven and caused some of the host and some of the stars to fall to the earth, and it trampled them down. It even magnified *itself* to be equal with the Commander of the host; and it removed the regular sacrifice

Ancient Prophecies Revealed

from Him, and the place of His sanctuary was thrown down. And on account of transgression the host will be given *over to the horn* along with the regular sacrifice; and it will fling truth to the ground and perform *its will* and prosper." *Daniel 8:10-12*

The Wrath of the Lamb and His God – starts in Revelation 6:16-17 and ends in Revelation 15:1

"and they said to the mountains and to the rocks, 'Fall on us and hide us from the presence of Him who sits on the throne, and from the wrath of the Lamb; for the great day of their wrath has come, and who is able to stand?'" *Revelation 6:16-17*

"Then I saw another sign in heaven, great and marvelous, seven angels who had seven plagues, which are the last, because in them the wrath of God is finished." *Revelation 15:1*

God's wrath ends with Armegeddon and the destruction of the Antichrist.

Days Shortened
When the plagues and disasters start in the middle of the tribulation, something causes the earth's axis to change. This is one thing that God does to slow down the Antichrist so that some flesh is saved. Ancient church father Lactantius is just one who interprets this as the actual shortening of days, months, and years. Notice before this occurs the church will have completely apostatized by allowing abortion, euthanasia, and children's rights to get out of hand.

"Unless those days had been cut short, no life would have been saved; but for the sake of the elect those days will be cut short." *Matthew 24:22*

"End times will manifest: Abortion, euthanasia, children carrying weapons, winter and summer will be confused, years months and days will be shortened," *Lactantius Epitome of Divine Institutes 71*

Antichrist's Destruction
Christ will destroy the Antichrist at His Second Coming (2 Thessalonians 2:8). The Antichrist will be thrown alive into the lake of fire, along with the false prophet (Revelation 19:20).

"Then that lawless one will be revealed whom the Lord will slay with the breath of His mouth and bring to an end by the appearance of His coming;" *2 Thessalonians 2:8*

"And the beast was seized, and with him the false prophet who performed the signs in his presence, by which he deceived those who had received the mark of the beast and those who worshiped his image; these two were thrown alive into the lake of fire which burns with brimstone. And the rest were killed with the sword which came from the mouth of Him who sat on the horse, and all the birds were filled with their flesh." *Revelation 19:20-21*

The Festival of Yom Kippur

During the festival of Yom Kippur there is a prophetic ceremony that involves two goats. Two nearly identical goats are selected and brought before the high priest. The high priest places his hands on one of the goats. Another priest brings out the Qalephi, a box containing two lots. One of the lots is randomly withdrawn by the high priest and placed with the first goat. Then the other is withdrawn for the second goat. On one lot is engraved לאדני, meaning "to the Lord." The goat that randomly acquired the lot "for the Lord" is sacrificed for

Newly created lots for the Yom Kippur ceremony

the sins of the people. This animal is a perfect representation of the Messiah dying for the sins of the world. The other lot is engraved with לעזאזל, meaning "to Azazel." This has commonly been translated "scapegoat," but Azazel actually is a proper name. Moses wrote about this ceremony in Leviticus 16 saying:

> "Aaron shall cast lots for the two goats, one lot for the LORD and the other lot for the scapegoat [Azazel]. Then Aaron shall offer the goat on which the lot for the LORD fell, and make it a sin offering. But the goat on which the lot for the scapegoat fell shall be presented alive before the LORD, to make atonement upon it, to send it into the wilderness as the scapegoat [to Azazel]." *Leviticus 16:8-10*

The Mishnah is a book written about AD 200. It contains the Oral Torah, or the exact details of how to perform the rituals mentioned the Old Testament. In Yoma 4.2 of the Mishnah, details are given concerning the ceremony of the two goats.

A scarlet-colored, wool cord was specially created for this ceremony. One piece of this cord was tied to one of the horns of the Azazel goat. One piece of the cord was tied around the neck of the Lord's goat.

In Leviticus, it describes the goat being sent into the "wilderness." But the Mishnah gives greater detail about that part of the ritual in Yoma 6. The two goats must be alike in appearance, size, and weight. The "wilderness" that the Azazel goat was taken to was actually a ravine. Between Jerusalem and this ravine were ten stations or booths. Since it was a High Holy Day one could not travel very far. One priest took the Azazel goat from Jerusalem to the first booth. Then another priest took it from the second to the third booth. This continued until a priest took it from the tenth booth to the ravine. Anciently this ravine was called Bet HaDudo. Its whereabouts is currently unknown. The Mishnah then says the priest took the crimson cord off of the goat and tied one piece to the large rock on the cliff of the ravine, and he tied the other piece to the horns of the goat. He then pushed the goat off the cliff. Before it would be halfway down the cliff, it was already torn into pieces.

If the ritual was properly done, the crimson cord would turn snow white. At that point the priest would signal the tenth booth, which would in turn signal the ninth, all the way back to the first booth, which would signal the high priest standing at the door of the sanctuary. When the high priest learned the crimson thread had turned white, he finished the ritual by quoting Isaiah 1:18

> "'Come now, and let us reason together,' says the LORD, 'though your sins are as scarlet, they will be as white as snow; though they are red like crimson, they will be like wool.'" *Isaiah 1:18*

The Meaning of the Ritual
It has been speculated that the scapegoat represents Jesus taking away our sin. That is one possible interpretation. If the information given in the Mishnah is correct, another picture emerges. Two identical goats, one dedicated to God, the other dedicated to Satan. One goat represents the Messiah and the other represents the Antichrist. The ravine represents, and probably is located in, the valley of Megiddo. The only way to tell the difference between the Messiah and the Antichrist is to know the Lord's will by carefully studying the Word of God. At the second coming, the Antichrist will be destroyed in Megiddo, in a battle called Armageddon.

Ancient Prophecies Revealed

The Millennial Reign
17 prophecies in 1,000 years

Date	Prophecy	References
	469. Jesus will return exactly the way He left	Acts 1:10-11; Zech. 14:4
	470. Messiah's feet will land of the Mount of Olives	Zech. 14:4
	471. Mount of Olives will split in two	Zech. 14:4
	472. Jesus will enter into Jerusalem through the Eastern Gate	Ezek. 43:1-5
	473. All nations will gather against Him - Armageddon	Rev. 19 (Ps 2:2)
	474. They will look upon Him whom they pierced	Zech. 12:9-10
	475. Israel cleansed of all sin	Rom. 11:25-27
	476. Times of the Gentiles will be over	Rom. 11:25-27
	477. 1000 year reign established	Rev. 20:6; Isa. 9:7
	478. Temple Mount will be cleansed and the foundation stone laid	Dan. 12:11-12
	479. New millennial Temple will be dedicated	Dan. 8:13-14
	480. All nations will receive the pure language of Hebrew	Zeph. 3:9-10
	481. Ancient relics will be brought back	Zeph. 3:9-10
	482. Israel will have new borders	Ezek. 47:15-20
	483. Human lifespan will return to the original length	Isa. 65:20
	484. Last Gog-Magog War	Rev. 20:7-9
	485. New Heaven and Earth	Rev. 21:1

Jesus Will Return Exactly the Way He Left
Jesus left earth ascending from the Mount of Olives into heaven. Then an angel told those watching that Jesus would come back *exactly* like He left. He will return in physical form, as John wrote in 2 John.

"And after He had said these things, He was lifted up while they were looking on, and a cloud received Him out of their sight. And as they were gazing intently into the sky while He was going, behold, two men in white clothing stood beside them. They also said, 'Men of Galilee, why do you stand looking into the sky? This Jesus, who has been taken up from you into heaven, will come in just the same way as you have watched Him go into heaven.'" *Acts 1:9-11*

"For many deceivers have gone out into the world, those who do not acknowledge Jesus Christ *as* coming [Back] in the flesh This is the deceiver and the antichrist." *2 John 7*

Zachariah writes Jesus' feet will touch the Mount of Olives when He descends at His Second Coming.

"In that day His feet will stand on the Mount of Olives, which is in front of Jerusalem on the east; and the Mount of Olives will be split in its middle from east to west by a very large valley, so that half of the mountain will move toward the north and the other half toward the south." *Zechariah 14:4*

Mount of Olives Spilt In Two
As Zechariah wrote (above), when the Messiah returns to earth and stands on the Mount of Olives, it will split into two parts from east to west, leaving two mountains out of what used to be the Mount of Olives. One new mountain will be on the north side and one on the south side.

Jesus Will Enter Into Jerusalem Though the Eastern Gate
The Eastern Gate has been sealed for generations. Ezekiel prophesied it will remain that way until the Messiah returns. The Messiah will travel from the Mount of Olives, which is east of Jerusalem, into the city of Jerusalem though the Eastern Gate. At this time the Messiah will unseal the gate.

"Then he led me to the gate, the gate facing toward the east; and behold, the glory of the God of Israel was coming from the way of the east. And His voice was like the sound of many waters; and the earth shone with His glory. And *it was*

The Millennial Reign

like the appearance of the vision which I saw, like the vision which I saw when He came to destroy the city. And the visions *were* like the vision which I saw by the river Chebar; and I fell on my face. And the glory of the LORD came into the house by the way of the gate facing toward the east. And the Spirit lifted me up and brought me into the inner court; and behold, the glory of the LORD filled the house. *Ezekiel 43:1-5*

All Nations Gather Against The Messiah – Battle of Armageddon
The Antichrist and his people will gather together to destoy the Messiah. The Messiah will destroy all the gathered people, including the Antichrist and the false prophet.

"The kings of the earth take their stand, and the rulers take counsel together against the LORD and against His Anointed, saying, 'Let us tear their fetters apart and cast away their cords from us!' He who sits in the heavens laughs, the Lord scoffs at them. Then He will speak to them in His anger and terrify them in His fury, saying, 'But as for Me, I have installed My King upon Zion, My holy mountain.' I will surely tell of the decree of the LORD: He said to Me, 'You are My Son, today I have begotten You. Ask of Me, and I will surely give the nations as Your inheritance, and the very ends of the earth as Your possession. You shall break them with a rod of iron, You shall shatter them like earthenware.'" *Psalm 2:2-9*

"And I saw heaven opened, and behold, a white horse, and He who sat on it is called Faithful and True, and in righteousness He judges and wages war. His eyes are a flame of fire, and on His head are many diadems; and He has a name written on Him which no one knows except Himself. He is clothed with a robe dipped in blood, and His name is called The Word of God. And the armies which are in heaven, clothed in fine linen, white and clean, were following Him on white horses. From His mouth comes a sharp sword, so that with it He may strike down the nations, and He will rule them with a rod of iron; and He treads the wine press of the fierce wrath of God, the Almighty. And on His robe and on His thigh He has a name written, 'KING OF KINGS, AND LORD OF LORDS.' Then I saw an angel standing in the sun, and he cried out with a loud voice, saying to all the birds which fly in midheaven, 'Come, assemble for the great supper of God, so that you may eat the flesh of kings and the flesh of commanders and the flesh of mighty men and the flesh of horses and of those who sit on them and the flesh of all men, both free men and slaves, and small and great.' And I saw the beast and the kings of the earth and their armies assembled to make war against Him who sat on the horse and against His army." *Revelation 19:11-19*

They Will Realize the Pierced One is the Messiah
This is a good example of a double fulfillment prophecy. The Jewish leaders looked on Jesus when He was pierced on the cross in AD 32. At His Second Coming, the Jewish people will see Jesus still marred from His scars from His sacrifice on the cross.

"And in that day I will set about to destroy all the nations that come against Jerusalem. I will pour out on the house of David and on the inhabitants of Jerusalem, the Spirit of grace and of supplication, so that they will look on Me whom they have pierced; and they will mourn for Him, as one mourns for an only son, and they will weep bitterly over Him like the bitter weeping over a firstborn." *Zechariah 12:9-10*

Israel Cleansed of All Sin and Times of the Gentiles Over
Jerusalem will be controlled by Gentiles until their time is over. Once the Messiah returns to reign on earth, the times of the Gentiles will end, and Israel will be forgiven for her sin.

"For I do not want you, brethren, to be uninformed of this mystery--so that you will not be wise in your own estimation--that a partial hardening has happened to Israel until the fullness of the Gentiles has come in; and so all Israel will be saved; just as it is written, 'THE DELIVERER WILL COME FROM ZION, HE WILL REMOVE UNGODLINESS FROM JACOB. THIS IS MY COVENANT WITH THEM, WHEN I TAKE AWAY THEIR SINS.'" *Romans 11:25-27*

1000-Year Reign Established
The Messiah will then set up a kingdom on earth that will last for 1000 years.

Ancient Prophecies Revealed

"For a child will be born to us, a son will be given to us; and the government will rest on His shoulders; and His name will be called Wonderful Counselor, Mighty God, Eternal Father, Prince of Peace. There will be no end to the increase of His government or of peace, on the throne of David and over his kingdom, to establish it and to uphold it with justice and righteousness from then on and forevermore. The zeal of the LORD of hosts will accomplish this." *Isaiah 9:6-7*

"Blessed and holy is the one who has a part in the first resurrection; over these the second death has no power, but they will be priests of God and of Christ and will reign with Him for a thousand years." *Revelation 20:6*

Temple Mount Cleansed

Ezra cleansed the Temple mount, gave a sacrifice to God, and taught the Torah to the people years before the Second Temple was built. I believe this gives us a pattern for the next Temple's restoration. In the section on the Tribulation, we saw Daniel's prophecy that from the time the Antichrist's abomination is set up to the time it is destroyed will be 1260 days. We saw this began 30 days before the middle of the Tribulation. Daniel then adds that people will be blessed if they wait until 1,335 days after the set up of the abomination. So 1,335 minus 1,290 is 45 days. The Temple Mount will be cleansed and the foundation stone laid 45 days after the Second Coming.

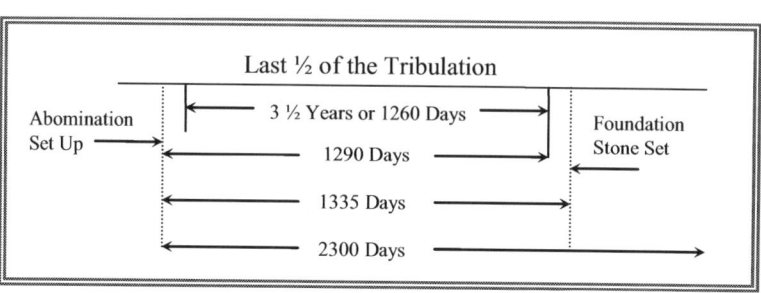

"From the time that the regular sacrifice is abolished and the abomination of desolation is set up, *there will be* 1,290 days. How blessed is he who keeps waiting and attains to the 1,335 days!" *Daniel 12:11-12*

New Temple Dedicated

Daniel taught that from the time the abomination is set up to the time the new Temple is dedicated will be 2,300 days. So, 2300 minus 1290 equals 1010 days. I believe Daniel's prophecy teaches that the new Millennial Temple described in Ezekiel 40-48 will be dedicated and in operation 1010 days after the Second Coming.

"Then I heard a holy one speaking, and another holy one said to that particular one who was speaking, 'How long will the vision *about* the regular sacrifice apply, while the transgression causes horror, so as to allow both the holy place and the host to be trampled?' He said to me, 'For 2,300 evenings *and* mornings; then the holy place will be properly restored.'" *Daniel 8:13-14*

Hebrew Language Restored

In Genesis, Moses wrote that all mankind spoke one language. Under the direction of Nimrod, most of mankind was involved in constructing the Tower of Babel in rebellion against God. In order to stop the building of the Tower, God instantly confused the minds of the people by turning the one original language into multiple languages. From that time on, there have been many languages in the world. When the Messiah returns, He will undo this action and all nations will once again speak the original pure language. In the section on Modern Israel we saw that the Hebrew language was restored to the nation of Israel, as prophesied in Jeremiah 31:23. Zephaniah predicts upon the Messiah's return, Hebrew (the original language) will be restored to the entire planet. The Hebrew of Zephaniah's prophecy actually says God will return the "pure language" to "all people" or "all nations."

"For then will I turn to the people a pure language, that they may all call upon the name of the LORD, to serve him with one consent. From beyond the rivers of Ethiopia my suppliants, even the daughter of my dispersed, shall bring mine offering. In that day shalt thou not be ashamed for all thy doings, wherein thou hast transgressed against me: for then I will take away out of the midst of thee them that rejoice in thy pride, and thou shalt no more be haughty because of my holy mountain." *Zephaniah 3:9-11 KJV*

The Millennial Reign

Ancient Relics Returned
These verses from Zephaniah also predict believers from the land of Ethiopia will bring an ancient relic to Jerusalem and present it to the Messiah after He has begun His rule. Zephaniah 3:8 describes the tribulation period and the return of the Messiah. *Then* verse 9 shows the return of the "pure language," and finally, the daughter of the dispersed, the Ethiopian Coptic Church, will bring an ancient relic back to the Messiah who is ruling on His throne in the city of Jerusalem, Israel. Isaiah 18:7 teaches the Ethiopians will bring this offering back to Mount Zion. See the section on Modern Israel – *Hebrew language Restored* and *Ethiopian Jews Fly Home* for full details.

Israeli Borders

The millennial borders of Israel are described in Ezekiel 47. On the next page is the map of what the borders will be. Notice the current borders expand to Sarafand in Lebanon during the upcoming Lebanese-Jordanian War and the border expands even further during the millennial reign.

"This *shall be* the boundary of the land: on the **north side**, from the Great Sea *by* the way of Hethlon, to the entrance of Zedad [Sadad, Syria]; Hamath [Hamah, Syria], Berothah [was between Hamath and Damascus], Sibraim, which is between the border of Damascus and the border of Hamath; Hazer-hatticon [south of Damascus], which is by the border of Hauran [southern Syria, bordering on Jordan]. The boundary shall extend from the sea *to* Hazar-enan [Kuryetein, about 60 miles east-north-east of Damascus] *at* the border of Damascus, and on the north toward the north is the border of Hamath. This is the north side. The **east side**, from between Hauran, Damascus, Gilead and the land of Israel, *shall be* the Jordan; from the *north* border to the eastern sea you shall measure. This is the east side. The **south side** toward the south *shall extend* from Tamar [18 miles ssw of the dead sea] as far as the waters of Meribath-kadesh [Rephidim is in the narrow gorge of Al-Watiyyah in the great Wady al-Shaikh], to the brook *of Egypt and* to the Great Sea. This is the south side toward the south. The west side *shall be* the Great Sea, from the *south* border to a point opposite Lebo-hamath. This is the west side." *Ezekiel 47:15-20*

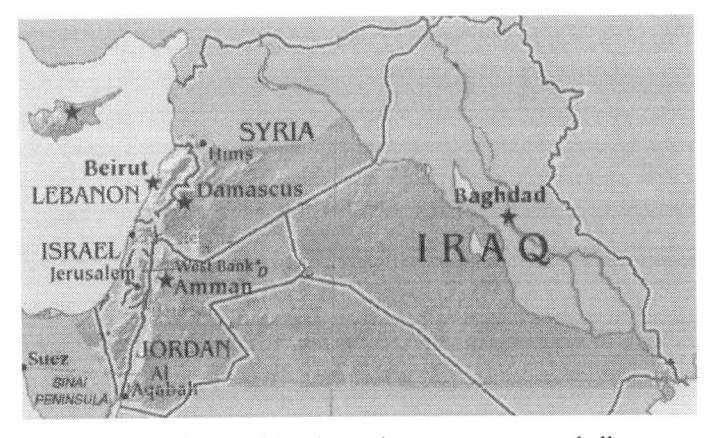

"On that day the LORD made a covenant with Abram, saying, 'To your descendants I have given this land, from the river of Egypt as far as the great river, the river Euphrates:" *Genesis 15:18*

Notice this area expands past the new borders of the Lebanese-Jordanian war. The Israeli borders during the Millennial Reign include all of Lebanon and over half of present-day Syria. Israel will have more land from the Sinai Peninsula, as well. As promised to Father Abraham, the land wil extend all the way to the Euphrates River.

Human Lifespan Increases
Before Noah's Flood, lifespans were close to 1000 years. After the flood, they immediately dropped to around 400 and within a few generations the average lifespan was only about 200 years. From that time on, life spans have continued to decrease and now they are only about 80 years. This is thought to be because of the destruction of the water canopy, and its residue decreasing over the centuries. This would allow more and more radiation to come into the planet's atmosphere.

Ancient Prophecies Revealed

When the Messiah comes back, He may reestablish earth like it was, restoring the canopy. The prophet Isaiah states our life spans will be lengthened again so that people will mature at about 100 years of age.

> "No longer will there be in it an infant *who lives but a few* days, or an old man who does not live out his days; for the youth will die at the age of one hundred and the one who does not reach the age of one hundred will be *thought* accursed." *Isaiah 65:20*

The Last Gog-Magog War

At the end of the one thousand year reign, Satan will be released and trick the hordes of Gog and Magog into another war against the Messiah. This last Gog-Magog war will result in the complete destruction of these satanic forces and the creation of new heavens and a new earth.

> "When the thousand years are completed, Satan will be released from his prison, and will come out to deceive the nations which are in the four corners of the earth, Gog and Magog, to gather them together for the war; the number of them is like the sand of the seashore. And they came up on the broad plain of the earth and surrounded the camp of the saints and the beloved city, and fire came down from heaven and devoured them. And the devil who deceived them was thrown into the lake of fire and brimstone, where the beast and the false prophet are also; and they will be tormented day and night forever and ever." *Revelation 20:7-10*

New Heavens and a New Earth
Then the time of godless mankind will be over and a new era of true righteousness will begin. This era will be called eternity!

> "But the day of the Lord will come like a thief, in which the heavens will pass away with a roar and the elements will be destroyed with intense heat, and the earth and its works will be burned up… looking for and hastening the coming of the day of God, because of which the heavens will be destroyed by burning, and the elements will melt with intense heat! But according to His promise we are looking for new heavens and a new earth, in which righteousness dwells." *2 Peter 3:10, 12-13*

> "Then I saw a new heaven and a new earth; for the first heaven and the first earth passed away, and there is no longer *any* sea. And I saw the holy city, new Jerusalem, coming down out of heaven from God, made ready as a bride adorned for her husband. And I heard a loud voice from the throne, saying, "Behold, the tabernacle of God is among men, and He will dwell among them, and they shall be His people, and God Himself will be among them, and He will wipe away every tear from their eyes; and there will no longer be *any* death; there will no longer be any mourning, or crying, or pain; the first things have passed away." *Revelation 21:1-4*

Other Books by Ken Johnson

Ancient Post-Flood History
Historical Documents That Point to a Biblical Creation.

Book Summary
This book is a Christian timeline of ancient post-Flood history based on Bible chronology, the early church fathers, and ancient Jewish and secular history. This can be used as a companion guide in the study of Creation science.

This revised edition adds the background history of nine new countries. Learn the true origins of the countries and people of France, Germany, Denmark, Sweden, Ireland, Scotland, Greece, Italy, Russia, Egypt, Israel, Iraq, Iran, China, the Arabs, the Kurds, and more.

Some questions answered: Who were the Pharaohs in the times of Joseph and Moses? When did the famine of Joseph occur? What Egyptian documents mention these? When did the Exodus take place? When did the kings of Egypt start being called "Pharaoh" and why? Who was the first king of a united Italy? Who was Zeus and where was he buried? Where did Shem and Ham rule and where were they buried? How large was Nimrod's invasion force that set up the Babylonian Empire, and when did this invasion occur? What is Nimrod's name in Persian documents? How can we use this information to witness to unbelievers?

Ancient Seder Olam
A Christian Translation of the 2000-year-old Scroll

This 2000-year-old scroll reveals the chronology from Creation through Cyrus' decree that freed the Jews in 536 BC. The *Ancient Seder Olam* uses biblical prophecy to prove its calculations of the timeline. We have used this technique to continue the timeline all the way to the reestablishment of the nation of Israel in AD 1948.

Using the Bible and rabbinical tradition, this book shows that the ancient Jews awaited King Messiah to fulfill the prophecy spoken of in Daniel, Chapter 9. The Seder answers many questions about the chronology of the books of Kings and Chronicles. It talks about the coming of Elijah, King Messiah's reign, and the battle of Gog and Magog.

This scroll and the Jasher scroll are the two main sources used in Ken's first book *Ancient Post-Flood History*.

Ancient Book of Jasher
Referenced in Joshua 10:13; 2 Samuel 1:18; 2 Timothy 3:8

There are thirteen ancient history books mentioned and recommended by the Bible. The Ancient Book of Jasher is the only one of the thirteen that still exists. It is referenced in Joshua 10:13; 2 Samuel 1:18; and 2 Timothy 3:8. This volume contains the entire ninety-one chapters plus a detailed analysis of the supposed discrepancies, cross-referenced historical accounts, and detailed charts for ease of use. As with any history book, there are typographical errors in the text but with three consecutive timelines running through the histories, it is very easy to arrive at the exact dates of recorded events. It is not surprising that this ancient document confirms the Scripture and the chronology given in the Hebrew version of the Old Testament, once and for all settling the chronology differences between the Hebrew Old Testament and the Greek Septuagint.

Ancient Prophecies Revealed

Third Corinthians
Ancient Gnostics and the End of the World

This little known, 2000-year-old Greek manuscript was used in the first two centuries to combat Gnostic cults. Whether or not it is an authentic copy of the original epistle written by the apostle Paul, it gives an incredible look into the cults that will arise in the Last Days. It contains a prophecy that the same heresies that pervaded the first century church would return before the Second Coming of the Messiah.

Ancient Paganism
The Sorcery of the Fallen Angels

Ancient Paganism explores the false religion of the ancient pre-flood world and its spread into the Gentile nations after Noah's Flood. Quotes from the ancient church fathers, rabbis, and the Talmud detail the activities and beliefs of both Canaanite and New Testament era sorcery. This book explores how, according to biblical prophecy, this same sorcery will return before the Second Coming of Jesus Christ to earth. These religious beliefs and practices will invade the end time church and become the basis for the religion of the Antichrist. Wicca, Druidism, Halloween, Yule, meditation, and occultic tools are discussed at length.

The Rapture
The Pretribulational Rapture of the Church Viewed From the Bible and the Ancient Church

This book presents the doctrine of the pretribulational Rapture of the church. Many prophecies are explored with Biblical passages and terms explained.

Evidence is presented that proves the first century church believed the End Times would begin with the return of Israel to her ancient homeland, followed by the Tribulation and the Second Coming. More than fifty prophecies have been fulfilled since Israel became a state.

Evidence is also given that several ancient rabbis and at least four ancient church fathers taught a pretribulational Rapture. This book also gives many of the answers to the arguments midtribulationists and posttribulationists use. It is our hope this book will be an indispensable guide for debating the doctrine of the Rapture.

Ancient Epistle of Barnabas
His Life and Teaching

The Epistle of Barnabas is often quoted by the ancient church fathers. Although not considered inspired Scripture, it was used to combat legalism in the first two centuries AD. Besides explaining why the Laws of Moses are not binding on Christians, the Epistle explains how many of the Old Testament rituals teach typological prophecy. Subjects explored are: Yom Kippur, the Red Heifer ritual, animal sacrifices, circumcision, the Sabbath, Daniel's visions and the end-time ten nation empire, and the Temple.

The underlying theme is the Three-Fold Witness. Barnabas teaches that mature Christians must be able to lead people to the Lord, testify to others about Bible prophecy fulfilled in their lifetimes, and teach creation history and creation science to guard the faith against the false doctrine of evolution. This is one more ancient church document that proves the first century church was premillennial and constantly looking for the Rapture and other prophecies to be fulfilled.

The Ancient Church Fathers
What the Disciples of the Apostles Taught

This book reveals who the disciples of the twelve apostles were and what they taught, from their own writings. It documents the same doctrine was faithfully transmitted to their descendants in the first few centuries and where, when, and by whom, the doctrines began to change. The ancient church fathers make it very easy to know for sure what the complete teachings of Jesus and the twelve apostles were.

You will learn, from their own writings, that the first century disciples taught on the various doctrines that divide our church today. You will learn what was discussed at the seven general councils and why. You will learn who were the cults and cult leaders that began to change doctrine and spread their heresy and how that became to be the standard teaching in the medieval church. A partial list of doctrines discussed in this book are:

Abortion	Free will	Purgatory
Animals sacrifices	Gnostic cults	Psychology
Antichrist	Homosexuality	Reincarnation
Arminianism	Idolatry	Replacement theology
Bible or tradition	Islam	Roman Catholicism
Calvinism	Israel's return	The Sabbath
Circumcision	Jewish food laws	Salvation
Deity of Jesus Christ	Mary's virginity	Schism of Nepos
Demons	Mary's assumption	Sin / Salvation
Euthanasia	Meditation	The soul
Evolution	The Nicolaitans	Spiritual gifts
False gospels	Paganism	Transubstantiation
False prophets	Predestination	Yoga
Foreknowledge	premillennialism	Women in ministry

For more information visit us at:

Biblefacts.org
Creationhistory.us
Wordofprophecy.net

Bibliography

1. Cruse, C. F., *Eusebius' Ecclesiastical History*, Hendrickson Publishers, 1998.
2. Eerdmans Publishing, *Ante-Nicene Fathers*, Eerdmans Publishing, 1886.
3. Whiston, William, *The Works of Flavius Josephus*, London, Miller & Sowerby, 1987. Includes Antiquities of the Jews.
4. Louis Ginzberg, *The Legends of the Jews*, Johns Hopkins University Press, 1948.
5. Ken Johnson, *Ancient Post-flood History*, Createspace, 2010
6. Ken Johnson, *Ancient Seder Olam*, Createspace, 2006
7. Ken Johnson, *Ancient Book of Jasher*, Createspace, 2008
8. Clarence Larkin, *Dispensational Truth*, Kessinger Publishing Company, 2005

Made in the USA
Charleston, SC
25 April 2014